The British Council and Anglo-Greek Literary Interactions, 1945–1955

In the immediate aftermath of the Second World War, and with British political influence over Greece soon to be ceded to the United States, there was a considerable degree of cultural interaction between Greek and British literati. Sponsored or assisted by the British Council, this interaction was notable for its diversity and quality alike. Indeed, the British Council in Greece made a more significant contribution to local culture in that period than at any other time, and perhaps in any other country. Many of the participants – among them Patrick Leigh Fermor, Steven Runciman and Louis MacNeice – are well known, while others deserve to be better known than they are today. But what has been less fully discussed, and what the volume sets out to do, is to explore the two-way relations between Greek and British literary production in which the British Council played a particularly important role until the outbreak of armed conflict in Cyprus in 1955, which rendered further contacts of this kind difficult. Close attention is paid to the variety of ways – marked by personal affinities and allegiances, but also by political tensions – in which the British Council functioned as an agent of interaction in a climate where a complex blend of traditional Anglophilia or Philhellenism found itself encountering a new post-war and Cold War environment. What is distinctive about the volume, beyond the inclusion of much recent archival research, is its attention to the British Council as part of the story of Greek letters, and not just as a place in which various British men and women of letters worked. The British Council found itself, sometimes more through improvisation and personal affinities than through careful planning, at the heart of some key developments, notably in terms of important periodical publications which had a lasting influence on Greek letters. Though in the cultural forum that influence was arguably to be less pervasive than that of France, with its more ambitious cultural outreach, or than that of the USA in later decades, the role of the British Council in Greece in this crucial period of Greek (and indeed European) post-war history continues to make a rich case study in cultural politics. This volume thus fills a gap in the bibliography on Anglo-Greek relations and contributes to a wider scholarly and public discussion about cultural politics.

Peter Mackridge was Professor of Modern Greek at the University of Oxford until his retirement in 2003 and is an Emeritus Fellow of St Cross College, Oxford.

David Ricks is Professor of Modern Greek and Comparative Literature at King's College London.

British School at Athens – Modern Greek and Byzantine Studies

Volume 6

Series editor: Professor John Bennet
Director, British School at Athens, Greece

The study of modern Greek and Byzantine history, language and culture has formed an integral part of the work of the British School at Athens since its foundation. This series continues that pioneering tradition. It aims to explore a wide range of topics within a rich field of enquiry which continues to attract readers, writers and researchers, whether their interest is primarily in contemporary Europe or in one or other of the many dimensions of the long Greek post-classical past.

THE BRITISH COUNCIL AND ANGLO-GREEK LITERARY INTERACTIONS, 1945–1955

EDITED BY
Peter Mackridge and David Ricks

LONDON AND NEW YORK

First published 2018
by Routledge
2 Park Square, Milton Park, Abingdon, Oxon OX14 4RN

and by Routledge
711 Third Avenue, New York, NY 10017

Routledge is an imprint of the Taylor & Francis Group, an informa business

© 2018 selection and editorial matter, Peter Mackridge and David Ricks;
individual chapters, the contributors

The right of Peter Mackridge and David Ricks to be identified as the authors of the editorial
material, and of the authors for their individual chapters, has been asserted in accordance
with sections 77 and 78 of the Copyright, Designs and Patents Act 1988.

All rights reserved. No part of this book may be reprinted or reproduced or utilised in any
form or by any electronic, mechanical, or other means, now known or hereafter invented,
including photocopying and recording, or in any information storage or retrieval system,
without permission in writing from the publishers.

Trademark notice: Product or corporate names may be trademarks or registered
trademarks, and are used only for identification and explanation without intent
to infringe.

British Library Cataloguing-in-Publication Data
A catalogue record for this book is available from the British Library

Library of Congress Cataloging-in-Publication Data
A catalog record for this book has been requested

ISBN: 978-1-472-47034-8 (hbk)
ISBN: 978-1-315-61414-4 (ebk)

Typeset in Palatino Linotype
by Apex CoVantage, LLC

Contents

Notes on contributors		*vii*
Acknowledgements		*xi*

Introduction   1
Peter Mackridge

1   The end of an affair: Anglo-Greek relations, 1939–1955   21
Robert Holland

2   'To cast our net very much wider': the re-opening of the
British Council in Athens and its cultural activities in Greece   39
Gioula Koutsopanagou

3   Steven Runciman at the British Council: letters from Athens,
1945–1947   69
Michael Llewellyn-Smith

4   Making a new myth of Greece: G.K. Katsimbalis as
Anglo-Greek Maecenas   111
Avi Sharon

5   Between propaganda and modernism: the *Anglo-Greek
Review* and the rediscovery of Greece   123
Dimitris Tziovas

6   The *Anglo-Greek Review*: Some residual puzzles   155
Dimitris Daskalopoulos

7   The magazine *Prosperos* and the British Council Corfu branch   159
Theodosis Pylarinos

8   The magazine *The Record* (1947–1955)   173
Dinos Christianopoulos

9   Making friends for Britain? Francis King and Roger Hinks
at the British Council in Athens   175
David Roessel

CONTENTS

10 Cultural relations and the 'non-political' problem:
    some personal reflections, with a glance at two novels
    from the period 1945–1955   187
    Jim Potts

11 MacNeice in Greece   201
    David Ricks

12 Kazantzakis in Cambridge   215
    David Holton

13 The Institut français d'Athènes 1945–1955:
    cultural exchanges and Franco-Greek relations   227
    Lucile Arnoux-Farnoux

Bibliography   239
Index   255

Notes on contributors

Lucile Arnoux-Farnoux is maître de conférences in comparative literature at the Université François-Rabelais in Tours. Her current work is concerned with questions of translation and reception, as well as modern Greek literature and cultural transfers between Greece and France in the twentieth century. She is coordinator of the research programme 'Athènes-Paris 1945–1975' at the École française d'Athènes, the successor to the 'Paris-Athènes 1919–1939' programme. She has published French translations of works by a number of contemporary Greek writers.

Dinos Christianopoulos is one of the leading writers and intellectuals in Thessaloniki, where he was born in 1931. His earliest published poem appeared in the British Council's magazine *The Record* in 1947. Since then he has published more than fifteen poetry collections and more than thirty volumes of essays and criticism. He has refused all offers of prizes, but he was awarded an honorary doctorate by the University of Thessaloniki in 2011.

Dimitris Daskalopoulos is an independent scholar, poet, essayist and biographer. He has published ten volumes of poetry and nine books of essays and has edited many works by George Seferis. His main interest is twentieth-century Greek literature, especially the Generation of 1930. His recent books (in Greek) include *C. P. Cavafy: His Poetry and his Poetics* (2013), *Wind's Net* (poems, 2015) and a bibliography of George Seferis (2016). He holds honorary Doctorates of Literature from the University of Thessaloniki (2006) and the University of Patras (2010).

Robert Holland has published widely on British overseas history in the nineteenth and twentieth centuries and has a special interest in the Mediterranean. His most recent book is *Blue-Water Empire: the British in the Mediterranean since 1800* (2012). He is a Visiting Professor at the Centre for Hellenic Studies, King's College London.

David Holton is Emeritus Professor of Modern Greek at the University of Cambridge and a Fellow of Selwyn College. His research and publications focus on Greek language and literature from late medieval to modern, particularly Cretan Renaissance poetry and drama. He is co-author of two grammars of Modern Greek and directed the research project that led to *The Cambridge Grammar of Medieval and Early Modern Greek,* to be published in 2018. He served as Chairman of the Society for Modern Greek Studies from 2012 to 2016.

NOTES ON CONTRIBUTORS

Gioula Koutsopanagou teaches European History at the Hellenic Open University. She is the founding director of the Greek Press History Workshop (ETMIET) at the Research Centre for Modern Greece (KENI), Department of Political Science and History, Panteion University. She is editor of the series 'Cultural Diplomacy-Cold War' (Papazisis Publishers). Her research areas include Cultural and Public Diplomacy, International Cultural Relations, Cultural Cold War, Culture and Mass Communication, Press History, Greek Diaspora and Migration, Youth and History.

Sir Michael Llewellyn-Smith served in the British diplomatic service and was ambassador in Poland (1991–96), and in Greece (1996–99). He is the author of *Ionian Vision: Greece in Asia Minor 1919–1922* and of other works on Greece; editor of *Scholars, Travels, Archives: Greek History and Culture through the British School at Athens*; Honorary Fellow of St Antony's College, Oxford; Visiting Professor at King's College London; and a Vice-President of the British School at Athens.

Peter Mackridge is Emeritus Professor of Modern Greek at the University of Oxford. His books include *The Modern Greek Language* (1985), *Dionysios Solomos* (1989) and *Language and National Identity in Greece, 1766–1976* (2009). He has co-written two grammars of Modern Greek and co-edited *Ourselves and Others: The Development of a Greek Macedonian Cultural Identity since 1912* (1997) and *Contemporary Greek Fiction in a United Europe: From Local History to the Global Individual* (2004). He has translated *The History of Western Philosophy in 100 Haiku* by Haris Vlavianos, stories by Vizyenos, Papadiamandis and Yorgos Ioannou, and the text of a forthcoming graphic version of Roidis' *Pope Joan*.

Jim Potts, OBE, worked for the British Council for thirty-five years, in the UK, Ethiopia, Kenya, Greece, Czechoslovakia, Australia and Sweden. His publications include *Swedish Reflections: From Beowulf to Bergman* (co-editor, 2003), *Corfu Blues* (Poems and Essays; 2006), *The Ionian Islands and Epirus: A Cultural History* (2010) and *Dorset Voices, with a Foreword by HRH The Prince of Wales* (co-editor, 2012). He contributed chapters to *Greece and Britain since 1945* (2nd edn 2014), *The Ionian Islands: Aspects of Their History and Culture* (2014) and *Travel, Tourism, and Identity* (2015).

Theodosis Pylarinos is Emeritus Professor of Modern Greek Literature at the Ionian University of Greece. He was a member of the advisory board of the journal *Porphyras*; editor of the journal *Ionios Logos*, published by the Department of History of the Ionian University; and President of the Organizing Committee of the 10th International Pan-Ionian Conference (Corfu, 2014). He is editor of the journal *Corfiot Chronicles (Κερκυραϊκά Χρονικά)*. His chief interests include the Ionian School of literature and the Greek Language Question in the nineteenth century.

NOTES ON CONTRIBUTORS

David Ricks is Professor of Modern Greek and Comparative Literature at King's College London. He has written widely on the fortunes of English poets in the Greek-speaking world, among them Tennyson, Browning and Arthur Symons, and has translated poems by Greek poets from Solomos to Nasos Vayenas.

David Roessel is the Peter and Stella Yiannos Professor of Greek at Stockton University in Galloway, New Jersey. He is the author of *In Byron's Shadow: Modern Greece in the English and American Imagination* and the co-editor of the recently published *Selected Letters of Langston Hughes*.

Avi Sharon taught Classics in Greece and the US before leaving academia for Wall Street. He has written widely on Greek topics, ancient and modern, and translates a number of authors and poets. He did a version of Plato's Symposium in 1998, and his rendering of the *Selected Poems of Cavafy* (Penguin, 2008) won the Harold Morton Landon Translation Award from the Academy of American Poets and the TLS Literary Translation Prize.

Dimitris Tziovas is Professor of Modern Greek Studies at the University of Birmingham and General Editor of a translation series of Modern Greek literature published by the university's Centre for Byzantine, Ottoman and Modern Greek Studies. His books include *The Other Self: Selfhood and Society in Modern Greek Fiction* (2003; Greek translation 2007); and the edited volumes *Greek Modernism and Beyond* (1997), *Greece and the Balkans: Identities, Perceptions and Cultural Encounters since the Enlightenment* (2003), *Greek Diaspora and Migration since 1700* (2009), *Re-Imagining the Past: Antiquity and Modern Greek Culture* (2014), and *Greece in Crisis: The Cultural Politics of Austerity* (2017).

Acknowledgements

In 2009 Peter Mackridge proposed that the British School at Athens host a conference on the activities of the British Council in Greece between 1945 and 1955, particularly in the realm of literature. Once the School had agreed to go ahead with the conference, he invited David Ricks to join him as co-organizer. The present volume consists of revised versions of the papers given at the conference, with the addition of the contributions by Gioula Koutsopanagou and Dinos Christianopoulos, which were commissioned especially for the volume.

The chapter by Theodosis Pylarinos was translated from Greek by Nicolas Philippakis and adapted for the volume by the editors, and the chapter by Lucile Arnoux-Farnoux was translated from French by Lucy Birot. The texts by Dimitris Daskalopoulos and Dinos Christianopoulos were translated by David Ricks.

The editors would like to express their thanks to Professor Cathy Morgan, FBA and her staff at the British School for hosting the conference on which this volume is largely based and providing the necessary organizational support, and to those who provided the funds needed to cover the expenses. We are particularly grateful to Matti and the late Nicholas Egon for their generous contribution to the conference expenses. In addition, the British Council made a major contribution to these expenses, while King's College London also contributed.

Peter Mackridge and David Ricks

Introduction

Peter Mackridge

The interaction between British Council officials and Greek intellectuals and artists during the period 1945–55 is a fascinating topic of study, and yet it has hardly been researched. The decade covered in this volume was a crucial one in Greece's history. It began soon after the withdrawal of German forces from the country and the return of the Greek government from its exile in Cairo, accompanied by British troops, in October 1944. The killing of unarmed demonstrators in Syntagma (Constitution) Square, Athens on 3 December 1944 began a period of violence (known in Greek as *ta Dekemvriana* [the December events]) during which Greek rebels fought against British troops and Greek government forces in December 1944 and January 1945. These events were followed, after an interlude, by the fully-fledged civil war between government and rebel forces from 1946 to 1949. The ten-year period ended with the outbreak of the armed struggle by EOKA for the expulsion of the British occupation authorities from Cyprus and for union of the island with Greece (*enosis*). Once the armed struggle in Cyprus had begun many Greeks who had hitherto been enthusiastically pro-British began to avoid contact with official British institutions, and during the following months British Council premises in Greece and Cyprus were attacked by protestors.[1]

British political and military power had made itself felt in Greece from the moment that British forces began to take over the Ionian Islands one by one from the French, beginning with Zakynthos in 1809 and ending with Corfu in 1814. The British participation in the Battle of Navarino, which destroyed the best of the Ottoman fleet in 1827, was decisive for the successful outcome of the Greek War of Independence against the Ottoman Empire, and Britain was to become the chief of the three 'protecting powers' of the nominally independent Kingdom of Greece. The British protectorate of the Ionian Islands lasted until 1864, the British having refused to hand them over to Greece until a king had been chosen who was favourable to British influence. Britain then controlled Cyprus from 1878 to 1960. Given the immense political influence of Britain, its literary and artistic culture made relatively little impact on Greece until the inter-war period, the most notable exception being Lord Byron. Among the earliest twentieth-century Greek writers to break successfully through the language barrier into English literary consciousness was C.P. Cavafy, who was more or less bilingual in Greek and English and was steeped in English literary culture.

As late as 1935 the knowledge of the English language came fourth in Greece, after French, German and Italian. But during the 1930s many leading Greek intellectuals began to be more interested in the English language, partly under the influence of Modernist poetry and fiction by Virginia Woolf, James Joyce and T.S. Eliot. George Seferis, who had held a diplomatic post in London in 1931–34, became a pioneering translator and critic of Eliot's poetry; he was posted to London again in 1951–53 and returned to become Greek Ambassador there from 1957 to 1961 during the crucial period of the Cyprus emergency. A number of his contemporaries had spent some time in Britain before the Second World War, thus preparing the way for a greater receptivity of British culture in Greece during the post-war years. The surrealist poet Andreas Embiricos studied at King's College, London during the academic year 1924–25. In 1928–29 the novelist George Theotokas spent the best part of a year in London, where he wrote his first book, *Free Spirit* (1929), an extended essay that has been called the manifesto of the Greek Generation of 1930. In it he called for a new creative reciprocal cultural relationship between Greece and contemporary Europe. His call appeared to be answered when the influence of Greek poetry and painting began to manifest itself in the work of British writers and artists during the 1940s.

In 1937 the Byron Chair, funded by the British Council, was established at Athens University for the teaching of English language and literature, and the Council continued to fund the post until 1963.[2] When the Council's Institute of English Studies opened in Athens in January 1939, demand for its English language courses exceeded all expectations. For the first time, the Institute's classes made the learning of English available to those Greeks who were not privileged to attend special commercial schools or élite private schools. Until 1940 French was the only language taught in state high schools (*gymnasia* and *lykeia*), while during the Axis occupation the only foreign languages that were allowed to be taught in Greek schools were German and Italian. In 1945, however, the teaching of English became compulsory, alongside French, in the *gymnasia*.[3]

In the first three months of 1941, the British presence in Greece was very noticeable, on a cultural as well as a military level. As Tina Krontiris writes, 'There was an intense interest in things relating to the British culture or to the connection between English and Greek literature. . . . The deluge of culture in Greek intellectual life was connected as much with the war as with the objectives of the British Council, which sponsored visiting professors and poets and appointed the person who occupied the Byron Chair of English Studies at the University of Athens.' The culmination of this enthusiasm for things British was the first-ever Greek production of Shakespeare's *Henry V*, translated by the left-wing author Vasilis Rotas, at the National Theatre in Athens in March 1941, which seemed to express a prevailing Greek mood at the time – just a month before the German invasion of the country.[4]

INTRODUCTION

Turning now to the other end of our period, the Cyprus conflict of 1955–59 followed a plebiscite in 1950, in which 96 per cent of the Greek Cypriot participants voted in favour of union with Greece.[5] Yet the Cyprus emergency also came after one of the high points in Anglo-Greek relations: when earthquakes and the subsequent fires devastated the islands of Zakynthos, Cephalonia and Ithaca in August 1953, the first foreign aid to arrive on the scene was provided by HMS Gambia, which happened to be nearby and immediately sailed to Zakynthos. This assistance by the Royal Navy and the Royal Marines was greatly appreciated by the people of Britain's former protectorate. In the minds of many Greeks, this British aid to stricken Greece seemed to be a fitting postscript to the beneficent efforts of the British to protect the country from a communist takeover.

The decade 1945–55 was a particularly fruitful period in the history of the British Council in Greece. Perhaps at no other time and in no other country did the British Council so successfully interact with local writers and artists, whose work the Council encouraged as vigorously as it promoted British culture.[6] A galaxy of British intellectuals worked for the Council in Greece during this period. They helped to promote knowledge and understanding of contemporary Greek culture within Greece itself as well as in Britain, while their experiences in Greece – their contact with the reality of modern Greece and their acquaintanceship and in some cases close friendship with leading Greek writers and artists – made a decisive contribution to their own subsequent careers. Francis King and Rex Warner, for instance, subsequently wrote a number of novels and stories inspired by their stay in Greece.[7]

The founding of the British Council before the Second World War was inspired by Reginald Leeper's recognition of the importance of 'cultural propaganda' in promoting British interests. Leeper went on to serve as British ambassador to the Greek government from March 1943 to March 1946 (first to the Greek government in exile in Cairo, then from October 1944 onwards in Athens), at a time when Greece was a bitterly divided country. Leeper played a crucial role in Greek political developments. However, in his memoirs of this period, Leeper doesn't mention the British Council or any of its employees.[8] It is not clear what role Leeper actually played in the activities of the British Council in Greece (including the choice of its personnel) in 1945 and the first weeks of 1946. It is certain, however, that he aimed to preserve the strength of British influence in Greece.

C.M. Woodhouse stresses the political importance of Greece for Britain from 1944 onwards:

> That Britain, not the USA, would remain the predominant power in the Mediterranean, was still taken for granted. . . . An American observer in 1947 wrote that, from 1942 onwards, 'London made most of the political decisions concerning the eastern Mediterranean, while Washington furnished much of the actual power needed for their enforcement.'

The same author goes on to say that

> up to 1947 the British Government appointed and dismissed Greek Prime Ministers with the barest attention to constitutional formalities. British experts dictated economic and financial policy, security and legal policy, trade union and employment policy.[9]

President Truman's declaration on 12 March 1947 that the US would support Greece and Turkey with economic and military aid to prevent their falling into the Soviet sphere shows how Greece was considered to be one of the two countries on the front line of the struggle between the US and the USSR for world domination. Although Britain handed over responsibility to the US for military and economic support to the Greek regime in 1947, it continued to wield soft power in Greece through the cultural diplomacy carried out by the British Council.[10]

In his contribution to this volume, which reflects personal knowledge of the issue, Jim Potts talks about the supposedly 'apolitical' nature of the British Council. It is obvious that there was a stark difference in perception between what British and Greeks considered to be 'political' and 'apolitical'. In Britain, 'apolitical' traditionally meant supporting the conservative status quo; with reference to Greece at the time, it therefore entailed supporting the monarchy. This applied to the activities of the British Council in Greece: it had highly political aims while claiming to be apolitical.[11] In some cases there was a fundamental difference between the assumptions of British officials and those of a significant proportion of the Greek population: the British saw the legitimate regime of Greece as being the *status quo ante bellum*, i.e. the situation before the German invasion, with King George II as head of state, while liberal and leftist Greeks considered that the king had forfeited whatever legitimacy he may have had by deciding to abolish parliamentary democracy and impose the Metaxas dictatorship in 1936; besides, EAM (the Communist-led National Liberation Front) had set up an alternative provisional government in the mountains of occupied Greece in March 1944 while the king and his government were safely living in exile. The British saw the Greek resistance against Axis occupation as being part of the Allied war effort, whereas many Greeks saw the resistance as being, at least in part, an internal Greek revolt against an old political order that the British were determined to reinstate. However, it should be said that the British tried to steer clear of both the extreme Left and the extreme Right and to lend most of their support to liberals.

One incident that illustrates the political nature of the British Council's activities is the dismissal of Paris Taveloudis from his post as an English-Greek translator for the British Council-funded *Anglo-Greek Review*. Taveloudis, better known by his *nom de plume* Kosmas Politis, was one of the leading novelists of the Generation of 1930, and he was subsequently to become one of the most prolific Greek translators of English and American literature. He had held his

INTRODUCTION   5

translating post at the *Review* for eighteen months before he was dismissed in the summer of 1946. He had briefly been a member of the KKE (Greek Communist Party) in 1944–45, and in June 1946 he was one of seventy-three Greek writers who signed a public protest letter against a government resolution stipulating the death penalty for 'those who conspired to undermine public order and the territorial integrity of the country'. The signatories to the protest letter included well-known writers who were not Leftists, including Angelos Sikelianos, George Theotokas, C.Th. Dimaras and Elias Venezis, whose names recur in several of the chapters in this volume. The plausible hypothesis that Taveloudis' dismissal was due to his leftist sympathies created a minor storm in the Greek press. However, Maurice Cardiff, Assistant Representative of the British Council, published a letter in a Greek newspaper in which he claimed that Taveloudis was dismissed not for political reasons but 'because he was carrying out his work as an employee inadequately'.[12] Taveloudis attributed responsibility for his dismissal to G.K. Katsimbalis, editor of the *Review*, though it has to be said that leftists were not the only people to criticize Katsimbalis for his actions and his views: in 1947, for instance, a number of articles against Katsimbalis were published by the writers I.M. Panagiotopoulos, M. Karagatsis, Michail Rodas and Eleni Ourani (who wrote as Alkis Thrylos).[13]

*

The topic of this book clearly has a personal dimension as well as a political and cultural one. There seems to be no doubt that to a large extent the British Council's activities in Greece were the initiative of the individuals who were employed by the Council on the spot rather than being decided by the Foreign Office in London, despite Steven Runciman's grumbles about central bureaucracy.[14] Some of these people had been in Greece (and some of them at the British Council) before the War. When the War broke out, British Council employees in Greece sought refuge in Egypt, where they found themselves stranded. These included Lawrence Durrell (1912–90), who from November 1939 onwards had been working in Athens, where he met Seferis as well as Bernard Spencer (1909–63) and Robert Liddell (1908–92), and subsequently in Kalamata; Spencer, who had previously been posted to Salonica [Thessaloniki] and came to know Seferis in Cairo; and Liddell (formerly in Athens), who remained in Cairo for twelve years, but then returned to a lectureship at the University of Athens from 1953 to 1972. Thus the Council had already had excellent people in Greece on the very eve of the Second World War. As Michael Llewellyn-Smith points out, 'the association of the British Council with literature, in particular poetry, was already established before the war'.

The first regular Representative of the British Council in Greece after the War was Steven Runciman (1903–2000), who had first visited Greece in 1924. By the time Runciman came to Athens to take charge of the Council in October 1945, having been professor of Byzantine art and history at the University of Istanbul, he had already published a number of books on Byzantine history, and he went on to become one of the world's leading authorities on Byzantine history and culture. In addition to his scholarly volumes, he published an article in 1953 in which he describes Zakynthos as he had seen it before the earthquakes, illustrating his brief text with two watercolours by Edward Lear and some of his own photographs of buildings, which act as a testimony to what had been destroyed.[15]

Rex Warner (1905–86) was the first Director of the British Institute of Higher Studies from 1945 to 1947. He had already published a volume of *Poems* (1937) as well as several novels, including *The Aerodrome* (1941). Soon after taking up his post in Athens, Warner met George Katsimbalis,[16] who introduced him to the poetry of George Seferis. Seferis wrote in 1949 that 'Rex is the *solidest* man I've met since the liberation [of Greece in 1944]',[17] and the two men remained lifelong friends. As George Thaniel notes, 'Warner seems to have been the only person celebrated by Seferis, in a poem written for a special occasion, Warner's sixtieth birthday in 1965: "Letter to Rex Warner, resident of Storrs, Connecticut, U.S.A. on his sixtieth birthday." '[18] Warner wrote the introduction to *The King of Asine and Other Poems*, the selection of Seferis' poems translated by Bernard Spencer, Nanos Valaoritis and Lawrence Durrell that was published in 1948.[19] Warner also wrote the introduction to *Poems by C.P. Cavafy* (1951), translated by John Mavrogordato, the first translation of the Alexandrian poet's collected poems to appear in English.[20] Thus the first volumes of Greece's two greatest twentieth-century poets to come out in English can be said to have been published under Warner's aegis.

In 1948 Warner gave a talk on the BBC entitled 'Aspects of contemporary Greek poetry'. In it he described Athens as 'to my mind . . . the most exciting city in the world' and conveyed the excitement he often felt in the company of its leading poets and writers.[21] In his contribution to the present volume Jim Potts talks about Warner's novel *Men of Stones* (1949), which was influenced by his experience of Greece. Warner also published his impressions of the country under the title *Views of Attica and its Surroundings* (1950). In the chapter entitled 'The British Institute' in that book, he rejects the allegation that Kolonaki (the district in which the British Council premises are situated) is Athens' equivalent of Mayfair.[22] Nevertheless, sixty years later, Geoffrey Graham-Bell, in a talk he gave at the conference (not published in the present volume), spoke about the snobbish atmosphere that prevailed at the Council in the late 1940s and the 1950s.

Warner later published a volume of his own translations of Seferis' *Poems* (1960),[23] which undoubtedly helped the Greek poet to win the Nobel Prize in 1963. In addition, in collaboration with Th.D. Frangopoulos, Warner translated a selection of Seferis' essays, which was published under the title *On the Greek Style*.[24] By this time Warner was well established as a leading translator of ancient Greek texts and a professor of Classics in the US. But he was able to appreciate modern Greek culture in itself, without always comparing it with

INTRODUCTION

ancient Hellenic civilization. His career is an example of the way the experience of working for the British Council in Greece could have a lasting and positive impact on Anglo-Greek cultural relations.

Bernard Spencer (1909–63) worked as a teacher and librarian at the Institute for English Studies at Salonica till 1940. He published only three books of poetry in his lifetime, including *Aegean Islands and Other Poems* (1946) and his translations of Seferis with Valaoritis and Durrell. A recent reviewer of Spencer's *Complete Poetry* writes that 'Spencer only really came into his own after he began living abroad as a lecturer for the newly founded British Council',[25] and much of his poetry is haunted by the landscape of Greece. On 6 September 1946 Spencer gave a talk on the BBC about the Greek poets Dionysios Solomos, Odysseus Elytis and Nikos Engonopoulos, with readings by Nanos Valaoritis. In 1955–56 the British Council posted him to Athens. There he witnessed demonstrations sparked off by the deportation of Archbishop Makarios from Cyprus to the Seychelles in March 1956. These events inspired him to write his poem 'The Rendezvous', which in an early, unpublished version indicated his sympathy with those who were demonstrating against the actions and policies of the British government.[26]

As I have already mentioned, Robert Liddell (1908–92) was another British writer who was brought to Greece by the Council, which employed him in Athens before the War. From 1953 to 1972 he taught in the English department of the University of Athens, which had been set up in 1951 around the Byron Chair of English, which, as we have seen, had been established by the British Council in 1937. After his retirement Liddell went on living in Greece until his death. Liddell came into close contact with Greek writers and artists both in Greece and in Egypt. His combined experience of these two countries inspired him to write his biography of the Alexandrian Greek poet Cavafy.[27] As well as a prolific output of novels and critical studies of English novelists, he published a series of guide books to Greece which were among the finest of their time.[28]

The poet Louis MacNeice (1907–63) worked for the BBC from 1941 to his death. In 1950, MacNeice was granted one and a half years' leave of absence to become Director of the British Institute (and subsequently Assistant Representative of the British Council) in Athens. David Ricks's chapter is devoted to MacNeice's time in Greece.

The subject of David Roessel's chapter, the novelist Francis King (1923–2011), worked at the British Council in Salonica in 1950–52, then in Athens from 1953 to 1957. He wrote a number of novels set in Greece, as well as editing a guidebook to Greece.[29] King was looking forward to taking part in the Athens conference, but sadly he died at the age of eighty-eight in July 2011.

Another erstwhile British Council employee who was invited to the conference but died before it took place was Patrick Leigh Fermor (1915–2011), who briefly – and rather ineffectually – worked for the Council in Athens. More importantly for his own career (and indeed for Anglo-Greek literary

8 PETER MACKRIDGE

relations), at various times during the period covered by this volume he was exploring unknown corners of Greece, gathering experiences and collecting material that would feed into his travel books *Mani* (1958) and *Roumeli* (1966).[30]

Lawrence Durrell (1912–90) only worked for the British Council in Greece for a short period before the War, and he was already living in the country when he was appointed to a post there. During the interregnum between the end of the Italian (then briefly German) occupation of the Dodecanese in 1945 and the handing over of the islands to Greece in 1947, they were temporarily administered by the British military authorities, and Durrell was stationed on Rhodes as director of public relations in the Overseas Information Service. Durrell had already begun to make a name for himself as a poet in the 1930s, whereas he is now chiefly known for the novels of his maturity, beginning with *Justine* (1957), the first volume of the *Alexandria Quartet*. It was Durrell who had invited Henry Miller to Greece in 1939–40 and had played a leading role in the American writer's friendship with Seferis and Katsimbalis. Durrell resumed his own friendship with Seferis in Cairo and remained a key figure in Anglo-Greek cultural relations.

Durrell had already published some translations of Seferis' poetry in *New Writing and Daylight* and in a privately printed pamphlet while he was living in Rhodes.[31] These were all included in *The King of Asine and other Poems*.[32] While in Rhodes he also translated Emmanouil Roidis' scandalous satirical novel *Pope Joan*, which was first published in Greek in 1866.[33] Durrell's residence on three Greek islands bore fruit in his trilogy *Prospero's Cell, Reflections of a Marine Venus* and *Bitter Lemons*, the first based on his experience of living in Corfu in 1935–40, the second inspired by his stay in Rhodes and the third inspired by his time in Cyprus in 1953–56, where, to the horror of his Greek friends, he worked as Director of Information Services for the British authorities during the Emergency.[34] These three volumes on Greek islands, together with Leigh Fermor's two volumes on the Greek mainland, have made the most significant contribution to the idealization of traditional rural Greece and the Greek landscape in the Anglo-American mind.[35]

Geoffrey Graham-Bell was in Athens from 1949 to 1952, and from 1954 to 1956 he ran the Anglo-Hellenic League School of English, which was assisted financially by the British Council. He knew the Council and its employees at the time, and he gave us the benefit of his memories of them at the conference.

One Englishman who did not work for the British Council in Greece but whose life and career were decisively influenced by it was John Craxton (1922–2009), one of whose pictures, painted in Greece in 1955 and now housed in the British Ambassador's residence in Athens, is reproduced on the cover of this volume. The cheaply produced but elegant tin olive oil can seems to encapsulate the frugal bounty of the Greek earth and the thriftiness of Greek life at

INTRODUCTION

9

the time. Craxton first visited Greece in 1946 on the invitation of Lady Norton (wife of Sir Clifford Norton, British ambassador in Athens from 1946 to 1951) to hold an exhibition at the British Council. Craxton spent much of the rest of his life in Greece, and it seems likely that his work from then on was influenced by his friend Nikos Hadjikyriakos-Ghika (1906–1994); if so, he is one of the very few English painters to have been influenced by contemporary Greek art. As Craxton wrote in his obituary for Ghika,

> Like so many of my fellow artists then I had a deep desire to go south to the Mediterranean. Greece was very much on my mind. To find a sympathetic artist who would welcome me in his native country gave me added impetus. I mention this first meeting with Ghika, for it is quite typical of how European painters are often cross-pollinated by chance encounters. Next year, in May 1946, it was my good luck to find myself in Athens. . . . It is to the credit of the English that the first retrospective exhibition of his [Ghika's] painting was held at the British Council in Athens in 1946.[36]

Ghika was a representative of a group of Greek writers and artists known as the Generation of 1930. Others included the future Nobel Prize-winning poets George Seferis and Odysseus Elytis, the novelist George Theotokas and the critic Andreas Karantonis. Some young writers of the 1930s realized that the old Greek nationalist ideals had been rendered obsolete by the catastrophic defeat of Greek forces by Turkish nationalist forces in Asia Minor and the consequent expulsion of almost all of the one and a half million Greeks living in Turkey. They therefore set about developing a new conception of Greekness that combined a cautious Modernism with the use of the language spoken by the Greek people, an aesthetic infused by the land, sea and islands of Greece, and a view of an unbroken Greek literary and artistic tradition – ancient, medieval and modern – that stressed its openness to fruitful foreign influences as well as its abiding concern with spiritual and moral equilibrium. The chief literary organ that published and promoted the work of the poets, critics and fiction-writers of the Generation of 1930 was the magazine *Ta Nea Grammata* (*New Letters*, 1936–40 and 1944–45), which was founded and edited by Karantonis and Katsimbalis. After being interrupted by the outbreak of war, *Ta Nea Grammata* resumed publication before the end of the Occupation, in January 1944, but it was again interrupted by the Communist uprising of December 1944, and its final issue, which was ready for distribution that month, was finally published with a cover dated July 1945.[37] Looking back to *Ta Nea Grammata* in 1949, Nanos Valaoritis wrote to Katsimbalis, 'Say what you will, that magazine created our new [literary] movement. You know that without *Ta Nea Grammata* it wouldn't have existed – neither Elytis nor practically anybody else. The influence of that magazine took what was diffused in the atmosphere and led it down a specific road.'[38]

10   PETER MACKRIDGE

Rex Warner's Introduction to *The King of Asine* (dated 1946) shows the influence of Seferis and other members of the Generation of 1930 in statements such as the following:

> The Greek land- and seas-scape, in its clarity and its mystery, its brilliance and its terror, in its stability and its hurrying movement, in all its contradiction is still the best basis for attempting to understand the Greek genius. . . .

> The distinction between the 'ancient' and the 'modern' Greeks is positively harmful, since it disguises the most obvious facts that the ancient Greeks were modern and that the modern Greeks are ancient.[39]

Among the most important manifestations to emerge from the collaboration between Greeks and British via the British Council were various lectures and exhibitions held in Athens, and the magazine bearing the indicative alternative titles *Αγγλοελληνική Επιθεώρηση* and *Anglo-Greek Review* (as it will be referred to in this volume).

Under the auspices of Rex Warner the British Institute not only held the first retrospective exhibition of Ghika's paintings in November 1946, but the first ever exhibition of paintings by Theophilos Chatzimichail (c. 1870–1934) to be mounted in Greece. Ghika was an obvious candidate for the British Council's patronage, since he was a member of the literary and artistic Greek Generation of 1930 whose work the Council tended to promote. The decision to put on the Theophilos exhibition in May 1947 was perhaps more surprising, since he was a naïve painter in the Douanier Rousseau mould.[40] However, Theophilos' work had come to be admired by members of the Generation of 1930 as well as by the Greek Left because he seemed to represent the brilliant native originality that untutored Greek peasants were capable of. While representatives of both Right and Left expressed the view that an exhibition of Theophilos was out of place at the Institute's elegant premises in Kolonaki Square, the centre of the richest residential area in Athens, Rex Warner claimed that the Communist Party newspaper *Rizospastis* actually encouraged its readers to visit the exhibition.[41] The Institute also put on a performance of the Karagiozis shadow theatre, a popular Greek tradition that goes back to the Ottoman period. Seferis gave two of his most important lectures at the British Institute: one on parallels between the poetry of Cavafy and T.S. Eliot, and the other on Theophilos at the opening of the exhibition; both of these lectures were subsequently published in the *Anglo-Greek Review*.[42]

One of the full chapters in this volume, by Dimitris Tziovas, as well as the short note by Dimitris Daskalopoulos, focuses on the *Anglo-Greek Review*, which was published in Athens. But the British Council was active in cultural relations in other Greek cities too, notably Salonica, Patras and Corfu. During the second half of the 1940s Salonica, the second largest city in Greece, situated not far from the country's borders with Yugoslavia and Bulgaria, was much

INTRODUCTION   11

closer to the hostilities of the civil war than was Athens. This made it a crucial and sensitive political, military and cultural centre. The port of Patras in the Peloponnese had historic ties with Britain because of the export of currants that has traditionally been carried on there. Corfu had a long-standing relationship with Britain, having once been the capital of the British-dominated United States of the Ionian Islands. The British Council published magazines in these three towns: *Prosperos* in Corfu – apparently named after Lawrence Durrell's *Prospero's Cell* – the short-lived literary magazine *Symposio* in Patras (1950–52) and *The Record* (1947–51) in Salonica. *Prosperos* is the subject of Theodosis Pylarinos' chapter in this volume. *The Record* hosted two poems in Greek by the eighteen-year-old Dinos Christianopoulos; this was his first appearance in print.[43] Christianopoulos was unable to accept our invitation to speak at our conference, but he has kindly contributed a short memoir to our volume.

In terms of prestige, the *Anglo-Greek Review* was the successor to *Ta Nea Grammata*. It was the most widely read Greek literary magazine of its time, though it published reviews and articles about literature rather than literary works as such. For instance, Katsimbalis was keen to publish Greek translations of reviews that had appeared in the British press about translations of Greek literature in English, and about exhibitions by Greek artists held in Britain. It is difficult to establish why and by whom the publication of the *Review* was originally planned, since there is no archive, and those responsible are no longer alive.[44] The first issue was published in March 1945, within weeks of the Varkiza agreement signed between the Greek government of Plastiras on one side and the KKE/EAM/ELAS on the other in an attempt to bring an end to hostilities, and two months before the end of the Second World War in Europe.[45] The first twelve issues were published by the Anglo-Greek Information Service (AIS, later AGIS), a propaganda organization set up by Leeper under the aegis of General Scobie, commander of the British forces in Greece, at a time when Greece was under British military occupation.[46] The head of the AGIS was Colonel Kenneth Johnstone,[47] who later became deputy director-general of the British Council in London from 1953 to 1962.

The AGIS was dissolved at the end of 1945, and responsibility for the publication of the *Review* passed to the British Council. Under the Council, the *Review* was less propagandistic than it had been under the AGIS, and it published a larger amount of original Greek material. Katsimbalis seems to have become editor after the third issue. He remained editor until 1952, when publication was interrupted for reasons that are not clear.[48] Seferis published two major articles in the *Review*, in addition to the lectures he gave at the Institute: 'Erotokritos', on the seventeenth-century romance by the Cretan Vintzentzos Kornaros, and 'Γράμμα για την "Κίχλη" ' ['Letter on "The *Thrush*" ']. The latter, the only commentary that he ever published on one of his own poems, was written after Katsimbalis invited him to publish a letter 'that might help the well-intentioned reader to read my poem "The Thrush" more easily'.[49] The *Review* resumed publication in summer 1953, with the young literary scholar

G.P. Savidis succeeding Katsimbalis as editor, until spring 1955, when it was decided to close it down because of the Cyprus emergency.

Anglo-Greek literary relations were not confined to activities taking place in Greece, even though there was nothing on the scale of the visits of Greeks to France organized by the French Institute.[50] For instance, some Greek writers visited England with bursaries from the British Council. On the eve of the war the poet and essayist Demetrios Capetanakis and the teacher and critic Elli Lambridi went to Britain with bursaries from the Council. Capetanakis was stranded in England when the war broke out, and he spent the rest of his tragically short life there, establishing himself, among other things, as a fine poet in English.[51] Nikos Kazantzakis, another Greek intellectual who had already spent a period in England at the invitation of the Council in 1939–40 (and had published a book based on his experiences), spent three and a half months there in 1946, which David Holton refers to in his contribution to this volume. It is interesting to speculate what some of the writers Kazantzakis met (among them John Lehmann and Stephen Spender[52]) would have made of the poetry that he had published up to that time – work that was as different as it is possible to be from the poetry of Seferis, with which they were already familiar. As Holton points out, it is significant that in Cambridge Kazantzakis drafted an early version of his novel *Kapetan Michalis* (*Freedom and Death*), in which he re-imagined his native Crete in the period before and during his childhood. The novelists George Theotokas, Angelos Terzakis, M. Karagatsis and Pantelis Prevelakis too (the last of these was an art historian by profession) visited England under the auspices of the British Council soon after the Second World War.

A major role in fostering Anglo-Greek literary relations in London was played by Nanos Valaoritis (b. 1921), who gave our conference the benefit of his vivid memories of the time.[53] He already knew Bernard Spencer and Lawrence Durrell in Athens before the War. In June 1944 the twenty-three-year-old Valaoritis escaped from occupied Greece to Cairo, where he contacted Seferis and met up with Spencer again. At Seferis' instigation he went to London to work at the Greek Embassy, with the aim of developing literary links between Greece and Britain, and eventually spent the next nine years there. He was highly successful in creating an Anglo-Greek literary network, meeting the most important British poets and publishers and introducing them to contemporary Greek poetry. His contacts in London included the poets T.S. Eliot, W.H. Auden (while Auden was visiting from America in 1948), Edith Sitwell, Dylan Thomas, Stephen Spender, Louis MacNeice, Roy Campbell, Kathleen Raine and George Barker, and the publishers and editors John Lehmann, Cyril Connolly and Tambimuttu. In fact, it was Seferis who put Valaoritis in touch with the literary impresarios Lehmann and Connolly, whom he had met on a flying visit to London on official Greek government business in the summer of 1944.[54] Lehmann went on to publish a number of books of Greek interest under his own imprint, while he included a substantial number of Greek

INTRODUCTION 13

poems and articles about Greek poetry in the magazines that he edited (particularly *New Writing and Daylight* and its successor, *Penguin New Writing*).[55] The March 1946 issue of Connolly's magazine *Horizon* contained an article by Valaoritis entitled 'Modern Greek poetry', which was, he rightly claims, the first article in Britain to focus on the work of the contemporary poets Seferis, Embiricos, Elytis, Nikos Gatsos and Nikos Engonopoulos.[56] The same issue contained an illustrated article on Ghika's painting. Valaoritis co-ordinated the volume of Seferis translations that was published under the title *The King of Asine and Other Poems*.[57] The volume consisted largely of new translations done jointly by Valaoritis and Bernard Spencer, supplemented with the already published translations by Durrell. It received what Eliot reportedly called 'eulogistic reviews'.[58] Seferis, who acknowledged Valaoritis' crucial role in this publication, wrote to him that 'it's the first time that a Greek poetic oeuvre has been judged and discussed in a large foreign country, not with the condescension of specialist scholars of modern Greek studies, but by literary men through and through, as an oeuvre equal to their own works'.[59] Valaoritis also published a number of translations of individual poems by Elytis and others in various magazines and gave a large number of talks about Greek literature on the BBC. A painting by John Craxton was used as the frontispiece for Valaoritis' first book of poems in Greek, *Η τιμωρία των μάγων* (*The Punishment of the Magi*), which was printed in London in 1947.

As I have already implied, another institution that made a major contribution to Anglo-Greek literary relations in Britain was the BBC.[60] Valaoritis worked there for Louis MacNeice after losing his job at the Greek Embassy, and other Greek intellectuals were employed there too for varying lengths of time; these included the critic Alexis Diamantopoulos (1945–51) and the poet and critic Zissimos Lorenzatos (1953). Among broadcasts of contemporary Greek interest was 'The Death of a Town', adapted for radio by Kay Cicellis from her story of the same name inspired by the 1953 earthquake in Cephalonia. Cicellis' drama was broadcast on the BBC Third Programme on 18 and 20 January 1954 and repeated on the Home Service on 23 August 1955. The leading role was played by Fay Compton, and the music was by Elizabeth Lutyens.

*

One conclusion that can be drawn from the contributions to this volume is that the British Council's Anglo-Greek literary interactions were at their most intense during the years 1945–47, under the aegis of Steven Runciman and Rex Warner, who were as committed to the encouragement and dissemination of modern Greek culture as to the promotion of British culture in Greece. These two remarkable men were succeeded by a series of top officials who were neither so much in sympathy with modern Greek life and culture nor so well qualified to carry out their duties with more than the minimum of competence. The period 1945–47 was what Dimitris Tziovas and David Roessel, in their contributions to the present volume, call the Golden Age of the British Council in Greece. The legacy of those early years, however, lived on till 1955 in the form of the *Anglo-Greek Review*, which, despite the mutual reluctance of the editors and the leftist intellectuals to collaborate with each other, provided a showcase for a rich harvest of literary and artistic activity and a forum for a fertile dialogue on cultural and intellectual matters. It is a tribute to the determination and discretion of all those involved with the *Anglo-Greek Review* that it managed to flourish and to maintain the high quality of its content for so long despite its financial and political link, obvious from its very title, with a foreign power.

The metaphor chosen by the editors of the present volume, of Anglo-Greek cultural relations being 'between two worlds', perhaps contrasts with the suggestive metaphor of the 'double voyage' proposed by Lucile Arnoux in her chapter on Franco-Greek cultural interactions. When one compares the activities of the British Council during the period 1945–55 with those of the Institut Français, one is struck by the obvious differences. The activities of the French Institute were equally dominated by the leadership of two men, but from there on the similarities disappear. Whereas members of the British Council staff who were married to foreigners were unlikely to be posted to their spouse's homeland, the French Institute's director, Octave Merlier, and his assistant, Roger Milliex, were both married to Greeks. And whereas the Council moved on its representatives after two or three years in order to avert the dreaded prospect that they might go native, these two Frenchmen remained in post for more than two decades, and indeed made Greece their permanent home. Merlier had been working at the Institute since 1925 (with a hiatus during the Occupation), and was already director when the war began. Milliex too was already working at the French Institute in Athens before the war, and he ran it in Merlier's absence throughout the Occupation, thus ensuring a personal and institutional continuity that was lacking from the British Council, which was forced to abandon its activities in Greece during the Occupation years. Merlier's wife Melpo (whom he married as early as 1923) was an expert on Greek folk music and the founder of the prestigious Centre for Asia Minor Studies, while Milliex's wife Tatiana (they married in 1939) became a well-known novelist and short-story writer. Thus both men were deeply embedded in contemporary Greek culture. In addition, because of their profound and intimate knowledge and experience of the Greeks, they were able to act in a more professional and open-minded manner than some of the rather aloof British Council representatives, who came and went without having the opportunity (and in some cases the desire) to participate closely in Greek social and cultural life.

Among the chief manifestations of Franco-Greek cultural relations were, first, the despatch of a consignment of one hundred and fifty young Greeks on the SS Mataroa in 1945 to study in France with French government scholarships

INTRODUCTION

and, second, a prolific programme of publications.[61] Instead of competing with the *Anglo-Greek Review*, the French Institute, on Merlier's initiative, launched a series of volumes under the title Collection de l'Institut Français d'Athènes as well as the annual *Bulletin analytique de bibliographie hellénique*. Between 1945 and 1955 the Collection comprised about a hundred volumes, beginning with Robert Levesque's French translations of Solomos and Seferis (1945) and continuing with books in Greek such as *Vyzantinon vios kai politismos* [*The Life and Culture of the Byzantines*], the massive and invaluable compendium of evidence on Byzantine social life and culture by Phaidon Koukoules (6 vols, 1948–57), the plays of the seventeenth-century Cephalonian dramatist Petros Katsaitis (1950), the etymological dictionary of Modern Greek by N.P. Andriotis (1951), the dramas of the contemporary poet Angelos Sikelianos (3 vols, 1950–54) and a ground-breaking French thesis by Thémis Siapkaras-Pitsillidès on a unique collection of poetry from sixteenth-century Cyprus, which included the first edition of the poems themselves (1952). Meanwhile the bibliographical bulletin continued to publish annual issues until 1973.

The fact that both Merlier and Milliex had left-wing sympathies made them different from most of the leading British Council employees in Greece at the time and afforded them access to a number of writers, artists and intellectuals who were largely shunned by the Council's representatives at a time of civil strife between Left and Right in Greece and the establishment of mostly conservative and anti-Communist governments in the country. This may reveal the fundamental difference between what the British Council and the Institut Français were ultimately aiming to do: while the Council's activities can be seen as part of an Anglo-American effort to keep Greece firmly in the Western political camp, the purpose of the French Institute was (and was perceived by Greeks to be) far less directly political and more cultural, aiming instead to perpetuate and reinforce an already long-standing Franco-Greek cultural relationship that was less dominated by Cold War confrontations – and also aiming to compensate for what could rightly have been perceived to be the post-War global ascendancy of the English language and the gradual dominance of American culture. Yet in the end, the Anglo-Greek cultural interactions examined in this volume were derailed not by factors directly related to the Cold War – the civil war and the schism between Left and Right in Greece – but by a manifestation of the worldwide decolonization movement, namely the Greek Cypriots' struggle for union with Greece, which became a national cause espoused by Greeks from all parts of the political spectrum.

I shall however close on a more positive note by quoting the view from the late 1940s, as relayed by Rex Warner, who wrote that the British Council 'is seldom given credit for an efficiency, a willingness to experiment, a tolerance and a responsibility which are seldom to be found in other organizations of the same kind.'[62]

PETER MACKRIDGE

Notes

1 The beginning of EOKA's armed struggle is conventionally dated to 1 April 1955. The British Institute library in Nicosia was destroyed by arson on 17 September 1955. The British Institute building in Patras was damaged by protestors on 1 November 1955 and a bomb exploded on the premises of the Institute of English Studies in Athens on 16 December 1955.

2 Gioula Koutsopanagou, 'Πολιτογράφηση και νομική θωράκιση του ελληνικού προσκοπισμού, 1917–1920', in Vangelis Karamanolakis et al. (eds.), *Η ελληνική νεολαία στον 20° αιώνα: Πολιτικές διαδρομές, κοινωνικές πρακτικές και πολιτιστικές εκφράσεις* (Athens, 2010), p. 394.

3 *Εθνικό και Καποδιστριακό Πανεπιστήμιο Αθηνών, Τμήμα Αγγλικής Γλώσσας και Φιλολογίας: 56 χρόνια παρουσίας* (Athens, 2008), pp. 5–6. For the connection between language teaching and the broader cultural activities of the British Council in Greece see Gioula Koutsopanagou's chapter in the present volume.

4 Tina Krontiris, ' "Henry V" and the Anglo-Greek Alliance in World War II', in Graham Bradshaw and Tom Bishop (eds.), *The Shakespearean International Yearbook*, 8 (London: Routledge, 2008), p. 34.

5 See, e.g., Alexander Kitroeff, 'Documents: Cyprus, 1950–1954: The Prelude to the Crisis, Part I: 1950', *Journal of the Hellenic Diaspora*, 15/1–2 (Spring-Summer 1988), p. 72.

6 This is borne out by the official history of the Council, Frances Donaldson, *The British Council: The First Fifty Years* (London, 1984). When I say 'British Council', I mean not only the Council *per se*, but also other related organizations in Greece, particularly the British Institutes set up in various parts of Greece under the Council's aegis.

7 Two of these novels are discussed by David Roessel and Jim Potts in their chapters in this volume.

8 Reginald Leeper, *When Greek Meets Greek* (London, 1950).

9 C.M. Woodhouse, *The Struggle for Greece, 1941–1949* (London, 1976), pp. 148–49.

10 The term 'soft power' (also used by Dimitris Tziovas and Jim Potts in this volume) was invented by Joseph Nye about 1990. The *Oxford English Dictionary* defines it as 'an approach to international relations which avoids coercion and relies on economic, ideological, and cultural influences, rather than on military action'.

11 The same could be said of Lawrence Durrell's *Bitter Lemons*, which the author claimed, at the beginning of the Preface, to be 'not a political book': see David Roessel, ' "This Is Not a Political Book" ': *Bitter Lemons* as British Propaganda', *Byzantine and Modern Greek Studies*, 24 (2000), pp. 235–45.

12 Politis' letters to the press are reproduced in Yiorgos Kallinis, *Σχεδίασμα Βιβλιογραφίας Κοσμά Πολίτη (1930–2000)* (Thessaloniki, 2008), pp. 56–58. The extract from Cardiff's letter is quoted from Dimitris Daskalopoulos, 'Βιβλιογραφία Γ.Κ. Κατσίμπαλη', *Νέα Εστία*, 108 (1980), p. 1530.

INTRODUCTION   17

13 For more on the attacks against the 'clique' allegedly headed by Katsimbalis see Avi Sharon's chapter in this volume.

14 See Michael Llewellyn-Smith's chapter about Runciman's experiences in Athens.

15 Steven Runciman, 'Zante and Its Capital Zakynthos Destroyed in the Recent Earthquake', *Architectural Review* (October 1953), pp. 214–20. For more on Runciman see Michael Llewellyn-Smith's chapter.

16 The bibliographer, raconteur and literary publicist Katsimbalis had already achieved international fame as the 'Colossus of Maroussi' in Henry Miller's memoir of the same name (1941).

17 Seferis to Katsimbalis, 2 November 1949, in G.K. Katsimbalis and Giorgos Seferis, Ἀγαπητέ μου Γιώργο': Ἀλληλογραφία (1924–1970), ed. Dimitris Daskalopoulos, vol. 2 (Athens, 2009), p. 142.

18 George Thaniel, *Seferis and Friends*, ed. Ed Phinney (Stratford, Ontario, 1994), p. 18.

19 George Seferis, *The King of Asine and Other Poems* (London, 1948).

20 Warner gamely undertook to write the Introduction (C.P. Cavafy, *Poems*, translated by John Mavrogordato (London, 1951), pp. 1–9) after E.M. Forster, followed by T.S. Eliot, had declined an invitation to do so (Bodleian Library, Papers of John Mavrogordato, MS Dep. Mavrogordato 51). Maurice Bowra was another who declined to write the introduction: 'Shamefacedly, Maurice pleaded that a Warden of Wadham could not be associated with such sexually explicit material' (Leslie Mitchell, *Maurice Bowra: A Life* (Oxford, 2009), p. 127). Warner was no doubt approached by John Lehmann, who had been Leonard Woolf's partner at the Hogarth Press from 1938 to 1946. It is significant that Warner's Introduction, dated 1949, makes no reference to the translations. In a review ('In the Rue Lepsius', *The Listener*, 5 July 1951), Forster was lukewarm about Mavrogordato's renderings. In a private letter he described the translations by 'Wooden cordato' as 'reliable rather than inspired' (Forster to G.P. Savidis, 25 July 1958, in Peter Jeffreys (ed.), *The Forster-Cavafy Letters: Friends at a Slight Angle* (Cairo and New York, 2009), p. 120).

21 The text of the talk is published in Rex Warner, *Personal Impressions: Talks on Writers and Writing*, ed. Marion B. McLeod (Sydney, 1986), pp. 15–20. The authors whose personalities and work he described in his talk are Sikelianos, Kazantzakis, Seferis and Elytis.

22 Warner, *Views of Attica and Its Surroundings* (London, 1950), pp. 73–74.

23 George Seferis, *Poems* (London, 1960).

24 George Seferis, *On the Greek Style: Selected Essays in Poetry and Hellenism*, translated by Rex Warner and Th. D. Frangopoulos, with an introduction by Rex Warner (London, 1967).

25 Mark Ford, review of Bernard Spencer, *Complete Poetry, Translations and Selected Prose*, ed. Peter Robinson (Tarset, 2011), in *London Review of Books*, 17 November 2011.

26 For this poem see Spencer, *Complete Poetry*, and Robinson's Introduction, ibid., pp. 23–24.

27 Robert Liddell, *Cavafy: A Critical Biography* (London, 1974, revised edn 2000).

28 Robert Liddell, *Aegean Greece* (London, 1954); *The Morea* (London, 1958); *Mainland Greece* (London, 1965).

29 Francis King, *Introducing Greece* (London, 1956).

30 For details of Leigh Fermor's life see Artemis Cooper, *Patrick Leigh Fermor: An Adventure* (London, 2012). See Chapter 11 of that volume for his career at the British Institute.

31 Lawrence Durrell, *Six Poems from the Greek of Sekilianos [sic] and Seferis* (Rhodes, 1946).

32 See Nanos Valaoritis, 'Remembering the Poets: Translating Seferis with Durrell and Bernard Spencer', in Anna Lillios (ed.), *Lawrence Durrell and the Greek World* (Selinsgrove, PA, 2004), pp. 46–53.

33 Emmanuel Royidis, *Pope Joan: A Romantic Biography*, translated from the Greek by Lawrence Durrell (London, 1954).

34 Lawrence Durrell, *Prospero's Cell: A Guide to the Landscape and Manners of the Island of Corcyra* (London, 1945); *Reflections of a Marine Venus: A Companion to the Landscape of Rhodes* (London, 1953); *Bitter Lemons* (London, 1957).

35 For more on Durrell and Greece see the contributions by Avi Sharon and Dimitris Tziovas in the present volume.

36 John Craxton, 'Obituary: Nikos Ghika', *The Independent*, 7 September 1994. For more on Craxton see Ian Collins, *John Craxton*, Introduction by David Attenborough (Farnham, 2011).

37 The source of the information concerning the final issue is Katsimbalis himself, quoted in Massimo Peri, *Τα Νέα Γράμματα: Lettere Nuove (1935–1945)* (Rome, 1974), p. 74.

38 Valaoritis to Katsimbalis, 4 December 1949, in Nanos Valaoritis and Giorgos Seferis, *Αλληλογραφία* (Athens, 2004), p. 207.

39 Rex Warner, 'Introduction' (dated 'Athens, 1946'), in Seferis, *The King of Asine and Other Poems*, p. 7.

40 The exhibition was curated by Ronald Crichton, who was later to become the music critic of the *Financial Times*.

41 Warner, *Views of Attica and Its Surroundings*, p. 75.

42 The first of these lectures was given at the British Institute on 17 December 1946 and published in the June 1947 issue of the *Anglo-Greek Review*, and the second was delivered on 2 May 1947 and published in the May 1947 issue. English translations of the lectures on Theophilos and on Cavafy and Eliot are included in Seferis, *On the Greek Style*, pp. 1–12 and 119–161. As Warner notes in his introduction to that volume (pp. VIII–IX), although the occasion for the essay on Theophilos was the exhibition in Athens, it was the fruit of Seferis' years-long admiration for the painter's work.

INTRODUCTION   19

43 'Ena tzitziki leei ton pono tou' and 'Topio Elliniko', *The Record*, 2/1 (December 1949).

44 Marina Kokkinidou, 'Το περιοδικό *Αγγλοελληνική Επιθεώρηση* (1945–1955): περίοδοι, στόχοι και συμβολή του στη μεταπολεμικη πολιτισμική ζωή', unpublished doctoral dissertation, Aristotle University of Thessaloniki, 2002.

45 KKE: Greek Communist Party; EAM: National Liberation Front; ELAS: Greek Popular Liberation Army (military wing of EAM). In his memoir Leeper (*When Greek Meets Greek*, p. 152) points out that both sides to the Varkiza agreement were republicans.

46 The AGIS, set up in Athens in October 1944, was an offshoot of the Political Warfare Executive.

47 Stephen Dorrill, *MI6: Fifty Years of Special Operations* (London, 2000), p. 313. Johnstone also went on to translate *The Tale of a Town* (London, 1976) by the Cretan writer Pantelis Prevelakis, as well as novels by the Bosnian Croat writer Ivo Andrić.

48 See the contribution by Dimitris Daskalopoulos in this volume.

49 'Erotokritos', a lecture given at the Parnassos society on 11 March 1946, was published in the June-July 1946 issue of the *Review*, while 'Letter on "The Thrush" ' appeared in the *Review* in July-August 1950. It was written in response to a review of the poem by Andreas Karantonis in the January-February 1950 issue (see Katsimbalis to Seferis, 29 November 1949, in Katsimbalis and Seferis, *'Αγαπητέ μου Γιώργο'*, vol. 2, p. 146). An English translation of the 'Letter' can be found in Seferis, *On the Greek Style*, pp. 99–105 and is followed by a translation of the poem (107–17).

50 For further details see the chapter by Lucile Arnoux.

51 John Lehmann edited and published a volume dedicated to Capetanakis' memory: *Demetrios Capetanakis: A Greek Poet in England* (London, 1947).

52 Spender's interest in modern Greece is suggested by the fact that he applied for the Byron Chair of English at Athens University when it became vacant in 1952. See Spender's letter to Seferis, 3 May 1952, reproduced in Thaniel, *Seferis and Friends*, p. 25. In the event, Bernard Blackstone held the post from 1952 to 1961.

53 Since Valaoritis' talk at the conference overlapped to some extent with a publish text entitled 'A Memoir', which he published in *Agenda*, 43/2–3 (2008), it is not included in this volume. Most of the information about him that I mention in my Introduction is drawn from his memoir.

54 Roderick Beaton, *George Seferis: Waiting for the Angel: A Biography* (New Haven, CT and London, 2003), p. 261.

55 Given the leading role played by Lehmann in the dissemination of contemporary Greek literature in Britain, research in his archives, kept at the University of Texas and Princeton University, is likely to yield rich pickings.

56 Nanos Valaoritis, 'Modern Greek Poetry', *Horizon*, 75 (March 1946), pp. 205–6. Valaoritis wrote in a letter to Seferis (10 February 1945) that this article was commissioned by Connolly (Valaoritis and Seferis, *Αλληλογραφία*, p. 45).

57 *The King of Asine and Other Poems* contains no indication as to which translators were responsible for which poems. All the translations are now reprinted in Spencer, *Complete Poetry*.

58 Valaoritis told Seferis that it was Lehmann who suggested a volume of latter's poems in English (10 December 1945, Valaoritis and Seferis, *Αλληλογραφία*, p. 47). For the reference to Eliot see ibid., p. 106.

59 4 September 1948, ibid., p. 103.

60 As far as I know, there is no complete list of BBC broadcasts on modern Greek topics between 1945 and 1955. These included brief talks by Seferis and Warner on Sikelianos to commemorate the latter's death in 1951, and by Seferis on Cavafy's poem 'Ithaca' in 1952. For information about articles of Greek interest that appeared in the BBC's magazine *The Listener* see David Holton's contribution to this volume.

61 For more details about the despatch of Greek scholars to France see the chapter by Lucile Arnoux in the present volume.

62 Warner, *Views of Attica and its Surroundings*, p. 72.

Chapter 1
The end of an affair:
Anglo-Greek relations, 1939–1955

Robert Holland

In her memoir *An Affair of the Heart,* published in 1957, the celebrated film critic Dilys Powell, who years before had been married to the Director of the British School at Athens, wrote of her return to the Greek capital in 1945. Still harbouring the 'remembered magic' of pre-war days, Powell conjured up her uneasiness at that time, even the consciousness of a threat. 'There was nothing to which one could point,' she wrote. 'Occasionally a sullen face, perhaps sometimes a blank [stare] instead of the old eagerness of manner. . . . It was . . . like a faint drum-beat in the air . . . I was horrified to find myself beginning to dislike my friends.'[1] It may be that Powell was here transposing onto her memories of 1945 tendencies that had by 1957 become more explicit because of recent Cypriot events. But in the years after the appearance of Powell's book any widespread remembrance, either British or Greek, that there ever had been 'an affair of the heart' between the two countries more or less dissolved. When the British Ambassador went to Corfu town in May 1964 for the centennial celebrations of Ionian accession to Greece, he was disappointed to find that there was little if any token that it had been a *British* cession in the first place; nor was there seemingly any recognition of a special historical tie between Britain and Greece.[2] And if we leap further ahead to the current trauma within the eurozone, there is almost no vestige in British public debate that Greece is a nation with which the United Kingdom had enjoyed over a long period an intimate, if always ambivalent, connection

Powell's 'remembered magic' of the 1930s need not be taken too much at face value. It was the magic of the expatriate archaeologists – her husband, Humfry Payne, had led digs on Crete and in the Gulf of Corinth – and in these circles engagement with anything other than ancient pots and pans in host societies can sometimes be limited. Anglo-Greek relations had often been anything but magical. After the Asia Minor disaster of 1922 there had been a strong reaction. Still, there had been something of a revival towards the end of the 1930s. The retiring British Ambassador in Athens, Sir Sydney Waterlow, writing his final despatch on 31 May 1939, credited a recent strengthening in Britain's standing, as he saw it, to the fact that it was no longer firmly tied to the faction of Eleftherios Venizelos.[3] The British had been careful not to extend any sympathy to Venizelos' botched coup in 1935, even though his usual Cretan sympathizers had signalled a willingness to 'raise the British flag'.[4] Ambassador Waterlow also noted the benefits from the cultural endeavours of the newly-founded British Council, for which Greece, and the Mediterranean in general, afforded an early focus. Great Britain now being equally popular, he claimed, with the two hostile camps in Greek political life, Waterlow concluded, 'There seems nothing in the situation to cause uneasiness as to the future course of Anglo-Greek relations. Their foundations are broad and firm . . . nothing but our defeat in battle is likely to shake them.'[5]

But of course the British were to be defeated in battle in Greece during the spring of 1941. The American Ambassador, Lincoln MacVeagh, attributed the surprising resilience of Greece in responding to Mussolini's attack across the Epirus frontier after October 1940 to the effects of 'national intoxication', a people united in 'one party, one class, one purpose'.[6] The phenomenon bore some similarities to Britain's own collective experience in the Blitz. But there was a resemblance rather than any lasting tie between these two experiences. In British diplomatic and military circles, the idea of diverting troops from the hard-pressed front in Egypt to Greece from the end of 1940 found many doubters. Such critics felt that the Greeks, like the Yugoslavs, must be left to their fate if and when German forces descended in overwhelming strength to make up for Italian feebleness. General Archibald Wavell, Commander-in-Chief in the Middle East, was instinctively opposed to his army being stripped for Greece's sake.[7] The decision to send a British Commonwealth expeditionary force (mostly Australian and New Zealand formations) to Greece was essentially political. Churchill said that it was necessary for Britain to 'share Greece's ordeal'.[8] But Anthony Eden's role as foreign secretary in this new intervention in Greece stands out just as significantly. More than any other British leader from the mid-1930s he had been committed to defending the country's stake in the Mediterranean. Eden's marked sympathy with Greece was consistent with that commitment. This is worth underlining because the gradual disintegration of Anglo-Hellenic friendship in the early and middle 1950s was to be closely linked to Eden's own person; his attitude then to Greece was often to be characterized by biting sarcasm, albeit tinged by a certain fond nostalgia.

But what did 'sharing Greece's ordeal' in 1940–41 mean for the British? It did not really mean saving Greece from Germany. Nobody thought that was actually possible. It was a moral, rather than immediately practical, argument, but moral in an inevitably subtle sense. Only by making its own blood sacrifice on Greek soil could the British Empire legitimate the later restoration of its influence in the southern Balkans if and when Germany should be defeated in other, more decisive, theatres. There were good reasons for the Greek leadership to doubt whether the 'saving' they were being offered in all those heated conferences with the British in Athens during February and March 1941 was really worth it. Going over yet again all those differences about troop dispositions, and whether the concentration should be on the Aliakmon Line or further to the north – 'haggling at an oriental bazaar', as it seemed to British participants – there is a constant implication that the sub-text was more telling than the text.[9]

The real test of the British commitment to Greece was the size of the expedition sent. This was enough to share Greek travails but not enough to seriously resist Hitler's 'Operation Marita'. Suggestively, and in contrast to what happened some months later when Japan attacked Malaya, once things went badly wrong Churchill did not send an order to General Wilson at the head of the expeditionary forces in Greece to make a last stand. It had been enough, symbolically, to go there in the first place. The story of the highly improvised, dispersed and varyingly successful evacuations in 1941 – things went very badly wrong at Kalamata – are well known. Some 58,000 troops got away. It might be easy for those of a cynical disposition to write off the frequent anecdotes of British and Anzac troop carriers passing through the villages of Thessaly and the Peloponnese, strewn with flowers by local inhabitants amidst calls to 'come back soon', as self-serving inventions to cover a catastrophic defeat, were it not that the evidence for such displays of local feeling is so plentiful.[10] But the psychology of the end-game in Greece during the spring of 1941 was extremely complicated, and its shadow was to hang over almost everything that came later.

Greece itself almost disappeared from British minds for some while thereafter. Insofar as the British kept a stake in Greek affairs, this was purely external. The role of the exiled Greek government from May 1941 was little more than to authorize the use of its national forces under British command in the Middle East. Greek politicians who left the country were helplessly subordinate to British civil and military authority, notably in Cairo, and one suspects that the petty humiliations they endured led to a hankering later on for a payback time. A British observer at Allied Forces Headquarters in the Mediterranean, perhaps with feminine intuition all the more astute in picking up purely personal vibrations, noted the growing mental distance between the British and counterparts from those countries undergoing physical occupation.[11] In the Greek case this had a special relevance.

Still, had the Anglo-Americans done what many anticipated and, after occupying Sicily in mid-1943, launched a full-scale Balkan offensive, subsequent events would surely have been very different. With a clearly superior force on Greek soil the Allies could have successfully imposed a new order of their own. This would have been extremely messy regarding governance and rehabilitation, probably even more so than the fairly dire experience of Sicily, but no local forces – not even the Communists (KKE) – would have dared to actually launch a counter-challenge. Instead the Allies got bogged down in mainland Italy from September 1943. Greece, admittedly, became an obsession with Churchill himself, though even for the British prime minister Greece would have quickly taken a back seat had he ever succeeded in his vision of getting Turkey to become a belligerent on the Allied side (Turkey entered the war, and then only nominally, in February 1945). The disastrous operation in the Dodecanese in the late summer of 1943 – one very much imposed by Churchill on his military advisers – had about it the air of 1941: another sharing of the ordeal by a force too small and vulnerable to sustain a strategic lodgement. By this time very few in Whitehall were party to Churchill's enthusiasm for the Aegean. The disillusionment about, and marginalization of, Greece was capped by the mutinies amongst the Royal Hellenic Forces, climaxing in April 1944. Richard Capell's scathing references recorded in his *Simiomata* to the formation of the Greek Mountain Brigade – later to have a notable fighting record in Italy – as being driven by the need to expiate the shame of the mutinies in Egypt were typical of the sharp feelings amongst soldiers in the field.[12]

Against that background, we can see that what happened inside Greece after 1941, including the resistance, or what passed for a resistance, including the role of the Special Operations Executive (SOE), was decidedly obscure so far as most Britons were concerned. SOE itself in this setting was a halfcock exercise run from Cairo with much bluster and what seems also to have been a degree of personal peculation, just when the Egyptian capital was being relegated in the wartime hierarchy: a backwater within a backwater. The British themselves, of course, were also being relegated within the wartime Grand Alliance, second-class players behind the Americans and Soviets. C.M. Woodhouse could still recall how 'In the name of the British' resonated with significance on Greek mountainsides, especially when lubricated by gold sovereigns.[13] Similarly, Richard Capell discovered on Chios the sentiment 'Dear England, you are beloved. . . . Your name spells hope', whilst on hungry Andros the islanders dreamed of British rule. But, touching and comprehensible though this might be, it was equally testimony to just how hermetically sealed off from the outside world Greece had been for four years whilst so much elsewhere had drastically altered.[14] The reconnect was bound to be fraught with miscalculations and false, even fatal, steps.

The constrained and highly tentative nature of British re-intervention on the Greek mainland after September 1944 – Operation Manna – flowed from much of this, as did a large degree of confusion amongst Greeks as to what was actually intended. This fresh expedition was little more than 8,000 troops at first, and not all of those were combatants. It had no heavy artillery. The overall force was very naval – 'a small Anglo-Greek armada' in one description[15] – and had the distinctly old-fashioned feel of a nineteenth-century limited pacification, a bit like the partial occupation of Crete by the local fleets of the Powers in 1897. Its very quaintness was one reason why the Americans regarded it with such disdain. The US Chief of Naval Staff, Admiral King, sarcastically remarked that the exercise being embarked upon 'does not appear to be part of a war in which the United States is participating'.[16] This was indeed the point. Churchill's new intervention in Greece had little to do with events which we today lump together as the Second World War.

Who was actually responsible for the bloodshed in Syntagma Square on 4 December 1944, and for the wider breakdown thereafter, is now beyond meaningful reconstruction. The British were not going to let themselves be written out of the script for Greece's future, especially once they had already been ejected from elsewhere in the Balkans. Likewise the Communists were not going to have prised from their grasp a prominence, perhaps the leading place, in the government of Greece, especially given their leading position in what sporadic resistance there had been to the occupation by the Axis states. Compared to these two actors, everybody else – including the liberal politician George Papandreou, Napoleon Zervas, leader of the non-communist resistance organization EDES, the King of Greece, *et al.* – were just bit-part actors. On the face of it, there was, or should have been, plenty of scope to make uncomfortable but workable accommodations. That this did not happen seems more than anything else due to sheer miscalculation and ignorance, a lack of basic information amongst the key parties and the uncontrollable fear and suspicion stemming from confusion about the real direction of affairs. The fog of the looming post-war was quite as thick as that which had enveloped the war itself.

The detailed events of December 1944 and their aftermath will not be repeated here. General Scobie's forces cleared Athens but not much more. Operation Manna had very clearly prescribed limits from the start. Progress outside the capital was patchy, especially in the north of the country, where British personnel fell back on Salonica. An uneasy stand-off prevailed in Greece's second city, though it is striking that here, where the raw material for an explosion was at least as marked as it was in Athens, local protagonists were able to come to an understanding. In other Macedonian towns those who had prematurely associated with the British immediately on their return sometimes had a hard time of it when the latter suddenly left again.[17] By the time of the Varkiza agreement in early February 1945 the British Army presence was around 80,000. But this was to be not a base-line for an expanding presence, but the peak of the British commitment. There was still a real war on elsewhere and British forces started to be withdrawn to western Europe almost immediately.

Post-Varkiza, British troops were involved in intensive patrolling of towns within the area from which KKE-ELAS forces had retired. Their essential achievement was to preside over the revival of a basic administrative and civilian shell, as well as to supervise distribution of emergency food supplies, principally via the United Nations Relief and Rehabilitation Agency.[18] Inevitably relief was inefficient and distorted in distribution, favouring Athens and especially groups connected to the shaky and in many ways still nominal government. Civil servants were invariably privileged. Attempts to correct this bias were never more than formulaic.

This was the stage at which the British Military, Police and Prisons and Naval Missions first took shape, charged with the reform of Greek institutions. Training was at the heart of the overall task. But under the circumstances this could not amount to much. The Naval Mission proved the most unproblematical. Here an established tradition was involved. British maritime missions to Greece went back to the early 1900s, though not without hiccups along the way. Royal Hellenic ships had served under the Royal Navy during the war at sea after 1940. A Greek battleship had been in the receiving line when the Italian Fleet surrendered in Malta's Grand Harbour in September 1943.[19] Against this background it is not surprising that Greek naval officers usually spoke English to some degree. The work of the Naval Mission – such as vital mine-clearance, essential if commerce was to revive – after 1945 was able to proceed unimpeded by events ashore. This did not mean that it was without tension or free from what in a characteristically waspish British assessment was termed 'the corrupt political game'.[20] In 1946 the Royal Hellenic Navy withdrew from exercises of the British Mediterranean Fleet. Still, until the end of the civil war in Greece the British Naval Mission was able to operate largely in a vacuum of its own.

The British Military and Police Missions were to prove more chequered. Greek Army officers tended to have French language rather than English (George Grivas, the leader of the virulently anti-Communist 'Chi', and eventually to cause the British so many problems in Cyprus, had once trained at the élite French military academy at Saint-Cyr). The introduction of a British brigade structure into Greek military organization did not go entirely smoothly.[21] On the other hand, British Army surplus – clothing, equipment, guns – was almost universal, and for most of the following period the Greek National Army looked like the British Army, as did some parts of its enemy, the Democratic Army. Amidst the chaos of the *Dekemvriana* the priority was large-scale emergency recruitment into Greek Government forces to bring them up to an operational level, necessarily with little regard to any real training.

At least after Varkiza the goal of creating a 'new model' Greek Army could make some modest progress. After October 1945 the British Military Mission was able to withdraw from operations proper into the advisory and logistical role that had been intended in the first place. The onset of real civil war, however, in mid to late 1946 brought about a further reversal of functions. For some time thereafter British officers were present at both brigade and corps levels, though scrupulously kept junior in rank to the Greek officers to whom they were attached. Because the *gendarmerie* under current Greek conditions played a military rather than strictly police role, the British Police Mission could hardly get on with its intended job of reform. All it could do was exercise a loose supervision over Government prisons, though these responsibilities did not extend to the political detention camps. Obtaining secondments to Greece from British Police Forces, including the Royal Ulster Constabulary – the long-time Head of the Mission in Greece, Sir Charles Wickham, was predictably an RUC man, a reprise of that Force's established role in underpinning the Palestine Police – always proved difficult.[22] Still, of all these activities, the British Police Mission in Greece was arguably the most effective and left the most distinctive legacy.

Suggestively, the work of these various British agencies was subject to a ban on any official news reporting back in the United Kingdom.[23] No official communiqués were issued at any point. The reasons were political. British actions in late 1944 had been intensely controversial at home, especially in the Labour Party, whose party conference at the time was as preoccupied with this matter as with the vision of a New Jerusalem at home.[24] This engagement with Greece, however, soon faded, and – to the bitter disappointment of the Greek Left – Ernest Bevin as foreign secretary in the Labour Government after July 1945 continued Churchill's policy on Greece without triggering a revolt in party ranks. But this did not mean that the moral and ideological rancour associated with Greece amongst leftists and progressives in Britain evaporated. As a result, the last thing the Labour Government wanted was to trumpet the effort being made there. The black-out policy on news continuing to the end of the civil war therefore arose from the need to keep embarrassments to a minimum. One subsidiary effect was that no British military medals were issued for service in Greece, in considerable contrast with American practice after 1948, where such medals abounded. The lack of any recognition caused resentment among British personnel. Such service in Greece certainly did little for individual preferment and careers; often quite the reverse, since to be out of sight was also to be out of mind.[25] Overall, in the British domestic setting, Greece quickly lost the transient salience it had possessed in late 1944 and early 1945. This contrasted keenly with the Spanish civil war ten years before, which had made such a lasting impact on highly polarized British imaginations and ideals. In effect, Greek affairs were tucked away in an obscure corner and covered over with a drape.

The British Information Services (BIS) – in which Osbert Lancaster was prominent, evoked in his *Classical Landscape with Figures*[26] – offered another aspect of intervention. It evolved out of the Allied information machinery (the Anglo-Greek Information Service, abbreviated as AIS and AGIS) with its wartime military intelligence bias, and the transition to a civilian role was never complete. After 'liberation' the local press was in disarray, and the only place that ordinary Greeks (certainly outside Athens) could get access to printed news was often in BIS and British Council provincial offices. Distribution of scarce newsprint was one means of encouraging a press of the 'moderate' sort that the British keenly wished to see. Articles were planted in 'friendly' papers. The BIS was also instrumental in establishing a national broadcasting authority, supposedly on the BBC model. What followed was a microcosm of the wider British experience. The capacity for detailed management or control soon disintegrated, and British oversight was withdrawn as a hopeless exercise. When Osbert Lancaster wrote an extended review for Whitehall of the BIS's work in mid-1946, his conclusion was that it had already failed in its political aim.[27] He advised that the whole thing should be scaled down to the narrower goal of promoting Anglo-Greek cultural ties, and the activities of the British Council and British Institutes (the latter concerned with English-language instruction) over the next few years followed naturally, until the Cyprus crisis came along and made their work almost impossible.

Certainly during 1945–46 anything British was still very much *en vogue* in Athens. There was even a new Chair in British Life and Thought at the University of Athens. The fact that the appointee was an English academic with hardly any credentials did not seem to matter ('obviously not first class', it was remarked in the Foreign Office).[28] In this the semi-farcical elements in Olivia Manning's portrayal of highbrow British propaganda in the Balkans, *Friends and Heroes*, had a post-war expression. In Anglo-Greek context highbrow also meant high-class. In the Foreign Office the Anglo-Hellenic League was scathingly termed as 'run by Mayfair for Mayfair' and was thought to have squandered an opportunity to break out of its narrow circles both in Athens and London.[29] Contemporary accounts and memories of the period – Capell's *Simiomata* has already been mentioned, and Mary Henderson's sometimes moving *Xenia*[30] – bring out something of this flavour. Such a constraint has perhaps never entirely gone away, as the cult around Patrick Leigh Fermor – with perhaps rather frozen conceptions of what both Britain and Greece were actually about as societies – also suggests.

The political narrative after Varkiza hinged on the elections of April 1946 and the ensuing September's plebiscite on the monarchy. By the start of that year the Labour Government began to look around for an elected Greek government onto which responsibility could be shoved. Having thereafter pushed through the elections, boycotted by the KKE, the British were not well placed to delay the plebiscite. Arguments at the time and since that further delay would have been preferable leave out of account the constraints operating on the British. Had the parliamentary elections provided for the ideal British outcome – a rough balance between the Right and the ostensibly Republican Left-Centre – they might have had the sort of equilibrium needed to secure their own purposes. But the dynamic unleashed proved far too strong for the British to manipulate in one direction or another. 'As usual,' Sir Harold Caccia at the Foreign Office commented, 'we are forced to make a choice of evils.'[31] There could not be much doubt which was the preferred evil in the circumstances. In making that choice, however, the abject dependence of the Greek Right on the British came to be offset by a degree of British dependence on the Greek Right – assuming, that is, that the British still wished to stay in the Greek arena at all.

The motif of a 'choice of evils' at this time regarding Greece is striking to anybody acquainted with the making of British policies regarding Cyprus a few years later. By the middle of 1958, as events span out of control in that island, the need to make a 'choice of evils' became central to the formulation of British dilemmas in the island.[32] Such a convergence of language and metaphors is perhaps logical, since the same officials were often involved, Caccia included. Just as one seemingly had to choose between repugnant Communists and only slightly more acceptable Rightists in Greece in 1946–47, so one had to choose between obdurate Greek-Cypriots and obstreperous Turks in 1958–59. In each case, the choice was purely theoretical, because it could only go one way under prevailing conditions. One is left wondering to what extent British images and formulations embedded in the Greek Civil War got transposed onto Cypriot developments later.

Meanwhile, to return to 1946 as it unfolded in Greece, Britain's standing with both the Left and the Right became subject to erosion. On the Left a basic paradox between a residual desire for British patronage and a deep resentment arising from recent events gave way to outright hatred. Yet although the Right might profess strong attachment to the traditional British connection, more equivocal feelings existed there also, and after parliamentary elections and the plebiscite these sentiments came more into the open. The British could be blamed for getting in the way of a draconian and swift liquidation of rebellion. It was in this milieu that Grivas, at the head of his Chi militia, began to develop strong anti-British traits. Already in 1947 Osbert Lancaster in his *Classical Landscape with Figures* could point out that although the British position in the country remained exalted thanks, as he expressed it, 'to Byron and all that', it was rather less secure than most people seemed to imagine.[33] If Sir Sydney Waterlow had been able in 1939 to find comfort in the fact that Britain had become equally popular with *both* mutually hostile camps in Greece, one aspect of the later 1940s was that the British were compromised whether they looked to the Left or to the Right, though the implications of this were not to be transparent for a few more years yet.

Questions of irredentism offered one expression for such unstable tendencies. In 1944–45 this was more than offset by the fact that Britain offered almost the only guarantee of keeping existing Greek frontiers intact, let alone expanding them. Nor did this factor altogether disappear afterwards. But British abstention on Greek claims concerning Epirus at the Paris Peace Conference during 1946 constituted an early turning point. In Salonica local people, both on Left and Right, stayed at home in mass protest.[34] The British were conscious that one way to make absolutely sure of Greek goodwill was to hand over Cyprus. Cretan autonomy after 1898 offered one possible model to adopt in this case.[35] But it did not take much discussion for the dominant view to form that the Greeks had a long way to go before becoming reliable recipients for such a new gift. Although the ex-Italian Dodecanese were handed over in stages during 1947–48, this was only because Turkey remained as yet still in the doghouse. It was axiomatic that the cession of the Dodecanese represented the last such extension of Greek territorial sovereignty, not a mere payment on account, as the Greeks hoped and believed.[36] British attitudes to what were designated as 'Hellenistic-Byzantine' ambitions took on an increasingly sarcastic tone.[37] The edginess over Cyprus on both sides by the end of the 1940s evolved in this setting, though in February 1950 the British Embassy in Athens could still feel 'that the average Greek is too much concerned with the internal situation . . . to work up much excitement over Cyprus'.[38]

Irredentism offered just one aspect of the basic problem at the heart of British engagements with Greek public affairs: a search for the ever-elusive grail of 'moderation' and the 'middle ground'. Geoffrey Chandler, with wide personal experience of northern Greece in the 1940s, later provided an assessment in *The Divided Land: An Anglo-Greek Tragedy*. From his position as a field officer in Macedonia, he had sent a series of pleas to the Embassy to come out more actively in favour of a Left-Centre coalition. They – and similar pleas by other British personnel out in the country – went unheeded. The enigma of the British presence was summed up in the contemporary anecdote, recalled by Chandler, that in London it was assumed that the Embassy had a policy without ever saying quite what it was, whilst the Embassy complained that London had a policy which it failed to communicate to them.[39] Suggestively, essentially the same anecdote was circulating at the same time in Palestine.[40] In Greece, as in Palestine, the fact was that nobody had any policy. But then for a policy you need raw materials to make one. Hector McNeil, the Labour minister, noted in March 1946 that 'The Centre [in Greece] have squandered every chance we have given them', and it is the case that 'moderates' – nice and cuddly though they may be made to appear to outsiders – are not necessarily or indeed usually any less venal or politically toxic than other contending factions.[41] In fact dependence on outside forces often makes them the *least* effective partners in building sustainable positions for the future.

'Our [British] duty,' the Permanent Under-Secretary at the Foreign Office, Sir Orme Sargent, said of Greece on the eve of renewed civil war, 'is to hold the ring and see fair play, not to take part in the battle ourselves.'[42] But the response of people like Chandler, then and in retrospect, was that the British *had* taken part in the battle over a long period, and most notably during the events of December 1944. There was no point, it seemed to some, in pretending otherwise. To act as the British had done, and then to draw back and claim just to 'hold the ring', as opposed to acting decisively to encourage and even impose a balanced approach to internal divisions, was to adopt the worst of all half-way-house policies. Had the British done nothing in the first place to stop an ELAS drive to power, at least an equilibrium with at least some semblance of representing Greek society as a whole might eventually have come about, albeit no doubt with victims along the way, but avoiding the extremities that subsequently occurred.

The variables here, however, could go round in endless debate. But the key fact regarding the evolution of British policy was that by mid-1946 the essential context had changed from eighteen months before. In late 1944 Greece had still seemed an important stake in British regional strategy. As such, London was still prepared to pay the price of finding scarce resources to intervene, however tentatively. From mid-1946, however, Greece increasingly counted for little in British Mediterranean calculations – and least of all with Prime Minister Attlee, sceptical towards all Mediterranean and Middle Eastern engagements.[43] Willingness to stump up hard cash was fast evaporating. As the Cabinet Secretary summed up to Attlee the financial pressures surrounding the Greek commitment, 'the time has come to stop this drain'.[44] Hugh Dalton – who as Minister of Economic Warfare a few years earlier had been against any easing of the wartime blockade on enemy-occupied Greece, which had contributed to the famine there in the winter of 1941–42 – now as Chancellor of the Exchequer pressed for a limit of 50,000 to be put on the strength of the Greek National Army, a number that could only mean defeat. 'Holding the ring', with all its failings, was in fact the utmost that the British had ever been willing to do, and even that was coming very much into question.

The British would soon have got out, bag and baggage, from Greece, as they eventually did in Palestine, if the Americans had not pressed them to stay, and then accepted much of the financial burden themselves under the Truman Doctrine. But the usual narrative that the Americans effectively *replaced* the British in Greece needs qualification. American marines did not arrive till the end of 1947, and they never did come in large numbers. The emphasis of the American effort throughout was on economics and reconstruction. Their achievements, especially in reviving the transport infrastructure, were considerable. But this priority had its limitations, and both the British and the Greeks came to share a concern that, strategically, Greece was regarded in Washington as a mere 'holding operation' in the nascent Cold War.[45] By early 1949 there was even anxiety that at the first opportunity General Van Fleet, the US Commander, and his men would 'weigh anchor and sail away' as soon as the chance arose.[46] This explains why Greek reliance on the British had such an after-life, principally as a kind of insurance policy, even when its material base had largely disappeared.

The *modus operandi* of the British and American Missions is important. The Greek authorities had no direct access on supply questions to London or, much more importantly from 1947, to Washington. The Greeks had to plead with the Missions for whatever they wanted, and, if convinced, the Missions then argued the Greek case with their own governments. This process was a key feature of the 'disabled' nature of Greek governance, and partly explains why genuine responsibility only developed in a partial and distorted manner. The British and American mission commanders were represented on the main Greek defence organs, and not much could happen without their concurrence. Much chafing arose, and in becoming Commander-in-Chief during January 1949 General Alexandros Papagos insisted on more autonomy for his own decisions.

Significantly, however, the British and American Missions were by no means integrated, leaving some limited room to Greek ministers for playing off one against the other. General Van Fleet was adamantly opposed to any Anglo-American integration.[47] Co-ordination was patchy at best. At ambassadorial level things were generally cordial. US Ambassador Grady had come from Delhi, where he had enjoyed good, if still guarded, relations with the Mountbattens.[48] But Van Fleet himself – who had learned his trade under the egregious Anglophobe General George Patton during the war – was 'universally disliked' in the British Military Mission.[49] Greece in the later 1940s offered a connecting stage in prickly Anglo-American relations in the wider Mediterranean from Operation Torch in North Africa during November 1942 through to Suez in 1956, and indeed beyond.[50] Greek beliefs in the seamlessness of 'Anglo-American' aims and ambitions in the region are invariably illusory, though in many ways an understandable expression of Greece's own recurring vulnerability.

British and American assessments of Greece and its prospects, nonetheless, certainly came to overlap, above all in their uniform direness. British Ambassador Norton's comment in June 1948 that 'nothing in Greece is quite as bad or as good as it appears on the surface' was about as sympathetic as things got.[51] Greek politicians and the Greek officer class were particular butts of opprobrium. An insidious threat to the survival of a democratic Greece was seen to be the basic failure to give the ordinary footslogger in the National Army a real reason for fighting.[52] Most Athenians, and that meant most politicians, in these years hardly ever set foot outside a tight circle around the capital, making any real empathy with the sufferings of the countryside limited at best. Against this background even seemingly good news was usually interpreted by outsiders as something else. The repulse of the 'rebel' attack on Florina in February 1949 was described as 'more depressing than a defeat'.[53] Politically, the ministerial crisis at the start of that year sparked a fresh wave of disillusionment, and introduced what Norton termed 'the shadow of a sort of dictatorship' that perhaps never entirely lifted before the Junta arrived eighteen years later.[54] Nor did the Communist defeat in the summer of 1949 lead to any revision of this pessimism, since it could be argued that henceforth the Communists might prove even more dangerous back in 'civvies' than they had been as ragged insurgents.[55]

By 1949, anyway, the British Army was on the sidelines of operations in Greece, whilst the Greeks themselves were 'quite capable of running their own show'.[56] By this time it was British military personnel who were driving around in bashed-up Second World War troop-carriers, and their Greek counterparts who instead possessed shiny new American transporters.[57] On the other hand, if it was not inconceivable that in some sudden crisis Greece might still need Britain, Britain no longer really needed Greece. This was not because the British had forsaken the broader regional stake underpinning the original re-intervention of 1944–45, but its shape had changed, and essentially disengaged from the Balkans. British Mediterranean, and increasingly Middle Eastern, interests were serviced through other partners – with Turkey gaining new salience – eventually to take shape in the Baghdad Pact of the mid-1950s. In this setting the Aegean itself slipped to the margins of British strategic cartography. Almost as soon as the Communist rump on Mount Grammos was liquidated, the War Office in London was keen to get British troops off Greek soil once and for all. They had for some months been planning to divert part

ANGLO-GREEK RELATIONS, 1939–1955

of the garrison in Greece to Malta, where they would be far better placed for redeployment in any regional emergency.[58] Nor were the Greek authorities at all reluctant. On 19 November the Minister of War hosted a farewell dinner for the British Military Mission at, inevitably, the Hôtel Grande Bretagne, attended by Marshal Papagos himself.

The following gloriously sunny day the British military departure from Athens was accompanied by an appropriate ceremonial, the Commander of the 1st East Surreys laying a wreath on the Tomb of the Unknown Warrior, after which King Paul inspected the troops.[59] There were, inevitably, many references to 1941 and to December 1944, whilst Queen Frederika told Lady Norton that she felt like crying (tears were always part of the emotional armament of Anglo-Hellenism). 'It was felt,' Ambassador Norton reported, not able to squash altogether a negative vibration, 'that this was the end of a chapter, and though the immediate future of Greece looks rosy so long as American help continues on the present scale, this solemn and memorable celebration has caused a good deal of heart-searching, coinciding as it does with . . . social and economic problems, not to mention the clouds on the northern horizon' (the latter being an allusion to Greece's exposed northern borders).[60] But the final British military withdrawal came in a freezing cold Salonica on 5 February 1950 when the 1st Battalion Bedfordshire and Hertfordshire Regiment similarly departed, several Greek women being said to have collapsed with emotion at the saluting base.[61] Taken together, these events might be said to have encapsulated the authentic end of the Anglo-Hellenic phenomenon with all its accompanying rituals and symbols.

This, however, did not mean the end of a British Mission to Greece entirely. It could, and was, argued that the real challenge of institutional modernization in the still crippled country was only just beginning. This had particular relevance for the Police and Prisons Mission, whilst as usual the British Naval Mission sought to position itself as having a long-term role immune from other developments.[62] Yet although the Greek Government was not going to turf these foreign agencies out, its own enthusiasm for their continuance was underwhelming, and expressed itself in growing resistance to meeting the bulk of their local costs.[63] For some while too there had been a growing feeling that the Missions were themselves pointless if the Greek Government consistently refused to follow any advice tendered to them.[64] In the end, after several extensions, the Police Mission was terminated, somewhat reluctantly in some quarters, in June 1951. The British Naval Mission hung on till September 1955 but fell into dormancy after the disastrous Tripartite Conference on Cyprus in that month. The effective end of a permanent British naval presence was taken as a blow to Britain's special position in Greece, but if Admiral Selby, the commander, stayed, it was felt 'he would be exposed to non-cooperation and even insults'.[65] Selby was brought home, allowing Prime Minister Eden to comment with what had become his habitual spite towards Greece that 'we don't want to spend money on unwilling Greeks'.[66] Still, vestiges of an old naval tie continued even into the era of the Greek Colonels after 1967. The Greek regime was by no means happy, for example, to see the end of a permanent British naval presence in the Mediterranean in 1968,[67] whilst subsequent visits by Royal Navy ships to Greek ports was one facet of the residual official links thereafter maintained between London and Athens. The cancellation of the visits to Greece by Her Majesty's Ships *Tiger* and *Charybdis* in March 1974 following the formation of a new Labour Government in Britain was one minor indication of the wider crisis in the eastern Mediterranean shortly to lead to the implosion surrounding Cyprus a few months later.[68]

Writing to his friend George Seferis in May 1956, Patrick Leigh Fermor stated that the first volume of his projected trilogy, that on the Mani, would soon be in the press. 'Although it is an extremely pro-Greek book as you can imagine,' he said, 'I tremble to think of the sneers and jeering and hatred that lie in wait for me in the columns of the *Estia*, the *Akropolis* and the *Apoyeumatini*. I could write them myself. I know it so well,' adding that the cheap English press was no better.[69] 'One of the many gloomy aspects of the present bloody situation,' Leigh Fermor went on, 'is that it seems to have turned both Greece and England into enlarged caricatures that their worst enemies have always pretended they were.'[70] These caricatures were set to become even sharper over time. But perhaps part of the problem was that what in 1956 Patrick Leigh Fermor thought was pro-Greek was, in Greek perceptions, only pro-Greek in a very old-fashioned, fuzzy and largely unhelpful sort of way; certainly *Mani*, readable though it remains, conveys something of that sense today. The truth was that by the mid-1950s neither Britain nor Greece had anything special to offer each other, and the gradual dawning of this fact was characterized by a disillusion that anyway had never been entirely absent from their interaction.

Cyprus indeed was to offer a medium through which this process worked itself out. Here, however, we arrive at a basic conclusion of our discussion. The conventional version is that it was the Cyprus issue after 1955 which progressively destroyed – to use Venizelos' old phrase – 'the traditional framework of Anglo-Hellenic friendship'. This seems to put the cart before the horse. Cyprus itself was never the determining factor in that relationship. What happened is that the Anglo-Greek relationship itself went into a sort of reverse by 1950, giving the subsidiary Cyprus issue the room to breathe it had never hitherto possessed. It is important to get the sequence in perspective. For their part, Greek-Cypriot radical protagonists of *enosis* after about 1950, watching other events in and around the Mediterranean, saw only a gathering British weakness, and thought that events were playing into their own hands. Thereafter they disdained negotiation that compromised their ideals. In this regard they fatally misjudged the leverage that they possessed.

This discussion, however, should end with Greece itself. It is impossible, in going back over the story of the 1940s, with a weakened and partially un-sovereign Greece, not to be struck in some respects by echoes of Greece's position today. Reading the official British records dealing with the years of civil war, one is struck by tics of analysis and commentary recurring much later. Underlying that analysis was the perceived statelessness of Greece. But perhaps most striking of all was the observation made by Ambassador Norton in December 1948 when things still looked decidedly bleak. He dismissed widespread talk of defeatism surrounding the Greek government. A much greater danger, Norton felt, however, was the 'feeling of hopelessness' amongst all Greeks as they confronted a seemingly unending stream of difficulties. This despair threatened to overcome the natural resilience of the people. No doubt, Norton said, Greeks could do more to help themselves; but it was also up to Britain and America not to let them down when it mattered most. Today Britain has become irrelevant to the future of Greece. But many of the same dilemmas and pitfalls in that country's relationship with the United Kingdom, often in dire circumstances, are still at play in altered contexts; and lack of hope remains the deadliest enemy in overcoming contemporary challenges, including its capacity to divide Greek from Greek.

Notes

1. Dilys Powell, *An Affair of the Heart* (London, 1957), p. 39. Powell's husband, Humfry Payne, had died suddenly in 1936. After 1941 she had worked on Greek affairs in the Political Warfare Executive in London, concerned with British propaganda in occupied Europe.

2. R. Murray to R. Butler, 25 May 1964 FO371/174838, The National Archives of the United Kingdom (hereafter TNA).

3. Sir S. Waterlow to Viscount Halifax, 31 May 1939 CAB21/1912, TNA.

4. James Barros, *Britain, Greece and the Politics of Sanctions: Ethiopia, 1936–36* (London, 1982), p. 119.

5. Waterlow to Halifax, 31 May 1939 CAB21/1912, TNA.

6. J.O. Iatrides, *Ambassador MacVeagh Reports: Greece, 1933–1947* (Princeton, 1980), p. 286.

7. Ronald Lewin, *The Chief: Field-Marshal Lord Wavell, Commander-in-Chief and Viceroy, 1939–1947* (London, 1980), p. 61.

8. Charles Cruickshank, *Greece, 1940–41* (London, 1976), p. 112.

9. Ibid., p. 109; also see Lord Henry Maitland Wilson, *Eight Years Overseas, 1937–47* (London and New York, 1950), pp. 69–72.

10. See, for example, 'Personal Diary of Captain Oliphant' in CAB 106/555, TNA describing experiences of the Australian Imperial Force during the retreat and evacuation.

11. Hermione, Countess of Ranfurly, *To War with Whitaker: The Wartime Diaries of the Countess of Ranfurly, 1939–45* (London, 1994), p. 242.

12 Richard Capell, *Simiomata: A Greek Note Book, 1944–45* (London: Macdonald, n.d.), p. 13.

13 C.M. Woodhouse, *Apple of Discord* (London, 1948), p. 25.

14 Capell, *Simiomata*, pp. 16, 38.

15 C.M. Woodhouse, *The Struggle for Greece, 1941–1949* (London, 1976), pp. 100–1.

16 Quoted in Robert Holland, *The Pursuit of Greatness: Britain and the World Role, 1900–1970* (London, 1991), p. 192.

17 Geoffrey Chandler, *The Divided Land: An Anglo-Greek Tragedy* (Norwich, 1994), p. 34.

18 See Richard Clogg, *Bearing Gifts to Greeks: Humanitarian Aid to Greece in the 1940s* (Basingstoke, 2008).

19 Robert Holland, *Blue-Water Empire: The British in the Mediterranean Since 1800* (London, 2012), p. 68.

20 Athens Embassy to Southern Department, Foreign Office, 27 December 1946 FO371/67054, TNA.

21 'The Work and Achievements of the British Military Mission to Greece, 1945–49', in FO371/87754, TNA.

22 P. Reilly to D.S. Laskey 21 February 1946 FO371/58684, TNA.

23 A. Rumbold to Brigadier Hamilton 25 May 1948 WO32/15547, TNA.

24 Andrew Thorpe, ' "In a Rather Emotional State": The Labour Party and British Intervention in Greece, 1944–45', *English Historical Review*, 121 (2006), pp. 1075–1105.

25 D. McCarthy minute, 12 November 1945 FO371/67052, TNA. In fact these special rules meant that not even the Head of the British Military Mission in Greece, Major-General E. Down, on leaving the post in 1949, received any mark of distinction. He had to make do with a letter thanking him for his services.

26 Osbert Lancaster, *Classical Landscape with Figures* (London, 1947), pp. 36–37.

27 Account of the British Information Services in Greece, December 1944 – May 1946 FO924/424, TNA.

28 British Council to Cultural Relations Department, Foreign Office, 25 February 1946 FO924/424, TNA. For more on this short-lived chair see Gioula Koutsopanagou's chapter in this volume.

29 Kenneth Johnstone (British Council) to W. Montagu-Pollock, 19 February 1946 FO924/424, TNA.

30 Mary Henderson, *Xenia: A Memoir* (London, 1988).

31 See the chapter on 'The Choice of Evils' in G.M. Alexander, *The Prelude to the Truman Doctrine: British Policy in Greece, 1944–47* (Oxford, 1982), pp. 109–39.

32 See Robert Holland, *Britain and the Revolt in Cyprus, 1954–58* (Oxford, 1998), pp. 236–62.

33 Lancaster, *Classical Landscape*, pp. 36–37.

34 Chandler, *The Divided Land*, p. 174.

35 J.R. Colville minute, 3 November 1947 FO371/58761, TNA.

36 Robert Holland and Diana Markides, *The British and the Hellenes: Struggles for Mastery in the Eastern Mediterranean, 1850–1960* (Oxford, 2006), pp. 194, 203.

37 Sir Charles Norton to C.H. Bateman, 15 July 1948 FO371/72349, TNA.

38 Athens Embassy to Southern Department, Foreign Office, 31 January 1951 FO371/78344, TNA.

39 Chandler, *The Divided Land*, pp. 157–58.

40 These frustrations in Palestine are expressed in Matti Golani (ed.), *The End of the British Mandate, 1948: The Diary of Sir Henry Gurney* (Basingstoke, 2009).

41 Note by Hector McNeil, 1 March 1946 FO371/15876, TNA.

42 Quoted in Alexander, *Prelude to the Truman Doctrine*, p. 142.

43 Holland, *The Pursuit of Greatness*, p. 205.

44 Sir Norman Brook to Prime Minister, 29 January 1947 PREM8/797, TNA.

45 Sir Charles Peak minute, 3 March 1949 FO371/78481, TNA.

46 G. Wallinger minute, 1 June 1948 FO1110/61, TNA.

47 Peak minute, 24 January 1948 FO371/78481, TNA.

48 Philip Ziegler, *Mountbatten: The Official Biography* (London, 1985), p. 467.

49 Brig. Hamilton to Peak, 28 January 1949 FO371/78481, TNA.

50 In this context Greece enters interestingly into Dionysios Chorchoulis, 'High Hopes, Bold Aims, Limited Results: Britain and the Establishment of the NATO Mediterranean Command, 1950–1953', *Diplomacy and Statecraft*, 20/3 (2009), pp. 434–52.

51 Norton to Sir Orme Sargent, 23 June 1948 FO1110/62. TNA.

52 Norton to Bateman, 22 December 1948 FO371/78393, TNA.

53 Athens Embassy to Foreign Office, 19 February 1949 FO371/78357, TNA.

54 Norton to Southern Department, Foreign Office, 8 January 1949 FO371/78341, TNA.

55 Embassy (Athens) to Foreign Office, 4 September 1949, FO371/78359.

56 'Work and Achievements of the British Military Mission', FO371/87754 (5), TNA.

57 Visit by Mr. Reilly to Central Macedonia and Salonica, 27 September 1948 FO371/72327, TNA.

58 E. Peck minute, 3 March 1949 FO371/78481, TNA.

59 'Departure of British Troops from Greece', Norton to Bevin 2 December 1949 FO371/78485, TNA.

60 Ibid.

61 H. Wolstan-Weld to Norton, 3 February 1950 FO371/187754, TNA.

62 See the discussions on the future of the Naval Mission in ADM116/6330, TNA.

63 D. Murray minute, 15 August 1951 FO371/95141, TNA.

64 J. McCourt minute, 16 February 1949 FO371/78495, TNA.

65 Foreign Office to UK Delegation at United Nations, 28 September 1955 ADM116/6330, TNA.

66 Minute by Prime Minister, 24 October 1955 PREM11/914, TNA.

67 Holland, *Blue-Water Empire*, p. 334.

68 Keith Hamilton and Patrick Salmon (eds.), *The Southern Flank in Crisis, 1973–6* (London, 2006), p. 25.

69 Fotis Dimitrakopoulos and Vasiliki D. Lambropoulou (eds.), *Γιώργος Σεφέρης, P. L Fermor & J. Rayner: Αλληλογραφία (1948–1971)* (Nicosia, 2007), pp. 94–95.

70 Ibid.

Chapter 2

'To cast our net very much wider': The re-opening of the British Council in Athens and its cultural activities in Greece

Gioula Koutsopanagou

British cultural diplomacy emerged in the 1930s, supported by two main pillars: the British Council and the BBC.[1] Developed for cultural propaganda in peacetime, the greater part of British Council work was financed by the Foreign Office. In 1941 a British Council Section of the Foreign Office was established which in 1943 evolved into a new and larger section called the Cultural Relations Department (hereafter CRD),[2] headed by William H. Montagu-Pollock. The CRD was to be the liaison between the Foreign Office and the British Council,[3] and its main task was to help give more political direction to pre-existing British Council work, to control its expenditure and to exercise close supervision over its activities.[4] By 1945, the CRD had been assigned to deal with various aspects of the growing cultural interaction with other countries and to promote Allied goodwill and understanding. It was also in the front line of the covert counterattack against Soviet action that had already begun in Britain.[5]

Although responsibility for the British Council remained within the Foreign Office, the 'rapid improvement' in its organization made close CRD supervision less necessary, and it too was reduced in size in 1947,[6] allowing the Council to stand on its own in regard to the detailed execution of its work.[7]

My chapter tracks the escalation of British interest in re-establishing the British Council's Athens branch in 1945 and upgrading it to a Grade I post. The Athens branch was one of the first to resume activities, owing to the direct mobilization of Sir Reginald Leeper, now in his last year as ambassador to Greece, who championed the political role played by Britain's cultural relations with other countries, and had essentially established the Council in 1934.[8] Its revival was regarded as 'badly needed' as a defence against the cultural activities of the rival foreign cultural agencies that had been re-activated in Greece after the war, and newer ones of that kind. The present study, based mainly on the archives of the Foreign Office in London, and in particular on those of the Cultural Relations Department,[9] sets out to explore the ways in which the Council's activities in Greece were planned in consultation between the British Council, the Foreign Office and the British Embassy in Athens.

Apart from its declared objectives, to project British institutions and to promote the English language, the Council also took particular interest in establishing British influence in the contemplated re-organization of Greek state secondary schools (*gymnasia*) and in reforms to the Greek education system. The British took the initiative of approaching the Greek government on this issue before the Americans, but in the long run the goal proved impossible to retain. The British Council had recognized early the significant role played by educational issues and cultural exchanges in the post-war period by organizing the Allied Conference of Ministers of Education (CAME) in London in 1943.

Several proposals for cultural activities were put forward in 1945 to be undertaken by the British Council in Greece. They included a project to establish a branch of Chatham House in Athens, or a National Institution of Research and Cultural Welfare, and a Modern Hospital and Nurses Training Centre in Salonica. The Council had also expressed interest in providing financial support to the British School at Athens[10] and had urged the speedy conclusion of a proposed Anglo-Hellenic Cultural Convention. Yet its main focus remained on educational matters. It was generally admitted that the success of the Council's endeavour would depend largely on the staff selected.

In April 1944 when the new National Government was formed under George Papandreou, Leeper, then in Cairo, felt that the time was ripe for the British Council to reactivate its activities and suggested that it should subsidize and provide 'carefully chosen British occupants' for two chairs at the University of Athens, in addition to the Byron Chair of Literature.[11] He was in agreement with Professor T.S.R. Boase, who was in charge of British Council activities in the Middle East, based in Cairo, that it would be useful to make the offer now and to hold it 'as a card in reserve for use when an opportune moment occurs'.[12]

Consequently the Foreign Office asked for the Treasury's consent to finance, 'at a later date', the resumption of the Council's activities in Greece and to approve the proposed establishment of two professorial Chairs, 'the subjects of [which] to be decided later'. Recently the Treasury had agreed in principle with resuming British Council activities in Italy[13] and the Foreign Office stressed that there were 'many reasons' why British policy must be 'to cultivate the goodwill of the Greek nation and to strengthen their cultural ties with Britain'.[14]

A few days after the Greek government was established in Athens, Leeper reported the 'undoubtedly very real wave of interest in everything English' which extended to a variety of persons who had been little affected by earlier activities of the British Institute in Athens. The Council should send a suitably qualified person, perhaps Boase, to explore the situation in person.[15] The Council was contemplating sending David Shillan[16] to visit the Mediterranean and report on the possibility of resuming Council work.[17]

For more than a year after the liberation, the British Council's functions were carried out by the Anglo-Greek Information Service (AIS, subsequently

THE RE-OPENING OF THE BRITISH COUNCIL 41

AGIS). Administratively this organization was under the British military authorities, while matters of policy were decided by the British Embassy. Leeper had the initiative of creating AGIS as an offshoot of the PWB[18] whose main responsibility was to direct British propaganda and information in Greece. AGIS operated on a very large scale in most of the principal towns.[19] Significant numbers of PWB officials worked for the Council; Colonel Kenneth Johnstone, their temporary representative in Athens, who had pre-war experience, was one of them. However, there was the 'thorny question' how much 'contamination the Council would suffer by association with individual officials or ex-officials of PWB', and the view in London was that this 'danger . . . need not be very great'.[20]

On the eve of the crisis of December 1944 Leeper presented in a letter to the Foreign Office the significance of re-activating the British Council as a factor in creating a climate favourable to Britain:

> We are so fully involved in Greek affairs we must decide very carefully how our influence is to be exerted. . . . At present our influence is associated with immediate political problems and with the sending of supplies. We need as soon as possible, if we are to strengthen our position, to cast our net very much wider and look beyond day to day problems. We start with so much goodwill here that we have a strong foundation on which to build. It is for this reason that I attach so much importance to the work of the British Council here. If this work is well done by really competent people who feel that they are here to render a public service, they can tap various strata of society especially younger people, who may soon have a political role to play and who, under the influence of British ideas, may form the nucleus of that Centre party whose absence at present is a serious weakness to stability and to our influence here.

He gave an assurance of the full support that would be provided to British Council people by the Embassy on which they would be able to rely for 'constant support and guidance'.[21]

In mid-November 1944, in a series of telegrams to the CRD, Leeper urged that immediate action be taken by the British Council. He stated that the French Institute was back in operation and public lectures in French were receiving notice in the press.[22] If the Council failed to respond, other 'undesirable bodies' might try to seize the initiative. He mentioned that there was a 'disturbing report' that EAM (National Liberation Front) was planning to found an Institute in which English and Russian would be taught.[23] In another telegram dated 18 November he criticized the Council for having failed to grasp how urgent it was to set to work.[24] A few days later, on 20 November, Leeper sent a list of activities that the Council should be urged to consider: re-opening the institute to students of English; sending British lecturers to Athens, especially to talk about Britain at war, reconstruction and social reform; and – since the University of Athens was contemplating changes in its constitution – the appointment of some senior British educational authority to renew contact and to explore what assistance could be provided to Greek universities and schools, and to exchange students.[25]

The Embassy's pressure for immediate action was discussed at a Foreign Office meeting on 20 November with Richard Seymour (Deputy Secretary-General), W.R.L. Wickham and David Shillan from the British Council, and Miss H.M. Hedley, CRD, and A.R. Dew, Head of the Southern Department from the Foreign Office. It was agreed that the Council should draft a telegram to Athens explaining the policy they proposed to adopt and asking for detailed proposals of what immediate action they should take to meet the demand for English classes, what the Embassy was doing about the two Chairs, and what were their recommendations for the Byron Chair. Shillan could then visit Athens to discuss long-term plans.[26]

Leeper's correspondence, 'increasingly irascible in tone', had reached the Foreign Office, but not the British Council, which received it two days later. The Foreign Office's view was that his criticisms of Council dilatoriness and procrastination were unfair. Moreover, both the Foreign Office and the British Council doubted the wisdom of approving his proposal that Johnstone act temporarily for the Council, since he was still in uniform and working for the PWB. It was also felt at the Foreign Office that Leeper was 'rather unreasonable at the start' with demands for Council work in 'very vague terms' and it was not until mid-November that his proposals become 'detailed and practical'.[27]

However, the CRD's delay in passing Leeper's telegrams to the British Council caused its Chairman to protest that it was 'most embarrassing and might well be damaging' for them.[28] Another cause for complaint was the deletion of a contentious passage in Sir Malcolm Robertson's reply to Leeper in which he explained that the Council had only just received his telegrams. This fact gave Robertson an excuse to add a 'monstrous' handwritten postscript recommending that 'perhaps the work of the British Council Section would diminish if they ceased to trouble about matters of detail which are no proper concern of theirs!' and an equally venomous comment by K.T. Gurney, Foreign Office, about Council personnel being criticized as untrained and incompetent.[29]

The British Council outlined their deliberations in a letter to Johnstone on 18 January 1945. They would allot a limited number of scholarships to Greece for 1945, and allow two former scholars who had been awarded British Council grants before 1940 to resume their studies.[30] The Council might also suggest brief courses of about four weeks' duration for teachers and other professional groups. Regarding foreign visitors to Britain, the Council would receive one or two as their guests, selected with 'the greatest care' owing to the 'odd state of public opinion here about Greece'. Then Wickham, the signatory of the letter, turned to the 'most important' of all proposals concerning the reform of the Greek education system. He linked together three matters, the renewal of the

THE RE-OPENING OF THE BRITISH COUNCIL

Byron Professorship and the creation of two additional Chairs at the University of Athens; the proposal that a competent person be sent out to study the future teaching of English in conjunction with the Greek Ministry of Education; and the rendering of British assistance to the contemplated reorganization of the University of Athens. The Byron Professorship should remain a Chair of English Language and Literature, one of the other chairs should be allotted to a scientific or technical subject and the third should be allotted to education. The candidate for this last Chair should have experience of educational administration as well as teaching experience; he should also have sufficient seniority to conduct negotiations with the Ministry of Education, and to assist in the reorganization the constitution of the University of Athens. Moreover, since the candidates the Council had in mind for this Chair were mostly humanists, the Council supported a visit by Professor S.J. Davies, Dean of the Faculty of Engineering in the University of London, who would be able to visit Greece in July and would pay special attention to scientific and technical aspects of the proposed reorganization. Wickham concluded that establishing British influence in the Greek state education system such as 'would affect not only the organization but the personnel of the Greek system' was of such 'very great importance' that the Council considered it an integral part of their wider scheme.[31] As for Leeper's request for books and pamphlets on education and for educational periodicals, the British Council Books and Periodicals Departments were about to send out a 'really good' collection of them.[32]

Choosing a permanent representative was to be critical in this regard. The sole British Council Representative in Greece, up to the end of July 1945, was the AGIS Commanding Officer Kenneth Johnstone, a Balkan specialist and, together with Leeper, one of the movers in establishing the British Council in London.[33] Johnstone was regarded as a provisional solution[34] because the Council was anxious to have him back in London to direct their European Division.[35] Pending arrival of a permanent staff member, Major M.H. Cardiff[36] took over as acting representative.

Selecting an appropriate representative proved to be a strenuous process that lasted for almost a year. Leeper was anxious to have a man of first-class calibre sent to Athens, preferably of intellectual standing. Various names were put forward for the post. These included those of the Instructor, Captain C.D. Howell, a man who, 'though useful, would carry little weight';[37] the man of letters William Plomer, who was then working in the information section with the Admiralty, though the London Office thought of him as a possible director of the Institute rather than as representative;[38] and the Shakespeare scholar M.R. Ridley, about whom Montagu-Pollock had spoken to Seymour.[39]

The Foreign Office proposal that Charles Melville Attlee,[40] Professor of Education at University College, Nottingham, should undertake the duties of Council representative, in addition to holding the Chair of British History and Institutions at the University of Athens, was ruled out by both the CRD and the Embassy. The latter considered that the work of the Council in Greece was too important to be a part-time job. Moreover, it was thought in the Embassy that, with the forthcoming reorganization of the University, 'it would be very difficult for him [Attlee], if he held this post in addition, to avoid implicating the Council in local politics.'[41] Evidently that was a misunderstanding on the part of the Embassy since the Foreign Office suggestion was not that Attlee combine the two posts but that he might be considered for one or other of them.[42]

The Athens Council post remained open. On a visit to London in March, Johnstone discussed it with Seymour and both were in favour of considering Professor J.C.S. (later Sir Steven) Runciman, who then occupied the Chairs of Byzantine Art and Byzantine History at the University of Istanbul. Wickham asked Michael Grant, the Council representative in Turkey and personal friend of Runciman, for a report on him and requested the CRD's views about him.[43]

Though there was no doubt about Runciman's academic qualifications, there were concerns about his experience and ability to undertake the arduous task of building up the Council's organization in Greece, especially in the early years, when a great deal of administrative work would be required. The Foreign Office found it difficult to discuss the merits of any candidate without knowing how the post was to be graded. The British Council was intending to make Athens a Grade I post, which meant equivalent in importance to Paris and Rome and a grade higher than Belgrade, Prague, Brussels or Oslo. In the CRD, Hedley doubted 'whether Athens merits such an outstanding position in the hierarchy of Council posts'. It was thought that the question of grading the post could be put off for a year or so, making it possible to appoint a very high-powered man to the position for the first few critical years, without entailing any Council commitment to keep Athens permanently as a Grade I post.[44] Montagu-Pollock considered that 'Greece is a country which should have high priority' and that the Council representative should 'be a Grade I man'.[45]

Montagu-Pollock, who knew Runciman personally, remembered him as 'a distinctly odd bird . . . with an extremely effeminate manner. I understand from Colonel Johnstone that he has become far more "normal" since those days, and this may well be the case'. He also had no high opinion of him as an administrator and in a personal and confidential letter to the Ministry of Information (MoI) asked about Runciman's record as Press Attaché at Sofia.[46] According to A.J. Henderson, Head of the MoI Balkan Section, he was 'very ill-suited to an administrative job'.[47] Wickham held the same view.[48] Another reservation was whether the state of Runciman's health would permit him to undertake such a demanding task.[49]

The Foreign Office and the British Council waited for Grant's report which confirmed 'that prima facie Runciman possesses requisite qualities in a high degree'.[50] Montagu-Pollock, still doubtful, asked Johnstone if he had further suggestions; he wrote in a postscript that 'my doubts are whether the directorship of the Institute is the right thing for him'.[51]

As the British Council was due to reopen in the autumn it was 'extremely urgent' that a permanent representative be appointed. In late September

THE RE-OPENING OF THE BRITISH COUNCIL

Seymour told Montagu-Pollock that 'in the difficult circumstances obtaining in Greece there is no doubt that a Grade I man is required, and we consider that this is the appropriate grade for Runciman'. Leeper too was in favour of his appointment. Montagu-Pollock replied subsequently that as the Council considered Runciman the best available candidate, 'we are prepared to waive our doubts and agree to his appointment'. Ruciman left for Athens on 2 October 1945.[52]

Meanwhile efforts were made to re-staff the Council, as was urgently needed to supervise the education programme, and to acquire new premises. In January 1945 Leeper sent the CRD his proposals for developing English language teaching in Greece. He stated that it was essential to start something, however modest, at once. As preparation for higher studies would take time, he proposed to initiate a three-month programme of English-language classes, both elementary and advanced, in Athens, Salonica, Patras and Corfu and estimated that the full costs of this programme, including teachers' salaries and junior administrative staff, would be adequately covered by pupils' fees. Shillan was expected in Athens and a further joint report would be sent to the Foreign Office.[53]

The enrollment of 13,000 pupils in these English-language classes made the need for textbooks more acute, as it had been further stimulated by the English lessons being broadcast on Athens radio. Leeper asked that adequate quantities of English language textbooks be sent to him,[54] and that permission be obtained from publishers to print them in Athens. In order to limit pirated editions of English textbooks, Leeper was considering applying through AGIS channels for the necessary authority to produce the books in Greece as AGIS productions instead of through Greek publishers. He also asked permission to produce a Greek edition of Evans'[55] *International English*[56] which he expected to promote through very large sales in Greece.[57]

Books too were required to train Greek teachers of English for the educational system that was due to begin in January 1946. AGIS were organizing a summer course in English on an island near Athens. The CRD asked Cairo, Rome and Ankara whether Council or other teachers would be willing to give instructions in the course[58] scheduled to start on 11 August.[59] The aim was to train fifty teachers by the following January. In addition, the Embassy requested sixty copies from a list of English language textbooks and literature titles, and 5,000 copies of each book were required to cover the needs of Greek secondary school classes.[60]

Due to the anticipated increase of English courses in secondary schools and the great shortage of teachers trained in English, Leeper very strongly recommended that, in addition to the ten scholarships for postgraduate research, six more scholarships be allotted for teachers, even if only for 1945. 'This would form a most valuable nucleus, as well as giving much needed psychological stimulus to Ministry.' Granting scholarships had always been one of the most effective aspects of the Council's work.[61] The Foreign Office agreed that six scholarships for teachers could be included instead of six postgraduate scholarships, although the total number for Greece could not be increased.[62] The Greek Ministry of Education agreed to pay their travel expenses.[63] They included Evangelos Papanoutsos, Director for Secondary Education, who was in charge,[64] and five others. Among them were Miss Doanidou, Miss Kalliopi Moustaka, Papelliou [Panayiotis Papailiou?] and Ojanetatos [?].

The successful organization of the summer English-language courses and the Council's considerable expansion of scholarships, which now included forty to fifty Greek students instead of the initial twelve,[65] were cited by Johnstone as 'major achievements' in a 'rather testy letter' to Montagu-Pollock on 2 August 1945 to defend the work already done by the Council in Greece by way of response to the Embassy's criticisms that the Council was being dilatory. Johnstone, now in the London Office, stated that the Council was already giving Greece the highest priority and everything possible was being done to ensure that they were able to operate on a fairly large scale in the autumn. Regarding books, a 'really first-class central library' was being assembled and shipped out to the British Institutes in Athens and Salonica; arrangements were being made for a lecture programme in the winter of 1945–46, and the acquisition of premises was a matter of urgency. The CRD was disturbed at not having been informed of the summer school and having only heard indirectly – through visa applications for the students – of the enlarged scholarship scheme.[66] This annoyance on the part of the Foreign Office over the British Council's tendency not to keep them briefed on their correspondence and their plans or actions was often expressed, as they were sometimes faced with the Council's tendency to assume greater independence in implementing its programme. 'They like to think they are independent. We must insist on being kept au fait with their plans,' wrote Hedley on one occasion.[67]

Before the war, English teaching had been closely connected with the Anglo-Hellenic League. The occasion for redefining Council's post-war relations with the League was provided by three letters addressed to Leeper, two from the Anglo-Hellenic League[68] and the third from a former teacher at the British Institute at Athens, George Georgiadis Arnakis.[69] Leeper supported the re-opening of the League,[70] but the Foreign Office thought it wiser not to make any arrangements with local teachers until Shillan had investigated the whole position in his exploratory visit to Greece and reported to the Council.[71] On the subject of the League, the British Council Chairman considered that they could take no action before the 110th Meeting of the Finance and Agenda Committee to be held on 13 February 1945.[72]

In the conclusions reached at the 110th Meeting of the Committee the English teaching enterprise was set up along the general lines of British policy in Greece. The Council's prewar policy of relying on Anglophile societies such as the Anglo-Hellenic League had involved them in local rivalries and had contributed to weakening the structure of the organization itself. It was now deemed preferable to establish independent Council Institutes in Athens and Salonica to be staffed with Englishmen and under the direct control of the Council representative's office. These Institutes would control all Council teaching activities; they would be focal points for the distribution of British material (books, periodicals, films, music) and would be the centres disseminating British cultural ideas throughout the country. Moreover, in view of the Greek government's intention to strengthen the teaching of English in high schools and universities from January 1946, this opportunity should be used as part of a coherent plan administered by the representative: he would coordinate activities such as university appointments and the appointment of a suitable adviser to the Greek government. Any economic support or special material (printed or audio) given to the Leagues in Athens and Salonica would be administered through the representative's office.[73]

The British Council initiatives addressed to the Greek government on teaching English and on training teachers of English took the Americans by surprise: they first saw in the press a reference to the introduction of English classes in Greek secondary schools. The Americans criticized the action of the Council which, 'for various reasons', had started negotiating with the Greek government on this matter without their knowledge. Professor Ernest Riggs[74] of Anatolia College 'came to call on us in a state of . . . indignation', Cardiff reported. With the main object of 'pacifying' them, he called a meeting on 26 June to which the heads of the American educational establishments in Greece were invited. They were Homer Davies[75] of Athens College, Professor Riggs and Dr Kathryn McElroy[76] of the Athens College for Girls.

At this meeting the Council made it clear that they welcomed American cooperation on the question of teachers of English and their qualifications. As Cardiff pointed out, no other attitude on the part of the Council was possible from the outset, because the influence of the three American schools on Greek life was so great that it could have a considerable impact, positive or negative, on the Council's work in Greece. It was also explained that discussions with the Greek government had been confined to the 'temporary' measures necessary to obtain a nucleus of teachers by January 1946; it was agreed on both sides that dealings with the Ministry regarding the long-term training of regular teachers should be made only after joint consultation. It was also agreed that, regarding diplomas and examinations or courses of study to train regular teachers, parallel American and English standards could be decided upon and would be regarded as equivalent. The Council sent translated copies of the draft Law and Decree to the three American educators, but requested that they not try to have these questioned or altered at this stage, since this might tend to postpone the whole Greek decision. Cardiff stated that the Americans were disturbed that their two Athens schools were still being used by the military, so that any action to free them would be very important in removing the suspicion of 'mutual intentions which sometimes hindered Anglo-American co-operation'.[77]

The Foreign Office entirely approved the action Cardiff had taken. They agreed with Seymour that the Americans should be given the opportunity to train some of the temporary teachers, but they disagreed that direct contact with the US Cultural Relations Department on this matter was necessary. McElroy was in London with a British visa and it was hoped that the Council could convince her of British willingness to work in close collaboration with the American educationalists in Greece.[78] Regarding any effect the Law might have on the teaching of French and the expected French reaction[79] in fighting to retain their language lead,[80] Montagu-Pollock disagreed with Seymour's view that the Council representative in Paris should be briefed, in the event that the Direction Générale des Relations Culturelles approached him on this subject. On the question of the British army releasing American buildings the CRD asked the Embassy whether there was any chance of doing so 'though . . . difficulties of finding alternative accommodation may rule it out'.[81]

The Law was finally passed on 21 December 1945.[82]

As noted earlier, the British Council took particular interest in establishing British influence in the contemplated reform of the Greek education system.

In the period leading up to the 1946 elections, the Greek Ministry of Education was staffed by persons whose educational ideology was in line with the forces of the so-called liberal 'centre'.[83] This climate reflected the line of British policy towards Greece at this period, which was to reinforce the 'centre' against the two other poles: EAM and the old-party political system. The immediate aim of British policy was to isolate EAM, to denounce it for having been dominated from its early development by the Greek Communist Party (KKE), and to try to win over its moderate elements. According to Johnstone, one of the factors affecting the Council's work in Greece was that EAM had attracted a very large segment of the younger generation and the 'tragedy of Greece' was that the KKE led this younger generation to extreme political theories and ideals.[84]

As expected, 'an entirely different set of personalities'[85] took office after the elections; they were to inaugurate a new educational reality by rescinding any attempt made in the previous fifteen months to reorientate the ideological content of education from its previous Metaxist legacy. The educational forces of the so-called 'centre', despite their institutional position, were ultimately unable to bring about the desired change.[86]

After consultation with 'the competent authorities' and with the British Consul-General in Salonica, the Embassy sent the Foreign Office detailed recommendations for the development of education in Greece. Regarding university chairs, the following points were agreed: (i) the Byron Professorship should be coordinated more closely with the university syllabus and be of benefit to students rather than to the cultured and leisured classes, as it had been formerly; (ii) a Chair of Science or Engineering was to be instituted at the University of Athens, details of which would be given when the Greek authorities had formulated clear plans; and (iii) Chairs of Education would be

THE RE-OPENING OF THE BRITISH COUNCIL 49

founded in Athens and Salonica. It was suggested that this title be avoided 'for fear of wounding Greek susceptibilities' and instead that there should be a title such as 'Chair of British History and Institutions'. The field of these two university posts would be 'roughly the same as that of Modern Greats at Oxford, namely History, Political Science, Economics'. Both Chairs would concentrate on the 'practical application of social principle' with particular reference to the development of British social institutions and their operation in modern practice. As much could be achieved in this regard by informal personal contact as by public instruction, in which case the professor's personality was as important as his academic qualifications. The work of both Chairs would be closely related to the work of the British Institute at Athens and Salonica. It would also have direct contact with Greek teachers' training colleges. As English was to be established as the main foreign language in the secondary schools, it was thought that the Ministry of Education would want the Athens Chair to coordinate the teacher training undertaken by British Institutes. Therefore choosing the 'right man' for this Chair with the widest possible knowledge of educational practice could 'do much by way of affording tactful and effective guidance to the Ministry of Education, and to the University'. Yet any suggestion that the Athens Professorship was 'specifically designed to help actively in the organization of the Greek educational system should be avoided for it will cause offence from the start'.[87] As the best alternative to any possible resentment by Greek authorities of British direct intervention in their educational matters, Leeper also suggested that a course of lectures be given by Professor Hamley[88] to Greek teachers on British educational methods and that through a tour of Greek schools and universities, opportunities would be provided 'for tactful guidance and offers of help'.[89]

In June the Council proposed that Professor Attlee be appointed to the Chair of British History and Institutions[90] at the University of Athens. The British Council felt 'fortunate' in having interested a man of Attlee's talents in the proposal. He had had previous experience of Greece[91] and had impressed them all 'with his keenness and energy.' Johnstone was asked to obtain official consent and a letter of appointment from the University of Athens.[92] In the event that the University had doubts about these professorships, F.Y. Thompson, British Council Regional Officer for the Balkans, pointed out that the most important thing was to get Attlee to Greece somehow.[93] In this connection the CRD asked Johnstone whether Attlee would be acceptable as representative. 'In our opinion Attlee would be more suitable than Runciman.'[94] But in the meantime, the Ministry and the University[95] finally agreed 'to proposed visits and Chairs'.[96] Attlee arrived in Athens on 16 August 1945; a military permit to enter the country was also issued for Professor Davies.[97] Attlee began his classes in November of 1945.[98] The official institution of his post as Chair of British Life and Thought took place two months later, in December.[99]

Soon, however, the British Council had to find a replacement for Attlee, who held the Chair for less than a year. The Council recommended H.M.

Butler, Headmaster of Queen Mary's Grammar School, Walsall.[100] It appears that in the end, Butler did not succeed Attlee[101] because the University of Athens decided, in September 1946, to amalgamate the Chair of British Life and Thought with the Byron Chair.[102] Given that the 1945 Law did not make the same provision for reciprocity as the 1938 Law on the founding of the Byron Chair,[103] the University proposed the merging of the two Chairs within the framework set out for the Byron Chair, so that this reciprocity would remain.[104] The issue of the Chair of British Life and Thought would be discussed again in October 1951 when the Royal Decree under Emergency Law 745/1945, drafted by the Faculty of Arts, came up for discussion in the University Senate.[105]

After some months of searching, a candidate for the Byron Professorship was found. In April 1946 the Council recommended the appointment of W.A. Sewell, since 1934 Professor of English at Auckland University College, New Zealand, for a period of three years.[106] Although the Foreign Office deemed that 'he does not seem absolutely first class', it approved his candidacy.[107] Runciman addressed the Senate of the University of Athens on 20 June 1946, requesting approval of Sewell's appointment, which was eventually ratified by the Ministry of Education for ten years.[108] Throughout his period of service, which lasted until the end of March 1952,[109] Sewell, who attended only the Faculty meetings on matters that concerned him, was extremely active in submitting reports, letters and requests, and indeed complaints.[110] His role was fulfilled when, in June 1951, the law was passed establishing two university Departments of English Studies,[111] in Athens and Salonica,[112] and the selection of his successor to the Byron Chair.[113]

Still pending was the appointment to the Chair of British Life and Thought at Salonica University. The Council recommended Dr W.H.C. Frend, whose recent field of interest was reported to be the study of modern European economic and social history, though Frend's distinguished academic career was to be in theology.[114] Even though Montagu-Pollock did not find him 'as strikingly suitable', he did not oppose Council's recommendation.[115] Eventually Frend came to Greece in 1956 – remaining until 1960, under the auspices of the British School at Athens – as director of the excavations of a fifth-century church at Knossos.[116]

The Council was prepared to meet the total cost of these Chairs. It was thought that considering the penury of the Greek government, any British pressure on them to provide even a 'microscopic sum' would very largely detract 'from the value of the gesture made in founding these Chairs, with no equivalent financial advantage to ourselves'.[117]

Regarding books, the British Council responded positively to specific requests from either individual university professors[118] or libraries. It contributed to re-establishing the Library[119] of the Hellenic Institute of International and Foreign Law,[120] and responded favourably to a request from the Library of the Greek Parliament for English books.[121] Parliament's request was considered of particular interest as it would have an excellent propaganda effect,

THE RE-OPENING OF THE BRITISH COUNCIL 51

'especially at the present very opportune moment when Greece is to have its first free elections for many years'.[122] Hector McNeil, MP, who was to become Minister of State in 1946, communicated with the House of Commons to this effect and a 'rather select presentation parcel' was to be sent to Athens. The British Council Books Department put together a collection of books and sent it off at the end of September.[123]

In July 1945, Harold Caccia[124] informed the Foreign Office of a marked increase in Soviet propaganda in Greece 'in the last few weeks', of which the most recent manifestation was the founding of a Greek-Soviet League.[125] Its aim was to further the good relations between the two countries, and it had developed an ambitious programme of conferences, lectures and discussions. The Greek sponsors were mainly Leftist and liberal academics and the open participation of the KKE had been 'carefully avoided'. The management of the League's affairs was entirely in the hands of Leonid Velitchansky[126] and Savvas Pylarinos,[127] the director of Sovfilm, a film company. He stressed that even the Greek government accepted the League at face value and that it had the blessing of the Minister of Information, Dionysios Zakythinos.[128] He then suggested that it was essential for the Council to receive all possible support. He requested that the supply of books, newspapers and lectures[129] be speeded up and, in particular, that the Council should quickly appoint their representative.[130] Laskey commented that, though the threat of Russian propaganda in Greece was not immediately visible, they could not 'afford to let the Russian challenge go unanswered'. He took up the matter with the CRD, which arranged to send propaganda material regularly to Greece, 'though probably not in sufficient quantities'. Hedley stated that she knew from the London Office that the work was still handled through the AGIS, as Cardiff was not acquainted with the Council's methods. It was essential therefore to send a full-time representative who 'has been coached in the London Office'. She also felt the time was right to re-open the question of the Anglo-Greek Cultural Convention, signed in 1940,[131] but never ratified. It was thought that whether or not such a convention was ratified would probably not have affected the volume of cultural exchanges in the years to come. Nevertheless, because Britain had conventions with other allied countries,[132] it was assumed that the Greek convention would probably also have to be revived eventually.[133]

Johnstone did not feel much alarm with regard to the points mentioned in a report by Constantine A. Trypanis,[134] dated 2 September 1945, about Soviet cultural activities in Greece.[135] In his report, signed with the pseudonym Ajax, Trypanis stated that the initiative for founding a Greek-Soviet League did not, 'oddly enough', belong to the KKE, though the League was 'now in its grip'. The idea had been introduced by the Sophianopoulos-Kafandaris circle, which favoured a Greek policy of friendship with both Great Britain and Russia. He gave details of the communist affiliations of some of the founders of the League with his personal comments on their personality; he considered Nikos Kitsikis, Dean at the National Technical University, Athens a 'man of no scruples' whose wife, Beata, was 'more Left than [he]!'; Ch. Theodorides, Professor of Philosophy at the Aristotle University of Thessaloniki, was 'a known Marxist', and his wife, Rosa Imvrioti, was 'one of the Chief Communist Instructors and Advisors of the Salonica branch of the KKE'. Although Nikos Kazantzakis and Elli Lambridi were not Communists, they nevertheless had '*a very strong anti-British feeling*' (Trypanis' emphasis), which they 'carefully conceal in public'. Professor Bensis, who 'is virtually in his dotage', was regarded as a misguided democrat. Trypanis considered that behind all this and the KKE stood Soviet agents such as Velitchansky. He noted that Velitchansky seldom met people, and appeared not to take any particular interest in local affairs, leaving to his chauffeur, 'who incidentally has not the hands of a chauffeur', to see all that was to be seen and meet anyone who should be contacted. Parallel to the Greek-Soviet League in Athens, a Greek-Soviet Youth League had also been formed. According to Trypanis it was conceived and founded by the KKE, led and guided by it, and was 'nothing else but another EPON under camouflage'.[136]

In winning the 'hearts and minds' of the Greeks, the British Council had to compete with the French as well. The success and influence of the French cultural appeal in Greece had been pointed out in an Embassy report sent to the CRD on 19 September 1945. According to this report French cultural contacts with Greece dated from the earliest days of Independence and had 'firmly established the respect for French civilization and the study of the French language here'. The French School was an educational institution of international prestige whose 'contacts' permeated the whole of Athenian educated society. Under its direction was the French Institute whose main task was to teach the French language in a 'thoroughly humanistic manner' and most of those who earned a diploma acquired a deep respect for and understanding of French culture as a whole. Thus 'those whose business is to present France to Greece are under the general direction of the senior French scholars in Greece among those studying Greece for its own sake, who may be presumed to be the best authority on local conditions, prejudices and psychology'. During the war, the French Institute in Athens continued to work to full capacity (3,000 students) with long waiting lists. Moreover there was a strong Franco-Hellenic League and a very active Ligue des Jeunes.

The French Government, according to the report, was now actively interested in revitalizing their cultural activity in Greece. An important step in this direction was the return early in June of Octave Merlier, the 'much-loved' Director of the French Institute since about 1920, who was welcomed by an 'enormous circle of friends'. He was 'a most remarkable character' with a 'clearly influential and attractive personality' and 'a thoughtful but convinced supporter of the Left'. The British thought that as Merlier had been 'appointed now Cultural Attaché[137] to the French Legation', he would certainly be 'his Ambassador's right-hand man as regards local intelligence, and . . . must certainly be one of the hundred most influential men in Athens as regards the forming of Greek political opinion'.

THE RE-OPENING OF THE BRITISH COUNCIL

The report concluded that with the re-opening of French cultural work 'of high quality', following on the foundation of Greek-Soviet League, 'to say nothing of the lavishly financed work of the Americans', the need for vigorous support for British efforts was becoming more acute than ever, if British cultural work in Greece was to compete with any success and if Britain's reputation was not to suffer.[138]

Two major schemes in the summer of 1945 were proposed to be undertaken by the British Council, providing they could be financed by non-governmental funds.

The idea of setting up 'a branch of Chatham House at Athens' or something along the lines of the Political and Economic Planning (P.E.P.) either originated with Leeper or was warmly supported by him. Philip J. Noel-Baker, the Minister of State for Foreign Affairs, was also interested in such a scheme. Its purpose would be to attract younger Greek intellectuals 'who are at present without any very definite political orientation'.[139] Montagu-Pollock pointed out that were the Council was to embark on this scheme it would be contrary to its aim, which was to teach the British way of life to foreigners and not to engage in political research. Noel-Baker countered that the Institute's intention would not be to 'propagate political doctrine but [to] promote discussion'.[140] He suggested that the Lord Mayor's Greek Relief Fund could make a contribution or could approach other charitable trusts.[141] The proposal was abandoned and in its place it was decided to form an International Research Institute if sufficient British and American non-governmental funds could be found. The prime mover in the scheme was Ioannis Georgakis,[142] who tried unsuccessfully to secure a sum from the Rockefeller Foundation. The whole scheme looked like falling through.[143] Since the Lord Mayor's Fund had now decided that all its funds would be required for strictly relief purposes, it was not prepared to subsidize the project as originally intended.[144] The Foreign Office were considering the possibility of interesting other similar Funds but before doing so they asked for Leeper's advice.[145] He and Runciman agreed that an organization would be useful that could deal with social welfare research in 'its broadest sense', aim to keep Greece informed about sociological studies in English-speaking countries, and work out how Greek welfare would be affected along these lines. Leeper suggested taking the matter up again after the elections.[146] But no one in the new Government seemed to be interested. The Minister of State dropped the project unless the Greeks raised it again.[147]

The other project concerned the establishment of a Modern Hospital and Nurses Training Centre in Salonica which could be used to train nurses, and as a supplementary teaching school for the final year medical students. As early as 1939, the British Council had shown interest in building a model hospital in Salonica.[148] The war prevented this plan from being fully explored and it was now being put forward again.[149] The Council deemed it 'a very worthwhile project'.[150] The CRD also found the plan an excellent scheme and approved the association of the British Council with the administration of the requested grant. The Southern Department also had no objection.[151]

The project was eventually abandoned by the British Council in September 1947 because of 'interminable delays on the part of the Greek Ministry of Health in putting into effect the necessary legislation and in providing their share of the money'.[152]

The British Council's work in Greece for 1945–46 and its future prospects in a country that was deeply engaged in civil war were presented in two lengthy reports by Kenneth Johnstone and Osbert Lancaster.

In his memorandum, discussed later in London with Wickham on the Council's general policy,[153] Johnstone mentioned the principal factors affecting the Council's work in Greece in 1945, certain basic facts that should be taken into consideration, and finally made some suggestions of his own. The foundations on which the Council's work in Greece rested were to be the country's enormous cultural reserves – similar in 'vitality and creativeness' to those shown by the French intelligentsia under German occupation – and its younger generation. The Council's work had to be part of a general plan for British aid to Greece. Basic facts to be considered were: the greatly expanding demand for instruction in English and for English books or books in Greek about England; 'the desperate need for the reconvention and enlightenment' of the younger generation, not only in Greek schools and universities but also that of the great majority of Greeks in their twenties and early thirties who had been brought up in wartime on 'extreme doctrines', and the pressing need to explain to them other 'more moderate points of view, particularly in questions of political and social organization'; and, finally, there was the British moral obligation to put Greece on the road to national revival or else publicly to admit failure.

Johnstone believed that what Britain could provide was less purely intellectual than what French or German culture, for example, had to offer: it was a practical method of dealing with life as a whole. The most important contribution that the Council could make to Anglo-Greek friendship would be to choose its staff carefully, since professional qualifications were less important than personality. 'We can concentrate on two things, quality and character. . . . In Greece particularly, where humanity is everything, it is even more essential to have men than to have books.'

Johnstone concluded that British-Greek cultural and educational exchange would have to be two-sided in order to make a full contribution to understanding between the two peoples. The personnel to be sent to Greece should be chosen for their ability to fulfil a twofold function; they should likewise be informed in advance that they should be expected to study some particular aspect of Greek life or thought and to write about it.[154]

The British Council's future role to be played in the political climate prevailing after the elections of 1946 was set out in 'an extremely interesting and valuable report'[155] by Lancaster of the Foreign Office News Department, the 'swan song' of his assignment to Greece from December 1944 to May 1946 when, at the request of Leeper, he was sent to Athens at the height of the crisis to help him keep the foreign press correspondents 'on the rails'.[156]

The report laid great emphasis on the role the Council could play as being of 'the greatest consequence'. Lancaster argued that experience had shown that the most satisfactory method of securing a better picture of Britain in Greece was indirect. British policy in Greece had pursued an active line in 1945, but had failed in its principal efforts. Therefore, in his view, the policy that should be adopted in the present circumstances should be radically different from that of the past and should be 'largely passive in nature'. From now on, Lancaster suggested, the two courses of action Britain should concentrate on were, in the short term, to counter propaganda, and in the long term, to ensure that 'a constant flow of books, articles, films and British cultural influences generally should be maintained at a steady level'.[157] In this connection he was convinced that 'the British Council, particularly through its language classes, has a more important role to play than the Press Department and that it is of the highest importance that the maximum degree of cooperation should exist between the two bodies'.[158]

The British Council's work was of primary importance for British policy in Greece. On this point there was no disagreement. Leeper was so anxious for the Council to start its activities that he often made unfair criticisms of its delays and indeed of its personnel. He preferred to trust people he had worked with in their capacity as PWB officials or ex-officials, such as Johnstone, Major Milne and Major Edward Malan, whom he regarded as 'good men' to hold responsible positions on the Council. But the Foreign Office and British Council both had serious reservations about employing men in uniform.

It was agreed that the Council's cultural programme should have its basis in British policy in Greece. Decisions as to what permanent form Council activities in Athens should take had been reached in February 1945, giving the British Council a central role in directing the entire new scheme. British influence and advice would need to make themselves felt in every branch of the Greek administration, especially education, sociology and the practical application of the sciences. Key sectors for its programme were education, the dissemination of English political thought and social welfare, reconstruction, health, law and public administration. The principal target social group was the younger generation who would play a political role in the future; their re-education with more modest political ideas was considered vital.

The British cultural effort faced two main competitors: from the Soviets and, in particular, the French. The French cultural appeal might be more intellectual and artistic: the British paradigm, on the contrary, was addressed to practical matters. Regarding the 'lavishly financed' American cultural programme, which was gradually gaining ground among the Greeks, the only possible course better to serve British interests in Greece was cooperation, not competition.

56 GIOULA KOUTSOPANAGOU

Yet a remark made by Kenneth Johnstone deserves further attention. He proposed that the British cultural programme in Greece should perform a dual function in order to establish an intellectual link between the two peoples.[159] Seen from today's perspective, it is precisely this distinction between ordinary intercultural communication and cultural relations that, in modern terms, defines what is called public diplomacy,[160] because it is based on 'cognitive experience', the so-called 'two-way street'.[161] The profound cultural and intellectual effect which France, a pioneer in this field of diplomacy, had in Greece would provide the model for British cultural diplomacy too.

Notes

1 J.M. Lee, 'British Cultural Diplomacy and the Cold War: 1946–61', *Diplomacy & Statecraft*, 9/1 (1998), pp. 112–34 (p. 116).

2 FO366/1452, Change of name of British Council Section to Cultural Relations Department.

3 FO366/1452, X3945/505, Office Circular No. 25, J.I.C. Crombie, 17 March 1945.

4 FO924/594, LC1916, Foreign Office Minute by William Montagu-Pollock, 19 April 1947.

5 Richard J. Aldrich, *The Hidden Hand: Britain, America, and Cold War Secret Intelligence* (Woodstock, 2002), p. 122.

6 When the new British propaganda policy was launched in 1948, the CRD's work was gradually transferred to the new Information Research Department (IRD), see Richard J. Aldrich, 'Putting Culture into the Cold War: The Cultural Relations Department (CRD) and British Covert Information Warfare', in Giles Scott-Smith and Hans Krabbendam (eds.), *The Cultural Cold War in Western Europe, 1945–1960* (London, 2003), pp. 109–33; Andrew Defty, *Britain, America and Anti-Communist Propaganda 1945–53: The Information Research Department* (London, 2004), pp. 9, 196.

7 FO924/594, LC1916, Minute by Montagu-Pollock, 19 April 1947. A Foreign Office Circular was issued on 22 August 1947 to this effect, informing all British Missions abroad that they should appeal to the Foreign Office only as a last resort (FO924/594, FO Circular No. 0149, and No. 71 [same text], signed by Ernest Bevin, entitled 'Relations between His Majesty's Missions abroad and the British Council', 22 August 1947).

8 Leeper commented in 1943 that 'the object was not culture for culture's sake, but culture for policy's sake' (in Louise Atherton, 'Lord Lloyd at the British Council and the Balkan Front, 1937–1940', *The International History Review*, 16/1 (1994), pp. 25–48. See also P.M. Taylor, *The Projection of Britain* (Cambridge, 1981), p. 150 especially from the chapter 'Cultural Propaganda and the British Council', pp. 125–78.

9 A previous study of mine approached mainly Greek archival sources and personal testimonies (Gioula Koutsopanagou, 'Προπαγάνδα και απελευθέρωση: Το Βρετανικό Συμβούλιο και ο Ελληνοσοβιετικός Σύνδεσμος στην Αθήνα στις παραμονές του εμφυλίου πολέμου (1945)', *Μνήμων*, 22 (2000), p. 172).

THE RE-OPENING OF THE BRITISH COUNCIL 57

10 In any event the Council was to contribute with practical assistance, in cooperation with the British Academy, cf. FO924/241 (1945).

11 Chairs of foreign literature were established at the University of Athens, Faculty of Arts by Emergency Law 1100, 23 February 1938, 'Περί ιδρύσεως εδρών ξένων λογοτεχνιών παρά τη Φιλοσοφική Σχολή του Πανεπιστημίου Αθηνών', Εφημερίς της Κυβερνήσεως [henceforth ΦΕΚ], Α 69, pp. 469–70. It was stipulated that both the establishment and the appointment of foreign professors would be 'on a reciprocal basis', meaning that a chair of Greek Literature would be established in British Universities and a Greek professor appointed on the recommendation of the Greek government.

12 FO924/36, LC16, Leeper to FO, tel. 464, 29 June 1944. Leeper's telegram referred to FO telegram No. 197 of 2nd May 1944.

13 The Foreign Office considered Greece and Italy two countries to which 'the highest priority should be given'. It is not accidental that there were strong communist parties in both these countries. In May 1945 Montagu-Pollock, in a politically significant text, analysed the role of cultural policy with respect to Britain's position after World War II. For the FO Directive regarding the activity of the British Council in Greece and Italy see D.W. Ellwood, " 'Showing the World What It Owed to Britain": Foreign Policy and "Cultural Propaganda", 1935–1945' in N. Pronay and D.W. Spring (eds.), *Propaganda, Politics and Film* (London, 1982), p. 72, n. 62.

14 FO924/36, LC16, Gurney to C.H.M. Wilcox, 14 July 1944. FO924/36, LC274, Wilcox to Gurney, 24 July 1944.

15 FO924/36, LC1343, No. 31, Leeper to FO, 26 October 1944.

16 The first and successful former British Council Representative in Yugoslavia (1940) who was now working in their London Office.

17 FO924/36, LC1343, No. 197, FO to Leeper, 16 November 1944.

18 Cf. Report by Osbert Lancaster, 'A Brief Account of British Information Services in Greece, December 1944-May 1946', (FO924/424, LC3333); Stephen Dorril, *MI6: Inside the Covert World of Her Majesty's Secret Intelligence Service* (New York, 2000), p. 313. The wartime Special Operations Executive (SOE) and Political Warfare Executive (PWE) had been largely disbanded in 1945 and would not be replaced until the formation of IRD in 1948.

19 FO924/424, LC3333, Report by Osbert Lancaster.

20 FO924/36, LC1488, 'Cancelled', Gurney to Wickham, n.d.

21 FO371/43735, R189671, No. 300, Leeper to FO, 21 November 1944.

22 For the French Institute see Chapter 13 below.

23 FO924/36, LC1489, No. 240, Leeper to FO, 16 November 1944. There is no evidence for EAM's plan to establish an Institute, other than a probable intelligence report regarding the Greek-Soviet League founded in July of 1945.

24 FO924/36, LC1506, No. 263, Leeper to FO, 18 November 1944.

25 FO924/36, LC1544, No. 287, Leeper to FO, 20 November 1944.

26 FO924/36, LC 1506, Minutes by Hedley. Outward Telegram, No. 1, FO to Athens, 24 November 1944.

27 FO924/162, LC402, Minutes by Hedley, 13 December 1945.

28 FO924/162, LC402, letters of Sir M. Robertson to Sir M. Palairet, 6 December 1944 and 16 January 1945.

29 FO924/162, LC402, Palairet to Robertson, 2 February 1945; Robertson to Palairet, 19 February 1945.

30 Among them was N.P. Constantinidis, who had headed the list of Greek beneficiaries from British Council scholarships in 1938 and been sent to the London School of Economics on a two-year grant. His request to come to Britain was strongly supported by the Embassy on the grounds that on his return to Greece 'he would be most useful in propagating British social and economic theory and thus in helping to counter Russian brands' (FO924/36, LC1504, E.R. Warner to Gurney, 8 November 1944).

31 FO924/162, LC276, Wickham's letter to Johnstone, 18 January 1945.

32 FO924/162, LC912, 'Educational Periodicals' Wickham to Johnstone, 6 March 1945. These included General (15 titles), Adult & Higher Education (4 titles) and Younger Children (4 titles).

33 Taylor, *The Projection*, p. 152.

34 FO 371/43735, R189671, Minutes. Johnstone rejoined the Foreign Office in 1945; he became Deputy Director-General British Council (1953–62) and Chairman of Council, School of Slavonic and East European Studies (1965–76).

35 FO FO924/162, LC1497, White to Leeper, 13 April 1945.

36 Maurice Cardiff worked for the British Council from 1946 to 1973 in several posts in Greece, Italy, Cyprus and elsewhere. He was attached to the PWE in Cairo in 1943 and was sent during the last months of the war to the Aegean Islands. In his capacity as a writer, under the *nom de plume* John Lincoln, he described his wartime experience in the Aegean in *Achilles and the Tortoise: An Eastern Aegean Exploit* (London, 1958).

37 FO924/162, LC398, No. 7, Athens to FO, 8 February 1945.

38 FO924/162, LC2222, Minutes by Hedley, 17 June 1945. Plomer's known homosexuality certainly affected his professional career; cf. Peter F. Alexander, *William Plomer: A Biography* (Oxford, 1989).

39 FO924/163, LC3062, Montagu-Pollock to Johnstone, 28 July 1945.

40 He was the author of *Philosophy in Educational Theory* (Birmingham, 1932).

41 FO924/163, LC2635, Athens (Caccia), to Montagu-Pollock, 22 June 1945.

42 FO924/163, LC2635, Montagu-Pollock's letter to Johnstone, 9 July 1945.

43 FO924/162, LC1416, Wickham to Gurney, 9 April 1945.

44 FO924/162, LC1416, Minutes by Hedley, 28 April 1945.

45 FO924/163, LC2635 Montagu-Pollock to Johnstone, 9 July 1945.

46 FO924/162, LC1416, Montagu-Pollock to Gerald Scott, Foreign Division, MoI, 1 May 1945.

47 FO924/162, LC1799/10/452, Personal and confidential handwritten note by Scott to Montagu-Pollock, 5 May 1945 and Henderson's comment written by hand on Pollock's letter to Scott, 1 May.

THE RE-OPENING OF THE BRITISH COUNCIL

48 FO924/162, LC2022, Wickham to Montagu-Pollock, 22 May 1945.

49 FO924/162, LC1416, Minutes by Montagu-Pollock, 1 May 1945.

50 FO924/162, LC1799/10/452 Confidential, Sir M Peterson, Ankara Embassy to FO, following from Grant, 4 June 1945.

51 FO924/163, LC2635 Montagu-Pollock to Johnstone, 9 July 1945.

52 FO924/163, LC4167, Seymour to Montagu-Pollock, 18 September 1945; Minutes by Hedley, 1 October 1945; Montagu-Pollock to Seymour, 1 October 1945.

53 FO924/162, LC397, No. 1, Leeper to FO, 22 January 1945.

54 FO924/162, LC397, Leeper to FO following for British Council from Johnstone, 25 and 28 January 1945, respectively. The books most generally required were Eckersley's English course, published by Longman and used in all British Council classes and Faucet's course, published by Oxford University Press, to be used in the English classes of Greek secondary schools.

55 Evans Brothers (1903–2012) was a publishing house specializing in educational books.

56 FO924/162, LC397, No. 17, Leeper to FO, 8 March 1945.

57 FO924/162, LC848, Harold Orton, British Council K.B. Robinson, Evans Brothers, 24 February 1946; Robinson to Orton, 24 February 1946; Orton to Johnstone, 1 March 1946; FO to Athens, 27 March 1946. Leeper attached particular importance to the form of the Greek language into which the book was to be translated by 'Dr Hourmouzios', that it had to be 'neither purely classic nor demotic Greek, but the everyday language of the people'. It seems most likely that the reference is to Aimilios Chourmouzios, who was involved with translating and was a well-known man of letters and supporter of the demotic. His cousin, Stylianos-Loukianos, who was living and working in London at that time – in late 1940s he was with the Greek Embassy Information Department in London – was also the author of a number of books, one of which was published in 1942 by Evans Brothers.

58 FO924/163, LC2748, FO to Cairo, 5 July 1945; FO to Ankara, 30 June 1945; FO to Rome, 5 July 1945.

59 FO924/163, LC2627, Athens (Caccia) to FO, from Cardiff, 15 July 1945.

60 FO924/163, LC2748, Athens (Caccia) to FO, 14 and 15 July 1945. The titles desired were: Scott's *English Conversations in Simplified Phonetic Transcription*, Palmer's *Colloquial English, Julius Caesar, A Tale of Two Cities, Pride and Prejudice*, also Faucet's *Oxford Reading and Language* (now approved for Greek schools) and Eckersley's *Brighter English*. See also FO924/163, LC2627.

61 Cf. FO924/162, LC1372, Johnstone's Memorandum, 'British Council Work in Greece: 1945/6', 7 March 1945.

62 FO924/162, LC886, Athens to FO, 19 March 1945. FO to Athens, 4 April 1945. Both the Council and the Embassy attached similarly great significance to awarding Council scholarships to Greek architects, many of whom, in addition to an academic career, were employed as state officials in major public works. The Council's list included well-known architects such as Dimitris Fotiadis, Rennos Koutsouris, Arthur Scheepers, Prokopios Vassiliadis, J. Papaioannou,

60 GIOULA KOUTSOPANAGOU

Paul Mylonas and Thucydides Valentis (FO924/163, LC2627, Athens to FO, 22 July 1945).

63 FO924/163, LC2627 Athens (Caccia) to FO, following for British Council to Foreign Office, 6 July 1945. Caccia to FO, following for Johnstone from Cardiff, 15 July 1945.

64 FO924/163, LC2627, Athens to FO, following for Thompson from Card, 18 July 1945.

65 The total number of French Institute scholarships – for twelve, six or three months – for 1945 was more than 150, selected from 60 fields and specializations (until 1937, the number of scholarships was ten), plus 70 more students who would have some facilities but at their own expense, see Koutsopanagou, 'Propaganda', p. 177. Cf. N. Manitakis, 'Ξένες κρατικές υποτροφίες: Πολιτιστική προπαγάνδα στην Ελλάδα του Εμφυλίου', in Christos Hatziiosif (ed.), Ιστορία της Ελλάδας του 20ου αιώνα: Ανασυγκρότηση-Εμφύλιος-Παλινόρθωση 1945–1952 (Athens, 2009), 4/2, pp. 133–57. On the other hand the American Government intended to make 160 scholarships available for Greece as stated in the press (point mentioned in Johnstone's Memorandum entitled 'British Council Work in Greece: 1945/6' dated 7 March 1945).

66 FO924/163, LC3307, Hedley to Johnstone, 17 August 1945.

67 FO924/36, LC1488, Minutes by Hedley, 17 November 1944.

68 The first signed by A.A. Pallis, Vice-President of the Athens Branch of the League (FO924/36, LC1386, J. Romanos to Laskey, 3 November 1944 and enclosed letters of Pallis to Leeper and to Sir M. Robertson, 26 October 1944); the other by A. Benakis, Hon. President and B.V. Melas, Hon. Secretary of the League to Leeper, 28 October 1944. Leeper to Antony Eden, 31 October 1944. LC1488, Leeper to FO, 15 November 1944 (FO924/36, LC1486).

69 FO924/36, LC1416, British Embassy, Athens to D.F. Howard, Southern Department, FO, 2 November 1944, enclosing letter from G. Georgiadis Arnakis to Leeper, 25 October 1944. For George Georgiadis Arnakis (1912–76) cf. 'An Autobiographical Sketch by George G. Arnakis', Neo-Hellenika, 4 (1981), pp. 9–28.

70 FO924/36, LC1488, Leeper to FO, 15 November 1944.

71 FO924/36, LC1416, Minutes, 17 November 1944.

72 FO924/162, LC307, Wickham's letter to Gurney, 23 January 1945.

73 FO924/162, LC664, Sir Robertson to Johnstone, copy for Gurney, 14 February 1946. See relevant Outward Telegram, No. 9, FO to Athens, 15 February 1945.

74 Ernest Riggs, grandson of the Presbyterian missionary in the Balkans Elias Riggs, was the third President of Anatolia College (1933–50).

75 Davies began his career at Robert College, Istanbul in 1920. In 1927 he was appointed Principal and in 1930 President of Athens College in Greece. At the outbreak of the World War II he went back to the US to become chief of project licensing division of the Board of Economic Warfare (1941–42) and executive vice president of the Greek War Relief. In early 1943 he joined the State Department as special assistant to the Foreign Service Auxiliary and was assigned to the American Consulate General in Istanbul. In 1944 he returned to Athens as

THE RE-OPENING OF THE BRITISH COUNCIL   61

Public Relations Officer with UNRRA and from 1945 until 1976 he returned to Athens College.

76 President of the American College for Girls (ACG) in Athens (1944–47). She taught art at ACG (1946–55).

77 FO924/163, LC2994, EDU/1/1, Secret, 'Impressions of a meeting with Mr Homer Davies (of Athens College), Professor Riggs (of Anatolia College), and McElroy (of the Athens College for Girls), 26th June, 1945'.

78 FO924/163, LC2994, EDU/1/1, letter entitled 'American Co-operation in the Teaching of English in Greece', Cardiff to Thompson, 3 July 1945. Seymour to Montagu-Pollock, 18 July 1945. H.D. Bryan, FO to Seymour 22 August 1945.

79 In the following excerpt from Merlier's annual report of the French Institute in 1947 one can discern French concern over the prospect of increased English language use in Greece. 'Britain and the US are the big winners. English competes with French in Greek education. All appears to be lost. France is no longer friends with the Greek administrative authorities, and the political world has decided to promote the richest and most powerful nations. An Anglo-Saxon department has been created at the University of Athens' (quoted by G. Kalpadakis in Nelli Andrikopoulou, *Το ταξίδι του Ματαρόα, 1945: Στον καθρέπτη της μνήμης* (Athens, 2007), p. 128.

80 FO924/162, LC886, Leeper to FO, 19 March 1945.

81 FO924/163, LC2994, FO924/163, LC2994, Minutes by Hedley, 31 July; by J.B. Donelly (Southern Department), 3 August; by Laskey, 7 August 1945. CRD to The Chancery, British Embassy, 22 August 1945.

82 Emergency Law 752, 21 December 1945, ΦΕΚ Α 311, p. 1565, 'Περί εισαγωγής της Αγγλικής Γλώσσης ως υποχρεωτικού μαθήματος εις τα γυμνάσια'. Regarding how Greek public opinion viewed the introduction of the English language as a compulsory secondary school subject, see the article in the Left-wing Greek newspaper, *Eleftheri Ellada* entitled 'Educational Acrobatics', 21 June, and the aggressive reply to it by the Right-wing paper *Ellinikon Aima*, 22 June 1945.

83 Evangelos Papanoutsos' long service in the post of director-general in the Ministry of Education is indicative. He retained this post from late December 1944 to its abolition on 30 April 1946 by the Populist government; see Charalambos Noutsos, *Ο δρόμος της καμήλας και το σχολείο: Η εκπαιδευτική πολιτική στην Ελλάδα: 1944–1946* (Athens, 2003), p. 153.

84 FO924/162, LC1372, Johnstone's Memorandum, 'British Council Work in Greece: 1945/6', 7 March 1945.

85 As Leeper had anticipated even before the elections (FO924/424, LC1236, Leeper to Montagu-Pollock, 1 March 1946).

86 Noutsos, pp. 154–69. See also Alexis Dimaras (ed.), *Η μεταρρύθμιση που δεν έγινε* (Athens, 1998), vol. 2 (1895–1967), pp. LIII-LIV.

87 FO924/162, LC886, Leeper to FO, 24 February 1945.

88 Professor Hamley was to arrive in Athens in early summer to stay about three months (FO924/162, LC942, FO to Athens, 15 June 1945).

89 FO924/162, LC1068, Leeper to FO, 16 March 1945.

90 It appears that, in the event, just one chair was instituted, that of 'British Life and Thought' which was passed by Emergency Law 745 of 19 December 1945, 'Περί ιδρύσεως νέων εδρών εν τω Πανεπιστημίω Αθηνών', ΦΕΚ, Α 309, p. 1560. By the same law, a regular chair of 'History of the United States and of American Letters' was likewise instituted. Attlee [he is referred to as Atli in the minutes] 'is to teach English literature' as announced by the Dean of the School, Professor A. Hatzis, at its 14th meeting on 29 October 1945, see Historical Archive of the University of Athens (hereafter IA.EKPA), Faculty of Arts, Minutes of Meetings, 21 (1945), p. 316. At his own suggestion, it was agreed that Attlee would not 'take part in the meetings [of the School], that his classes [would] be optional and that the students could attend them without being examined'.

91 No data has so far been found on what kind of previous experience of Greece Attlee had.

92 FO924/162, LC2287, R. Davies, British Council, London to Montagu-Pollock, 'Proposed Chair of British History and Institutions, University of Athens', 7 June 1945.

93 FO924/163, LC2430, Minutes by Hedley, and by Montagu-Pollock, 15 June 1945.

94 FO924/163, LC2430, FO to Athens, 15 June 1945. See also FO924/162, LC2287, FO to Athens, 23 June 1945.

95 IA.EKPA, Minutes of the University of Athens Senate Meeting, 56 (1944–1945), Rector I. Politis, 7th Meeting (Extraordinary), 18 October 1945, p. 78. It was also announced that Attlee would give six lectures 'to all students' in the university's main Assembly Hall on the topic 'British Life and Thought' and would in addition conduct 'special tutorials for persons who wish to become teachers of the English language' in another hall.

96 FO924/163, LC2430, Athens (Caccia) to FO, 23 June 1945.

97 FO924/163, LC2755, Athens to FO, 18 July 1945.

98 IA.EKPA, Faculty of Arts, Minutes of Meetings, 17th Meeting, 5 November, 21 (1945), p. 319.

99 The chair 'British Life and Thought' was instituted by Law 745/1945 (see footnote 91). Regarding the appointment of professors for the English and American chairs, their qualifications, duties and rights were to be determined by Royal Decree upon a proposal by the Ministry of Education and the University Senate (see footnote 105).

100 He was recommended for the post not for his high academic qualifications but for his personal qualities and administrative ability 'for the difficult pioneering work . . . in establishing a school of British History at the University'. It was thought that after three years, the academic standard of the Department would have risen high enough to justify the appointment of a historian more highly qualified academically (FO924/424, LC1292, Letter from H.G. Wayment, Education Division, British Council, London to Montagu-Pollock, 13 March 1946. Minutes by Laskey, 19 March 1946. Montagu-Pollock to Wayment, 21 March 1946).

THE RE-OPENING OF THE BRITISH COUNCIL 63

101 There is no reference to the name of H.M. Butler in the Minutes of the Faculty of Arts and University Senate meetings during the critical period from 3 December 1945, in which the name of Attlee is mentioned for the last time in the minutes, until the first reference to the name of W.A. Sewell on 3 March 1947.

102 IA.EKPA, Faculty of Arts, Minutes of Meetings, 1st (Extraordinary), 9 September 1946, 22 (1945–1946), pp. 9–10.

103 See footnote 11.

104 The reciprocity issue was reintroduced into the discussion on a proposal by Dean S. Marinatos and at the 2nd Meeting, 16 September 1946, after approving the Minutes of the previous Meeting (see note 102), the School decided 'that the two English chairs be merged into one and that the reciprocity defined by law 1100/1938 be retained', IA.EKPA, Faculty of Arts, Minutes of Meetings, 22 (1945–1946), p. 12. However, the University Senate 'decided not to retain reciprocity', IA.EKPA, Faculty of Arts, Minutes of Meetings, 3rd Meeting, 14 October 1946, 22 (1945–1946), p. 19.

105 Up to that point the Faculty of Arts had not yet reached a conclusion 'because we regarded the issue as very important . . . and that it had to be studied and was indeed studied . . . at length . . . from all viewpoints and from every aspect', see IA.EKPA, Minutes of the University of Athens Senate, Rector K. Moutousis, 3rd Meeting, 2 October 1951, 63 (1951–1952), p. 42.

106 FO924/424, LC1763, R. Davies, British Council to Montagu-Pollock, 9 April 1946.

107 FO924/424, LC523, Wayment to Montagu-Pollock, 4 February 1946. Minutes by Laskey, 9 February 1946 and by Montagu-Pollock, 15 February 1946. Montagu-Pollock to Wayment, 20 February 1946.

108 IA.EKPA, Minutes of the Senate of the University of Athens, 57 (1945–1946), Rector D. Balanos, 40th Meeting (Extraordinary), 25 June 1946, p. 405. The Ministry of Education approved Sewell's appointment in its document No. 55515 dated 18 July 1947(sic) (1946), 57 (1945–1946), 47th Meeting, 29 August 1946, p. 467. Ratification of the contract for a ten-year appointment was announced by the Ministry of Education to the Senate on 22 October 1946, 58 (1946–1947), Rector S. Dontas, 10th Meeting (Extraordinary), 9 November 1946, p. 78.

109 IA.EKPA, Faculty of Arts, Minutes of Meetings, 14 and 21 January, 24 (1952), pp. 129, 137.

110 Sewell's interventions concerned proposals to change the programme of English language teaching which, under the regulations in force then, was not compulsory, to increase the number of classes (in fact he asked for approval to teach '7–8 classes for the public from November to December, on the topic of English thought in the 17th century and 12 classes in the months of January, February and March on the topic of the tragedies in Shakespeare's works'). He complained 'because the class in English Literature is not equivalent to those taught at the University', asked that certification of English language studies be granted, and requested that persons attending his classes not be required to pay fees. He also proposed that the contract be for at least three years' duration with the prospect of renewal. Cf. the minutes of Meetings

of the Senate and the Faculty of Arts in the period 1947–53. Some information about English studies at the University of Athens can be found in *Εθνικό και Καποδιστριακό Πανεπιστήμιο Αθηνών, Τμήμα Αγγλικής Γλώσσας και Φιλολογίας: 56 χρόνια παρουσίας* (Athens, 2008). It is my intention to examine this subject in a future article, with emphasis on the establishment of English and American chairs.

111   It is worth noting that a Chair of French Literature did not yet exist at the University of Athens, 'at least legally', until its official establishment under the Royal Decree of 19th June 1953, ΦΕΚ, Α 161, p. 1015, 'Περί ιδρύσεως έδρας Γαλλικής Λογοτεχνίας παρά τη Φιλοσοφική Σχολή του Πανεπιστημίου Αθηνών'. Until 1953 the regulations governing this Chair had been defined in the Greek-French Agreement on educational and cultural relations, dated 19 December 1938 and ratified by Emergency Law 1608 of 14th February 1939, ΦΕΚ, Α 57, pp. 385–89. The Department of French Studies was instituted at the University of Athens through Law 3107 of 30 December 1954, ΦΕΚ, Α 314, pp. 2573–74 in accordance with which the above-mentioned Chair was abolished and in its place two Chairs were established: the Chair of French Language and Literature, and the Chair of French Civilization.

112   Emergency Law 1858, 23 June 1951, 'Περί τρόπου μορφώσεως καθηγητών της Αγγλικής εν τοις σχολείοις της Μέσης Εκπαιδεύσεως', *ΦΕΚ*, Α 185, pp. 1318–19. The title of the law is characteristic, since emphasis is placed on training future secondary school teachers of the English language, who in accordance with the law, in addition to the English language, could also teach other humanities classes in high schools, especially in remote areas. It is interesting to note that in the first university entrance examinations for the academic year 1951–52, just one candidate appeared, and the Senate extended the deadline for writing the entrance examinations to 20 February 1952.

113   Sewell was present in person at the Meeting on 21 January 1952, at his own request to the Dean of the Faculty of Arts, to announce that 'telegrams were received in London . . . that distinguished scholars submitted their candidacy for the Byron Chair', 24 (1952), p. 137. Sewell's successor was selected from 43 candidates, foremost among whom were the following: Bernard Blackstone, David Hardman, Robert Gus Wowarth (sic, for Howarth) and Stephen Spender. Taking part in the special council meeting on behalf of the Greek embassy in London was George Seferiades (Seferis), later Ambassador to London (1957–62) and Nobel laureate (1963). Eventually Blackstone was selected. Twelve of the faculty members voted affirmatively, one (N.B. Tomadakis) did not vote for any candidate because 'there were no criteria' and one (S. Marinatos) cast a blank ballot because he could not vote as his 'conscience dictated'. It is worth mentioning that in the discussion, all the faculty members agreed with the view of Professor Marinatos that 'the election of professors of foreign literature must in future be done by university professors who will also bear the responsibility for their choice'. IA.EKPA, Faculty of Arts, Minutes of Meetings, 28 April, 24 (1952), pp. 191–94.

114   His earlier interests were archaeological and mediaeval. A couple of theological items on his curriculum vitae (FO924/424, LC 2254) also indicated

THE RE-OPENING OF THE BRITISH COUNCIL 65

theological interests. He became acquainted at school with C.P. Mayhew, later Labour MP and Parliamentary Under-Secretary of State for Foreign Affairs from 1946 to 1950. From 1942 to 1946 he served as intelligence officer in the Foreign Office. He was to become one of the leading historians of the Early Church and 'one of the scholars of early Christianity to use archaeological material in a 'scientific' way. See *Proceedings of the British Academy*, 150 (2007), pp. 37–54.

115 FO924/424, LC2254, Wayment to Montagu-Pollock, 8 May 1946. Montagu-Pollock to Wayment, 17 May 1946.

116 *Proceedings*, pp. 44–45.

117 Cf. Johnstone's Memorandum on 7 March 1945.

118 Cf. FO924/162, LC531, Athens to FO, 31 January 1945; FO to Athens, 27 February 1945.

119 FO924/706, LC61.

120 This had been established in 1939 to contribute to promoting legal studies in Greece and knowledge of Greek law beyond national borders. The first Institute Director was Professor Petros Vallindas (1939–60). After the Liberation the Institute resumed its activity up to this day.

121 FO924/163, LC4475, N. Verros (Director of the Library of Greek Parliament) to British Ambassador, Athens, 3 August 1945.

122 FO924/163, LC4475, Chancery, Athens to British Council Section, Foreign Office, 1 October 1945.

123 FO924/163, LC5380, letter, M. MacLeod, Books Department, British Council to Hedley, 26 October 1945.

124 Caccia took charge of the British Embassy in Athens during Leeper's leave of absence in Britain until September 1945.

125 Koutsopanagou, 'Προπαγάνδα', pp. 171–90.

126 See Phivos Economidis, *Πόλεμος, διείσδυση και προπαγάνδα* (Athens, 1992), pp. 86-93.

127 Koutsopanagou, 'Προπαγάνδα', p. 188.

128 Among his other activities, he was also professor of Byzantine and Modern Greek History in the University of Athens (1939–70) and at the Panteios School (1951–65).

129 The lecture programme on literary subjects to a wider audience proved to be highly successful as recent experiments with a 'Shakespeare Week' had showed. This was a series of seven lectures about Shakespeare in English by British (Kenneth Johnstone, Osbert Lancaster, Derek Patmore) and Greek scholars (C.A. Trypanis and Tentes Rodokanakis) before the production of *Twelfth Night* by the Manolidou-Aroni-Horn company at the Pantheon Theatre in February 1945, on the initiative of the theatrical agent Theodoros Kritas in conjunction with the British Council. The lectures were introduced by Georgios Melas, Deputy Minister of the Interior, see Koutsopanagou, 'Προπαγάνδα', p. 177.

130 FO371/48238, R11703, Caccia to FO, 7 July 1945 in P. Koutsopanagou, 'The British Press and the Greek Crisis, 1943–1949', unpublished Ph.D. Thesis, LSE, University of London, 1996, pp. 182–83.

131 Atherton, 'Lord Lloyd at the British Council', pp. 34–35.

132 Conventions were signed by Britain with Belgium (April 1946), Brazil (April 1947), Czechoslovakia (June 1947), Norway (February 1948), France (March 1948) and the Netherlands (July 1948). Drafts on similar lines were under consideration for Conventions with Luxembourg, Italy, Greece and Portugal.

133 FO924/163, LC3062, Minutes by Laskey, 12 July 1945 and by Hedley, 19 July 1945. Montagu-Pollock to Johnstone, 28 July 1945. The Anglo-Greek Cultural Convention was finally signed in September 1951.

134 Constantine Athanasius Trypanis (1909–93). Classical scholar, translator and poet, the last primarily in English. In 1947 he went to Oxford as an assistant to John Mavrogordato, whom he soon succeeded as Bywater and Sotheby Professor of Byzantine and Modern Greek Literature, a post for which Steven Runciman had also been considered. In 1974–77 he was Minister of Culture and Science in Greece. He became Secretary General of the Academy of Athens (1981–85) and its President in 1986.

135 FO924/163, LC 4491, the report sent to Johnstone and Michael Grant was transmitted to Montagu-Pollock on 8 October.

136 FO924/163, LC 4491, AGIS, CMF, Trypanis' report, 'The Greek Soviet League', signed by AJAX, 2 September 1945.

137 Actually this appointment never materialized. Despite his 'enormous circle of friends in Athens, ranging politically from Archbishop Chrysanthos to Professor Svolos and M. Porphyrogennis', according to the report, Merlier, who was censured as being a supporter of EAM and a pro-communist, was unable to avoid becoming involved in a lengthy public dispute that eventually cost him his position as cultural attaché at the French Embassy; cf. Andrikopoulou, pp. 132–34. See also Chapter 13 of the present volume.

138 FO924/163, LC4172, Chancery, British Embassy to CRD, Report entitled 'French Cultural Work in Greece', 19 September 1945.

139 FO924/163, LC3909, Minutes by F.R. Cowell, 19 June 1945.

140 FO924/163, LC3909, Minutes by Montagu-Pollock (addressed to J.G. Tahourdin, Private Secretary to the Minister of State), Minutes by Noel-Baker?, 18 September 1945.

141 FO924/163, LC3909, Minutes by Noel-Baker, 14 September 1945. The Nuffield and Wall Foundations were mentioned.

142 In 1941 he was elected Professor of Law at the Panteios School. In 1944 he became Chef de Cabinet of the Regent, Archbishop Damaskinos, and took part in the Varkiza agreement as an observer. In 1945 he was appointed Governor General of the Ionian Islands. He played a major role in the Panteios School, having been elected rector twice in 1963–64 and 1974–75. It is worth noting that Georgakis approached the British Council in 1950, expressing the

THE RE-OPENING OF THE BRITISH COUNCIL   67

School's desire 'to have closer contact with English culture in general, with the English language and with English thought on political economy and economics'. The Embassy in Athens considered the Panteios School an 'important organization which it will well repay us to cultivate since it provides the training ground for the great majority of Greek civil servants' and suggested that the British Council should meet, at least in part, the School's request set out in Georgakis' letter (FO924/791, L23/3).

143 FO924/163, LC5009, Leeper to Montagu-Pollock, 22 October 1945.

144 FO924/163, LC5009, Pollock to J.A. Romanos, Greek Embassy, London, 6 November 1945 and FO924/163, LC5504, O. Contostavlos (Romanos was absent in Greece), First Secretary, Greek Embassy, London to Montagu-Pollock, 21 November 1945.

145 FO924/163, LC5504, Montagu-Pollock to The Secretary, Lord Mayor's Greek Relief Fund, 5 December 1945; No. 306, FO to Athens, 13 February 1946.

146 FO924/424, LC1236, Leeper to Montagu-Pollock, 1 March 1946.

147 FO924/424, LC3371, LC1236, Montagu-Pollock to Norton, 12 June 1946; Patrick Reilly, British Embassy to Montagu-Pollock, 25 June 1946; Montagu-Pollock to Reilly, 25 July 1946.

148 This model hospital was to be run along the lines of the agreements between the Greek government and the Rockefeller Foundation, the Health Organization of the League of Nations and the Wellcome Research Laboratories, which worked satisfactorily from 1931 to 1939.

149 About the politics of health in the post-war Greece see indicatively Dimitra Giannuli, ' "Repeated Disappointment": The Rockefeller Foundation and the Reform of the Greek Public Health System, 1929–1940', *Bulletin of the History of Medicine*, 72/1 (1998), pp. 47–72; David H. Close, 'War, Medical Advance and the Improvement of Health in Greece, 1944–53', *South European Society and Politics*, 9/3 (Winter 2004), pp. 1–27; Maria Vassiliou, 'Politics, Public Health and Development: Malaria in 20th Century Greece', D.Phil. Thesis, University of Oxford, 2005; Katerina Gardikas, 'Relief Work and Malaria in Greece, 1943–1947', *Journal of Contemporary History*, 43/3 (2008), pp. 493–508; Violetta Hionidou, *Famine and Death in Occupied Greece, 1941–1944* (Cambridge, 2006; Greek edition, Athens, 2011).

150 FO924/163, LC4225, Seymour to Montagu-Pollock, 14 September 1945.

151 FO924/163, LC4225, Minutes by Hedley, 18 September 1945; by Laskey, 21 September 1945. Montagu-Pollock to Seymour, 24 September 1945.

152 Seymour, Sir G. Wilkinson of the Lord Mayor's Fund and Dr. Henry Foy, director of the Wellcome Research Laboratories in Salonika, agreed that the Council should transfer its responsibility in administering the grant to the Wellcome Trust, see FO924/706, LC651, Confidential, British Embassy to CRD, 3 February 1948. Minutes by J.A. Aitken, 11 February 1948. See also FO924/706, LC933, Sir Henry Dale to B.C. MacDermot, Foreign Office, 25 February 1948.

153 FO924/162, LC1372, Wickham sent a copy of Johnstone's memorandum to Gurney, 7 April 1945.

154 FO924/162, LC1372, Johnstone's Memorandum, 'British Council Work in Greece: 1945/6', 7 March 1945.

155 FO924/424, LC3333, Norton to Bevin, 21 June 1946.

156 British cultural and publicity policy in Greece in the first decade after the World War II is the subject of a forthcoming book of mine.

157 As an immediate response to Lancaster's report, Norton pointed out a number of severe handicaps that still hindered British Council work in Greece, notably in relation to translation rights of English books for Greek publishers, supplies of English textbooks, delay in appointing the Council staff (FO924/424, LC3145, Norton to Bevin, 20 June 1946). These handicaps were eventually removed; as regards the staff appointment of the 43 London-appointed Council posts in Greece 35 had already been filled, and appointments to four more were about to be made (FO924/424, LC3145, Montagu-Pollock to Johnstone, 8 July 1946. Johnstone to Pollock, 26 August 1946. Montagu-Pollock's draft letter to Johnstone, 25 September 1946. FO to Norton, 30 September 1946).

158 FO924/424, LC3333, Minutes by Hilton Young, Hedley, Dudley, Johnstone, Lowell (EEID), Montagu-Pollock, from 2 to 23 July 1946. However, Lancaster's recommendations in attempting to pool personnel between the Press Department and the British Council in the provinces were treated sceptically. The CRD wanted to keep information in the hands of Foreign Office staff. Johnstone agreed that the points raised by the report regarding the close cooperation between the cultural and information staff should be considered at a meeting. In future, the activities of the British Council and the FO Information Policy Department would be more coordinated than before. The 'illegal' Kavala experiment – in which, after its closure, the British Information Centre housed its activities in the British Council representative's building – met with considerable success and set a good example for similar future collaborations (cf. FO930/422, R.T. Eland's Report, Press Department, British Embassy, 30 June 1946, and FO924/706, LC18962).

159 FO924/162, LC1372, Johnstone's Memorandum on 7 March 1945.

160 The term 'public diplomacy' was coined in 1965: see Nicholas J. Cull, 'Public Diplomacy Before Gullion: The Evolution of a Phrase', in Nancy Snow and P.M. Taylor (eds.), *Routledge Handbook of Public Diplomacy* (London, 2009), pp. 19–23.

161 H.N. Tuch, *Communicating with the World: U.S. Public Diplomacy Overseas* (New York, 1990), p. 9; cf. G.D. Malone, *Political Advocacy and Cultural Communication: Organizing the Nation's Public Diplomacy* (Boston, 1988), pp. 1–11.

Chapter 3

Steven Runciman at the British Council: Letters from Athens, 1945–1947

Michael Llewellyn-Smith

Steven Runciman,[1] the historian of Byzantium, was an inquisitive and observant traveller. He divided his book *A Traveller's Alphabet*, which he called 'Partial Memoirs', into sections by the alphabet, for example 'Thailand, Ur of the Chaldees, Vancouver Island, West Indies, Xanadu, Yucatan, and Zion'. The Greek sections are Athos under A – a sparkling piece – and Morea: Monemvasia and Mistra under M. There is no entry for Athens. The simplest explanation for this absence is that he had decided to have one entry only for each letter of the alphabet, and Athos had priority (though he cheated over the Ms by including both Monemvasia and Mistra under the umbrella of the Morea). Mount Athos responded to his feeling for the Orthodox faith and for Byzantine architecture and mysticism. He knew what he wanted to write about them. Athens did not strike a similar bell.

However, Steven spent more than a year and a half in Athens at a critical period of Greek history, as 'Representative' (Director) of the British Council. His letters home, to his mother Hilda, Viscountess Runciman, are a main source for this period.[2] She was living at Doxford, the family home in Northumberland, and caring for her husband Walter, the 1st Viscount (1870–1949). Walter Runciman was the long-serving Liberal Minister who is most famous for leading the unsuccessful 'Runciman Mission' to Czechoslovakia in 1938. By 1945 he was suffering from the degenerative illness from which he died in November 1949.

Steven was forty-two years old when he went to Athens. After Eton and Trinity College Cambridge, where he took a First in History, he had travelled extensively between the wars and spent eleven years as a Fellow of Trinity. As he was fond of saying when explaining his special interest in Byzantium, he had persuaded the great historian of the late Roman empire J.B. Bury to take him on as a pupil. A generous legacy from his grandfather, the shipping magnate, enabled him to resign his fellowship in 1938, and from then on he was a private scholar of independent means.[3] After short spells as Press Attaché in Sofia, and in a similar role in Cairo, he spent the years 1942–45 as Professor of Byzantine Art and History at the University of Istanbul.[4] This led to his appointment as Representative of the British Council in Athens. He already had a reputation as a Byzantinist, based on publications from his period at

Cambridge. *Byzantine Civilization* (1933)[5] was the first of his books that was addressed to a wide reading public as well as to specialists. The Istanbul post was an ideal vantage point from which to enlarge his knowledge of Byzantium and of the Islamic world. At the time when he went to Athens he had published nothing substantial since *Byzantine Civilization*, but we know that in Athens he was working on what became his three-volume history of the crusades.[6]

The British Council was established in 1934, at the initiative of Reginald (Rex) Leeper, a British diplomat of Australian origin with a background in political intelligence. As head of the Foreign Office News Department, he saw the need to develop cultural diplomacy and propaganda to assert 'British Values' in a world staggering towards war.[7] In 1940 the Council became a corporate body under Royal Charter, independent though funded by government – a status that many people have found hard to understand.[8] The Foreign Office was its sponsoring department. By a happy coincidence, Leeper was British ambassador to Greece at the time Runciman was appointed Representative.[9]

The Council had operated in Greece before the war. An early token of cultural diplomacy was the establishment in 1937, with a Council subvention, of the Byron Chair of English Language and Literature at Athens University. In 1939, in the course of a mainly political visit, the Council's maverick Chairman, Lord Lloyd, smoothed the path for the Council at meetings with King George II and the dictator Ioannis Metaxas.[10] The Representative in Greece until the evacuation of Council staff in May 1941 was A.R. Burn, the historian of ancient Greece.[11]

The most important aspect of the Council's work in Greece was the English language, as appeared when its Institute of English Studies (IES) threw open its doors to English language students, having taken over this function from the Anglo-Hellenic League, which operated out of 9 Ermou Street.[12] 'It immediately became evident,' wrote the Council employee Anastasios (Tassos) Sagos, 'that an enormous demand for English teaching existed in Athens, which had somehow to be met. Staff recruitment went on rapidly in England, and in November 1939 occurred the amazing scenes when thousands of would-be students packed the entire street in an attempt to register. In the end some 4500 students were accepted and a separate annexe was set up in Philhellinon Street near Syntagma Square for children's classes.'[13]

Between the outbreak of war and the German invasion of Greece in April 1941 the staff was augmented by various 'refugees' from other countries. Burn thus found himself in charge of a varied group of teachers, many of whom were budding writers. Among the names of teachers cited in the Council's files and by Mr Sagos[14] are the literary critic Terence Spencer and the historian Douglas Dakin, both transferred from Rome; Lawrence Durrell; the poet Bernard Spencer; Robert Liddell; Robin Fedden; Julian Pring, who subsequently wrote the small Greek-English and English-Greek dictionaries published by Oxford University Press; C.M. Woodhouse; Reginald Close, later to be Representative of the Council in Greece in the 1960s; and other refugees from Belgrade and Bucharest.[15] Of these Pring was in Salonica, Liddell was sent to teach in Crete and Durrell to Kalamata.

Thus the association of the British Council with literature, in particular poetry, was already established before the war. The flavour of this period of nervous waiting and shifting population is conveyed by Olivia Manning's *Balkan Trilogy*.[16] Reginald (Reggie) Smith (1914–85), Manning's communist husband, was one of the Council refugees from Bucharest.

Robin Burn had an exceptionally difficult job, dealing with staffing problems both normal and unusual, including security, the rapidly increasing cost of living, a dispute over the attempt by the Council to impose a standard contract on teachers, preparations for evacuation and keeping the show on the road after the Greek government closed all teaching institutions in November 1940. The answer to this last was to arrange teaching in private houses.

The staff were dispersed with the German invasion of Greece, several of them migrating to Egypt. Normal service, if it can be called that, resumed after the war, with the reopening of the Institute for English language teaching. The demand proved even greater than in 1939 – more than 7,000 applications within seven days, of whom 3,651 were accepted for the first term (November 1945–January 1946) at a fee of £1. Soon afterwards, the IES was split up, and a separate British Institute of Higher Studies (BIHS) established in an elegant house at 17 Philikis Etairias (Kolonaki Square) combining diploma tuition with lecture courses and study groups. Rex Warner was the first Director of this, followed by Malcolm Welland and Louis MacNeice.[17]

While the English language and literature operation was based in Kolonaki Square, the main British Council office was then at 4 Vassilissis Sofias. It was here that Steven Runciman took up his duties, succeeding Prudence Wallace, the widow of Major David Wallace, who had been killed in the mountains during the war.[18]

There were special factors that affected the still young British Council in Greece in this strange post-war period.

First, the Greek operation had to be rebuilt virtually from scratch. There had been a gap in operations of more than three years since the evacuation of May 1941. Moreover, for reasons that remain somewhat mysterious, the Council took the view that the pre-war staff in Greece were unsatisfactory. This view was put most pungently by C.A.F. Dundas (known as 'Flux'), the Council's Middle East Representative, in a letter to the Council's chairman, the redoubtable Lord Lloyd, in 1940:

> I feel very strongly that some of the Council's Greek staff have gained (and a few deserved) a reputation for qualities which make their position untenable in the especially difficult and delicate circumstances of the present time. It is variously said that they are indiscreet, extravagant, lack any serious purpose, do not consider the public effects of their personal behaviour, or are irresponsible in financial matters. It is, too, repeatedly said, however slanderously,

72 MICHAEL LLEWELLYN-SMITH

that they are 'pansies', 'longhaired' or 'soft'. This unsavoury reputation unhappily found its way both to Egypt and to Cyprus this summer.[19]

I have found no evidence in the files to support these charges. But they affected the attitude of the Council to restaffing after the war – in theory at least; in practice, the Council had some difficulty in finding the right teaching staff in the disturbed post war conditions.[20]

The second factor was the omnipresence in late 1944–45 of the British military. At the end of the war they had established a large-scale information effort, the Anglo-Greek Information Service (AGIS), and a teaching operation which extended beyond Athens and Salonica as far as Rhodes. (This was the period in which Rhodes and the Dodecanese were under British military administration pending their union with Greece.)[21] Much energy therefore went into dealing with lines of demarcation between the Council and the military over information work and teaching. This was still the case in the early stage of Runciman's tenure.

The third factor was the condition of Greece, unsettled throughout Runciman's period, with changes of government, rapid inflation of prices and towards the end civil war.

The way had been well prepared by two impressive individuals. The first of these was Colonel Kenneth Johnstone, who put the British Council operation on its feet in 1944–45.[22] Johnstone was a Foreign Office official who had worked closely with Leeper before the war and been seconded to the British Council in 1938 as one of its two Deputy Secretaries General. The second was Major Maurice Cardiff, an officer in the Scots Guards who had been involved in political warfare in Cairo and had been sent into the Aegean islands. He was summoned to Athens in 1945, invited to take over as Acting Representative of the British Council, and briefed on the job in the course of an hour by Johnstone, who was packing his suitcase the while. Cardiff described this curious scene in his memoir *Friends Abroad*.[23] He later joined the British Council as a permanent member of staff.

The efforts of Johnstone and Cardiff included reopening the major teaching operation of the British Institute, restarting a programme of lectures by both resident staff and visiting lecturers from Britain, finding a new building for the Institute, supporting libraries and the distribution of books and periodicals and initiating a modest cultural and arts programme.[24]

Johnstone returned to London in summer 1945 and resumed service as a senior member of the Council's headquarters staff, as Director for Europe. This meant that there was someone in London who well understood the Council's Greek operation and its problems. This was important in an organization where 'them' and 'us' feelings between London and Athens staff were typical. In a memo on 'British Council Work in Greece, 1945–6', endorsed by the London office, Johnstone expressed the enlightened spirit that inspired the appointment of, for example, Rex Warner. Under the heading 'intellectual liaison', he wrote of the need to send to Greece 'men who are as ready, and as competent, to give as to take, men, that is to say, who are prepared as much to take an active interest in modern Greek literature, science, agriculture or music, as to inform the Greeks about British achievements in these various fields'.[25] In London Johnstone rose to the point where he was considered a potential Director General of the Council, but never quite made it.[26]

The Council had been searching since 1944 for a new Representative to take over from Johnstone. Several names emerged in correspondence between London and Athens, including the Hellenist Romilly Jenkins;[27] the Roman historian Michael Grant;[28] the historian of ancient Greece Nick Hammond,[29] who had been with SOE in the Greek mountains; Professor C.M. Attlee of University College, Nottingham; and the literary critic M.R. Ridley. Each of these was either unavailable or judged unsuitable.[30]

By 1945 the matter was becoming urgent, since the Council wanted Johnstone back as soon as possible – though ambassador Leeper wanted him to stay in Athens.[31] Steven Runciman's name came up in March 1945 and his appointment soon followed, though not without considerable hesitation in London, which seems to have been largely on the grounds of his homosexuality.[32] He took over in October 1945, initially on a one-year contract, and directed the Council in Greece until July 1947 when he returned to the UK.

In his letters home Steven described mainly the representational duties of his job, his own domestic affairs, the social life of Athens and his regional visits. There is not much about the day-to-day administrative tasks of a British Council director, but there are many insights into the work and the political and cultural setting. He mentions his own lectures and those of visitors and colleagues. His interest in the Greek royal family emerges clearly.

In a note which accompanies Steven's letters, his niece Ann Shukman describes the period as 'a time of political instability in Greece: governments came and went, the King returned only to die soon after, and the Civil War broke out in the north. Hardships – electricity cuts and difficulties of transport – were a feature of the time, but so was the vibrant social life of the capital.' That sums it up well. The flavour of the period comes through in memoirs and letters by a number of the British writers who played a part, including Rex Warner.[33]

Steven described in January 1946 the waves of strikes affecting the telephone, trams, taxis, electricity and water ('the water company employees tried to turn off the water supply but they made a mistake and turned the tap the wrong way, so that Athens, which is strictly rationed for water, enjoyed a welcome flood'). He found these strikes more irritating than serious. 'EAM, the communist party of Greece, is thus hoping to obtain power.'[34] Inflation was a threat and he liked to record prices. It took him a long time to find an apartment suitable for entertaining, which he rightly saw as an important part of the job.[35]

By virtue of his position and personality, Steven had access at the highest level. On the British side, General Scobie, 'the most popular man now in

Greece (though more typically the nice simple British soldier than you could believe possible)', came to a reception he gave in October 1945.[36] In January he had a long talk with the Ambassador, Rex Leeper, while returning from a reception in the car. He found him 'cordial, but depressed and . . . almost pathetic – not a strong man, physically or otherwise'. Leeper, who was not as weak as this suggests, was soon succeeded by Sir Clifford Norton with his flamboyant wife 'Peter'.[37]

In April 1946 Steven lunched with Constantine Tsaldaris, the Prime Minister designate and leader of the People's Party, and found him 'very genial and well intentioned and I fear quite remarkably stupid. . . . The power in the house is Mme Tsaldaris who is just the type of woman whom I adore. . .'[38]

The highest level of all was the Greek royal family. Steven was fascinated by royalty, in Britain as much as in Greece. He came to know Princess Andrew, Princess Catherine, Aunt Helen (wife of the late Prince Nicholas), King George II and Crown Prince, later King, Paul and his wife Frederika. When the old king died on 1 April 1947, the day after visiting the British Embassy for a showing of the film *Henry V*, Steven wrote, 'I am very sorry that he is dead. He was doing his job extremely well, in a quiet unglamorous and even uninspiring way . . . I am a little nervous about his successor, who is anxious to be a 'progressive' King while the new Queen is rather too clever to be a good queen. . .'[39] The funeral, at which the six-year-old Constantine accompanied his father Paul, the new king, in the cortège, brought Mrs Britten-Jones, the dead king's English lady friend, out from London. She attended discreetly. Steven thought that they had at some point quietly got married.[40]

A month later he conceived the idea of writing a life of King George II and talked about it to Colonel Levidis, the late king's friend and Master of Ceremonies. Levidis was enthusiastic and reported that King Paul was equally keen. Steven had in mind 'something short and human'. The book would not be 'official', and he would have to have freedom to write what he wished. But he would try to avoid controversial political issues. There would be tricky questions such as how to deal with the king's relationship with Mrs Britten-Jones.[41] The project never materialized, which is a pity but not at all surprising. Given the royal family's attitude to Mrs Britten-Jones, it would have been impossible to produce an acceptable and also truthful record.[42]

Almost on the eve of his departure from Athens, Steven was invited to a lunch with the new king and queen – just the three of them, in a family atmosphere. He found the king 'a little guileless though very good hearted', and the queen 'dangerously clever for a Queen, a little hard, . . . not much humour – he has more – but bright and quick. They obviously love being King and Queen – fortunately – though they rightly hate their politicians.'[43]

Steven's interest in Greek royalty had a professional justification in the importance of the king's political role (though the British Council was specifically excluded from political activity).[44] But his main motive was fascination with royalty as such. Snobbery played a part. He was alert to social

STEVEN RUNCIMAN AT THE BRITISH COUNCIL

distinctions, as suggested by his remark about Alethea Hayter, who visited Athens in March 1947: 'still, she is a *lady*, which is rare, and anxious to be helpful'.[45]

Steven revelled in his invitations to the palace. They allowed him also to exercise his talent for fortune-telling on King George, who proved to be interested not in revelations about affairs of state but only in his own private affairs.[46]

Steven got to know all the personalities in the world of Athenian culture. He continued to see some of them after leaving Athens, for example George Seferis, whom he described as 'the nicest Greek I know' and with whom he established a warm and lasting relationship.[47] The literary party he gave in April 1946 was 'very chic – only the accepted great masters were invited and all except the doyen of Greek poets (M. Sikelianos) accepted – and he invited me instead to visit him on Monday at his retreat on Salamis. M. Kazantzakis, the epic poet who has written the longest poem in all the world's literature, even put off his departure to his country seat to attend'.[48] His engagements notebook records the names, besides Kazantzakis, of Seferiades (i.e. Seferis), George Katsimbalis, C.Th. Dimaras, Panayiotis Kanellopoulos, George Theotokas and Konstantinos Tsatsos as being present, with spouses. The occasion of the party was a visit by Raymond Mortimer, literary editor of the *New Statesman*. The only other British guests were Rex Warner, director of 'my Institute', whom Steven liked, and his wife Frances.[49] This party was a tribute to the strength of the links between the literary world and the British Council, and to Steven's drawing power as host.

Warner's role was equally, or more important, in forging close links with the Greek literary world. In fact Runciman and Warner were complementary. Warner combined scholarship in Ancient Greek, later put to good use in his translation of Thucydides, with distinction as a writer of poetry and avant-garde novels. His circle included Seferis, Katsimbalis, Theotokas, Professor Angelos Katakouzinos and the artists Fotis Kontoglou and Nikos Hadjikyriakos-Ghika. Katsimbalis and Seferis, and for a time Ghika, were particularly close to him. He played the key role in presenting the Institute's cultural programme, built around lectures by Council staff including Runciman and Warner himself; Greek writers including Seferis and Katsimbalis; and visitors from England including Maurice Bowra, John Lehmann and the actor Robert Speaight. Warner's secret was his affability, which enabled him to get on with virtually everyone. His deputy and fellow carouser in the Grande Bretagne bars, Apotsos and the Plaka tavernas was Major Patrick Leigh Fermor.

John Lehmann in particular was bowled over by Greece and by Warner's performance. His description of his lecture tour, which he called 'one of the most passionately interesting episodes in my whole life', contains a warm tribute to Cardiff; Ronald Crichton, 'expert in many facets of Greek art and the traditional dancing of the Greek sailors'; Brian de Jongh, 'student and lover of Pausanias'; and above all to Rex: 'Undoubtedly my visit was made by Rex,

MICHAEL LLEWELLYN-SMITH

and the band of young ex-soldiers, lecturers and enthusiasts all for Greece.' According to Lehmann,

> they were supported, on a higher level, not only by the wordly-wise [sic], amusing, scholarly personality of Steven who was *persona grata* with the Greek Royal family, but also by the charming ambassador, Sir Clifford Norton, and his wife 'Peter', who had a passionate interest in modern Greek art and also in the art of young Englishmen, in particular John Craxton. Gigantic, brilliantly coloured pictures of young Greek shepherds, in curious perspective with their sheep and the Greek landscape, decorated the august walls of the reception rooms in the British Embassy, where elegant eighteenth century portraits had hung before. Britain was fortunate in having these men and women to represent her at that particular time: if their appointment was not the result of extremely skilful choice by some anonymous genius in the Foreign Office, it was certainly an exceedingly lucky chance.

Lehmann added that Rex's good humour never failed:

> The atmosphere in his office when visitors called – and they called very often – was indeed more like that of a taverna than a centre of administrative organization. This the Greeks immensely appreciated. . . . He imposed authority as much by his sturdy physical build as by his obviously deep classical learning, his devotion to Greek civilization, and his reputation as an outstanding imaginative author.[50]

As friend and publisher of the young poet Demetrios Capetanakis (who went to London in 1939 on a British Council scholarship and died there in 1942) and later of Seferis, Lehmann was a working part of the Anglo-Greek literary engine of these years.

Steven regularly complained in his letters about the constant social round, which he actually enjoyed although it was tiring and bad for his health. He suffered from irregular bouts of stomach complaints, as well as other ailments including at one point a nasty case of herpes on his back. Like some others whose health in their youth was delicate, he lived to a great age.

But there was more than one sort of social life. That of Steven moved in parallel with the social life of a diplomat, centring on professional and governmental contacts in relatively formal surroundings. The other sort was the looser life of the literary and cultural world, the lunches at Apotsos and taverna evenings in the Plaka of Warner, Katsimbalis and their friends, who included, sporadically, Seferis, Elytis, Ghika, Lawrence Durrell, Leigh Fermor and Xan Fielding.[51] Though Steven occasionally took part, this was not his natural scene. There was a strait-laced aspect to his character, perhaps inherited from his Nonconformist parents.

Any British Council director has to establish a relationship with the British ambassador and the embassy. Steven's early references to the Nortons are disobliging. He saw 'Peter' Norton as a vulgar exhibitionist who lowered the tone of the embassy, and he thought that the ambassador was in thrall to his wife.[52] He had no time for Lady Norton's cavorting on the dance floor with John Craxton (nor did the ambassador). Only towards the end of his stay did he allow that Lady Norton was not so bad after all. This was as a result of sitting next to her at a lunch and getting from her the full story of Mrs Britten-Jones, which delighted him.[53] He criticized the embassy for their failure to attend some social functions. And he saw British policy towards Greek governments as a hopeless attempt to find and support a centre that did not exist. It should be remembered that Britain was still – just – top country in Greece. Truman's famous declaration about Greece and Turkey came late in Steven's time, and he noted the immediate effect on Greek officials, who began to pay less attention to the British.[54]

Steven's initial judgements of people and their offerings tended to be acerbic or dismissive, but he was prepared to change his mind. A lecture by Harold Nicolson on Byron was 'not very good'. The critic Raymond Mortimer was 'a rather foolish man'. John Lehmann was a 'pompous, didactic, self-opinionated bore', but a good editor. Arthur Sewell's inaugural lecture as the Byron Professor of English at Athens University was 'pretentious, second rate but reputable'.[55] On the plus side, Dilys Powell was 'a great success here and very pleasant'.[56] These letters were not written for publication and Steven was more positive in public and official documents. His confidential report to the British Council on the period January to May 1947 is complimentary about the embassy, the Nortons and the visits of the chairman of the British Council, Miss Hayter and others.[57]

His sharpest comments spring from a professional disappointment. In 1946 Steven put himself forward as a candidate for the Bywater and Sotheby Professorship of Byzantine and Modern Greek Language and Literature at Oxford University, to be vacated on the retirement of John Mavrogordarto. Though clearly a strong candidate, he failed to secure the chair and wrote to his mother, 'I can't say I mind at all, except for a feeling of indignation that it has been given to a Greek, a philologist, an oily unpleasant man with not a very good record in the war (he managed to grow sleek and fat and prosperous when most Greeks were starving) and a scholar who is considered bogus even by Athenian standards.'[58] These remarks are unfair to the winning candidate, C.A. Trypanis, who was a respectable scholar, a poet, an effective minister of culture in Constantine Karamanlis' government following the fall of the junta and a decent man. Steven's attribution of a poor war record to Trypanis must have come from the Athens rumour machine.[59]

The Athens operation was seen by the British Council in London as an important weapon in the British politico-cultural armoury. This reflected the

Foreign Office view of the political importance of Greece, from which the Council inferred that the promotion of culture and the English language was correspondingly valuable.[60] It is ironic that this view seemed not to be shared by the British Embassy. The ambassador, Clifford Norton, commented that British Council work, in these 'very hard times', is 'a bit of a luxury out here'.[61] Such a view, undermining the whole *raison d'être* of the British Council, was much resented both in Athens, by Runciman's successor W.G. Tatham, and in London. Kenneth Johnstone rebutted it firmly.[62]

In 1946 Sir Malcolm Robertson retired as Chairman of the British Council after a less than brilliant period of office. The new Chairman was Sir Ronald Adam, formerly Adjutant General to the armed forces.[63] He visited Athens in February 1947. Steven did not warm to him. He seemed slippery, opportunist and a bad listener.[64] Again Steven's view improved on further acquaintance. 'Yes, I think I can say I liked him, but . . . I didn't (arrogantly) respect the integrity of his character.'[65]

On his return to London, in a note on his visit, Sir Ronald described Rex Warner as 'first-class and must not be lost'.[66] This confirmed Steven Runciman's own assessment. It was his task, as line manager, to report on Warner. In his last annual report, before Warner left in May 1947, he judged him as A for Personality, Initiative, Tact and Zeal and Extra mural activities and relations; B for Accuracy; and C for Judgment, Power of taking responsibility, Power of supervising staff and Linguistic ability in relation to country. His general assessment was that 'Mr Warner is proving an immense success at his job. He is an extremely popular figure in Athens, where his obvious distinction and his personal friendliness impress all types and classes. His personality has done a great deal to build up the Institute to be a feature in Athens life. He is not himself an administrator, but he has good [rapport] and is in every way most co-operative. . .'[67] This judgement does credit to both Warner and Runciman.

Runciman's view of Maurice Cardiff was also positive. Cardiff's view of Runciman was wary. He wrote, 'Personally I was terrified of Steven. Friendly and charming though he was at our first meeting, I was prompted to attach a mental label to him; "handle with care".'[68]

It was Warner on the British side, and Katsimbalis and Seferis on the Greek side, who were at the centre of the network of literary and artistic relationships that are the subject of this book. The *Anglo-Greek Review*, established in Johnstone's time, was a key ingredient of this network. Most of the writers mentioned in this chapter, Greek and British, contributed to it. Katsimbalis played the dominant role for a time as editor. The centrality of Seferis and Warner can be seen also in the early history of translations and publication of Seferis' poetry in English. Runciman's role was to give Warner his head, to encourage contacts and to ensure that the Council continued to fund the *Review*.[69]

One might have thought that Paddy Leigh Fermor, in his position as deputy to Warner at the British Institute, might have played a Warner-like role also in fostering literary friendships and collaboration. Such was not the case, although he became friendly with most of the Greek and English writers mentioned. He gave a number of lectures, mainly about the war and SOE.[70] But he failed to find a role at the Council, and both Runciman and Warner thought he was wasting his and the Council's time. This was obvious even to outsiders. Maurice Bowra, reporting on a lecture tour to Greece made under the Council's auspices, praised the work done by Cardiff and some other members of staff, and added, 'A misfit is Mr P. Lee-Fermore [sic] who has many excellent gifts but is unfit for office work. With his experience in Crete he has many unusual Greek acquaintances, which is a great asset, and might be better employed on a roving commission of making contacts, for which he is admirably fitted.'[71] In the end, to Paddy's annoyance, Steven Runciman gave him the push.[72]

By 1947 one senses in Steven's letters that he is getting tired of his work in Athens, though not of Greece or the Greeks. One factor in this was the nature of the work, primarily administrative, to a large extent bureaucratic. He hated bureaucracy. And although a man of wide general culture, well placed to encourage the Council's work in the cultural field, he was not himself a poet, novelist or artist, nor did he enjoy roistering evenings in tavernas with Greek poets. 'That evening there was another big intellectual party in a bohemian tavern, which dragged on for ever,' he remarked in November 1946, 'We were still sipping coffee at 1.30 a.m.'[73]

His growing impatience to get away from Athens showed itself in disparagement of the British Council itself. This started as soon as Easter 1946, in an attack on the Council's incompetence and bad treatment of junior staff.[74] It continued with grumbles about the increasing bureaucracy of modern life, including at the British Council, which he called 'this unhappy organisation'. 'We really have fought this war to make the world safe for bureaucracy.'[75] He wrote to Leslie that he was 'more and more horrified by the British Council (which is coming all out for the Common Man)'.[76] The immediate cause of this outburst was a visit by a Council officer whom he found insular, left-wing, offensive and altogether unsuitable for his post. This was Dr Morgan, the director of education. Warner was even more scathing.[77]

Steven worked hard at the office and enjoyed himself despite health problems and exhaustion. Travel to the regions was, at this unsettled time, absorbingly interesting, and important in showing support for the regional officers. It led Steven to make recommendations for the reorganization of work in the provinces, which were overturned when the civil war made the necessary travel impossible.[78]

The main 'official' picture of his and the Council's work is in his confidential report for the period January to May 1947.[79] This comprehensive document covered the functional activities of the Council in Athens, fine arts, books and periodicals, music and films, scholarships, visitors both ways (Angelos Terzakis, 'probably the leading Greek novelist', was visiting England at the time) and the regions.

'The British Council has now had two years of activity in Greece since the liberation of the country,' Steven wrote, 'and I think that we can say that it has achieved a certain standing and reputation. . . . This reputation largely rests on the personal contacts made by officials of the Council and is therefore not entirely secure, though unless such contacts are maintained we might as well close down in this country. . .' To put the work of the Council on a secure basis he recommended the negotiation of a British-Greek Cultural Convention.[80] It was impossible to assess the Council's effect on the Greek public, but 'the presence of a certain number of British men and women with a large circle of friends and known sympathies and interest in Greece does an immense if intangible amount of good'.[81]

Apart from this assessment on the Council's general impact, Steven's most significant comments relate to the British Institute and the *Anglo-Greek Review*.

On the former, he wrote, 'Our main centre of activity in Athens is the British Institute, which under Mr Warner's directorship has come to play a noticeable part in Athenian intellectual life. Its work falls under two headings, first, the regular courses for advanced students of English with an examination in view, and secondly, public lectures and exhibitions and the provision of a library. The regular courses are attended by a steady collection of pupils drawn from many types of home and supply an urgent need. Akin to them are the lectures of the Functional Officer, Mr Crichton, on English music, which . . . secure a regular audience and are the more important in that no other foreign Institute provides anything parallel. But I should place more emphasis on the public lectures and exhibitions. . . . The bulk of the lectures are in English and therefore limited to the English-speaking world of Athens; but even so a well-known lecturer such as Mr Warner himself fills our lecture-hall to capacity, while a Greek lecturer or a concert means that we are overcrowded . . . in addition to English lectures, there was one Greek lecturer, Mr Prevelakis, the art-critic, a former British Council visitor to Britain, who lectured on Modern British sculpture;[82] two concerts, given by Greek performers with programmes in which British music played the important part; one film-show of British Council films; and one show of Karaghieuzi, the Greek shadow-marionette form of Punch and Judy. In addition the Institute rooms were used for a Book Exhibition, . . . an exhibition of the recent works of the living Greek artist, Hadjikiriakos Ghika, and of the works of the Greek popular artist, Theophilus. It might be argued that the Karaghieuzi show and the exhibitions of Greek art are not within the scope of the Council; but I most firmly support Mr Warner's policy in introducing them, partly because it is very necessary for our work to show a practical interest in Greek art and life, and partly because every such activity makes the Institute known in circles that would otherwise never trouble to go there. This has been particularly true of the Theophilus exhibition. Theophilus was a definitely 'popular' painter, untrained, – a Greek Douanier Rousseau, – but a born artist, who died some 15 years ago. Connoisseurs have collected his work. But this is the first exhibition of them and as such has aroused enormous interest.' One side effect of the exhibition was to bring readers of the communist newspaper *Rizospastis* into the British Institute for the first time, with the grudging approval of the KKE. A practical result was an increase in the number of visitors and subscribers to the Institute's Library.

On the *Anglo-Greek Review*, Steven wrote, 'It continues to be the leading intellectual periodical in Greek and to reach Left-wing circles that are otherwise untouched by British propaganda. Indeed, though it is completely non-political, we have been occasionally accused by the extreme Right of sponsoring a crypto-Communist publication. Owing to the axing of the Press Department's provincial organization, we anticipate a temporary falling off in circulation for the next one or two numbers, but I do not think that the use or value of the *Review* will be seriously impaired.' Steven's commendation of the *Review* was shared by his successors, as was the difficulty of sustaining the Council's subsidy.

Steven wrote that the Council had been fortunate in the attitude shown by the British Embassy:

> Its policy has been to take an interest in our work but never to interfere unless we ask for advice or assistance; which has always been readily given. In return, I think that we have through our contacts sometimes been of use in supplying information to the Embassy. The Ambassador himself and Lady Norton whenever they can patronize our lectures and exhibitions and other functions. The Press Department, both at Athens and in the provinces has been especially co-operative. . .

'It has been our policy to attempt no sort of rivalry with other foreign cultural organizations,' he wrote. The French, who used to dominate Greek cultural life, had lost ground for political reasons. The Americans relied on their material assets and their schools. The Russians were active but their efforts only reached their political sympathizers. The danger for the British was loss of prestige owing to the greater expenditure of others (a familiar story).

Steven recorded that 'we are on cordial terms with all the leading political figures in Greece with the exception of the extreme Left', with which no contact was then possible. The Minister of Education was amiable but unintelligent and had politicized education. The Council's long-term hope of providing teachers of English to schools all over Greece must be put on ice in view of other priorities (rehabilitation) at the Ministry. Relations with the Ministry of Health were bad, owing to the minister himself, an unpleasant individual. (There was a major long-running row over the provision of a hospital in Salonica.) Relations with the universities of Athens and Salonica were good. The Byron Professor's lectures were well received, but the audience small. Professor Sewell had persuaded the university to institute a diploma in English, the first such. Classes in English were also provided to the Polytechnic (National Technical University).

A few days later, Steven left for a short break on Andros, and on 17 June he began the long journey home, via Rome, Venice, Asolo (staying with Freya Stark), Milan and Paris.

On their side, the British Council respected Runciman's management of the Athens operation. There is a cryptic observation in Frances Donaldson's book, that 'the record suggests that Messrs Runciman, Warner and Leigh Fermor may not have been by nature suited to the administration of the Council finances'.[83] In Runciman's case this seems to me most unlikely; he had an orderly and practical mind.[84]

Steven's time in Athens was a transitory episode in his life and career. It confirmed his love of Greece, its landscape and people and history. It confirmed his dislike of bureaucratic organizations and his resolve to continue his path as a gentleman scholar. It confirmed also that when he set his hand to it he could be an effective manager. Unlike Rex Warner, he had good bureaucratic skills, as well as literary talent, self-confidence, scholarly expertise and a wide general culture.

The flourishing of literary and artistic collaboration between Greek and British writers at this period was a product of the presence in Athens of a number of extraordinary Greek writers and artists, and of talented British intellectuals who were keen to work in Athens, both for love of Greece and out of need for a congenial job in the unsettled post-war period. It has already been explored fruitfully from the point of view of individual writers and artists, by Roderick Beaton, Edmund Keeley and others.[85] The institutional framework revealed in the British Council files and the Runciman letters underpinned the informal networks. It was not accidental that writers and artists clustered round the British Council in Athens. Careful thought went into the selection of Steven as Representative, and of Rex Warner as Director of the Institute (though Warner says he was surprised by the proposal and thought at first he should turn it down.) At least one officer at a senior level in London, Kenneth Johnstone, saw 'intellectual liaison' as important and was in a position to do something about it. But it was hardly part of a grand plan on the part of the Council that they should strike sparks off their Greek colleagues, and generate such fruitful collaboration. For Warner and others, this was a more entertaining and inspiring use of their time than more routine but necessary and important Council activities. For the Greeks, it was a lucky chance that in this difficult period, when they yearned for contact with the literary world of the west, such men were brought to them by the Council, which also had the resources, in books, periodicals, library, lectures, exhibitions and funds for visits to Britain. Katsimbalis, Warner and Seferis were the men primarily responsible, and Steven Runciman and Kenneth Johnstone the talented and necessary facilitators. Once Runciman and Warner left, much of the impetus was soon lost, as Warner himself had predicted. With the arrival of W.G. Tatham as Representative a chillier note enters the minuting.[86]

STEVEN RUNCIMAN AT THE BRITISH COUNCIL

Perhaps it was too good to last. The British Council is a very different organization today from the British Council of the 1940s – not so much in its mission and ethos as in the ability of a young organization still in the process of formation to absorb the unusual personality and allow room for the creative in its own ranks. The combination of circumstances that brought this company of talent to Athens and threw them into creative contact with Greek writers and artists will not recur. The old order changeth, yielding place to new; happily the old speaks to us through not only the archives but also the few survivors from those times.

Annex

Extracts from Steven Runciman's letters from Athens

Letters are to Viscountess Runciman (HR) except where the recipient is specified as WLR, i.e. Leslie Runciman, Steven's elder brother.

Work and the British Council

Steven makes frequent references to British Council administration and events such as lectures and exhibitions. He also comments freely, particularly to his brother Leslie, on his view of the Council as an institution. His first work-related entry, in Letter 2 of 16 October, records that 'the whole organisation has been chaotic. My excellent Assistant Representative [Maurice Cardiff] came in after the chaos had started and had neither the time, the experience nor the authority to clear much up; and I am unearthing all sorts of mess' (Letter 2, 16 October 1945).

His contract with the Council was due to end on 31 August 1946. They asked if he would be prepared if necessary to stay on for some months. He wrote to his mother in April, 'I am torn between family affections and a desire to get on with my own work on the one hand, and on the other a conscience about the present job and a liking for Greece, which is a much nicer country than modern England and where I not only feel physically well . . . but also believe (conceitedly) I am more of a success and more useful than many of my compatriots.' He described the British Council as 'so incompetent that I couldn't stay with it for long' (Letter 20, 12 April 1946). He filled this out in a letter to WLR on Easter Sunday 1946, after a visit to England in which much time was taken up with 'trying to cope with the British Council in London . . . they try to cheat and exploit the humbler members of my staff – more, I think, from incompetence than from malice, – but the incompetence is getting worse, as the great British bureaucracy puts its *main morte* firmly down on it all with a Treasury control on details of expenditure that bears no relation to practical

84 MICHAEL LLEWELLYN-SMITH

needs and hasn't even the excuse of being economical. So, though I very much enjoy being here and quite enjoy most of the local work and feel that if you are going to live abroad nowadays you must have a semi-official position, I shan't be sorry to be set free. . . . England seems to me such hell now, that I really can't contemplate living in London. . . . It is shocking to have become so *dépaysé* and it is doubtless very demoralizing to live in a country where it is much too easy to be Somebody – but it is very agreeable. Indeed I find life in Athens very delicious. The climate is the best in the world, and the country the loveliest. The people, for all their obvious faults, are very *sympathique*. I have a most desirable and comfortable flat, with a view that is unsurpassed – the Acropolis, the sea, the islands and the Peloponnese. So what more could one want?'

By early July, he was troubled by staff problems: 'quite unnecessary if my London office allowed me to handle things here, but they will attempt (with this present mania for bureaucratic centralization) to organize it from London and send out people who cannot fit into the jobs . . . how I hate bureaucracy' (Letter 35, 6 July). A fortnight later he wrote to Leslie that he had decided to stay on and spend the winter in Athens: 'Quite apart from my desire to winter out of England, I have a conscience about getting the work here finally on to a better basis . . . I am getting a little weary of administrative work, but that is largely due to being short-handed in this heat. I even find I have at times a certain most unwarrantable nostalgia for Britain, and a more justifiable one for a quiet literary life' (Letter 34, 21 July 1946).

Steven's discontent with the Council reached a peak with a visit to Athens by the Council's Director of Education, Dr Morgan. Morgan came at the same time as the Council's Auditor-General Sir Cameron Badenoch, a 'grim humourless son of the manse of quite incredible meanness, but I think very competent' (Letter 44 of 28 November 1946). Steven described Morgan at first as 'a provincial University type, amiable, pompous, boring, personally easy but disastrous for work, as he cannot see that foreign countries can possibly be different from England. His rigid obstinacy is most remarkable. His social ideas are of the half-baked leftishness, so fashionable in England and so utterly inapplicable elsewhere'. A few days later he called Morgan 'about the most unsuitable man for such a post that you could imagine. He knows nothing of foreign countries and refuses to learn – he cannot see why they should [not] be just like the rather sloppy left-wing Britain that he represents. He never listens to anything that he doesn't wish to hear. He is offensive (though I'm sure he means to be genial) out of sheer arrogance; he is tactless to a wonderful degree; he is obstinate, and he is patronizing. Many of his ideas are not unsound, but he leaves us all so angry that it is difficult to do them justice; and most of his ideas seem to me to be nonsense. He has infuriated every member of my staff and is resented by the Greeks that he meets. He also has a way of mixing himself up with all the most undesirable Greeks, without referring to me, and making plans of an appallingly unsuitable nature, behind my back. I have so far curbed my temper. . . . But it all seriously makes me wonder if I can last out even another 6 months with the Council.'

It was no doubt this visit that led Steven to his severest strictures on the British Council: 'I have too much dreary office-work and am more and more horrified by the British Council (which is coming all out for the Common Man). I shall leave its service without the slightest regret, though I shall be sorry to leave Greece. The end of May seems the best time to do so. . . . I think I can hide from the Greeks till then how awful this organization really is' (Letter 47, 15 December 1946).

Steven's next senior visitor, in late January 1947, was the new Chairman of the British Council, Sir Ronald Adam, a former Adjutant-General of the armed forces. Steven did not take to him. He wrote to his mother, Letter 54 of 31 January, 'He is not difficult to deal with, as he is anxious to please, but I do not like him. He seems to me rather slippery, he has one eye the whole time on the Labour Government, with which he is doing very well. He doesn't want to learn, but to show off ("Mr Bevin himself said to me the other day . . ."). . . . In some ways it is rather nice to see someone who so loves his position; and he is certainly clever. But, I think, no good and not honest. . . . He turns on charm much too artificially and I find that he is not cutting much ice with the Greeks. . .'

Steven changed his mind on much of this. He wrote on 6 February, 'My chairman left today. . . . I really quite enjoyed his visit and grew almost to like him. He was so determined to make himself pleasant, and I think genuinely thought that we were doing well here, which is always gratifying. But he is a little too anxious to agree, and you inevitably suspect that he will show the same *complaisance* with the next man who may say the opposite thing to yours. He is moreover a bit gullible – not, I think, a good judge of people. . . . But he *is* clever and quick – a little eager to sidestep if he sees an awkward point coming; but I don't altogether mind that – it meant that he understood a hint. Without saying a single unpleasant word I think I was able to make him appreciate how disastrous I thought his Educational Director who visited us in December. I should naturally have preferred to talk frankly, but perhaps, for a man running an organisation full of people who hate each other, his technique is wise.' Sir Ronald turned out to be good with the Greeks after all. He spoke well to a brief. He paid lip service to the Leftish ideas that were modish in Britain. He loved the High Society parties he was taken to. Steven concluded, 'Yes, I think I can say I liked him, but while I respected the quickness of his brain, I didn't (arrogantly) respect the integrity of his character' (Letter 55, 6 February).

Steven's considered views on the British Council in Greece, and on some of the persons mentioned here, are in his confidential report to the Council on the period January to May 1947, which he wrote as a valedictory. Not surprisingly, it lacks the personal touch and the bite of his letters.

Political and economic situation

Steven recorded the main political developments such as elections, strikes, the union of the Dodecanese with Greece and the Truman declaration, and commented on personalities such as Tsaldaris, the Prime Minister and the young Markezinis. He comments frequently on price inflation, noting in one of his earliest letters (Letter 6, 19 November 1945):

> Here we are in full crisis. The Greeks won't cooperate about any government. They lament the rise in prices and help it on by their hoarding and blackmarketing. All prices now are calculated on the gold pounds, of which there are vast hoards in the country. The drachma is officially fixed at 2000 to the £ sterling, but the gold pound, which was at 32,000 drachmas when I arrived 6 weeks ago is now at 78,000 and still rising. Everything is priced accordingly and only to be bought on the black market; and I really can't understand how any of the poorer people live.

He notes that British officials, who are not allowed to use the Black Market, pay four times as much for everything as they should. The situation greatly complicated his administration of the British Council finances and staff salaries.

Strikes were an intermittent nuisance. 'Life is a little difficult here at the moment, owing to strikes – E.A.M., the Communist party of Greece, is thus hoping to obtain power. Yesterday we had no telephone, for two days no trams, last week no taxis (but they reappeared this week), today no electric light, and the water company employees tried to turn off the water supply but they made a mistake and turned the tap the wrong way, so that Athens, which is strictly rationed for water, enjoyed a welcome flood. There is a fortunate lack of coordination in the strikes which has made them so far more irritating than serious; but God knows when they will stop' (Letter 10, 8 January 1946).

He criticizes British policy, in forcing on the Greeks a centrist government which no one wanted: 'The political situation gets worse and worse. I think our embassy has gone mad. They are determined to keep in office a left-centre government which represents nobody and is a laughing-stock. The Prime Minister, poor man, is 84, the Secretary to the Navy a mere 87. Most of the other ministers are irresponsible left-wing journalists, while the Foreign Minister's one passion is M. Molotov, to the fury of the Greeks who know that Molotov held up the cession of the Dodecanese to them. Meanwhile the Monarchist right and the republican right-centre have united, largely from fear of the foreign Secretary's policy. For years the British have rightly said that the tragedy of Greece was the presence of too many parties, and now that two great parties have united, the British Embassy is *furious*. The present Prime Minister seems to have accepted office on condition that Britain gives Greece a loan. But I doubt if the loan will be given. He too will be let down, a loan might save the economic situation, which depends on the political and is appalling. Prices mount and mount, being all calculated in gold sovereigns. For those of us who law-abidingly have to use the drachma, the official currency, it is most inconvenient. For example, if I negotiate for a flat, the price is quoted in gold pounds, and as the drachma falls continually in relation to gold, I find the price vastly increasing while the negotiations are in progress. As a result I cannot afford and cannot ask H.M. Government to afford a flat for me. Strikes add to the variety of life. At the moment the whole hotel staff is out, which doesn't add to the general comfort' (Letter 11, 14 January 1946).

In mid-March Steven notes that 'we are said to be on the verge of an economic crisis, and there will be civil war in early April'. At the end of the month, on election day, after a lack-lustre campaign he expects a right-wing Populist party victory and predicts that the next problem will be the king: 'a good majority of the Greeks want him back; but unfortunately he isn't very good as a King' (Letter 18, 31 March 1946). Later he reported, 'To the fury of the British correspondents who have been sending to London all the propaganda poured into their ears by the Left, the Election Observers' mission has made what seems a very just report of our elections, proving that the abstaining Communists represented at most 20% of the electorate and more probably 9% or 10%. Greece understandably wants the Monarchy, at least at the moment, but I rather wish that the King would abdicate in favour of his stupid but more genial brother Paul' (Letter 20, 12 April 1946).

Soon Steven was on terms with the Prime Minister designate and leader of the People's Party, Constantine Tsaldaris: 'very genial and well intentioned and I fear quite remarkably stupid. None of our diplomats has taken the trouble to get to know him. . . . I am the first British official to be invited to the house and am it seems high in favour. The power in the house is Mme Tsaldaris who is just the type of woman whom I adore. They say she came off the streets, but a long, long time ago. Actually I believe she was the daughter of King George I of Greece's Dutch housekeeper, but she certainly had a full career before she married Agamemnon Schliemann, the son of the archeologist, and then passed on to M. Tsaldaris. She is highly decorated and dyed and wears portentous hats' (Letter 21, 18 April 1946).

As time passed Steven reflected on the Greek monarchy: 'I think the King of Greece will certainly come back in the autumn. But he is an unalluring figure and I doubt if he'll stay long. However the Communists here by their outrages have really killed Republicanism in Greece, at least for the next few years. The present Royalist government, though rather stupid, is not doing so badly. The Prime Minister [Tsaldaris] cannot be described as clever but he is genial and genuinely anxious not to be petty – though some of his underlings are not so sensible, and there have been foolish "purges" not only of the civil service but of such bodies as the Board of Directors of the National Theatre. Everyone not 100% Royalist has been removed. . .' (Letter 40, 4 August 1946).

In early November, 'The political situation here is unsettled, as the opposition Centre is being very coy about coming in to a coalition [which the British had favoured, though not to the point of pressing the opposition]. The Liberal leader Sofoulis (aged 87) whose party comprise at most 15% of the electorate

88   MICHAEL LLEWELLYN-SMITH

will only join if he can be Prime Minister, confident, so he declares, that it is he that Greece really wants whatever recent elections may have said. I think some of the other Opposition leaders will consent. Meanwhile prices are rising fast. I have had to raise my maid's wages more than double. . .' (Letter 40b, 2 November 1946). A week later, 'Our political crisis is over. Every single politician involved behaved frightfully badly – the Prime Minister swaying weakly between a genuine desire to broaden the government, or rather a genuine desire to meet the King's wishes for it, and a fear of the extremists of his party – the opposition leaders thinking of nothing but their own personal advantage in the narrowest and most immediate and short-sighted sense. The result is that we have a reshuffled government that is slightly stupider and less able to deal with the difficult situation than before. Meanwhile things are not going well, prices soaring and brigandage in the north increasing. Arms are smuggled in from over the frontier, and as every Greek would really rather be a brigand than a soldier it is difficult to use the soldiers against the brigands – they are so apt to desert' (Letter 41b, 9 November 1946).

On 28 March 1947 Steven noted, 'Truman's declaration on Greece and Turkey has been widely welcomed here, and rightly. It is perhaps a little galling for us to find all the time-serving Greeks at once neglecting us in favour of the Americans, and minor Government officials (always an unpleasant race) have been rather chillier to us lately – I notice it in my official relations with them. But most Greeks tell us frankly that after a few months of American occupation all Greece will so love the British that Britain could not have made a cleverer move! . . . Still I hope that the Americans won't make too much of a mess, as their presence is really necessary to keep the Russians out' (Letter 56b, 28 March 1947).

In May Steven noted the rising of a new star in the political firmament: 'Only one of them [i.e. recent dinner parties] was really amusing – given by a youngish man called Markezini (with a very nice wife who is more English than Greek) who is considered the cleverest and most promising politician in Greece. He leads a right-centre opposition to the Government, but is in very close touch with the Palace. He is suspected of wishing to be dictator, but he simply hasn't the presence, being small, hideously ugly and I believe a bad speaker' (Letter 61, 1 May 1947).

Steven closed his reflections on politics with a down-beat assessment of the future, noting 'the gradual closing down of the British Economic Mission and the gradual influx of Americans, who will soon make Greece a much less pleasant place. Prices, especially rents, are rising at once' (Letter 64, 18 May 1947).

People and their lectures

Lectures were an important part of the work, by Steven himself, his colleagues and visitors. He reported on them regularly, e.g. on 10 February 1946, Letter

14: 'I gave a lecture on Thursday at the University in its big lecture room which was very full. It was a pretty stiff lecture (on Byzantine Education) as I wanted to appear in the role of a serious savant. It all went down quite well, except that the hall is acoustically difficult. . . . I had two Orthodox bishops, bearded and black-robed, sitting in the front, both apparently understanding English. They crossed themselves whenever I mentioned the Church. But fortunately I did not slip into heresy. . .' (Letter 14, 10 February 1946).

He lectured also, at the British Institute, on British Historians of Medieval and Modern Greece, on Greece and Western Christendom and on Barbarian Invasions of Greece, 'not so much historical as a theory of history, ending up with a plea for better education than modern educationalists provide. It went down quite well – the more intelligent Greeks saw that I was attacking modern Greek education (which is deplorable), the less intelligent thought that I was attacking either the Americans or the Russians, while the American wife of the Swedish Minister thought my peroration (on what education really is) so beautiful and so true that to my embarrassment I had to dictate it to her all over again' (Letter 53 b, 6 March 1947). He gave lectures also to audiences of soldiers and of interpreters, and at Salonica University, to 250–300 people in an unheated amphitheatre, on the evils of materialism. 'The Greeks, being more materialistic than most people, love moral uplift.'

The lecturing workload was shared by Rex Warner, Paddy Leigh Fermor and Ronald Crichton from the Council staff. There was also Arthur Sewell, the Byron Professor. And there were the visiting firemen and women: Dilys Powell, whom Steven liked; Harold Nicolson; John Lehmann; and Maurice Bowra (on whose lectures we do not have Steven's comments since he was away at the time).

Royalty

Steven went about cultivating the Greek 'royals' in a deliberate way, starting with a contact with Princess Alice, whom he calls Princess Andrew, in May 1946. This led to further contacts, with King George's sister Princess Catherine, and then with the king himself and with Crown Prince, later King, Paul and his wife Frederika. He describes these contacts with enjoyment and a certain fascination at the institution of the Crown and the idiosyncrasies of the royals, sometimes stupid, often genial, sometimes insensitive, liking practical jokes and lavatory humour, ambivalent about Greece.

On 18 May 1946, Letter 26, he reported on 'a long interview with Princess Andrew of Greece (she was a Battenburg, a sister of the Crown Princess of Sweden and of Lord Louis) who is going to found a woman's college on Oxford and Cambridge lines here. She is almost stone deaf but gets over the difficulty by talking all the time herself – a wonderful mixture of shrewd sense and the royallest of platitudes. Her son Prince Philip (now in the British Navy)

90   MICHAEL LLEWELLYN-SMITH

is said to be the man that our Princess Elizabeth wants to marry – he is remarkably good looking and charming.'

In August Steven talks of 'going to try to see the King when I pass through London – he has asked me to do so. They say he is very obstinate and it is no use trying to talk freely to him' (Letter 40, 4 August 1946). The meeting probably never happened. The rhythm of his contacts with royalty accelerates from the autumn. On 2 November, Letter 40 b, he reported a small lunch-party at the Embassy to meet the Crown Prince and Princess. 'The Crown Prince is very likeable, much more genial than his brother and, though stupider, perhaps less foolish. He talked very soundly about his plans for Greece and seems far fonder of the country than his brother is. The Princess is a bright little thing. They all say that she is the cleverest of the whole Royal family, though I believe rather tyrannical with her staff. They were very cordial and had, I discovered, taken a lot of trouble to find out exactly who we all were.'

On 14 November he dined at the Palace (Letter 42 of 15 November). 'It was an intimate party, just the king, his youngest sister Princess Catherine, a girl of 33, rather silly and very plain but a nice, good girl; his Aunt Helen (Princess Nicholas, mother of the Duchess of Kent) – née a Russian grand-duchess, rather racy and a good royal manner; M. Pipinelis, the Chef du Cabinet of the King . . . with his tall blonde Swedish wife; and General Clark, head of the British Economic Mission . . . and his wife, a large amiable army lady rather of the battleship build. It was all very genially done, good food, English servants, and the general atmosphere of a comfortable English country house. . . . The King was very pleasant. I thought him less trivial than when I saw him before. . . . It was really a very nice party. . .'

In December Steven reported that he would be giving a small lunch party to meet Princess Catherine, the King's sister, and was 'planning to have a Princess a week to lunch' (Letter 46, 14 December 1946). He was pleased when Princess Andrew was most enthusiastic about his book *Byzantine Civilisation* which she had read during the summer.

The lunch party for Princess Catherine turned out 'a terrific success' (Letter 49 of 26 December 1946). 'The Princess talked and laughed and giggled without stopping, and asked me to invite her again very soon. She told me that she was engaged to a British officer now in Iraq [Major Richard Brandram] but there were difficulties. (I had heard of it and knew that the King, her brother, disapproved. I knew her fiancé when he was a gay, rather disreputable but charming under-graduate at Cambridge many years ago but I think there must be something odd in a young man who gets engaged to a really very plain Princess aged 33, without any money. She hasn't even many jewels; for when her mother Queen Sophie (who had inherited most of her mother the Empress Frederick's wonderful collection) died she was very young and her elder sisters said to her: "You were Mother's favourite, so you must have the dear little string of pearls that she always wore", while they made off with the great ceremonial ropes, and "you must have that sweet little brooch that she

STEVEN RUNCIMAN AT THE BRITISH COUNCIL

was so fond of", while they took the tiaras and parures; and so on.) However she is a very nice girl and quite amusing in a simple way. She says that life in the Palace is terribly complicated because the English butler is called King. My maid, though she has Republican sentiments, was thrilled to entertain Royalty.'

The contacts continued, suggesting that Steven ranked only after the ambassador in the unofficial rankings of Athenian society. He gave lunch for Princess Alice, who had to climb five flights of stairs in the absence of electricity – 'she is slightly crazy – for 10 years (1926–36, I think) she was completely mad and locked up – but extremely kindly and very popular here, she does her good works very nicely.' There was dinner for Princess Catherine, at which Steven told her fortune with the cards. This led on to a summons to dine at the Palace to do the same for the king. After dinner, 'I retired into a separate room with the King and took out my cards. What was interesting was that he didn't want to hear anything about affairs of state – not that I felt I could venture far on that line – but he did want desperately to know about his future private life, a subject on which I felt I had to tread with even more delicate care. It was a fascinating interview. He seemed content with what I told him; and I certainly learnt a lot about him. I hear I am in extremely high favour in Royal circles. Perhaps too high, for the Chairman of the British Council has been informed, I'm told, that we are too right-wing here' (Letter 51, 15 January 1947).

If Steven saw the king's death in the cards, he gave no sign of it. But three months later he wrote to his mother that 'Our great event here is the sudden death of the King, which was so unexpected that many people thought it at first an April Fools' Day joke.' He had looked ghastly for some time but no one knew that his heart was so weak. Steven reflected, 'He was not a popular man, and one did not see much signs of distress, apart from flags at half mast from almost every house. But he was respected, particularly so recently; and many people, even republicans, were saying it was a tragedy. My maid, who was a republican till I took to entertaining princesses, – now she is rather monarchist, – snivelled quite sadly. There were well-behaved crowds outside the Palace, unusually quiet for Greeks . . . yesterday was a holiday for the procession when the body was taken from the palace to the Cathedral. It was a very moving procession, excellently managed; and I was surprised to see how big the crowds were, and how silent when the cortège passed – very moving . . . the coffin on a gun-carriage followed by the new King and his 6-year-old son on foot (a touch that produced many sobs from the onlookers). . . . The Greeks, if they choose, can carry out such a ceremony with magnificent dignity' (Letter 57, 4 April 1947).

'I am very sorry that he is dead,' Steven wrote. 'He was doing his job extremely well, in a quiet unglamorous and even uninspiring way; and he was obviously beginning to feel more self-confident and to make a few more appearances. The night before he died he came to a Gala Performance of the film Henry V, organized by the British Embassy for charity, and was very well received, though I thought he looked awful. I am a little nervous about his successor, who is anxious to be a "progressive" King while the new Queen is rather too clever to be a good queen. My republican friends are against the new man, because, they say, he will want to assert himself too much, whereas George was as good a King as any King could be from their point of view because he kept so quiet and only intervened recently in politics in order to broaden his government towards the left. . . . He was always extremely nice to me; so indeed are the new pair, but I feel their friendship depends too obviously on their sense of who is important. He was more genuine.'

He added, 'When I told Princess Catherine her fortune a month ago, I said that she need not worry so much about financial affairs as some sudden event would result in her receiving a gift or a legacy.'

A few days later Steven described the funeral: 'We are still mourning our King here. The funeral on Sunday was impressive. The first part of the procession was really beautiful, with the dark blue and white of the sailors, the red black white and royal blue of the Evzones, some 100 priests and bishops in brocades of every colour and the bishops and the archbishop in great jewelled mitres, and the gun-carriage and the royal mourners all in uniform. The new King brought his little son with him again and the boy (aged 6) insisted on walking all the way. . . . What was most impressive was the behaviour of the crowd – the biggest crowds that Athens has ever seen, all in perfect silence except for a few sobs. . . . One got the feeling that though the late King did not seem popular in his lifetime, he was fundamentally popular and very much respected. . . . The King's lady friend from London [Mrs Britten-Jones] came out and drove discreetly in the funeral in a closed car as a lady-in-waiting. As, so I believe, she had been legally married to him, that was only right. But no mention was made and no one is supposed to know' (Letter 58, 9 April 1947).

In an intriguing postscript to the king's death, Steven floated with Colonel Levides, the Chamberlain, the idea of his writing a Life of the late king. 'He took up the idea enthusiastically, and rang me up this morning to tell me that the present King was very keen that I should, and so was the late King's political adviser, M. Pipinelis whom I knew well when he was Greek Minister in Bulgaria. So I am more or less committed to it. I have said that it must be clear that it is not official but my views are my own and that I want as far as possible to avoid controversial political issues; and that it must be short and human. It is rather a formidable task, but interesting. It gives me a wonderful excuse for coming out to Greece for a month next spring! There are certain difficult passages to consider – not least the question of Mrs Britten-Jones' (Letter 62, 7 May 1947).

Steven followed this ten days later with a long talk with Levides about the late king. Levides 'talked to me all about the King, very frankly and freely and very intelligently. It was fascinating. They all seem at the Palace very much to like the idea that I should write about him. . .' (Letter 64, 18 May). Later, at an intimate lunch *à trois* with King Paul and Queen Frederika the question of the biography of King George apparently did not arise. It was still in his mind when he left Greece because he recorded on 10 June that he was leaving some money in Greece to enable him to return in the spring to discuss the idea of the biography further. But at some point the idea was abandoned. It probably foundered on the rocks of Mrs Britten-Jones, possibly on the further obstacle of writing an interesting book without addressing the political dimension. But the lunch gave Steven a further chance to assess the couple in a wholly informal atmosphere of free discussion: 'He is genial but I think may make mistakes, as he is a little guileless though very good hearted and anxious to do the right thing. She is extremely clever, dangerously clever for a Queen, a little hard, (but I found her more *sympathique* than I had previously) not much humour – he has more – but bright and quick. They obviously love being King and queen – fortunately – though they rightly hate their politicians' (Letter 66, 31 May).

As a postscript to these dealings with Greek royalty, it is worth recording Steven's reflections on the marriage of Princess Catherine to Major Dick Brandram. He attended a party given by Lady Norton to meet the Princess and her fiancé. 'I was amused to see the young man again, after having met him once or twice in his undergraduate days. He was as I had remembered him, good-natured, gay, good looking in a slightly coarse way, a heavy drinker but not a drunkard, and very, very common. He greeted me as an old friend (glad, I think, to have someone fairly reputable with whom he could claim acquaintance) and whenever he caught my eye at that rather stiff gathering he would give me a broad wink. He told me with childish delight how amusing it was to find himself in parties that consisted only of royals. It was rather endearing but really very shocking. He is marrying the poor girl entirely out of naïf snobbery. I think he'll be quite nice to her, but maybe when they are not asked every weekend to the Duchess of Kent's (who says she does not wish to have that common man in her house) his attentions will diminish. She is clearly desperately in love. The wedding, on Monday, was very quiet. . . . The bride, by a special arrangement, keeps two passports, one Greek in which she is still H.R.H., and one British in which she is just Mrs Brandram' (Letter 60, 23 April 1947).

The ambassador and Lady Norton

Steven took an interest in the personalities and doings of Sir Clifford and Lady ('Peter') Norton, who succeeded Sir Reginald and Lady Leeper in March 1946. His first impressions were unfavourable: 'They say she wears the trousers, literally as well as figuratively. He looks fairly nice, not distinguished and very stupid; she seems a heavy-built blear-eyed old battle-horse with 1920s Chelsea leanings – not quite eccentric enough to go down well with the Greeks, who like the British to be smart or mad' (Letter 17, 24 March 1946).

A week later he lunched with them. 'The impression that he gives is of a hen-pecked, kindly half-wit, but politically he is showing a canny caution which is all to the good. She could I suppose be called a 'good sort' and she certainly wants the Embassy to be a centre of hospitality. But she is impossible, blowsy and opinionated and utterly without dignity or discretion. . . . It is a disastrous pity, as the Ns had a wonderful opportunity of being really popular. I must say I do hanker for reforms in the Diplomatic Service – but not the reforms that I think we are going to have' (Letter 18, 31 March 1946).

'I must say our Embassy is a curious place nowadays. What do you think of an Ambassadress who gives a public display of dancing the jitter-bugs with a disreputable young artist as partner in a night club that isn't even the most chic? He seems quite a nice little man and not altogether foolish politically, but weak – and domestically entirely under her thumb. He looks exactly like a suburban bank manager' (Letter 29, 7 June 1946).

In the autumn Lady Norton, apparently as wild as ever, decided to take the British Institute under her wing, and therefore featured more in Steven's life. In late November he dined *en intimité* at the Embassy after giving a lecture at the British Institute on 'Greece and Western Christendom'. '*Intimité* meant that the ambassadress (who was wearing bare legs, skiing socks and no visible knickers (and you could see a long way up) kicked off her shoes after Dinner. Doubtless they were tight, but I found it unsavoury. However, the dinner was good; and I seem to be in high favour there – rather to my embarrassment as I cannot wholeheartedly return the compliment' (Letter 43, 23 November 1946).

In April the ambassador fell ill. 'It had been thought to be typhoid but turns out merely to be flu. Many British Patriots are a wee bit disappointed' (Letter 59, 17 April). What redeemed Lady Norton in the end was gossip. Steven sat next to her at a small dinner in April. 'She was at her brightest. Though mad and rather bad she is no fool and can be most entertaining. She poured into my willing ears, most indiscreetly, the full account of the visit of the late King's lady friend to Greece for the funeral. The lady had stayed at the Embassy. Contrary to the usual situation in such cases, his family were furious with her for not having been with him all the time and for not having returned here with him. She, poor women, had been kept in England first by her own illness and then by the death of her father. (I had said this when reading his cards but hadn't known that it was true.) There were several painful scenes of hysteria, it seems. He died intestate and she gets nothing. The house that he bought for her in London goes to Catherine. But I believe that the family will be generous. Lady Norton made me promise to see her when I go to London. I shall.

'Our Ambassador is better. For a week no one was allowed to see him, and I had a theory that he was dead and Lady N. was hiding it, so as not to stop being ambassadress. But alas – or, rather, happily – he has been seen again on his way to convalesce by the sea' (Letter 60, 23 April 1947).

By May Steven's belated approval of Peter Norton was confirmed: 'Even our mad Ambassadress is most cordial.' She was to give a large farewell supper party for him, 'so I feel I must retract all the unkind things that I've said about her' (Letters 65 & 66, 25 & 31 May). The party turned out to be a very grand affair, with diplomats, courtiers and high society. 'I do like diplomats and courtiers, they flatter one so well.' Lady Norton, eccentric to the last, missed the party, having hopped onto an aeroplane sent to fetch back the Duchess of Kent who was in Athens on a visit (Letter 67, 10 June 1947).

Writers and artists

'My literary party was very chic – only the accepted great masters were invited, and all except the doyen of Greek poets (M. Sikelianos) accepted – and he invited me instead to visit him on Monday at his retreat on Salamis. M Kazandzakis, the epic poet, who has written the longest poem in all the world's literature, even put off his departure to his country seat to attend. I had eight of them, with wives. The occasion was the visit of a rather foolish man called Raymond Mortimer, Literary Editor of the *New Statesman*, who has come out here (and to Italy) to lecture for us. I was glad to have him because he is less prejudiced than most of his paper and himself has strong anti-Russian views, and he is learning a lot. He's a good lecturer and an easy visitor. . . . The only other British that I had to my party were the Director of my Institute, a British novelist called Rex Warner (who is a good writer and a very pleasant person) and his wife. It all went with a swing, though I had to prepare Lenten fare for the ladies. . . . I heard today that it was considered a very distinguished affair and that my flat was much admired' (Letter 21, 18 April 1946).

'That evening there was another big intellectual party in a bohemian tavern, which dragged on for ever – we were still sipping coffee at 1.30 A.M.' (Letter 40b, 2 November 1946). The party included the Katsimbalis couple, Rex Warner, Basil Wright, Dora Stratou, Lawrence Durrell, May Hodgkinson, Chas Frier, Captain Antoniou and Maurice and Leonora Cardiff.

Travel and the countryside

Steven travelled a lot: on business to Patras, Salonica, Rhodes, Kavala, Ioannina, and for pleasure to Euboea, Olympia and Gastouni, Aegina, Andros, the Peloponnese, and to most corners of Attica.

'I drove down to Patras on Sunday morning, to attend the opening of a British Academy there – a most lovely drive all along the north coast of the Peloponnese, which is fertile with orange and lemon trees, and the vines on the lower hills were all golden, with dark pine-covered crags above. But the road was vile. I was in a military car with the Colonel of the A.G.I.S. (Anglo-Greek Information Service – the military organisation which we are gradually taking over.) It was an exhausting visit. At 4 P.M. the Academy was opened in style by the British Consul, the Prefect (who quoted all of Kipling's *If* in Greek), the Mayor (whose eloquence was interrupted when he lost his notes after arriving at the passage "All the great English authors whose names we know so well . . .") and the Archbishop, who blessed us all very resonantly. Then we hurried off to a Girl Guides' performance at the local theatre – including some very pretty national dances – then a cocktail party at the Greek naval headquarters; then a dinner given in our honour by the local journalists, which lasted till 1.30 A.M. Next day we drove back taking the Archbishop with us. He stood us lunch on the way. I tried to pay for it, but he said he was my spiritual father and it would be unfilial of me to do so' (Letter 4, 31 October 1945).

In late November Steven travelled by ship via Izmir to Istanbul where he spent a week clearing up the remnants of his years at the university there, packing and despatching. He gave away some of his furniture, but sent the better pieces, his linen, china, pots and pans, most of his books and all his icons to Athens to furnish his flat once he had obtained one. The return journey was uncomfortable and not without incident: 'I left Istanbul with indigestion, rheumatism and a bad cold on Monday evening (the 10th) – an enormous party of Turks, Greeks and British coming to see me off with chocolates and even flowers (such a difficult adjunct to one's luggage – I had already 7 pieces, with all my linen and blankets, etc.) I spent the night in a comfortable Turkish Wagon-Lit (only 2 bugs), but at 4.30 a.m. I was woken by the Turkish Customs, and at 6 a.m. I was deposited at Pythion, the Greek frontier station. It was pitch dark, there was 6 inches of melting snow on the ground and rain pouring down in torrents. At Pythion, which is just a small station and three cottages, on a bleak plain beside a flooded river, I stayed till 3 p.m. in a cold stuffy station café, chatting to my fellow passengers – a Greek colonel of gendarmerie, a Greek business man from Istanbul, and an Istanbul-Greek old body called Madame Olga. The frontier police, the customs officials, the railway staff, etc. were all very matey (so unlike Turkey) and we were all a happy party – but scarcely comfortable.

'At 3 we got into a small train, unheated and unlit and only 3rd class compartments, which took us in about 6 hours, the 75 miles to Alexandroupolis. It was like travelling by stage coach. At every station the engine was unharnessed to be groomed and watered. We were packed tight (which perhaps kept us warmer, and I was wedged between two quite clean Greek officers), with chickens tethered under the seats, whose unseen cluckings made me think at first that everyone had indigestion. So we chugged along, on a viaduct through endless floods' (Letter 8, 14 December 1945).

At Alexandroupolis (Dedeagatch) Steven was met by Elliott, the efficient director of the Salonica British Council office, who accompanied him by train, on a 'cold bright day, the great mountains along the Bulgarian frontier glistening with snow and the streams all flooded and the forests still golden-brown', to Salonica, where he looked into the Salonica operation and lectured, despite a sick headache and gastric flu.

Weekend excursions, with Rex Warner, Maurice Cardiff and Greek friends, were a refreshing change from city life: 'I went with a British officer to a village he knew well, having visited it with an archaeologist before the war . . . where therefore we were received with the upmost hospitality. It was a delightful drive, over bumpy roads but through the loveliest scenery and fields of poppies and other flowers as rich as ever you see when you pass Sutton's Seeds gardens near Reading. We visited the town of Chalcis, as I wanted to see the only Gothic cathedral in Greece. . . . I spent the night in a peasant's house. I had the bed, the peasant and his wife had the floor and the baby the cradle, while the old parents had the kitchen next door. It was spotlessly clean. The baby when awake screamed and when asleep snored louder than any adult. The bed was a board overlaid with magnificent woven blankets (family heirlooms). . . . Next day we rowed out to a nearby island overgrown with flowers. . . . I got terribly sunburnt with the first bathe. Also, as the village fed us on nothing but eggs – masses of them – and cuttle-fish dripping in oil, I came back terribly liverish. . .' (Letter 24, 4 May 1946).

'On Friday I motored over to the town of Kavalla – 5 ½ hours of an appalling road through perfectly lovely country – where we have a small establishment. It is a charming town, on the sea – the great tobacco port of Greece – one of the prettiest in the country – and you will be glad to hear, the strictest in its morals being under the moral dictatorship of an energetic and extremely severe Archbishop. For example, any young person under the age of 20, out of his house (or her house) after 9 P.M. is excommunicated along with his parents! Nowhere else in Greece does one see so sober and demure a population. The Archbishop, whom I interviewed, is a magnificent old man' (Letter 31, 16 June 1946).

Steven had the benefit of an official car and driver. This proved a useful asset. 'I am just back from a pleasant week-end – I set off in my car on Saturday afternoon with a friend in the Greek Foreign Office and two Greek army officers, instructors in the Cadet School, to visit the home of one of the latter – very pleasant simple men with beautiful manners and so much more to say for themselves than the equivalent British officer. I have found these Greek officers about the best educated class (as regards general education) here, because their school is the only one that is properly disciplined. They are all extremely monarchist and right-wing, saying, with some truth, that only a rather authoritarian government can get anything done in Greece. We spent Saturday night at Loutraki, near Corinth. . . . Then on Sunday we went over to spend the day at a village on the Peloponnesian coast with the family of one of the officers – a house that had been, for Greece, a large and comfortable house but now, after occupation by Italian, German, Communist Greek, and finally British troops, was in a horrible state and the family were living in what had been the servants' quarters. There were just the old parents there, and they too were looking rather shabby after it all. But the hospitality was prodigious – *far* too much to eat – and all done with such simple friendliness. The fact that I had provided a car to enable the officer to visit his parents (communications being very bad nowadays) made them treat me as a tremendous family benefactor' (Letter 32, 24 June 1946).

'I spent last weekend staying with one of my Greek officer friends and his family. . . . Everything was very simple (they have lost much of their money and the house is badly damaged by a series of requisitioning) but spotlessly clean; and I was given a touchingly cordial welcome. The only contretemps was that my officer friend was not up in time to go to church on Sunday morning (at 7 A.M.!). To make up, we had to go and light the lamps in a family chapel in a village where the mother comes from, some miles away inland, up one of the loveliest valleys that I have seen. The chapel was on a cypress-clad hilltop, with the family farmstead perched half way up. It was a very refreshing weekend – exhausting in a way, as I had to speak Greek all the time, but otherwise reposeful. The sea is a few yards from the house, and was deliciously warm' (Letter 39, 29 July 1946).

'Tuesday was the Greek National Day . . . and in the afternoon we drove out to Megara where there is usually very fine dancing on this feast – all the women of the town in their costumes take part. But we found that the local Governor had banned it as being unsuitable with a civil war raging in the north; so we went on disconsolately to sit by the sea at a little port close by, where we found the local tavern-keeper entertaining his father-in-law who had just arrived with his shipmates from the Dodecanese (they were sponge-fishers). In the hospitable Greek country way we were made to join the party. . . . On our way back we came upon a group of peasants dancing really beautifully at a wayside inn, so were not entirely deprived of our objective' (Letter 56 b, 28 March 1947).

I recall Steven saying in Athens in 1997, at the age of 94, that though this might be his last visit to Greece, he would like once more to see the spring flowers in the Peloponnese. Perhaps he was recalling the week's visit he made in April 1947, of which he left the longest of his descriptions (Letter 59, 17 April 1947). 'We set off on Thursday a week ago – at noon, I with two of my staff, my Music and Arts officer, an extremely intelligent sensible and civilized young man, of gentle birth (called Crichton) and the Deputy Director of my Higher Institute – equally intelligent and cultivated but of less gentle birth and education, which showed in a certain lack of adaptability in little things (he was miserable if he couldn't get his egg at breakfast, for example) – and this in spite of the fact that he knows Greece well and is an excellent Modern Greek speaker. It wasn't enough to be irritating, but it interested me. We took an ex-R.A.F. truck, large, rattling and sturdy, which we have just bought and wanted to try out. It stood up to the quite appalling roads very well indeed, without a single mishap. Our chauffeur was the British Council mechanic, a well-mannered Greek youth who drove carefully enough, not giving us more than half a dozen bad frights. But how we bumped about!

'The first day we went to Argos, and slept, three in a room, in a simple but clean enough hotel. I say slept, but in fact the bus stop was just outside our windows, and all through the night buses arrived on their way to Athens, each one laden with lambs tied on the roof going to be slaughtered for Easter; and each lamb being very uncomfortable and perhaps foreseeing its fate, bleated without ceasing. It was not a tranquil night. Next day, Greek Good Friday, we drove over the hills to Tripolis, the capital of Arcadia. It was misty and growing colder, and the views were hard to see. At Tripolis there is a smart hotel where you can even have a not very hot bath. We were two nights there – the first to see the Good Friday processions. . . . On Saturday it was pouring with rain and distinctly cold. However we decided to drive down to Sparta to see the Byzantine churches and ruins of Mistra which I hadn't visited for 17 years and the others not at all.[87] The Sparta road is occasionally attacked by Communist brigand bands, and our chauffeur was frankly nervous; but with a huge Union Jack pasted on our wind-screen I felt it unlikely that we should be molested. It was a bit wet at Mistra and the mountains looked tremendous in the mist; but it was worthwhile. That night at Tripolis we celebrated Easter, attending the mid-night service; but the ceremonies were spoiled by the bitter cold – the Bishop did not come out onto the square to announce the Resurrection. It was all done inside the Cathedral amongst a crowd huddling together for warmth.

'On Easter Sunday it was gently snowing, but we started out to drive over the Arcadian mountains, despite rumours of a bandit attack on the road the previous evening. We climbed up through great forests of oak and pine and desolate mountain villages where the cold kept people from their usual Easter celebrations of roasting lambs out of doors. We hardly saw a soul. At last, in a sinister clearing in the forest we saw a bus, deserted by the wayside, its wheels punctured and its doors left open and the wooden seats stained with blood. A little later, as we went down to the next village, we met a crowd of men, with rifles, wheeling two tyres up the hill, to recover the bus. They told us that it had been a bandit attack late the previous afternoon, and four passengers had been killed. When we reached the little town of Dimitsana – an extraordinary place perched on a ridge sheer above a torrent 2000 feet below, and full of old churches and a surprising municipal library – where we had hoped for an Easter lunch, we found it all in mourning. Two of the dead had come from there, a woman and a soldier on Easter leave; and they were waiting for the funeral. We passed on and picnicked by the way – on a sensational and terrifying and winding [road] high above the gorge, far too narrow for our truck. Mercifully we met nothing. (We had ample provisions with us all the time.) So we went on, through another superb hill town, Karytaena, with lovely churches and a great Frankish castle, to Andritsaena, a similar hill town where we spent the night, in the most primitive of inns but very clean. There we were out of the brigand country, and though it was icy and wet, the inhabitants were gayer and extremely friendly.

'On Monday the weather changed, and we walked through sunshine with the view clear all round and the mountain tops glistening with snow to the Temple of Bassae, some 10 miles away. The temple itself is well preserved but not an exciting building, but the situation, on a hilltop without a house in sight and views for miles all round and the sea on the horizon, was magnificent; and the walk was through country that is just how one dreams of Arcady – glades of oak and plane and sycamore, with bubbling streams and no other sounds except sheep-bells and the cuckoo, and a laughing muleteer to guide us and a mule to carry our lunch. It was so beautiful that we never felt tired, though the going was rough and the path very steep. We came back in time to drive down through gorges and then a smiling plain to Megalopolis, a small town next to huge ruins – ruins of the sort that I like, romantically overgrown with trees and wild flowers. . . . On Tuesday we went to Tripolis and retraced our steps to Argos, spending the night at Nauplia. . . . Then yesterday (Wednesday) we drove to Corinth, indirectly, so as to see three Byzantine churches and I had long wished to visit (one of them very pretty) and the temple of Nemea, (a few well-situated columns), to Corinth, where we saw the ruins of old Corinth, rather too much dolled up by the American archaeologists that cleared them, and spent the night. And so back here this morning. The weather was excellent these last days and I am painfully sunburnt. The open air and the simple fare have been most healthful' (Letter 59, 17 April 1947).

Health and safety

Steven suffered at various times from gastric flu, colitis, bug bites, colds and herpes, and spent more than one period in bed. Christmas 1946 was a bad time: 'I have been pursued by ill-luck since last I wrote. It began with losing cigarette lighter on Sunday evening; on Monday morning I dropped an essential part of my razor irretrievably down the sink; on Monday evening I tripped up in a dark street and fell hard on my face and still have a swollen nose and a black eye (as though I had been involved in a disgraceful brawl); on Tuesday morning my hot water system struck a leak; and yesterday I had my overcoat stolen from the hotel where I was lunching. (It was a deliciously warm day, so I had left it there, rashly, while I went for a walk.) However my servant tells me that if I burn a little money to the New Moon (which I unluckily saw through glass yesterday) my luck will change, so I shall solemnly do so at sunset tonight' (Letter 49, 26 December 1946).

The most awkward of his ailments was a sore toe which at first he thought was broken: 'I now have another complaint, far more ridiculous but rather painful. I appear to have broken or anyhow cracked my little toe. It is a terribly aristocratic injury. I think it got kicked in a crowd . . . at least it had been sore for some time. Then the Crown Prince at his party a fortnight ago, as I was sitting on the floor at his sister's feet, backed into me and trod right on it. As he is a very large man the impact was very painful; but I thought nothing of it. However it continued to hurt a bit. The day before yesterday was a lovely day, and having stayed indoors for two days with my cold I decided to go out for a long walk – wearing a not very comfortable shoe. The result was enormous agony after I returned: so I went to the military doctor here, who prodded it a bit and said it was a break or more probably a crack and all one could do was to bandage it tight to the foot (which was done by a very clumsy orderly; I had some difficulty in not screaming) and to walk as little as possible' (Letter 52, 19 January 1947).

The toe continued to be painful. An orthopedist pronounced that the nerve had been crushed. The remedy was bandages and soft shoes. Steven was told that the story had reached the ears of the King, who 'laughed more heartily than he had for years. It is of course just the sort of joke that Royals really like'. On 27 February Steven pronounced, 'My toe at last seems cured, and I can now wear all my shoes again without agony.'

Bywater and Sotheby professorship of Byzantine and modern Greek language and literature

In January 1947 Steven noted that he was glad his mother approved of his application for the Bywater and Sotheby Chair at Oxford University. 'If they want a modernist and a philologist they won't choose me; if they want a Byzantinist they probably will.' He wrote that though he would certainly accept the Chair if offered it, he did not really want to live in Oxford.

On 21 February he wrote to his mother that the Oxford chair had not been offered to him, and offered uncomplimentary comments on the favoured candidate, Constantine Trypanis, but without naming him. 'It brings out all one's worst prejudices against Oxford to see how he has taken them in there, which again is a consolation – it makes me realize how speciousness always triumphs there. I remain more loyal to Cambridge than ever! My real embarrassment is that when I write to my backers to thank them I simply cannot make the proper gentlemanly remarks about what a good choice has been made' (Letter 56, 21 February 1947).

Unpublished primary sources

Steven Runciman letters from Athens, unpublished, to his mother Viscountess Runciman (Hilda) and brother Leslie; referred to as 'SR to HR' and 'SR to WLR' and numbered in a series. Quoted by kind permission of Ann Shukman.

British Council files at The National Archives, Kew, in the British Council series BW. The British Council's Records Management Officer, Peter Bloor, has provided helpful advice. I have consulted the following files:

BW 34/1	Institute of English Studies Athens, 1939–1946
BW 34/10	British Cultural Propaganda 1945–1946
BW 34/11	British Cultural Propaganda 1946–1947
BW 34//19	General Policy 1948–1949
BW 34/20	Annual Reports 1947–1950
BW 34/23	Representative's confidential six-monthly reports: correspondence 1947–1948
BW 34/13	Fine Arts: 1937–1945
BW 83/1	Specialist lecture tours (includes Maurice Bowra's 1946 tour)
BW 83/4	Specialist lecture tours (includes John Lehmann's 1946 tour)
BW 83/6	Specialist lecture tours (includes Robert Speaight's tour)

Notes

1 Steven Runciman was born in 1903 and died in 2000. The *Oxford Dictionary of National Biography* (ODNB) contains a short biography by Averil Cameron, and *Proceedings of the British Academy*, 120 (2003), pp. 365–81, an extended account of him by Anthony Bryer, 'James Cochran Stevenson Runciman'. Minoo Dinshaw, *Outlandish Knight: The Byzantine Life of Steven Runciman* (London, 2016), which appeared after this chapter was written, is the only biography of Runciman and essential reading on his life and work.

2 Steven's letters from Athens have been kindly made available to me by Ann Shukman, his niece and literary executor. He wrote 76 letters home, 72 of which were to his mother, Hilda, to whom he wrote regularly every week, and 4 to his elder brother Leslie ('Lellie') (1900–89), the 2nd Viscount, who went into the family shipping business. Lady Runciman (1869–1956) was a public figure in her own right, and had been member of parliament for St Ives in 1928–29. In my references to the letters, SR denotes Steven, HR his mother Hilda and WLR his brother Leslie.

3 SR to WLR, 11 July 1946, about the family finances: 'I shall always probably have more money than I'll actually need.' Cameron's entry for Runciman in the ODNB records his substantial wealth at death.

4 Michael Grant, the historian of the ancient world, who worked for the British Council in Turkey, suggested this post to Runciman.

5 Steven Runciman, *Byzantine Civilization* (London, 1933). His scholarly reputation was established by *The Emperor Romanus Lecapenus and His Reign* (Cambridge, 1929) and *A History of the First Bulgarian Empire* (London, 1930).

6 Steven Runciman, *A History of the Crusades* (3 vols, Cambridge, 1951, 1954, 1955). The story is that protocol required visitors to knock at his office door to allow time for him to put away the manuscript before they entered.

7 For the early history of the Council see Frances Donaldson, *The British Council: The First Fifty Years* (London, 1984).

8 Jim Potts, 'Truth Will Triumph: The British Council and Cultural Relations in Greece', in David Wills (ed.), *Greece and Britain Since 1945* (Newcastle upon Tyne, 2010), pp. 99–129, quotes from the Charter at p. 110.

9 Sir Rex Leeper (1888–1968) joined the Diplomatic Service in 1918 and spent most of his inter-war career in political intelligence and propaganda work. He was appointed ambassador to the Greek Government-in-exile in 1943, and served in Athens from 1943 to 1946, writing a memoir of his Greek experience, *When Greek Meets Greek* (London, 1950).

10 Louise Atherton, 'Lord Lloyd at the British Council and the Balkan Front, 1937–40', *The International History Review*, 16/1 (February 1994), pp. 25–28.

11 A.R. (Robin) Burn (1902–91), schoolteacher and classical scholar. After his spell at the British Council he spent the war years in intelligence in Cairo, Bletchley Park, and Aleppo, before returning to Greece with the British Embassy, witnessing the British confrontation with EAM/ELAS in December 1944. After the war he taught at Glasgow University, and later in Athens. Among his many published books were *The Modern Greeks* (London, 1944), and *A Traveller's History of Greece* (London, 1965). His wife Mary was an assistant keeper at the Victoria and Albert Museum and taught Greek and Byzantine art.

12 The Anglo-Hellenic League, established in 1913, had more or less lively branches in the main Greek towns at this time. There was debate in the British Council as to whether they were overly 'social' as opposed to professional.

13 Anastasios Sagos, *A Chronicle of the British Council Office in Athens, 1938–1986* (Athens: privately reproduced typescript, 1995), p. 8: a useful, quirky book.

14 There are some discrepancies between Sagos' account and the various indications in the British Council files, in particular BW 34/15, which lists teaching staff as at 27 August 1940. This is not surprising, given that many early Council papers were destroyed and that this was a time of rapid movement and change.

15 Robert Liddell's *A Treatise on the Novel* was published in 1947, so he must be presumed to have been working on it while he was teaching for the British Council. The same is the case with his subsequent novels, books of criticism, and several travel books about Greece. Potts, 'Truth will Triumph', p. 109, records that Terence Spencer worked on *Fair Greece, Sad Relic* (London, 1954) in the Council's Library. I have seen no evidence other than one reference by Sagos that Woodhouse worked at the British Council.

16 Olivia Manning, *The Balkan Trilogy: The Great Fortune* (London, 1960); *The Spoilt City* (London, 1962); *Friends and Heroes* (London, 1965).

17 Rex Warner (1905–86), novelist, poet, classical scholar and translator, wrote a memoir of this period, *Views of Attica and its Surroundings* (London, 1950). His translation of Thucydides, famous in the Penguin edition, was published in 1954. Stephen Tabachnick, *Fiercer than Tigers: The Life and Works of Rex Warner* (East Lansing, 2002) describes Warner's time in Athens, fuelled by drink and good company.

104 MICHAEL LLEWELLYN-SMITH

18 Major David Wallace, attached to SOE, was parachuted into Greece on 18 July 1944 and killed on 18 August while observing an attack by EDES forces on Menina on the Igoumenitsa – Ioannina road, in which there were numerous German casualties. His widow Prudence was temporarily in charge of the Athens office when Steven arrived.

19 Donaldson, *British Council*, p. 95, Dundas to Lloyd, 31 October 1940.

20 BW 34/10, A.J.S. White (BC) to Sir R. Leeper, 10 March 1945: 'Our pre-war organisation in Greece was, as you know, not altogether satisfactory, and it is so important for us to start well this time.'

21 Robert Holland and Diana Markides, *The British and the Hellenes: Struggles for Mastery in the Eastern Mediterranean 1850–1960* (Oxford, 2006), ch. 8, 'The Dodecanese Experience, 1939–1948'.

22 Kenneth Johnstone (1902–78), after Eton and Oxford, entered the diplomatic service in 1926. He served in Warsaw, Oslo, Sofia and London and was seconded to the British Council in 1936, working under Rex Leeper. He joined the Welsh Guards in 1939 and served in France, North Africa, the Middle East and Greece, rejoining the FO in 1945. He was Deputy Director-General of the Council, 1953–62. In his retirement he became Chairman of the Council of the School of Slavonic and East European Studies (SSEES) of London University. His wife Pauline, an expert in textiles and embroidery, worked at the Victoria and Albert Museum for ten years. She wrote the classic *Greek Island Embroidery* (London, 1961).

23 Maurice Cardiff, *Friends Abroad* (London, 1997), pp. 1–2. Cardiff also wrote a memoir of his war experiences in the Aegean under the pen name John Lincoln, *Achilles and the Tortoise: An Eastern Aegean Exploit* (London, 1958).

24 For Johnstone, Cardiff and the period 1944–45 see also Gioula Koutsopanagou's contribution to this volume.

25 TNAC, BW 34/10, Johnstone to A.J.S. White, Secretary General, British Council, 7 March 1945, enclosing memorandum 'British Council Work in Greece 1945–6'.

26 Donaldson, *British Council*, p. 146.

27 Romilly Jenkins (1907–69), Emmanuel College Cambridge; Student at the British School at Athens (BSA) 1930–34; Chairman of the BSA 1951–58; 1936, Lecturer in Modern Greek at Cambridge; 1946, Koraës Professor of Modern Greek and Byzantine History, Language and Literature at King's College, London; 1960, Professor of Byzantine History and Literature at Dumbarton Oaks.

28 The historian Michael Grant served the British Council in Turkey during the war. Like Runciman he was a fellow of Trinity College, Cambridge. He wrote numerous books about the classics and ancient history, and held posts at Cambridge, Edinburgh, Khartoum (as the first Vice-Chancellor of the university) and Queen's University Belfast (Vice-Chancellor), before moving to Italy.

29 N.G.L. (Nicholas) Hammond, Fellow of Clare College Cambridge, 1930; headmaster of Clifton College, 1954; Professor of Greek at Bristol University, 1962, was a historian of ancient Epirus, and doughty mountain walker. He served

in SOE in the Pindus mountains, 1943–44, and wrote the memoir *Venture into Greece* (London, 1983).

30 Details in BW 34/10, R. Seymour (BC) to Johnstone in Athens, 2 December 1944, writing that there was no obviously suitable candidate: 'We must be particularly careful in our choice of a permanent Representative . . . a person of some academic reputation, for preference not a classical scholar, who is a competent administrator, knows the Greeks and can speak modern Greek. In temperament he should be the kind of person to whom people like to take their grievances.' Romilly Jenkins had been suggested but was not available until the end of the war. 'Nor do I think he would be suitable.' Michael Grant 'has the capacity', but was he suitable for Greece by temperament and experience? Jenkins had suggested Nicholas Hammond, but following his wartime experience in the Greek mountains he would probably be identified with one Greek faction. Seymour added that the Council wished to appoint only a minimum of pre-war Greek staff.

31 BW 34/10, A.J.S. White, Secretary General, BC, to Leeper, 13 April 1945, commending Runciman and saying that Johnstone might be left in Athens until the end of July.

32 Koutsopanagou, in her contribution to this volume, quotes the Foreign Office official Montagu-Pollock on Runciman's 'extremely effeminate manner'.

33 Rex Warner, *Views of Attica and Its Surroundings* (London, 1950). John Lehmann, *The Ample Proposition: Autobiography III* (London, 1966). Cardiff, *Friends Abroad*, for an account of the early post-war days, and pen pictures of Patrick Leigh Fermor and Lawrence Durrell. Tabachnick, *Fiercer than Tigers*. See also Ian MacNiven, *Lawrence Durrell: A Biography* (London, 1998), Roderick Beaton, *George Seferis: Waiting for the Angel* (New Haven and London, 2003), Edmund Keeley, *Inventing Paradise: The Greek Journey 1937–47* (New York, 1999), and David Roessel, *In Byron's Shadow: Modern Greece in the English and American Imagination* (Oxford and New York, 2002).

34 SR to HR, letter 10, 8 January 1946. EAM was not the Communist Party as such, but the political wing of the Communist-led resistance organization during the Axis occupation of Greece.

35 Inflation and prices: letters 4, 6, 12, 17 (all to HR). Accommodation, letters 3, 10.

36 SR to HR, letter 4, 31 October 1945. General Sir Ronald Scobie (1893–1969), commander of the British force sent to Athens to hold the ring after the withdrawal of the Germans, and thus in effect military governor during the confrontation with EAM/ELAS in December 1944: a respected figure for the honest and straightforward way he managed this difficult task.

37 SR to HR, letter 10, 8 January 1946. Sir Clifford Norton (1891–1990) was British Ambassador to Greece, March 1946 to 1951. His wife Noel Evelyn née Hughes, generally known as 'Peter', was a 'character', with artistic interests and bohemian manners. She had co-founded the London Gallery, and befriended the artists John Craxton and Lucien Freud, whom she brought out to Greece.

38 SR to HR, letter 21, 18 April 1946. Constantine Tsaldaris (1884–1970), leader of the Popular Party, was nephew of the pre-war leader Panagis Tsaldaris

(1868–1970). His wife Nadine had a colourful career (as did Lina, the daughter of Spyridon Lambros and wife of Panagis). She was apparently born Nadine de Bornemann, of at least one Danish parent (but other sources call her British or Austrian), had an affair in Paris with Agamemnon Schliemann (1878–1954), son of the great archaeologist Heinrich, and eloped with him to New York, where the young couple were forced to contract a civil marriage. Agamemnon became deputy for Larissa, and in 1914 was appointed Greek Minister in Washington. He and Nadine were divorced some time in the 1920s, after which, in 1926, she married Constantine Tsaldaris. Nadine died in 1973. Agamemnon committed suicide in 1954. Thus Steven in letter 21 gets the story right, except for the rumours about Nadine's origins ('daughter of King George I's Dutch housekeeper'), which are unsubstantiated, though the uncertainty of the sources as to her parentage and nationality suggests that anything is possible. (*The New York Times*, 22 June 1902, reports on the elopement. The British Embassy's report 'Leading Personalities in Greece, 1947', calls Tsaldaris' second wife 'the divorced Austrian wife of Agamemnon Schliemann', and writes that she 'wears the trousers'. Their wedding is the 'culmination of a long love story, and they are devoted to each other, in spite of Mme Tsaldaris's caustic tongue, which is feared and detested by his colleagues.' National Archives, FO 371/67128, 24 April 1947.) I am grateful to Helen Gardika-Katsiadakis and Petros Petrides for helping me to untangle this story.

39 SR to HR, letter 57, 4 April 1947.

40 SR to HR, letter 58, 9 April 1947. In 1921, when he was Crown Prince, George had married Princess Elisabeth of Romania. The marriage was dissolved in 1935, without issue. He took up with Mrs Britten-Jones in the 1930s. She seems to have been a discreet and sensible lady.

41 SR to HR, letter 62, 7 May 1947.

42 SR to HR, letter 60, 23 April 1947.

43 SR to HR, letter 66, 31 May 1947.

44 SR to HR, letter 7, 28 November 1945, 'Fortunately politics are right outside my scope, specifically outside, and I can refuse to discuss them.'

45 SR to HR, letter 56 bis, 28 March 1947. Alethea Hayter (1911–86), the sister of Sir William Hayter, British ambassador to Moscow and later Warden of New College Oxford, was working for the Council in London at the time. She wrote the fine book *A Sultry Month: Scenes of London Literary Life in 1846* (London, 1965). Mr Sagos makes a similar observation about Miss Hayter, calling her 'the most representative Lady of English society I have met in my life': Sagos, *A Chronicle of the British Council Office in Athens*, p. 20.

46 SR to HR, letter 51, 15 January 1947.

47 Beaton, *Seferis*, pp. 300–1, citing Steven's memories of a month he spent in Beirut in 1953 when Seferis was ambassador there. Steven published a short, warm memoir of Seferis: Steven Runciman, 'Some Personal Memories', *Labrys*, 8 (1983), pp. 47–49. 'Nicest Greek I know' from SR to Stewart Perowne, 12 October 1952, cited in Bryer, 'Runciman 1903–2000', pp. 365–81.

48 SR to HR, letter 21, 18 April 1946.

49 Rex Warner was married three times, but to only two women: first to Frances Grove, by whom he had three children; the marriage was dissolved in 1949, in which year he married Barbara Rothschild née Hutchinson: this marriage was dissolved in 1962, after which Barbara married Nikos-Hadjikyriakos-Ghika the artist. Warner remarried Frances in 1966. She visited him twice in Athens, but spent more time in England with the children.

50 Lehmann, *The Ample Proposition*, pp. 59–60. The section on Lehmann's visit in the British Council file BW 83/4 contains no information other than the titles of his two lectures, 'English Letters and European Vision 1930–1946' and 'The Pursuit of the Myth', and a note by Lehmann himself about his publication of poetry by Seferis, Elytis, Sikelianos and Prevelakis as well as Capetanakis.

51 Tabachnick, *Fiercer than Tigers*, pp. 205–6, quotes a description by Leigh Fermor of a typical evening's schedule: starting in one of the Grande Bretagne hotel's two bars; on to the Plaka tavernas, usually Platanos or The Seven Brothers, for singing and *retsina*; and sometimes on to a dive in Piraeus for dancing and *bouzoukia*.

52 For Steven's views on the Embassy see Anthony Bryer, 'Steven Runciman – Proem: The Problem of Oratory; Being a Brief Thesis on the World, Oral, Written and Remembered; in a Word History', in Αφιέρωμα στον *Sir Steven Runciman*, special issue of *The New Griffon* (Athens), new series, no. 5 (2002): 'he thought that the people at the British Embassy then might have had more cultural or social sense'. For a more favourable view of Peter Norton see Cardiff, *Friends Abroad*, pp. 6–7: 'Eccentric and self-willed, she had an impulsive drive and vitality, which could be overwhelming, but beneath it lay a warm and generous nature.' Her patronage of the arts, and particularly her support of Craxton, were a service to the arts in Greece and Britain.

53 SR to HR, letter 60, 23 April 1947.

54 SR to HR, letters 56 bis of 28 March 1947 and 64 of 18 May 1947. President Truman declared in a speech on 12 March 1947 that the US would support Greece and Turkey with military and economic aid to prevent their falling into the Soviet sphere. It outlined what became known as the Truman Doctrine. Britain had asked the US in February to take over her role as chief supporter of Greece, and from now on played a secondary role.

55 Nicolson: letter 4 of 31 October 1945; Mortimer: letter 21 of 18 April; Lehmann: letter 42, 15 November 1946; Sewell: letter 45, 6 December 1946.

56 Dilys Powell: SR to HR, letter 6, 19 November 1945.

57 BW 34/23, 'The Work of the British Council in Greece, January 1st to May 31st, 1947', sent by SR under cover of letter to White, Secretary General of the BC, dated 31 May 1947.

58 SR to HR, letter 56 of 21 February 1947.

59 The target of Steven's comment must be presumed to be Constantine Trypanis (1909–93), who succeeded Mavrogordato as Bywater Professor. The obituary of Trypanis by Peter Levi in *The Independent*, 21 January 1993, casts light on Steven's strictures: 'His first marriage was a disaster: the honeymoon was a fortnight in the Grande Bretagne Hotel, but the marriage lasted less long.

Unfortunately his wife kept a successful night-club, at which she indoctrinated Osbert Lancaster and a long succession of others with monstrous stories about him, the echoes of which were believed in England.' Steven described Trypanis as 'my old friend' in his description of his visit to Mistra in September 1976, accompanied by Trypanis who was then Minister of Culture, for the naming of a street after Steven: *A Traveller's Alphabet* (London, 1991), p. 97. See Koutopanagou's chapter in the present volume for Trypanis' reporting to the British Embassy, under the pseudonym 'Ajax', on Soviet cultural activities in Greece.

60 BW 34/1, minute by Deputy Secretary General, BC, 10 August 1945, referring to Cabinet decision that 'the highest importance is attached to the extension of British influence in Italy and Greece'.

61 BW 34/11: the Ambassador's view was passed on to the Council in a letter of 20 December 1947 from Macdermot, FO, to G.H. Shreeve, BC.

62 BW 34/19 for Johnstone's stalwart comment of 6 January 1948 on ambassador Norton's view that costs could be cut by cutting lectures on poetry and the arts. He pointed out that not long before Norton had asked the BC to substitute T.S. Eliot, Sir Laurence and Lady Olivier, and Gilbert Murray for technical and scientific lectures.

63 General Sir Ronald Adam (1885–1982), Adjutant-General to the Forces, 1941–46, where he was a reforming influence on the army; Chairman of the British Council, 1946–55: 'an able administrator and a man who is remembered with much affection by his staff', Donaldson, *British Council*, pp. 160–61.

64 SR to HR, letter 54, 31 January 1947.

65 SR to HR, letter 55, 6 February 1947.

66 Tabachnick, *Fiercer than Tigers*, p. 229.

67 Ibid., ch. 7, p. 338 and n. 75. See also ch. 7, n. 40, for an earlier assessment of Warner by Runciman.

68 Cardiff, *Friends Abroad*, p. 17.

69 For more on the *Anglo-Greek Review* see the chapters by Dimitris Tziovas and Dimitris Daskalopoulos in this volume.

70 Leigh Fermor lectured, for example, to troops in Salonica on 30 November 1947, on Resistance in Crete, and repeated this to an audience of about 1500 in the Attikon cinema, Kavalla, where he lectured also at the British Institute on the Philhellenes of 1821. BW 34/11.

71 TNA, BW 83/1, Bowra's three-page report on his visit, which was judged a great success. He gave two lectures, on Modern English Poetry and The Debt of English Literature to Greece, and met Seferis and other literary figures. Bowra was Chair of the British Council's Humanities Advisory Committee, as well as being Warden of Wadham College Oxford, and Professor of Poetry at Oxford University. He became friendly with Leigh Fermor, and had a soft spot for Leigh Fermor's wife Joan, but there was always an undertone of ambivalence in the relationship of the two men, attested by Leigh Fermor's attitude to Bowra's light, and often obscene, verses about his friends. He refused to allow Henry Hardy, editor of a collection of these verses published as *New Bats in*

Old Belfries (Oxford, 2005), to include two verses about Paddy himself in the collection. Following Paddy's death Hardy published one of these in *The Spectator*, 17/24 (December 2011), p. 77, and followed this by publishing both poems ('The Wounded Gigolo' and 'On the Coast of Terra Fermoor') with annotations, in the *Oxford Magazine*, no. 329, 5th week, Michaelmas Term, 2012. Given the obscene and highly personal content, it is not surprising that Leigh Fermor blocked publication.

72 Artemis Cooper, *Patrick Leigh Fermor: An Adventure* (London, 2012), pp. 205–13, gives a lively account of this disappointing period in Leigh Fermor's life. He had been recruited in London by Col Johnstone, and took the job in order to be close to Joan Rayner (née Eyres-Monsell), his future wife, who was working for the AGIS at the British Embassy in Athens. Rex Warner thought that Paddy was useless in this job. 'Paddy Leigh Fermor (though very charming & mad) does nothing at all, so I've won over to my side a beautiful & efficient woman from the Embassy, who, I hope, will organise everything, leaving my mind free for higher things.' Warner to Pam Morris, 31 January 1946, quoted in Tabachnick, *Fiercer than Tigers*, p. 215. Maurice Cardiff, *Friends Abroad*, ch. 2, pp. 11–21, 'A Tour of the North with Patrick Leigh Fermor' gives an entertaining portrait of Leigh Fermor at this period.

73 SR to HR, letter 40b, 2 November 1946. The party included the Katsimbalises, Rex Warner, Basil Wright, Dora Stratou, Lawrence Durrell, May Hodgkinson, Chas Frier, Captain Antoniou and Maurice and Leonora Cardiff.

74 SR to HR, letter 20 of 12 April 1946; SR to WLR, letter 22, Easter Sunday 1946.

75 SR to HR, letter 40 of 4 August 1946.

76 E.g. SR to HR, letter 35 of 6 July 1946; SR to WLR, letter 47 of 15 December 1946. See also Bryer, 'Steven Runciman'.

77 SR to HR, letter 45, 6 December 1946, on Dr Morgan's visit; the 'common man' in SR to WLR, letter 47, 15 December 1946. Warner called Dr Morgan 'stupid & arrogant . . . obviously disapproves of everything we do here. What we actually have done in a year is to wrest from the French the intellectual leadership of Greece'. Tabachnick, *Fiercer than Tigers*, p. 226.

78 BW 34/11, SR to Director, Foreign Division C, BC, 6 March 1947, enclosing 'Plan for the Reorganisation of the Regional Offices of the British Council in Greece'.

79 BW 34/23, 'The Work of the British Council in Greece, January 1st to May 31st, 1947', sent by SR under cover of letter to White, Secretary General of the BC, 31 May 1947.

80 There is a long previous and later history to this. See BW 34/12, 'Anglo-Greek Cultural Convention, 1939–1941'; BW 34/28, 'Anglo-Greek Cultural Convention, Mixed Commission Correspondence, 1944–1960'.

81 He particularly commended Elliott in northern Greece, Batty in the west, and Forster in the Aegean islands, to which names he might have added Marie Aspioti in Corfu.

82 Pantelis Prevelakis (1909–86), Cretan author of novels, poetry and plays, and art historian; a close friend and disciple of Kazantzakis. His younger brother Eleftherios was a distinguished historian.

110 MICHAEL LLEWELLYN-SMITH

83 Donaldson, *British Council*, p. 147.

84 One reference that may be relevant but does not bear it out is in BW 34/11, a critical comment on 2 January 1947 by the financial officers in London on a loan of £50 authorized by Steven to a teaching institute in Patras to help them over a cash flow problem. This looks like a bureaucratic objection to an innocent transaction.

85 In Beaton, *Seferis*; Keeley, *Inventing Paradise*; Roessel, *In Byron's Shadow*.

86 E.g. Tatham's confidential report on the six-month period February – July 1948, on which the BC Director for Southern Europe commented that 'all these points [viz on staffing, finance and administration] are obstructed by the very uncooperative Athens Embassy'.

87 Steven revisited this trip in the chapter 'Morea: Monemvasia and Mistra', in *A Traveller's Alphabet*.

Chapter 4

Making a new myth of Greece: G.K. Katsimbalis as Anglo-Greek Maecenas[1]

Avi Sharon

When a character in Lawrence Durrell's novel *Tunc* (1968) managed to liken the Parthenon to 'the last serviceable molar in some poor widow's gum',[2] a minor revolution was signalled. For no other place or people has been so shackled by the vaunted repute of their ancient past as Greece and the Greeks. 'Classic' was the operative term in most tourist accounts of the country, where visitors tend to have eyes only for the relics of antiquity, the Parthenon foremost of all. The effort to unearth and celebrate (and transmit) the achievements of contemporary Greek culture, buried under the suffocating prestige of its classical forebears, was a gargantuan task. It became the lifelong labour of G.K. (George) Katsimbalis (1899–1978) and was central to the rediscovery of Greece by English and American writers during and after the Second World War. Philip Sherrard wrote of this rediscovery: 'One day . . . historians will speak of how in the late thirties, and through the two succeeding decades, a number of English writers began to discover a Greek world of a kind totally different from what had become the stereotype of the Classical tradition. They began to discover a living Greece. . .'[3]

The work Katsimbalis did with the British Council after the war, in particular his editorship of the *Anglo-Greek Review*, has been examined by others in this volume. In this essay I hope to convey some sense of what Katsimbalis was able to accomplish outside the bounds of any institutional role – as friend and literary gadfly for so many English writers of the period. Two of them, Lawrence Durrell and Rex Warner, were very much a part of the British Council effort of cultural exchange, and it is their collaboration with Katsimbalis in the promotion of Greek letters that I will focus on. Though Durrell had no formal involvement with the Council in the period covered by this volume, no account of the latter can fail to bring him into the story.

Before World War II the literary and cultural life of contemporary Greece was hardly a matter of general interest outside the country's borders, much less within those of England.[4] Early signs of a mutual acquaintance between the two had begun in the teens, in a courtship which the Great War helped accelerate. In 1915, Churchill's Gallipoli campaign brought Rupert Brooke via his burial to the Aegean island of Skyros, rendering a part of Greece forever England, and recalling Byronic memories among the Greeks themselves.

A year later, E.M. Forster shipped out to Alexandria, where he found the Greek poet C.P. Cavafy standing motionless at a slight angle to the universe. But otherwise English literary sympathy for the place remained slight. The only Greece that reached English letters in those years, apart from the old imaginary Hellas, was insubstantial and sometimes disparaged as in Yeats's Byzantium poems, or Eliot's Mr. Eugenides, 'unshaven, with a pocket full of currants'. But the reality of modern Greek culture was still largely blocked from view by the towering prestige of its ancient forebear and any acquaintance with its modern poets was virtually non-existent. Yet only a generation after those Anglo-American modernists, England's leading writers, W.H. Auden and Stephen Spender, were composing verses inspired by Cavafy and George Seferis, while Henry Miller and Lawrence Durrell were celebrating the modern poets and landscape of Greece in their books.[5] By the end of the 1940s John Lehmann, Cyril Connolly, Bernard Spencer, Louis MacNeice, Rex Warner and other members of their literary generation in England all shared to a large extent the feelings expressed by John Waller in his poem 'Spring in Athens' (1945), in which 'Athens for me was Katsimbalis, Seferis, Antoniou/ New friends for new places'. This sudden and extraordinarily personal discovery of Greece by the Anglophone west, capped in 1948 by the first volume of George Seferis' poetry to come out in English, prompted the young Greek poet and translator Nanos Valaoritis to announce from London: 'I tell you, George, the wall is cracking, it's falling. The seed has been cast beyond our borders.'[6] I would argue that much of the credit for this re-discovery of Greece is due to Katsimbalis and his rapport with his English friends.

The inspiration for Henry Miller's *The Colossus of Maroussi*, for long the most popular book about modern Greece, was a man whom Miller (and later Warner, Spender, Patrick Leigh Fermor, Durrell and others), thought the most Greek of Greeks. Colossal in size and in his passions, Katsimbalis is portrayed by Miller as a man of many words in the best sense, both a teller of tales and a modern Maecenas. Friend and mentor to two Nobel laureates (George Seferis and Odysseus Elytis), founding editor of the most influential literary journal in Greece and the country's first bibliographer, this eternal dawdler in the taverns of Athens was in himself a national circulating library, a Greek Dr Johnson. But above all Katsimbalis was an inspirer, his Socratic nature ever drawing people out, discerning their talents, listening, directing and, in due course, publishing. Hundreds of works owe their existence to his sympotic grumbling, yet (save for a number of translations done with his friend Theodore Stephanides) no more than Socrates has he written. For Miller the voice of Katsimbalis was, like the Greek landscape itself, a revelation: 'Nobody can explain it satisfactorily. Nobody can explain anything which is unique. One can describe, worship and adore. And that is all I can do with Katsimbalis' talk.'[7]

Katsimbalis devoted his life to the idea of a renascent Greece, and he spent his energy and his dwindling fortune working to that end. In defining his modern Greek project, Katsimbalis persistently urged his stable of artists and writers to focus on what he saw as the vital core underneath the classical husk, the naked constant of Greek earth and Greek sun. And it was that landscape that he himself was considered, like a human colossus, to incarnate. It is no wonder that so many imagined him in petrified form. Spender compared him to 'one of the gigantic stone lions over the entrance to ancient Mycenae', while the English publisher and editor, John Lehmann, described him as 'an archaic statue . . . roaring to the waves and the wind'.[8] In his person he was said to have given rise to an authentically Greek literature and art, like a voice emerging out of the stones, 'rumbling in the depths of the distant mountain sides', as Miller tells it. From that inspiriting voice would come a resurgent Greek version of Modernism, where the poet Seferis would be the parallel to Eliot, the painter Ghika to Picasso, the photographer Nelly's to Stieglitz, the novelist Kosmas Politis to Joyce and so on. Conveniently employing the devices of Modernism to remove the old museum-like carapace, these men enabled a new, more vital Greece to come to light, emancipated finally from the dead weight of its classical inheritance. And of this troupe Katsimbalis was the undisputed Diaghilev.

The Katsimbalis family came from an eponymous village in the real Arcadia in the Greek Peloponnese, though he was brought up on the imagined Arcadia of Belle Époque Paris. Like his father (the translator of FitzGerald's *Rubáiyát* into demotic Greek in 1919), the younger Katsimbalis was equally at ease among the Parisian salons and the taverns of Athens. In the twenties he translated the French moderns (Valery Larbaud, Paul Morand) into Greek and the national poet of Greece, Kostis Palamas, into English, while persistently soliciting for a Nobel Prize for the latter. But it was in the thirties in Athens, mostly through his friendship with the poet Seferis (which we can follow at close hand in their correspondence over fifty years),[9] that his work would take on its definitive form. There Katsimbalis founded the crucial organ of his renaissance, the journal *Ta Nea Grammata* (*New Letters*), and set out on his cultural mission. Miller and Durrell caught him at his zenith in Athens in September 1939, just before the war put a temporary halt to that effort.

Durrell described his landfall on Corfu as being as much a matter of hap as destiny. At first the place, 'unbelievably primitive', appealed simply because it happened to offer a good rate of exchange. Other explanations followed. In one Durrell claimed that in Corfu he was seeking his own genealogical roots and the Minoans, a famously diminutive group of *islomanes*, provided him with a suitable and probable pedigree. Arguably more fateful, however, was his discovery of several lifelong friends during his formative years there on the island, characters who helped render the place 'miracle ground' for Durrell. Indeed, one wonders whether Greece could ever have become a place that offered, as Durrell notoriously put it, 'the discovery of yourself', had it not been inhabited by these friends, mentors who 'stretched out hands – touch, touch – and I felt in contact'.[10] As a result of the fellowship that grew up among Durrell and these men the young writer was able to become the thing he was:

he discovered himself as he found these friends. The story of their affection for one another (as much as their reciprocal influence) is one with the image and idea of Greece which they lived with and conjured up throughout their work.

Durrell's acquaintance with these beneficent figures followed swiftly on his arrival on the island:

> By some fluke of fate I found myself, within a week of setting foot in Corfu as a young man, the possessor of a small green covered volume of modern Greek poetry translated by two unknown persons – Theodore Stephanides and George Katsimbalis.[11]

Soon Durrell would come to meet Stephanides, the saintly zoologist, doctor and patriot, in the flesh, and later discovered Miller's *Tropic of Cancer*, heraldically, in an island outhouse, after which he began an excited correspondence with the author. Stephanides later introduced Durrell to George Katsimbalis and, through him, to Seferis. Over time this growing circle of friends would evolve into a kind of Greek chorus, Durrell's 'industrious singers', all happily employed in making a new myth of that 'enormous blue', while they themselves became deeper and deeper friends in Hellas.

The 1939 visit of Henry Miller and Durrell to Athens and their subsequent friendship with Katsimbalis and Seferis ushered in a burst of mutual creative activity among this foursome, and Katsimbalis, colossus-like, straddled most of their joint creations. Miller, for one, would never have written his 'favourite book', *The Colossus of Maroussi* (1941), without Durrell's invitation to Corfu and his friendship with Stephanides, who led them both to Athens and hence to Katsimbalis. An equally circuitous and shared provenance marks Seferis' poem 'Les anges sont blancs', the Greek writer's poetic conversation with Balzac and Miller and a memento of their joint visit to Hydra in November 1939. Later that year Durrell unintentionally began his own published work in the collective, in the form of a letter from 10 August 1940, which describes the famous scene of Katsimbalis waking the cocks of Athens with his shrill cry, which Miller thought fit to publish as the culminating epiphany of his Greek travelogue. Durrell's August letter goes on to close with the news that he is writing from a ship bound for Mykonos, along with Bernard Spencer and Nanos Valaoritis, further traceable evidence of how these friendships slowly wound their way to literary collaboration. For together that same trio of writers, Durrell, Valaoritis and Spencer, would translate and publish the first collection of Seferis' poetry in English in 1948, in a volume which included the poem dedicated to Miller, 'Les anges sont blancs'. The list of shared efforts and joint devotions would continue to grow: Katsimbalis translated and published Miller's 'Thoughts on Writing' in *Ta Nea Grammata* (1939) and seeded in Durrell the idea to translate E.D. Roidis' *Pope Joan* (London 1954), while years later that obstreperous 'leader' or *archigos*, as Katsimbalis was almost universally called in Greek, would turn up as the character Caradoc in Durrell's 1968 novel *Tunc*. While the months from September to December 1939 proved the most intense period of their corporate friendship, these men, in their deep affection and nostalgia for one another and for the country in which they met, created a lively and long-lasting literary cooperative for Hellas.

Durrell's poem 'Mythology II' (1943) offers a particularly good illustration of the shared and reciprocal nature of the creative output of this foursome. The poem is a summing up of Durrell's past in Greece, a declaration of identity and fellowship and a work in common. As Durrell set out 'to make a new myth of Greece', he could not do so without the patron divinities of his own landscape, including Miller, Eliot, Katsimbalis and Seferis. Sitting alone in Alexandria, separated from his wife Nancy and nostalgic about his days in Greece, Durrell summed up his life so far along with his most crucial benefactors.

Mythology
All my favourite characters have been
Out of all pattern and proportion:
Some living in villas by railways,
Some like Katsimbalis heard but seldom seen,
And others in banks whose sunless hands
Moved like great rats on ledgers.
[. . .]
The poetry was in the pity. No judgement
Disturbs people like these in their frames
O men of the Marmion class, sons of the free.

The poem was written early in 1943, in Alexandria, in a mood and environment which Durrell would later draw with greater candour and clarity in his 'epilogue in Alexandria', from *Prospero's Cell*: 'The loss of Greece has been an amputation. All Epictetus could not console one against it.' Later in the same passage he writes of his Greek friends in Egypt but seems, in part, to describe himself: 'I see them (the Greeks) daily recovering by their acts, their songs and poems, the whole defeated world of acts and thoughts, into a small private universe, a Greek universe.'[12] The poem has (not so) veiled references to Eliot ('whose sunless hands moved like great rats. . .'), Miller ('living in villas by railroads'), Katsimbalis ('heard but seldom seen') and Seferis (who had referenced Ramon Gomez de la Serna to Durrell in a delirious conversation after an anti-typhus injection taken in Athens). Durrell sent this poem of his own private Greek universe, while still in manuscript, to Seferis in Cairo. Of all Durrell's poems, Seferis translated only this.[13] The poem constitutes a credo of his apprentice years, and a loving memento of the men whose table talk and affection helped him find his own voice.

Now to Rex Warner, who, along with Steven Runciman, was arguably the most visible and consequential member of the British Council in Greece in the years just after the War. If Runciman managed the diplomatic and political imperatives of the Council during that time, it may be that Warner provided the lifeblood of the cultural exchange the Council espoused. Warner's relationship with Greece and Katsimbalis coincided from just after the end of the War. Warner recalls the beginning of that relationship in a Third Programme BBC radio talk ('Aspects of Contemporary Greek Poetry'), which aired on 27 September 1948.[14] Based on this text, it seems his interest in and support of Greek literature went well beyond any official mandate:

> I cannot claim to be able to put before you an accurate, balanced, objective criticism of the state of literature in Greece today. Neither my knowledge of the language, nor my study of the literature is great or profound enough for that. I can only give you my personal impressions for what they are worth, personal impressions partly of the literature itself, partly of the scene and atmosphere, partly of a few of the leading poets and writers with whom I was happy enough to make friends during the two years from 1945 to 1947 which I spent in Athens.

It did not take long for Katsimbalis to identify Warner as valuable quarry for his modern Greek project: any talented foreign writer would be a reasonable target for him.

> It was quite soon after my arrival and at one of the taverns near the Acropolis, that I first met my friend, the great critic and talker George Katsimbalis . . . this large man, with egg-shaped head and mouth like a fish, brandishing his enormous walking stick or pausing suddenly for a few contemplative sentences, escorted me through the maze of streets to his favourite tavern and never stopped speaking for an instant.

It was during these literary perambulations that Katsimbalis' evangelizing work took place, and soon Warner would be introduced to a rich company of friends in Athens: 'It was very often in the company of Katsimbalis that I met other writers and poets of Greece.'

But it was not simply as a literary matchmaker that Katsimbalis excelled. His introductions came with guidance, whether a fervent request or a downright command, to understand Greece and Greek letters in his terms. This meant, first and foremost re-directing his classically trained travellers towards the moderns. Warner provides evidence of this in his BBC talk:

> Katsimbalis recognised but only remotely approved of my classical enthusiasms. What interested him most was the modern movement in Greek poetry, the movement that had started with Palamas, and was now represented by Sikelianos, Seferis, Elytis and other poets, different enough among themselves but all of them creating the language and literature of modern Greece.

G.K. KATSIMBALIS AS ANGLO-GREEK MAECENAS 117

And the lesson took hold in Warner, himself a leading translator of ancient Greek literature in England: 'Perhaps in speaking of a people so ancient as the Greeks, it may sound odd to talk of creating the language, but in fact it is only in recent years that the popular spoken language has, for the purposes of literature, replaced the academic style and dialect, which for all its echoes of ancient Greek, could have no direct or vital connection with the minds of the living people.'

And so Warner became, as had Miller, Durrell and many others, a friend and ally of Katsimbalis in his larger project. But with Warner the personal bond seems to have grown particularly close. In a letter Katsimbalis wrote to his wife Aspasia during a British Council-sponsored trip to London in 1948 we get a glimpse of the warmth of affection for Katsimbalis felt not just by Warner, but by a large swath of literary England of the time:

> After the embassy I went to [the editor John] Lehmann's who had invited me to his house for lunch. There were two of the better known poets there: Laurie Lee (you can see his photograph in AE [the *Anglo-Greek Review*] no. 12 and Alan Ross (with whom I ate the previous day at the Brown's hotel luncheon). Then, suddenly from behind the door, appeared Rex. You can imagine what happened next! The house and the meal both were out of this world. As for good spirits, that you can imagine. Rex's endless laughter. accompanied by that of Lehmann, stories, jokes, etc. Rex wanted to spend the afternoon together, just the two of us, and I agreed. But then suddenly came a phone call: 'Lady Rothschild for Mr Warner', and the whole plan for the afternoon dissolved. Rex fled like a madman pleading to be excused and whispering vague excuses. In the evening I dined with Cyril Connolly (editor of *Horizon*). The wife of Stephen Spender was there, Peter Watson, Pryce-Jones (with whom I ate at Brown's) and Joan [Rayner, companion and later wife of Patrick Leigh Fermor] and Xan [Fielding]. Unbelievable hospitality and rivers of French wine, liquor and champagne.[15]

Several days later, Katsimbalis was at Lady Rothschild's Oxfordshire estate with Warner and Rosamund Lehmann:

> We spent all Saturday and Sunday the four of us together from morning to evening, walking, talking, reading. The ladies were crying with laughter from my stories, and Rex was cackling continuously with that warbling laugh of his. Later he read some poems for hours and passages from his novel, where I appear as a Captain Nicholas!

The novel in question was the allegorical *Men of Stones* (discussed by Jim Potts in Chapter 10 of this volume) a portrait of a Greek island prison and a 'young lecturer in literature . . . attached to one of the foreign cultural missions', who

118   AVI SHARON

is enlisted to help direct a prisoner production of *King Lear*. Katsimbalis' copy
in the archive is inscribed by the author: 'To George (Captain Nicholas) from
Rex (Mr. Goat), with love, Rex'.[16] In Mr. Goat's first meeting with Captain
Nicholas, we see the lineaments and hear something of Katsimbalis' gifts as a
raconteur:

> The elder man, tall, stout and wearing a thick overcoat, stood still, leaning
> sideways on the exceptionally thick walking stock which he carried. His
> large and egg-shaped head was inclined slightly backward, his small mouth
> pursed, as he examined the general scene in a critical manner. His eyes fol-
> lowed the curves of the elongated figures of engraved saints, some upside
> down, some leaning at crazy angles, all on the ground, lying unnaturally
> away from the high belfries where in past ages they had been devoutly
> hung and where their workmanship had been admired. When he spoke, he
> spoke loudly and with great rapidity. This, he said, making a sweeping ges-
> ture with his walking stick, is astounding; it is terrific; it is all wrong. I am
> not a religious man. I never have been. My family were always against the
> church. Priests, I hate them. And saints days. I've always been very unlucky
> on saints days. There is a story I must tell you some time about what hap-
> pened to me on a saints day. But with bells it is different. The villagers like
> them. They must have them. It is part of the tradition. When I commanded
> a company of mountain infantry in the war before last, we always rang the
> bells before going into action. Very wonderful music. We would weep and
> cry and embrace each other as we heard those bells. They were the voice of
> our country.[17]

Like Miller before him and Durrell after, Warner has become the vessel through
which Katsimbalis' message of a more vital and relevant Greece would be
translated. It also confirms Warner's own surmise about Katsimbalis in the
radio talk: 'The influence of this Greek Dr Johnson depends, I think, more on
his spoken than his written words.'

We have focused on Lawrence Durrell and Rex Warner as two representative examples of Katsimbalis' work as an 'Anglo-Greek Maecenas'. But there
were many others, including Patrick Leigh Fermor, John Lehmann, Robert
Liddell, C.A. Trypanis, Philip Sherrard, Bernard Spencer, William Plomer and
others who attest to his efforts to celebrate and transmit modern Greek culture
outside the borders of Greece. And this tally does not even begin to include
the many French, German, Italian, Swedish and other 'collaborators' in the
drama that Katsimbalis inspired and directed. That's why it may be useful to
get the perspective of the Greek literary community itself regarding Katsimbalis' outsize role in Greek literary culture of the time. A useful reference for that
is the explosive dispute that arose in 1947 among the Athenian literati, when
the poet, novelist and critic I.M. Panagiotopoulos wrote to the chief literary
magazine of the day, *Nea Estia*, complaining of a 'clique' that controlled the

dissemination of modern Greek literature. The most creative response to the charge was a parody of it, written by George Theotokas, one of the founding members of the literary journal *New Letters*. It is a passionate and effective apologia for Katsimbalis and his maieutic role in Greek letters, and stands as the best possible conclusion to my essay:

> Our intellectual life is in great danger. The entirety of Hellenic Culture is at risk. There is a Clique, a horrible cancer, a dark Machiavellian mafia, a secret organization held together by diabolic machinations that has succeeded in wrapping its tentacles around all the intellectual manifestations of our nation. It exploits every opportunity to serve its unspoken ends. It mercilessly destroys whomsoever does not render it service. It is on its way to monopolizing the intellectual life of Greece, here and abroad. It employs gangs of international adventurers to spread its own fame to the ends of the civilized world while it stifles without mercy every other Greek voice . . .

> It is a matter of utmost concern to the nation, as anyone will immediately realize. It's obvious that, to have managed such frightening achievements the Clique must have great resources, and no doubt it receives from the hands of its constituents a sizable fund for its operations. For it is no slight achievement to have monopolized all the foreign scholars of Greek and all the foreign publishing houses interested in international literature, for all of them to be persuaded that they are to concern themselves only with the work of Clique members and that in no way, shape or form should the name of a certain I.M. Panagiotopoulos appear in Roman letters. . .

> In the end, all were acquitted and fled. Excuse me. All except one. In the hall remained one man, with his cane in one hand and his cigar tilted at an oblique angle to his huge head: George Katsimbalis. And in this way it was discovered that the secret yet notorious Clique had but a single member. One figure alone was Leader, Guide, Follower and Autocratic Master of the Clique, and the source of all its crimes.[18]

As Hugh Kenner said of Wyndham Lewis, 'One man cannot make a Renaissance, but he may be indispensable to it.'[19]

Notes

1 For the 'new myth of Greece' see also Dimitris Tziovas' contribution to this volume (ch. 5).

2 Lawrence Durrell, *Tunc* (London, 1968), p. 29.

3 Philip Sherrard, 'Γιώργος Κατσίμπαλης', *Νέα Εστία*, 108/1278 (1 October 1980), pp. 1426–27.

4 An interesting testimony from the period can be found in a letter from Robert Byron to Theodore D. Stephanides, dating to 1925: 'If time and money ever permit, I hope to add two volumes to *The Byzantine Achievement*, and thus complete the original scheme. The first is to be a study of Greek life from 1453 to 1861; the second a lesson in amoral Western diplomacy. It was the latter which I thought I was beginning when I began the *Byzantine Achievement*. But what was the use of writing about modern Greece, when no one knew what modern Greece was?'

5 See Auden's 'Atlantis' and Spender's 'Messenger', along with Henry Miller's *The Colossus of Maroussi* (San Francisco, 1941) and Durrell's poetry (passim) and his books *Prospero's Cell* (1945) and *Reflections on a Marine Venus* (1953). Bernard Spencer's collection *Aegean Islands and other Poems* (London, 1946) and William Plomer's *Collected Poems* (London, 1960) also testify to the sudden explosion of interest in modern Greece and its poets.

6 Valaoritis to Seferis, 15 March 1948, in Nanos Valaoritis and Giorgos Seferis, *Αλληλογραφία* (Athens, 2004), p. 86.

7 Miller, *The Colossus of Maroussi*, p. 29.

8 Stephen Spender, ' "Brilliant Athens and Us" ', *Encounter*, 2/1 (January 1954), p. 78. John Lehmann, *The Ample Proposition: Autobiography III* (London, 1966), p. 68.

9 G.K. Katsimbalis and Giorgos Seferis, *'Αγαπητέ μου Γιώργο': Αλληλογραφία (1924–1970)*, ed. Dimitris Daskalopoulos (2 vols, Athens, 2009).

10 Lawrence Durrell, *Blue Thirst* (Santa Barbara, 1975), p. 17.

11 The book in question was *Modern Greek Poems, Selected and Rendered into English by Theodore Ph. Stephanides and George C. Katsimbalis* (London, 1926). The quote is from Durrell's Preface of Stephanides' translation of the Cretan romance, *Erotokritos* (Vitzentzos Kornaros, *Erotocritos: circa 1640 A.D.*, translated by Theodore Ph. Stephanides (Athens, 1984), p. 15.

12 Lawrence Durrell, *Prospero's Cell* (London, 1945), p. 131.

13 As Durrell recorded in *Tunc*, p. 53, it was the Katsimbaline Caradoc who used to say 'the poetry is in the putty', a variation on a phrase from Wilfred Owen's preface to his poems: 'Above all I am not concerned with Poetry. My subject is War, and the pity of War. The Poetry is in the pity.'

14 The transcript of the BBC talk and the annotated copy of *Men of Stones* were found in the Katsimbalis archive, a collection held privately by the Katsimbalis family. The talk has been published in Rex Warner, *Personal Impressions: Talks on Writers and Writing*, ed. Marion B. McLeod (Sydney, 1986), pp. 15–20.

15 Another window onto this trip is provided in the following excerpt from an earlier letter to Aspasia: 'This morning I was presented to Colonel J.C. Smuts (the nephew of the other [Field-Marshal J.C. Smuts, the South African statesman]) who runs the Visitors' Division of the British Council and then I went to Brown's Hotel (one of the most chic in London) where Kenneth Johnstone had organized a lunch in my honour (he's the former director of AGIS with whom we first started the *Anglo-Greek Review*), with Alan Pryce-Jones, editor of the

Times Literary Supplement, Alan Ross, a young poet and critic, and the famous Tambimuttu, the editor of *Poetry London.'*

16 Rex Warner, *Men of Stones* (London, 1949).

17 Ibid., pp. 58–59.

18 Giorgos Theotokas, 'Η φοβερή κλίκα', *Νέα Εστία,* 42 (1947), pp. 969–71.

19 Hugh Kenner, *The Pound Era* (London, 1971), p. 240.

Chapter 5

Between propaganda and modernism: The *Anglo-Greek Review* and the rediscovery of Greece

Dimitris Tziovas

Since the beginning of this century a number of books and articles have been published on Anglo-Greek relations.[1] Understandably these studies tend to focus on military operations and political developments, but some of them explore the cultural aspects of those relations or analyse the attitudes of British travellers to Greece.[2] The studies by Richard Clogg on the role of the British School at Athens in promoting the study of modern Greece and by Jim Potts, who worked for the British Council for thirty-five years and has charted its presence in Greece from the late 1930s to the present day, offer useful surveys of the contribution made by British institutions to strengthening Anglo-Greek ties.[3] However, there is still scope for more detailed studies, focusing on cultural activities such as the publication of the magazine *Anglo-Greek Review/ Αγγλοελληνική Επιθεώρηση* (1945–52 and 1953–55).

The *Anglo-Greek Review* should not be treated in isolation, but as part of the wider cultural developments of the 1940s and early 1950s, a period marked by the re-opening of the British Council in Greece and a new kind of rediscovery of the country by the British, which saw a growing number of translations of Greek texts into English and cultural exchanges between the two countries. Hence, before embarking on a closer examination of the magazine's contribution to the cultural interaction between Greece and Britain, it is important to look at the broader picture and early efforts by the British to promote their culture in Greece.

Before the First World War Britain's main preoccupation was the consolidation of its geopolitical interests, and any cultural achievements were generally left to speak for themselves. By contrast, the French were the first to recognize the value of international cultural exchanges with the establishment of the Service des Œuvres Françaises à l'Etranger, which operated through the Alliance Française (founded in 1883) and French missionary schools all over the world. Similarly, the Germans started their efforts to spread German *Kultur* abroad through the Verein für das Deutschtum im Ausland and the Italians did the same with the foundation of the Società Dante Alighieri in 1889. Italy and Germany achieved national unification rather late and had large ethnic or expatriate communities outside their national territories. For this reason, their efforts at promoting their culture abroad had anti-assimilationist objectives, aimed at trying to prevent these communities from being integrated into foreign cultures or states. Britain remained aloof and indifferent to international cultural diplomacy until it acknowledged the need to counter the growing cultural propaganda of France, Italy and Germany with the establishment of the British Council in 1934.[4] There was an upsurge in cultural propaganda in the 1940s, and the example of the British was followed in 1940 by the Danes, who set up the Danish Society, and the Swedes, who established the Swedish Institute in 1945.

The British Council's involvement in Greece started in 1937 by funding the Byron Chair of English at the University of Athens, newly established to mark its centenary, and continued with the opening of the Institute of English Studies in January 1939.[5] The Council was closed in February 1941 because of the war and re-opened in 1944 when British troops became involved in the civil fighting that broke out in Athens in December 1944. When the British Council reopened, the crowd of prospective students gathered in the square outside was so large that 'the police had to be called out to deal with them'.[6] As a result a tug-of-war for cultural influence started between the British and the French. The French tried to stem the Anglo-American drift of the post-war world by offering French state scholarships. In December 1945 the ship Mataroa sailed from Piraeus carrying over 200 young Greeks who had won such scholarships to study in France.[7] The large number of scholarships and the manner of the students' mass transportation across a war-wrecked Europe demonstrates the increased efforts being put into cultural diplomacy.

It should be noted that Greece and Italy received special attention from Churchill and the British Council due, among other things, to the fact that they had strong Communist parties and to the fear of Russian infiltration, which was intensified by the founding of the Greek-Soviet League in July 1945.[8] The British Council, however, was always at pains to demonstrate that it was an organization promoting cultural dialogue and not an instrument of propaganda. In December 1940 A.R. Burn, the Representative in Athens, wrote in a letter to Lord Lloyd:

> Perhaps my chief difficulty is that the British Council gets no credit whatever for its scrupulous refusal to take part in politics. . . . The strongest evidence of this is that our best friends, the most enthusiastic Anglophiles among Greeks frequently reproach us of the Council for not 'making propaganda' as they put it. . . . Our friends also in general criticize us for the supineness of British propaganda, and seem to have difficulty in taking in any explanations offered.[9]

A few years later in an anonymous article in the *Anglo-Greek Review* the impartiality and non-political role of the British Council are emphasized once again:

> The main purpose of the British Council is to give the inhabitants of the other countries of the world the opportunity to understand British culture and the

BETWEEN PROPAGANDA AND MODERNISM

British way of life, and to give the British the opportunity to understand the cultures of other countries. . . . What needs to be remembered above all the details is the ultimate aim of the Council's activities; that is, the spreading of mutual understanding, respect and love between the peoples of the world. And that, above all, is the Propaganda of Peace.[10]

Indeed the first issue of the *Anglo-Greek Review* opens with two texts which highlight the emotional ties between the two peoples: one by Britain's Ambassador to Greece Reginald Leeper ('Anglo-Hellenic Friendship', a speech at a reception given by the Council and the Anglo-Hellenic League on 22 November 1944 in Athens), and the other by Costas Ouranis ('What we Feel for England').[11] Leeper started by saying that both peoples were going through an emotional phase of their friendship, but that this was not enough since emotions could change. He was keen to present Britain as a model democracy and the British as a model people: tolerant towards others, hating hyperbole and violence and respecting individual rights. He also stressed the importance of freedom, something which Britain had enjoyed for centuries, and that it was now the turn of Greece, after years of oppression, to take full advantage of its benefits. By relying above all on the emotional language of friendship, he then proceeded to vaunt the superiority and generosity of the British and assure his Greek audience that 'we must provide you with what we think the best in our modern life and thought which we have to offer'. Though careful to avoid any suspicion of propaganda, Leeper did not escape a condescending and patronizing tone, urging Greeks to follow the British example.

Leeper had earlier played an important role in setting up the British Council and had strong views on cultural diplomacy.[12] In April 1934 in a memorandum to the Foreign Office he formulated the guiding principles of British cultural propaganda by supporting qualitative rather than quantitative propaganda and the avoidance of the one-sided methods of cultural infiltration 'which French, Germans and Italians are apt to pursue so vigorously'. In his memorandum he outlined his ideas on cultural relations, which could well have been part of an editorial in the *Anglo-Greek Review*:

> In conducting cultural propaganda, we should avoid the idea that it is directed against any other country or indeed that it is competitive. Cultural relations will only improve political relations if they are maintained on a basis of strict reciprocity. It is just as good propaganda for this country to bring distinguished foreigners to lecture and meet people here as it is to send our own speakers abroad. We shall obtain better publicity for our own culture in other countries if we take an equal interest in their culture.[13]

After leaving Athens, Sir Reginald published his book *When Greek Meets Greek* (1950) in which he deals with the policies pursued by Greek Governments, first in Cairo and later in Athens, at a time when the British connection with them was particularly intimate. Adopting a different line from the one he had taken in his speech on 'Anglo-Hellenic Friendship', he makes a comparison between the Greeks and the British in the book's introduction, pointing out that the latter had enjoyed greater security throughout their history than most other nations and had learnt to prize continuity and stability. The Greeks, on the other hand, whose historical background had differed so profoundly from that of the British, were inclined to the opposite way of thinking and found stability rather boring. And he concludes his analysis by emphasising the difficulties involved with collaboration between the two peoples:

> The Englishman, who spends some time amongst the Greeks and has to do business with them and get drawn into their affairs, will either become exasperated, lose his patience, and exclaim that he never wants to see another Greek, or he will keep his temper, pit his wits against theirs, and discover how much he has to learn and how much he can find to like in this wayward and never boring people.[14]

Yet these differences in mentality did not prevent them from working together, promoting cultural interaction and publishing the *Anglo-Greek Review* for some years.

The *Anglo-Greek Review*

The first issue of the *Anglo-Greek Review* came out in March 1945.[15] The first volume (12 issues up to February 1946) was published by the Anglo-Greek Information Service and subsequent volumes, starting with the first issue of the second volume (March 1946), by the British Council.[16] As stated on the cover of the first two issues, it was intended to be a fortnightly publication, but this ambition was never realized and the magazine was produced once a month (and later once every two months). In its early period the front cover of the *Review* stated that it covered art, literature, science and everyday life and featured (until March 1946) a drawing of a head (probably of the goddess Athena) wearing an ancient Greek helmet and with a lion depicted on a smaller scale in front of it, thus trying to combine Greek and British symbolism (Figure 5.1). Though there are references to Scotland and Wales, the term 'English' (rather than 'British') was commonly used throughout the magazine's history. From volume 2 (March 1946) the hyphen in the word Αγγλοελληνική of the title is removed and the magazine is described as a 'Monthly publication of intellectual culture' ('Μηνιαία έκδοση πνευματικής καλλιέργειας').[17] This description of the magazine tries to shift attention from politics to culture.

All the articles in the first three issues were published in both Greek and English, but from the fourth issue (June 1945) onwards the publication was exclusively in Greek. On the last page of the third issue it was announced that the *Review* would be published monthly and would 'be enlarged to 32 pages'.

Figure 5.1 The front cover of the *Anglo-Greek Review* in its early period

It also stated that the 'new review will provide its readers with nearly three times as much material as is possible in the present formation [format]'. However, what was not spelt out in this note was that one of the magazine's original three aims was being dropped. In the editorial for the first issue the magazine's second stated aim was 'to give the British reader some idea from contemporary sources of what Greece is thinking and feeling today about the problems which confront her'. But almost from the very beginning the *Review* focused exclusively on its Greek readership and the aspiration to 'be of interest and use to readers of each country who are learning the language of the other' or 'to promote a still closer understanding between two peoples' had to be abandoned to some degree. The list of contents in each issue continued to be published in both languages, but it was no longer possible for someone with no knowledge of Greek to read the *Review*.

128   DIMITRIS TZIOVAS

The magazine was rather unusual in not identifying its editor or editorial board during the first period of its publication. Surprisingly the translators of the articles are not mentioned either, apart from those who translated poetry. From recently published correspondence it has emerged that George Katsimbalis himself and Nikos Gatsos were doing the translations, though it is not clear who translated the texts of the first issues from Greek into English.[18] The novelist Kosmas Politis, who worked for the British Council from 1945 to 1946, also translated for the magazine. Though it has been alleged that he was sacked for his Communist sympathies, the Assistant Representative of the British Council (Maurice Cardiff) claimed in a letter to the newspaper *Eleftheria* (27 August 1946) that he was not efficient at his job.[19]

The *Review* ceased publication in September 1952 after having published fifty-nine issues. It began publishing again on a quarterly basis in the summer of 1953 for a short period (1953–55) under the editorship of G.P. Savidis (whose name was mentioned on the last page of each issue), who was at the time in his twenties. After consulting Seferis but nobody else, Savidis decided to suspend publication of the *Review* after the Spring 1955 issue.[20] Seferis, though a regular contributor to the magazine from 1946 to the summer of 1954, had refused to publish two poems 'Νεόφυτος ο Έγκλειστος μιλά – ' ('Neophytos the Cloisterer Speaks – ') and 'Πραματευτής από τη Σιδώνα' ('Pedlar from Sidon') as a protest against British policy in Cyprus.[21]

The *Anglo-Greek Review* included contributions primarily from English and Greek writers, which were not separated in the main body of the magazine but were listed separately in the table of contents in each volume. On one occasion, in addition to the English and Greek contributors, Swedish contributors to a special issue on Sikelianos formed a distinct category in the table of contents. At least in the first few issues the magazine tried to maintain some sort of balance between the two cultures, with for example a piece on the English landscape by Edmund Blunden in the second issue and 'The Landscape of Attica' by Costas Ouranis in the third. Later, an article on 'The English and their Country' by Thomas Burke (vol. 1, no, 4, June 1945), which tried to depict the English character and capture the essence of British life, was matched by a similar article by Dimitris Loukatos 'Folklore and the Unity of Greek Tradition' (where the Greek title refers to the homogeneity of the Greek character).[22] In the next issue Elizabeth Bowen's essay on the English short story is followed by Apostolos Sachinis' outline of Greek prose fiction.

In its early issues the *Anglo-Greek Review* makes its readers aware of postwar problems such as achieving full employment, referring to the report by Sir William Beveridge, describing how Britain was trying to cope by building new houses (1/4, June 1945), publishing Bertrand Russell's reflections on the post-war situation ('Where do we go now', 1/5, July 1945) or raising dilemmas about the economy ('Inflation or Self-control' reprinted from *The Economist*, vol. 1, no. 8, October 1945). Though the word 'science' featured on the cover of the magazine throughout its first period and although after the war there were

BETWEEN PROPAGANDA AND MODERNISM

wider concerns about the uses of science or the freedom and the responsibilities of scientists, the relevant articles in the magazine are limited to the early issues.[23] There were regular contributions on theatre, painting, music and radio programmes, but surprisingly very little on cinema, a growing popular entertainment and medium of propaganda.[24]

The *Review* includes a large number of photographs of individuals, buildings or landscapes. Apart from the photographs of Greek writers and paintings, there are no photographs of Greek life. On the other hand, there are a number of photographs of British buildings, landscapes and streets which play an important role in providing information and constructing an image of Britain. In the second issue, for example, a picture of King's College, Cambridge is printed with the rubric: 'A scene typical of English dignity and peace'. In the fourth issue the high street of a typical English country town is depicted. An article on modern architecture in Britain (2/3, May 1946) is accompanied by photographs of the Queen Elizabeth Hospital in Birmingham, a Guinness factory and a recreation centre for miners in Lancashire.

During the course of its publication the price of the magazine went up considerably, going from 20 drachmas (March 1945) to 300 drachmas in March 1946. A particularly sharp rise occurred after issue 8 (October 1945) when the price doubled (from 30 to 60 drachmas) in November 1945, reaching 500 drachmas in December 1946 only to go up to 1,000 the following month. By December 1947 the magazine cost 1,500 drachmas and in early 1950 the price had doubled yet again to reach 5,000 drachmas by July-August 1951. For the second period the subscription in Greece started at 25,000 drachmas per year (£1 for abroad), but it is not clear whether the rate remained stable thereafter. The price of the magazine, of course, reflects the volatility of the Greek economy in the period but the low price in its early days might explain the claim in the Report of the British Council 1945–46 that 'the *Review* has the highest circulation of any magazine of its kind in Greece, and since it was taken over by the Council has greatly increased its scope and gained a wider interest among serious intellectual circles'.[25] The Report of the British Council for the following year 1946–47 cites very high circulation figures by Greek standards: 'The *Anglo-Greek Review*, produced locally by the Council with a high standard of contributions, reached a circulation of about 5,000 and penetrated even to remote areas in Macedonia.'[26] Similarly in the next year's Report we read: 'One of the Council's most valuable contributions has been the publication of the *Anglo-Greek Review*, a cultural journal which has a circulation larger than that of any Greek literary review.'[27] There is no way to ascertain the veracity of these claims or to come up with accurate data concerning the magazine's circulation.

However, in a report dated 31 December 1948/4 January 1949 by Ian Scott-Kilvert, it is stated that the *Review*, like all other magazines in Greece, had gone through a difficult period and 'its circulation is now between 1750 and 2000 per number (six numbers p.a.) which after deduction of all agency expenses

130 DIMITRIS TZIOVAS

leaves us with net receipts of £37.40 per number'.[28] The same report mentions that 80 per cent of the circulation is in Athens and 10 per cent in Salonika while the hoped-for sales outside the Greek mainland, e.g. in Turkey, Cyprus and Egypt, have been negligible. In Turkey 'the local authorities were apparently not in favour of its distribution and in Egypt the Information Department were not disposed to promote its sales'. It is surprising that the Council was expecting to sell a magazine, which by 1948 was entirely in Greek, to other countries, unless it was aiming at Greek residents of those countries. It is not clear whether the dissemination of the magazine beyond the borders of Greece was intended for cultural or propaganda purposes. It is true, however, that the *Review* was reaching remote areas in Greece.

Propaganda and the *Anglo-Greek Review*

To what extent was the *Anglo-Greek Review* an instrument of political or ideological propaganda? It was not like Metaxas' *To Neon Kratos* (1937–41) which tried to impose a cultural ideal and to instil in the minds of its readers an ideological agenda. Primarily the magazine aimed at providing a forum for liberal Greek voices and helping to consolidate the non-left-wing intelligentsia during a period in which the country was ravaged by civil war. This support for liberal institutions, democracy and freedom of speech is particularly evident in the early issues.[29]

In the second issue (April 1945) of the magazine one finds articles on 'How Britain's Parliament Works', written by an anonymous British MP, and 'Free Speech'. In both articles Britain is associated with freedom of speech and the British parliamentary system is praised thus: 'This practice of Parliamentary Questions is perhaps the most important of all rights of the House. . . . It lies at the very root of the Briton's conception of liberty. It is what renders the House of Commons the most vigilant and the most effective legislation assembly in the world.'[30] In another article on 'National Unity in Britain's Government' extracts from speeches of three leading British political figures are quoted in order to 'show that, though at present under a united Coalition Government, there is a healthy freedom for sane expression of purely Party opinion in Great Britain' – surely a coded message to Greek politicians to follow the example of Britain and overcome their differences. The article by Sir Bernard Pares on 'Soviet Russia and England' (1/6, August 1945) could also be seen as a form of political propaganda: it starts with the reception of communism in pre-war Britain and ends by advocating rapprochement with Russia and the post-war cooperation between the two countries for peace and stability.

While German censorship is condemned, the association of freedom with England is further emphasized in an article by M. Rodas 'The Theatre during Occupation: Shakespeare under Ban [banned]'. Rodas reports that during the German occupation the Greek National Theatre repeatedly sought permission

BETWEEN PROPAGANDA AND MODERNISM   131

to perform *Macbeth, Julius Caesar* or *King Lear* invariably only to be refused by the German censor. A production of Oscar Wilde's play *The Importance of being Earnest* was at first allowed on the grounds of Ireland's neutrality, but two days before the opening the Germans banned it thinking that 'they saw British propaganda through Wilde's soothing and beautiful spirit'. The same applied to Bernard Shaw, who was of Irish birth and upbringing: the Germans 'allowed only those of his plays where satire was made of the English [the English were satirized]'.[31] One could read these articles as a subtle form of British propaganda and a way of highlighting the importance of freedom of speech in a politically polarized period in Greece.[32]

The issue of intellectual freedom was discussed in Greece at that time and Andreas Karantonis, a regular contributor to the *Anglo-Greek Review*, wrote an article called 'The Ivory Tower' (1/6, August 1945) where he argued that the main role of the writer is to prepare his position in the history of literature and not to beg it from the political demagogues, thus giving them the opportunity to proudly claim that they control, among other things, cultural and artistic life.[33] Though Karantonis suggested artists should stay in their ivory towers and later (in 1947) published a book on intellectual freedom, which was adver-tised on the back cover of the *Review* (3/2, June 1947),[34] he himself played the role of the propagandist, writing a pamphlet in the form of a letter to all those who had been seduced by the communists or forcibly recruited to act against their own country.[35]

It should be noted that both editors of the magazine refer implicitly to its political and propagandistic character. In a letter to Seferis in November 1946 Katsimbalis boasts that the *Anglo-Greek Review* is not only growing and improving, having gained pre-eminence in literary circles, it has even started attracting contributions by communists.[36] Moreover, in his application for a chair at the University of Thessaloniki in 1966, his successor G.P. Savidis stated that he had 'managed to completely stamp out the propagandistic character of the magazine and secure its reputation as an instrument of both English and Greek humanist culture'.[37] It is true that in the second period under the editor-ship of Savidis the *Anglo-Greek Review* was opened up to younger writers and critics, some of who were Left-leaning. For example, the magazine published a book review by Nikos Svoronos, an exile in France who had been stripped of his Greek citizenship by the Greek government in 1955.

To what extent did the *Anglo-Greek Review* represent a form of cultural propaganda? In order to answer this question we need to start with a broad definition of cultural propaganda. Philip Taylor has described it as being 'the promotion and dissemination of national aims and achievements in a general rather than specifically economic or political form, although it is ultimately designed to promote economic and political interests'.[38] By this definition it could be argued that the *Anglo-Greek Review* is a good example of an attempt at cultural infiltration by a foreign power and of promoting a political agenda through culture. The magazine certainly supported British cultural activities in Athens by publicizing the cultural activities of the British Council and publishing a number of lectures delivered at the British Institute by English and Greek scholars, writers and artists, thus giving Greeks from all over the country the opportunity to read them. It also helped to familiarize the Greek public with aspects of British life, the arts or its institutions and publicized art exhibitions such as those by the sculptor Henry Moore or the painter John Craxton. During the *Review*'s second period the programme of events of the British Council (January-March 1954, October-December 1954, January-March 1955) was printed at the end of issues 3, 6 and 7. The issue of cultural propaganda also features in T.S. Eliot's essay 'The Responsibilities of the Man of Letters', where he warns that 'modern governments are very much aware of the new invention "cultural propaganda", even when the governors are not remarkably sensitive to culture: and, however necessary cultural propaganda may be under modern conditions, we must be alert to the fact that all propaganda can be perverted'.[39]

It could be said that the *Review* started with the aim of promoting British culture and the values of liberal democracy and gradually developed into a magazine which fostered cultural communication, giving the opportunity to intellectuals and artists from both countries to develop closer links. In the early volumes one can find articles on British universities (Oxford, Cambridge, London, St Andrews), museums (British Museum, Victoria and Albert Museum), galleries (Royal Academy, Tate Gallery, England's National Gallery), the Covent Garden Opera House, Fleet Street, cathedrals, theatres, libraries, clubs or rural colleges, whereas the later volumes focus more on literature and the arts. In terms of cultural institutions or modern buildings, Greece had very little to offer but in the areas of literature, painting and music there was an opportunity to present its heritage.[40] The *Review* was instrumental in highlighting some manifestations of modern Greek culture (Theophilos, *Erotokritos*, Makriyannis) which some of the writers of the 1930s considered not only important but also representative of popular culture. In the third volume Avra Theodoropoulou presented some leading modern Greek musicians in each issue.[41]

The *Anglo-Greek Review* poses other questions which are not easy to answer. Was it more of a British than a Greek journal? In other words, was the *Review* part of the British effort to win hearts and minds in Greece, or was it a magazine primarily controlled by Greek intellectuals? Who determined its editorial policy: its invisible Greek editor or the British who funded its publication? It is an open secret that George Katsimbalis was the driving force behind the magazine, but he never signed an editorial, an article or a translation (apart from the 'Hymn to Liberty' by Solomos which he did jointly with Theodore Stephanides). The Report of the British Council of 1945–46 states that the *Anglo-Greek Review* 'is edited by George Katsimbalis, the leading Greek literary critic and a well-known translator of modern Greek verse into English'.[42] It is not clear why he wished to remain anonymous as the editor of the magazine. Was it to avoid any accusations of serving the British or was it for some other reason? It appears that Katsimbalis took on the editorship in order to earn a living, as it transpires from a letter he wrote to Seferis.[43] Though he considers it one of the best Greek magazines, in his correspondence with Seferis he often appears tired of editing it and on the verge of giving up.[44] Writing to Seferis in May 1952 he mentions some uncertainty regarding funding, but later in the same month he confirms that London is determined to continue publishing the magazine at all costs.[45]

The *Review* seems to have tried to be educational and informative by offering surveys of developments in English literature and short articles on different aspects of British life, rather than to generate debate or introduce new literary trends. Apart from a few articles by Karantonis, it avoided becoming involved in current controversies.[46] Unlike other Greek magazines of the time, the *Anglo-Greek Review* was not concerned with the social role of art. The magazine was careful to avoid any provocations and was gradually adopting a more conciliatory attitude to the Left, in an attempt to culturally counterbalance the political and military involvement of Britain in Greece at the time. The British contributions to the magazine tended to be short, low-key, encyclopaedia-style articles rather than pieces intended to express a contentious viewpoint. It is not clear who chose these pieces or where they came from. To what extent it was Katsimbalis himself, the British Council or other sources who chose them is difficult to say at this stage. Generally speaking, it appears that the Council's role was limited to funding the *Review*, and generally promoting it. It was not 'their' publication, as some other publications (e.g. *Britain Today*) were.

In sum, the *Review* should not be seen on its own but as part of a nexus of public lectures, visits, exchanges, translations and reviews and the wider British strategy (involving the British Council and the BBC External Services) of promoting liberal democracy and offering a taste of British life and culture. It therefore contributed to the efforts made to create a conducive atmosphere and a favourable backdrop to the stage upon which politics and diplomacy were conducted. A kind of 'soft power', which was crucial at a time when Greece was ravaged by civil war and liberal democracy, was at stake. One can, of course, debate whether there are any clear lines between cultural propaganda, cultural diplomacy or image making, but it can be argued that the magazine did not so much represent a form of British propaganda as an attempt on the part of the British to support the liberal intelligentsia of Greece and offer them a respectable forum in which to express themselves and promote the country's cultural achievements. The success of the magazine lies in the fact that it was not uni-directional.

Modernism and canon consolidation

The *Anglo-Greek Review* is more of a critical review than a literary journal; it contains more critical essays than literary works. In its first period one can find very few literary texts, especially poems, in the magazine.[47] During that first period the *Review* focused exclusively on writers who had first appeared before the war and who engaged very little with contemporary literary developments. This suggests that the aim of the magazine was to present a number of English writers, mainly of the inter-war period, to the Greek public and to consolidate the canon of modern Greek poetry by promoting established Greek poets such as Dionysios Solomos, Kostis Palamas and Angelos Sikelianos, but no post-war poets.[48] During this period there was a renewed interest in Solomos' poetry thanks to the studies of Linos Politis, the book by Romilly Jenkins (*Dionysios Solomos*, 1940) and the translations of Robert Levesque into French (1945), Sikelianos had been nominated for the Nobel Prize for literature and Dimaras published his *History of Modern Greek Literature* in 1948–49.

On the other hand, Cavafy did not receive the attention that Sikelianos, Palamas and Seferis enjoyed. Though a few articles on the poet were published in the *Anglo-Greek Review*, there were undoubtedly reservations about his poetry, once again calling into question any modernist label which might otherwise be attached to the magazine. In particular Elytis' stance towards Cavafy was rather ambivalent, describing him as a great decadent poet but doubting his appeal to younger generations.[49]

Katsimbalis claimed that the *Anglo-Greek Review* was an important magazine comparable to *Ta Nea Grammata*. Indeed it could be argued that the *Review* contributed more to the reputation of Seferis than did *Ta Nea Grammata* and that it was instrumental in canonizing Greece's literary past. This canonization was supported by reprinting articles on Seferis by foreign critics and Andreas Karantonis, Dimitris Nikolareizis and Mitsos Papanikolaou. In a letter to Seferis in 1949 Katsimbalis wrote: 'we should make people followers of Seferis in small doses, otherwise a violent inoculation might kill them'.[50] In view of the magazine's strong support for Seferis it is surprising that Katsimbalis kept Alkis Thrylos on as its main book reviewer, given that she had been expressing reservations about Seferis' poetry since 1931. She even repeated her anti-modernist views in a brief review of *Logbook II* and '*Thrush*' published in the *Review*, claiming that Seferis was primarily an essayist and that poetry for him was just an experiment.[51] As an Anglophile she might have been imposed on Katsimbalis by the British Council, but her reviews further obfuscated the literary orientation of the *Review*.

How far, therefore, can the *Anglo-Greek Review* be seen as a magazine promoting modernist modes of writing? The magazine looked to the recent cultural past, and tried to canonize it, rather than addressing the present or the future. With the exception of Karantonis, who praised Lorentzatos and Sachinis[52] as promising critics and essayists, the *Anglo-Greek Review* avoided promoting any young post-war writers or challenging critical voices during its first period, relying instead on writers and critics of the 1920s (Thrylos,[53] Kleon Paraschos) and the 1930s (Karantonis, Aimilios Chourmouzios, Papanikolaou) or other rather more traditionally-minded critics and scholars (Michalis

BETWEEN PROPAGANDA AND MODERNISM

Peranthis, Vasilis Laourdas, Fanis Michalopoulos, Nikolaos Tomadakis). In the second period, under the editorship of Savidis, things changed and we come across contributions by post-war women writers such as Margarita Lymberaki, Kay Cicellis and Mimika Kranaki, a poem by Takis Sinopoulos, articles by Alkis Angelou and reviews by Alexandros Argyriou.

Katsimbalis' sensibility was more in line with the poetry of Palamas than with any modernist experimentation, which tended to leave him cold, if not outright hostile. He followed closely what was being published in the English press on modern Greek literature and tried to orchestrate its promotion as he saw fit or correct any 'misguided' assessments. In November 1950 he considered Rex Warner's usefulness as a publicist (and possibly as translator) for contemporary Greek poetry in Britain had run out of steam. Instead he turned his attention to Kenneth Young, though he did not know him personally. Young had recently published an article on the influence of Greek poetry in the work of Durrell and Bernard Spencer. Seferis did not think highly of this article. Katsimbalis claimed in a letter to Seferis that he had 'practically dictated' a subsequent article to Young.[54] He also hoped that MacNeice might write the book on Greece that Warner could not.[55] The *Review* helps us to understand Katsimbalis' approach to modern Greek literature and his attempts to promote it abroad. Taking all these things into account, one could argue that the *Review* presents us with a paradox. On the one hand, it was looking to the past and relying on traditional and conservative critics, and on the other it tried to promote Eliot and Seferis as modernist poets by focusing on the relationship between them. To what extent then can the magazine be seen as torn between traditional and modernist poetics?

In fact, I think the *Anglo-Greek Review* and more particularly its editor George Katsimbalis avoided such a conflict by focusing not on movements or trends but on individual writers and poets. Though the *Review* included a number of articles on Eliot and references to other modernists (Woolf, Joyce and, in its second period, Yeats),[56] it did not concern itself with poetic experimentation as such but with the relationship between Seferis and Eliot and how this relationship might be perceived or interpreted. Therefore, the focus was on Seferis and Eliot as leading poets rather than on literary modernity as a broader trend. Katsimbalis' primary concern was to promote Seferis' poetry and to show its international appeal and at the same time to refute any claims that Seferis was imitative of Eliot.

The study by Malanos on Seferis and Eliot further exacerbated the issue by suggesting that the former had imitated the latter and provoked a response from Philip Sherrard.[57] In his lecture to the British Institute published in the *Anglo-Greek Review*, Sherrard highlighted instead the contrast between the two poets, claiming that their poetry represented two different systems of thought and attitudes to life.[58] Seferis and the Greeks, he argued, were closer to the natural world and more 'primitive' compared to people in the West, who had lost touch with nature as a result of industrialization. Sherrard described what

136   DIMITRIS TZIOVAS

he called 'neo-paganism' as being healthier than the western detachment from nature, the senses or the body. Seferis belonged to a different intellectual tradition, and his quest was more earthly than the metaphysical and theological preoccupations of Eliot. Warner too points out that 'there is nothing mystical in Seferis' approach to his problems and here he differs profoundly from Eliot'.[59] Thus Seferis emerged not as an imitator of Eliot but as the representative of a cultural tradition distinct from that of the West. It was this cultural difference that attracted to Greece in the 1940s a number of British intellectuals, who tried to explore and define this exuberant neo-paganism.

Seferis was very cautious as to how the English reviews of his poetry were presented in the *Review*. To avoid any misunderstandings or accusations of interference he suggested to Katsimbalis that he should reprint in full only four or five, which he would select, and that he should simply mention some of the others.[60] The correspondence between Seferis and Katsimbalis reveals how methodically the image and reputation of Seferis was constructed both in and outside Greece and how the *Anglo-Greek Review* played a significant part in this process. Katsimbalis even claims that Dimaras waited for the issue on Seferis to be published before finalizing his history of Greek literature![61]

Undoubtedly everything submitted for publication on Seferis was carefully vetted. It is interesting to note that Spandonidis sent Seferis a review of *Thrush* in August 1948 for publication in the *Anglo-Greek Review* or elsewhere.[62] It was never published in the *Review* but it appeared later in *Makedonika Grammata*.[63] Reading it one can understand why it was not published in the *Review* and also why it attracted attention and praise from Malanos (though we cannot be sure that the published review is the same text as the one sent to Seferis).[64] The same vetting procedure was applied to translations of Seferis' poetry into English. Seferis considered Warner's translations the best and, along with Katsimbalis, expressed reservations about those by Kimon Friar and Rae Dalven.[65]

In general, it could be argued that the *Anglo-Greek Review* was not a modernist magazine as such, but aspired to consolidate the canonization of certain modern Greek poets and that it contributed enormously to constructing an international image for Seferis through a careful process of selection and networking. The so-called generation of the thirties owes a great deal of its reputation to the efforts of Katsimbalis who, in his role as editor, orchestrated its promotion in Greece and abroad. It can be said that the magazine represents one of the best illustrations of the mechanisms of canonization, manipulation and literary promotion.

The golden age of Anglo-Greek cultural interaction

Despite the fact that there were significant cultural contacts between Greece and Britain in the nineteenth century, due to the British presence in the Ionian Islands, the setting up of the British School at Athens in 1886 and the role

BETWEEN PROPAGANDA AND MODERNISM 137

played by certain individuals such as Andreas Kalvos, Alexandros Rizos Rangavis, Ioannes Gennadius, Dimitrios Vikelas and others, the period from the late 1930s to early 1950s could be claimed to be the golden era of Anglo-Greek cultural contacts.[66] During the 1940s a number of well-known scholars, writers and artists either worked in the British Institute or British Council in Athens, or lectured or exhibited there.[67] The leading Byzantinist Steven Runciman went to Greece in 1945 as British Council Representative and remained there until 1947.[68] The classicist Rex Warner was appointed as first Director of the British Institute of Higher Studies (1946) and was joined by Major Patrick Leigh Fermor as his deputy. In late 1945 and early 1946 both Runciman and Leigh Fermor lectured at the University of Athens, together with Harold Nicolson.[69] Runciman, Warner and Leigh Fermor may not have been great administrators, but they left their mark on Greek cultural life and on Anglo-Greek relations. They also contributed to the *Anglo-Greek Review*.

The same applies to Maurice Bowra, who came to Greece for the first time in September 1946 and gave two lectures at the British Institute in Athens. One of them, on 'Contemporary English Poetry', was published in the *Review* (2/9, November 1946) while his book *The Creative Experiment* (1949) included a chapter on Cavafy and the Greek past. Though a number of these people were classicists (Warner, Bowra, Scott-Kilvert) or Byzantinists (Runciman, Jenkins), they had a wide range of interests and were well-versed in modern literature. Rex Warner was a novelist himself. They also translated modern Greek poetry (Warner) or wrote articles (Bowra on Cavafy) and introductions to works of fiction (Scott-Kilvert in Kazantzakis' *Zorba the Greek*, London 1952).[70]

Other important figures who either visited Greece during the 1940s or contributed to the *Review*, or on whose work the magazine published articles included the Anglo-Irish poet Cecil Day-Lewis, who had an article published about him in the *Review* (4/10, April 1950); Stephen Spender; John Lehmann; and Louis MacNeice. Together with W.H. Auden, they shared left-wing views and became celebrated as the 'Thirties Poets'. Their verse, modern in its industrial imagery but traditional in form (against the prevailing modernist mood of the time), was polemical and articulated a wider unease at the political, economic and social crisis in Europe.

On the other hand, during the 1940s and early 1950s a number of Greek scholars, writers and artists visited, lived, worked or exhibited in London either as guests of the British Council or independently. Amongst others one could mention Nikos Kazantzakis, George Seferis, Zissimos Lorenzatos, Linos Politis, Nanos Valaoritis, Michael Cacoyannis, Yannis Tsarouchis and Apostolos Sachinis. Nanos Valaoritis also published an article in *Horizon* on modern Greek poetry 'as it has developed between the two wars and as it has emerged now out of this War' together with translations of poems.[71]

Studying the *Anglo-Greek Review* can offer a useful perspective on this golden age, and an article by Tasos Athanasiadis published in the magazine in December 1945 might serve as a starting point. In his article 'The Message of

English Prose Fiction in Greece' he makes the point that, until the 1930s, when there were growing signs of a shift towards Anglophone literature, French literature and German scholarship had been dominant in Greece.[72] According to Athanasiadis, Seferis was instrumental in this shift, and the translations of Eliot, Pound and Joyce also revitalized literary sensibilities in Greece, while the fiction writers of the 30s started to become aware of recent developments in English fiction.

A year later, in March 1946, Kleon Paraschos put forward a similar argument. He pointed out that, with the exception of the Ionian Islands, and some short periods around 1900 when German and Scandinavian literatures had made their presence felt in Greece, the dominant outside 'influence' on Greek literature had been French. After emerging from four years of occupation which, as Paraschos points out, hindered contacts with European cultural developments, Greece had an opportunity for a new cultural departure. Immediately before and after the war English literature started providing new directions for Greek writers to go in and once again Paraschos mentions Seferis and his translations of Eliot and Pound. He also claimed that fiction writers too were turning their attention to English-language fiction, because English and American fiction writers were the most innovative at that time. He predicted that English literary influence would soon oust the French and concluded, with reference to Goethe, that hybridization involving several totally different cultures was the most productive and rewarding process.[73]

It seems that the *Review* was making an effort to promote cultural interaction and understanding. English critics and scholars wrote on modern Greek poetry (Rex Warner on Seferis, Bowra on Cavafy) or novels (Romilly Jenkins on Ion Dragoumis' *Samothraki*) and Greek critics tried either to trace points of contact between modern Greek and English literature[74] or draw parallels between Greek and English poets.[75] Efforts were gradually made to break through the existing boundaries and Greeks started writing on English literature and arts (Sachinis on the English novel, Seferis on a Greek traveller to England, Terzakis on Ben Jonson, Valaoritis on Dylan Thomas and Lawrence Durrell, Chourmouzios on George Bernard Shaw, Skiadaresis on English music, Prokopiou on English art, Makris on English cinema) while the English continued to review Greek prose writers and poets.

In addition to the articles by Athanasiadis and Paraschos mentioned above, the publication of English critical views on Seferis and Swedish reviews of Sikelianos indicate an increased literary and critical exchange. In particular Seferis' 'Letter to an Englishman on Eliot' (4/1, January-February 1949) can be seen as a turning point.[76] This was Seferis' contribution to a volume dedicated to T.S. Eliot to mark his sixtieth birthday, and for the first time a Greek poet was writing in English for an English audience on a major modernist poet. Following Seferis' article the *Review* reprinted in volume 5 the views of foreign critics and scholars on Greek writers such as Elias Venezis, George Theotokas and Cavafy.

BETWEEN PROPAGANDA AND MODERNISM

One could argue that the level of cultural interaction between Greece and Britain increased from 1948 (the year the English translation of Seferis' poems was published[77]) onwards, as can be seen in the pages of the *Review*, and that it reached its peak in the succeeding years when a number of Greek novels were published in English translation (Elias Venezis' *Aeolia* (1949), George Theotokas' *Argo* (1951), Kazantzakis' *Zorba the Greek* (1952)).[78] It was even claimed in the *Review* that Venezis' novel was the first Greek novel to be translated into English, but, of course, this is misleading since earlier translations had appeared of Dimitrios Vikelas' *Loukis Laras* (1881) and Emmanouil Roidis' *Pope Joan* (one in 1886 and another in 1900). Nevertheless these translations were indicative of the impetus created by the magazine for cultural extroversion and interaction.

During this period there was an increasing emphasis on Europe, and this is reflected in a number of articles published in the *Review*. T.S. Eliot refers to it in his essay 'The Responsibility of the Man of Letters',[79] arguing that its cultural health was 'incompatible with extreme forms of both nationalism and internationalism'. And he concluded his article by saying that 'we have a mutual bond and a mutual obligation to a common ideal; and that on some questions we should speak for Europe, even when we speak only to our fellow-countrymen'. John Lehmann also wrote on English letters and the European vision (2/10, December 1946) while Linos Politis described Solomos in an essay as both a national and a European poet (2/8, October 1946) and later published his inaugural lecture at the University of Thessaloniki on modern Greek and European literature (4/3, April 1949). Karantonis also argued that the tendency until then had been to see Solomos in a kind of isolation and not working in the 'workshop of universal poetry'. Seferis, he claimed, was the first to place him in the context of European poetry and thanks to the contribution of others, such as Robert Levesque, Solomos was no longer seen as marginal and isolated but as a mainstream and contemporary European.[80] Papanoutsos also saw Seferis as somebody who combined being Greek (and proud of his nation), with being European (something better informed and more advanced),[81] while Rex Warner argued that 'it is because Seferis is so much a European that he is so aware of being Greek'.[82] In a way the *Anglo-Greek Review* expressed the cosmopolitanism and Europeanism which emerged after the Second World War, and it made a genuine effort to place modern Greek culture within a larger European context.

However, from the mid-1950s onwards 'the halcyon days of the Anglo-Greek honeymoon', in John Lehmann's words, were overshadowed by the Cypriot struggle for independence.[83] In his unpublished chronicle Anastasios Sagos, a British Council employee at the time, described that difficult period for the British Council, claiming that even the movement of its cars in Athens had to be restricted for fear that the occupants might be lynched by crowds of students enraged by the sight of British number plates. A bomb exploded on the premises of the Institute of English Studies on 16 December 1955 and mobs

140   DIMITRIS TZIOVAS

frequently attacked the British Embassy and the British Council.[84] After the deportation from Cyprus of Archbishop Makarios in March 1956, the Greek Government advised the British that they could not be responsible for the safety of those using the British Institute buildings in Athens and Thessaloniki and as a result both closed.[85]

Apart from the Cyprus troubles in the 1950s, the US was seen to play an increasing part in the region from the end of the forties, as they began to take over the cultural role hitherto played by Britain. In 1948 the Fulbright Foundation opened in Greece its second office worldwide and Elias Venezis was the first European writer to be invited to visit the US in the context of a programme of cultural exchanges set up by the State Department. M. Karagatsis was invited the following year and George Theotokas in 1952, while Katsimbalis wrote to Seferis that the Americans were not counting on him because they considered him a venal agent of the British Empire.[86] The discontinuation of the *Review* marked the waning of British cultural influence in Greece and its supplanting by the growing American cultural and political supremacy. It should be noted that culture during the Cold War was less something to be exchanged, and more a weapon in the battle to win hearts and minds. This battle was not so much concerned with promoting a country's best side, as to win the competition of two contrasting 'ways of life'.[87] Thus the humanist notion of culture ('the best of everything') gave way to its anthropological definition ('a way of life').

From Shelley's hell to a new myth of Greece

In the 1940s and early 1950s a new confidence is evident among Greeks and a re-appraisal of their relationship with Europe, involving efforts to shift attention from the ancient past to the present. The war and the Greek resistance effort had turned Europe's attention to Greece and made the Greeks more self-confident, encouraging them to see themselves increasingly as part of Europe. During the subsequent internal strife both camps looked to forces outside the country for support, accepting to some extent the idea that they were part of a wider ideological and cultural struggle. By publishing or reprinting certain articles, the *Anglo-Greek Review* played a crucial role in this new openness and the search for a new myth of Greece.

In the third issue of the *Anglo-Greek Review* an essay by Demetrios Capetanakis was reprinted from *Daylight* (1941). In this essay he calls for a new understanding of Greece and her people, a departure from the classical ideal, the prejudices of the past and the stereotypical clichés. He invited his readers to see Greeks not as history but as human beings and calls for a history of the Greek sensibility, from the Homeric age to the twentieth century, proposing something along the lines of what Virginia Woolf had attempted in *Orlando*. He pointed out:

> The Greeks of today are neither lingering specimens of a race that worked wonders two thousand years ago, nor a Balkan people, without any past and without any roots in the history of their land. If one wants to understand them, one must connect them to the whole rather than to some periods of their history, and see them at the same time as modern Europeans. It would be a great pity if the Greeks were still what they were at the time of Pericles. The history of their sensibility would be much too poor [sic].[88]

The modern Greek was very proud of his ancestors, Capetanakis claimed, but he did not much like to be considered only in relation to them.

Though the *Anglo-Greek Review* had published several articles on antiquity,[89] Byzantium appears to receive increasing attention with articles by Steven Runciman, V.N. Tatakis, P.A. Michelis, Dionysios Zakythinos, Nikos Veis (Bees), Emmanouil Kriaras, Manolis Chatzidakis (mainly in the second period) and others. In an article on English historians of medieval and modern Greece, Steven Runciman points out that the English contribution to the study of classical Greece is well known and valued, but the corresponding contribution to the study of medieval and modern Greece is little known and could be further developed. He concluded his article by saying that Greece was not only its classical past but its great monasteries of Hosios Loukas and Mount Athos, the churches of Thessaloniki, the heroic sites of Missolonghi, Souli and the Pindos and the villages burnt out by the Germans.[90] This emphasis on Byzantium continued during the second period when Yeats's poem 'Sailing to Byzantium' (translated by G.P. Savidis) was published along with articles on Byzantine art including photographs of paintings and frescoes.[91]

In the periods immediately before and after the Second World War there was a rediscovery of Greece driven by an interest in modern literature, combined with an emphasis on the country's material distinctiveness (landscape, light, food, pleasure).[92] This rediscovery was different from the one in the early nineteenth century, which was based on the ideal of antiquity, or the survivalist-inspired one of the early twentieth century, which highlighted, for instance, the connections between ancient religion and modern folklore.[93] If the former rediscovery was based on a humanist conception of culture and the latter on an anthropological one, the one in the 1940s tried to combine both notions. The architects of this new Philhellenism, such as Henry Miller and Lawrence Durrell, came to Greece with little, if any, classical baggage. The post-Byronic cliché of disparaging the modern Greek and comparing them to their ancient ancestors is replaced in the writings of Miller and Durrell by 'a new perspective and a new mode of imagining the country based on what they could actually see and what might then be translated into a contemporary idiom'.[94] And this new mode of writing about the country had a strong influence on the post-war new philhellenes.

Idealism and survivalism seem to give way to existentialism, while a different appreciation of modern Greek culture, particularly literature, was under

142 DIMITRIS TZIOVAS

way, a process in which the *Anglo-Greek Review* became involved. This is signalled in an article by Lawrence Durrell, 'Hellene and Philhellene', published anonymously in the *Times Literary Supplement* in 1949 and soon afterwards published in translation in the *Anglo-Greek Review*, which shifted the focus from classical antiquity to the exuberance of contemporary Greeks, the radiance of Greek light and, most importantly, modern Greek literature as something worth reading, studying and translating.[95]

In his article Durrell drew a distinction 'between the Philhellene of yesterday and the Philhellene of today', arguing that almost up to 'the present generation the passionate bias of the English writer and scholar has been towards the classical world'.[96] He claimed that the classical bias had tended to blindfold the traveller who had been tempted to dismiss the Greeks of their own day with contempt. Durrell reminds his readers of how Trelawney recorded Shelley's emotions on being taken aboard a dirty Greek caique at Leghorn. When Shelley was asked: 'Does this realize your idea of Hellenism?' he replied, 'No. But it does of Hell.' Starting from the Victorians and making reference to Sir Rennell Rodd, G.F. Abbott and Virginia Woolf, he reviews attitudes to Greece in order to show that the classical scholar gradually began to find himself no longer at sea in modern Greece but rather at home. They had begun, Durrell points out, 'to see the Greeks as something more than Homeric silhouettes'. Durrell's rediscovery of Greece is completed by a sketch of modern Greek literature since 1821 in order 'to try to establish whether there are signs that Greek writing has begun to assume a European, instead of a purely national validity'.

The new Philhellenism advocated by Durrell represented a radical change in the sense that 'the modern Greek has become more than worthy of the admiration that was too often in the past reserved for his ancestors'. The new Philhellenes do not search for the idealized Hellas without setting foot in the country or look to discover traces of antiquity in ruins or modern folklore; instead, according to Durrell, they appreciate modern literature as it 'is struggling out of the swaddling-clothes of purely political or national aspiration towards a universalist validity, a European significance'. Modern literature brings Greece closer to Europe and for the new Philhellenes this connection seems more relevant than that with antiquity. Interviewed in 1947 for the position of deputy editor of the Greek Section of the BBC External Services, Durrell said: 'When I first went to Corfu in 1935 I began to realise that England constricts the sensibilities of man, whereas Greece opens them out.'[97]

In a turbulent period of war and civil conflict what mattered for the new Philhellenes was personal discovery and not political action. The new geography of Greece was masculine and some of these new Philhellenes were gay. As David Roessel points out: 'When politics mattered in the English and American construction of Greece, the country was routinely personified as female. Greece gained a masculine personification abroad when political concerns were not taken into account.'[98] Most of the texts written by the new

BETWEEN PROPAGANDA AND MODERNISM

Philhellenes engage neither with Nazi violence nor with that of the Greek Civil War, but try to separate the sights and sounds of Greece from its politics. The sacred landscape seems impervious to the atrocities of war, as in the following disclaimer by Rex Warner in his book *Views of Attica* (1950):

> It is by no means my purpose to attempt any kind of description of the civil war in Greece. I shall be chiefly concerned with sights and sounds, colours and places. Violence, savagery, poverty, irreconcilable hatreds are not part of my theme, yet it is only too true that they exist.[99]

It could be said that the *Anglo-Greek Review* contributed to this shift from politics to landscape and the appreciation of modern literature by reprinting or otherwise promoting the views of the new Philhellenes.

In 1949 Ian Scott-Kilvert, in an article tellingly entitled 'Hellenic Revival', discusses 'the amazing and too little-known development of contemporary literature in Greece' with reference to the work of Sikelianos, Seferis, Kazantzakis, Capetanakis, Elytis and Engonopoulos. There he argues that veneration for the classics 'led too many to exalt the ancients as a breed of Aryan demi-Gods and write off the moderns as a race of Balkan shopkeepers'.[100] Again we witness a shift away from antiquity towards modernity, and this is expressed in terms of discovering modern Greek literature.

A year later, in 1950, Kenneth Young adopted a similar line, talking about the rediscovery of Greece.[101] Not what E.M. Forster called 'public school Greece', but a country where 'the people open up like flowers' and where, in the words of Henry Miller, 'every event no matter how stale is always unique'. This rediscovery is much concerned with 'the reality of the self', and Young illustrates this by quoting Durrell: 'Other countries may offer you discoveries in manners of lore or landscape; Greece offers you something harder – the discovery of yourself.'[102] An appreciation of the 'real' Greece, according to Young, constituted an implicit criticism of and a desire to escape from life in the western world. Far from being a retreat or a throw-back to an earlier stage in European history, Greece offered an answer to the 'problem of philosophical *angst*'. Modern Greek poetry in particular 'is built upon, and impregnated with, angst', Young claims, and thus the existentialist rediscovery of the country goes hand in hand with the discovery of its poetry. Young notes the diffusion of knowledge about Cavafy, Seferis and other Greek poets outside Greece and tries to trace Greek influences on British poets such as Durrell and Spencer. It appears that for the first time modern Greek literature was not only being taken seriously, but was being seen as capable of having an impact on foreign writers.[103]

Indeed during the 1940s and 50s there seems to have been a new appreciation of the Greeks themselves and the country's landscape by certain scholars, artists and travellers as can be seen in the book *Eternal Greece* (1953) with text by Rex Warner and photographs by Martin Hürlimann. In his Introduction

144 DIMITRIS TZIOVAS

Rex Warner also tries to counterbalance the schoolmaster's picture of classical Greece with that of a modern anthropologist. The emphasis is no longer on harmony but on contradictions, not on statues inside the walls of a museum but on the intense life, radiant light and unique landscape. Though the book contains photographs of and chapters on ancient sites, Rex Warner tries to define 'eternal Greece' in the following way:

> When we say that the achievements of the Greeks or that Greece herself is 'eternal' we mean, among many other things, that the place and spirit, even the achievements themselves, extend both forwards and backwards in time. We also mean to suggest by the word 'eternal' a quality of intense and radiant life, something that scarcely suits with a museum or, at any rate, a museum in northern Europe. . . . In fact museums are not always enlightening and however necessary it may be to put statues in cages, it must still be remembered that they were meant for a free and brilliant air and to be seen against a landscape that is absolutely unique. Sea, rocks and islands, that golden light, the perfume of aromatic shrubs – none of these are to be found inside the walls of a museum.[104]

The classical Greece of museums in northern Europe is contrasted with the liveliness of the contemporary landscape, inviting people to study Greece in situ and not in vitro. This is what Robert Liddell does in his idiosyncratic travel book *Aegean Greece* (1954) (reviewed in the *Anglo-Greek Review*) where he celebrates the Aegean as 'a type or foretaste of Paradise'. His travel guide-cum-ethnographic study combines topography with anthropology by focusing on landscape and trying to offer insights into the Greeks and their culture: 'I love the Greeks, though not quite blindly, and I usually dissent from unflattering generalizations about them, nevertheless one such generalization I must venture to make: they have no interior life.'[105]

Earlier, in a similar vein, in his book *Classical Landscapes with Figures* (1947) Osbert Lancaster, who had been Press Attaché at the British Embassy in Athens in 1944–45, claimed:

> The Greeks are of all people the least inhibited (it is significant that the only two professional psychoanalysts practising in Athens have large private incomes) and their passions, both amorous and political, are seldom indulged under a bushel. But whereas elsewhere politics may do little to enrich the landscape, here they find visible expression in a variety of ways all of which lend character to the scene and which to omit would falsify the whole.[106]

Adopting a humanist perspective, he tried to see landscape and people, past and present as inseparable, pointing out that the inhabitants were part of the landscape and 'that were they omitted the picture would take on an unreal lunar bareness carrying no conviction to those acquainted with the reality'.[107]

BETWEEN PROPAGANDA AND MODERNISM 145

Without ignoring antiquity, Lancaster placed the emphasis on the present and argued that history is a 'meaningless fantasy if not interpreted in the light of present-day experience'.[108]

Landscape emerges as a hybrid topography of aestheticist purity and orientalist pleasure, the crucial link between Greece as a still sacred precinct and as a modern Dionysian place[109] or 'a private country' (the title of Lawrence Durrell's first poetry collection [1943]). The celebration of the Greek landscape and its people leads to a revitalization of the past through the present and to a 'new philhellenism which has grown up during and since the war' and of which Stephen Spender speaks with reference to the book by Rex Warner and Martin Hürlimann.[110] He argues that in this book the classical element has been given new life from contemporary Greece and that this rediscovered love of Greece has nothing to do with current Greek politics: 'Modern Greece opens on to the "eternal Greece" not through politics, but through the landscape and the people, and through modern Greek poetry.'[111] Spender considers that the nineteenth-century English public school ideal of Greek moderation or Nietzsche's discovery of the Dionysian aspect of Greek poetry were of little use in the 1950s. According to him Greece held the secrets of life by treating artistic creation and the enjoyment of life as parts of the shared life of the community.

In an unpublished draft of an essay in French Seferis has described the enterprise of the new Philhellenes as 'une nouvelle sorte de Byronisme', and David Roessel adopted the term 'new Byronism' to define the rediscovery after the Second World War of Greece as a land of sensation and rough physicality.[112] However what he does not mention is that the new Byronism was first outlined in the *Anglo-Greek Review* in articles such as the one by Nanos Valaoritis on 'Lawrence Durrell and the Myth of Greek Landscape' with its references to Byron. Interestingly Valaoritis' article was published in the same issue (4/5, July-August 1949) as Durrell's anonymous, but influential, article 'Hellene and Philhellene'.

From the foregoing it could be concluded that in the 1940s and early 1950s there was an anthropological rediscovery of Greece, blending the aesthetics of landscape with homoerotic hedonism,[113] amplified by a new appreciation of modern literature (e.g. the English translation of *Zorba the Greek*). It is important to stress that, unlike earlier ones, this rediscovery did not assign priority to antiquity at the expense of modernity. Instead it tried to discover the 'eternal' Greece through the perspective of the present, and the country was seen emerging as a modern site of energy, creativity and pleasure and not simply as a site of ancient ruins and past glories. During the 1940s and 1950s 'the geographical center of Greece had shifted from the Acropolis, Marathon, or Missolonghi to the tavernas and cafes of Athens'.[114] The image of Greece as an exotic land for tourists and an earthly paradise for intellectuals has its origins in this period. The *Anglo-Greek Review* was part of this wider process and made a significant contribution to this new myth of Greece and its culture.

DIMITRIS TZIOVAS

Notes

1 The most comprehensive of these studies is the book by Robert Holland and Diana Markides, *The British and the Hellenes: Struggles for Mastery in the Eastern Mediterranean, 1850–1960* (Oxford, 2006). See also the study by Marina Petraki, Βρετανική πολιτική και προπαγάνδα στον ελληνοϊταλικό πόλεμο (Athens, 2011).

2 Thomas W. Gallant, *Experiencing Dominion: Culture, Identity, and Power in the British Mediterranean* (Notre Dame, IN, 2002), David Wills, *The Mirror of Antiquity: 20th Century British Travellers in Greece* (Newcastle, 2007), Vassiliki Kolocotroni and Efterpi Mitsi (eds.), *Women Writing Greece: Essays on Hellenism, Orientalism and Travel* (Amsterdam and New York, 2008), Mary Roussou-Sinclair, *Victorian Travellers in Cyprus: A Garden of Their Own* (Nicosia, 2002).

3 Richard Clogg, 'The British School at Athens and the Modern History of Greece', in *Anglo-Greek Attitudes: Studies in History* (Basingstoke, 2000), pp. 19–35 and Jim Potts, 'Truth Will Triumph: The British Council and Cultural Relations in Greece', in David Wills (ed.), *Greece and Britain Since 1945* (Newcastle, 2010), pp. 99–129, and his chapter in the present volume. See also Michael Llewellyn-Smith, Paschalis M. Kitromilides and Eleni Calligas (eds.), *Scholars, Travels, Archives: Greek History and Culture Through the British School at Athens* (London, 2009).

4 Philip M. Taylor, *The Projection of Britain: British Overseas Publicity and Propaganda 1919–1939* (Cambridge, 1981), pp. 125–78.

5 Frances Donaldson, *The British Council: The First Fifty Years* (London, 1984), pp. 58, 60–61. Anastasios Sagos offers further details in his unpublished study *A Chronicle of the British Council Office in Athens 1938–1986* (Athens: privately reproduced typescript, 1995).

6 Donaldson, *The British Council*, p. 147.

7 See the chapter by Lucile Arnoux-Farnoux in this volume.

8 Gioula Koutsopanagou, 'Προπαγάνδα και απελευθέρωση: Το Βρετανικό Συμβούλιο και ο Ελληνοσοβιετικός Σύνδεσμος στις παραμονές του εμφυλίου πολέμου (1945)', *Μνήμων*, 22 (2000), pp. 171–90, and the same author's chapter in this volume.

9 Donaldson, *The British Council*, p. 89. It should be noted that during the 1940s and early 1950s a number of books in English on modern Greece were published, particularly by classicists such as A.R. Burn (*The Modern Greeks* (London, 1944)) and A.W. Gomme (*Greece* (London, 1945)) who both taught Ancient History at the University of Glasgow.

10 'Το Βρετανικό Συμβούλιο', *Anglo-Greek Review*, 2/1 (March 1946), p. 27.

11 Ouranis' praise of England verges on hyperbole: 'When a Greek, whether belonging to the people or to the educated classes, pronounces the word "England", the tone of his voice is entirely different from when he pronounces the name of any other country. . . . All that England represents for us is the ideal to which a nation can strive – and reach. . . . We admire everything of hers and all that is English – from her institutions to her manufactured goods.

"English" is for us synonym[ous] with the best and the strongest that exists of its kind' (Costas Ouranis, 'What We Feel for England', *Anglo-Greek Review*, 1/1 (March 1945), p. 4).

12 In his article ('British Culture Abroad', *Contemporary Review*, 148 (July-December 1935), pp. 201–7) Leeper drew attention to what other countries such as France, Germany and Italy had been doing for a long time.

13 Quoted in Taylor, *The Projection of Britain*, p. 144.

14 Reginald Leeper, *When Greek Meets Greek* (London, 1950), p. XXII.

15 The first issue of the *Anglo-Greek Review* is not very diverse or ambitious in its scope. Apart from the articles by Leeper and Ouranis, it includes the first fifteen stanzas of the 'Hymn to Liberty' by Solomos translated by Theodore Stephanides and George Katsimbalis, an article by George Theotokas on 'The Fate of John Keats' reprinted from *Ta Nea Grammata* (January 1935), a couple of sonnets by Keats, a theatre review, extracts from the Greek underground press of 1943, brief reports on the British burden of war, Britain's war achievements, British aid to its allies, exploits of Greek submarines, and a piece from the House of Commons on septennial Parliaments dated 13 March 1734.

16 One can find further details regarding the magazine and its contributors in the unpublished doctoral thesis of Marina Kokkinidou, 'Το περιοδικό Αγγλοελληνική Επιθεώρηση (1945–1955): περίοδοι, στόχοι και συμβολή του στη μεταπολεμικη πολιτισμικη ζωή', unpublished doctoral dissertation, Aristotle University of Thessaloniki, 2002.

17 It is surprising that the magazine was called Anglo-Greek and not Anglo-Hellenic, following the example of the Anglo-Hellenic League, founded in the aftermath of the 1912–13 Balkan wars in order to counter anti-Greek propaganda in Britain. The League published the biannual *Anglo-Hellenic Review* (1990–2014).

18 G.K. Katsimbalis and Giorgos Seferis, 'Αγαπητέ μου Γιώργο': Αλληλογραφία *(1924–1970)*, ed. Dimitris Daskalopoulos (Athens, 2009), vol. 2, p. 16, vol. 2, pp. 36, 218, 220. It should be noted that the English translations of the Greek texts published in the *Review* are often somewhat shaky.

19 See Peter Mackridge, 'Χρονολόγιο Κοσμά Πολίτη (Πάρι Ταβελούδη)', *Διαβάζω*, 116 (10 April 1985), p. 11 and Yiorgos Kallinis, ' "Αγαπητή Μέλπω": Οκτώ επιστολές του Κοσμά Πολίτη προς τη Μέλπω Αξιώτη', *Νέα Εστία*, 155/1767 (May 2004), pp. 741–53. The letters of Kosmas Politis in the Greek press regarding his dismissal by the British Council are reprinted in Yiorgos Kallinis, *Σχεδίασμα Βιβλιογραφίας Κοσμά Πολίτη (1930–2000)* (Thessaloniki, 2008), pp. 56–59. In his letters Politis blames Katsimbalis for his dismissal and attributes a favourable review of his own work in the *Anglo-Greek Review*, immediately afterwards, to the tricks and manoeuvres of British propaganda.

20 See Katerina Kostiou (ed.), 'Κυπριακές' επιστολές του Σεφέρη *(1954–1962)*: *από την αλληλογραφία του με τον Γ.Π. Σαββίδη* (Nicosia, 1991), p. 30.

21 Though he stresses his long-standing ties with England in a letter to Savidis (29 November 1954), Seferis expresses his disappointment at British propaganda with regard to Cyprus and the role they were playing there and states that

148   DIMITRIS TZIOVAS

his refusal to publish his poems in the *Anglo-Greek Review* is a 'matter of conscience' for him (Kostiou (ed.), *'Κυπριακές' επιστολές του Σεφέρη*, pp. 56–61).

22 We observe a similar change in the Greek title of the article by Dilys Powell 'Nationality and Cinema' which is rendered in Greek as 'The National Character in Cinema' (1/9, November 1945). It appears that there is a preoccupation with the national character or the national psychology at the time, to judge by the reprint of an article by George Theotokas 'Some Questions of Modern Greek Psychology' (1/5, July 1945) first published in English in the magazine *The Link* (June 1938) and an article by N.B. Tomadakis entitled 'The National Character of Cretan Literature' (1/8, October 1945).

23 Sir Henry Dale, 'International Activities in Science' (1/5, July 1945) and 'Peaceful Uses of the War Discoveries' (1/10, December 1945), J.D. Bernal 'Science and Human Affairs', F. Sherwood Taylor 'The M & B Discover' (both in 1/7, September 1945) and R. McNair Wilson, 'Lord Lister, the Father of Modern Surgery', (2/2, April 1946).

24 'Development of the British Cinema' (1/8, October 1945) by an anonymous critic from the Anglo-Greek Information Service [A.G.I.S], Dilys Powell, 'British Film Today' (1/11–12, January-February 1946) and later G.N. Makris, 'Ο αγγλικός κινηματογράφος' (5/11, May-June 1952).

25 *Report of The British Council 1945–1946* (Name of Representative: The Hon. Steven Runciman) (London, 1946), p. 37.

26 *Report of The British Council 1946–1947* (Name of Representative: W.G. Tatham M.C.) (London, 1947), p. 53.

27 *Report of The British Council 1947–1948* (Name of Representative: W.G. Tatham M.C.) (London, 1948), p. 55.

28 Ian Scott-Kilvert was then working at the British Council in London and had gone out for a period of temporary duty to help out the Athens office of the Council when they were 'stretched'. His report is available in the British Council files at the National Archives in London (TNA, BW 34/19: 'Greece: General Policy').

29 Though he contributed to the magazine during its second period, Alexandros Argyriou calls *The Anglo-Greek Review* a 'propagandistic periodical of English culture' with almost exclusively English themes in its first volume (Introduction to *Η μεταπολεμική πεζογραφία: Από τον πόλεμο του '40 ως τη δικτατορία του '67* (Athens, 1996), vol. 1, p. 97).

30 'How Britain's Parliament works', *Anglo-Greek Review*, 1/2 (April 1945), p. 22.

31 M. Rodas, 'The Theatre during Occupation: Shakespeare Under Ban', *Anglo-Greek Review*, 1/2 (April 1945), p. 16.

32 In 1/4 (June 1945) of the *Anglo-Greek Review* there are two other articles on freedom, one by Cyril Forster Garbett, 'Freedom that Came from Faith' and the other by John Lehmann 'These Pens Wrote for Freedom'. In the following issue (1/5, July 1945) there is an article by Kent Cooper on the freedom of the press.

33 Defending the autonomy of art, Apostolos Sachinis also argued that sociopolitical events have little significance for art ('Η αυτονομία της τέχνης', *Anglo-Greek Review*, 2/2 (April 1946), pp. 60–61).

BETWEEN PROPAGANDA AND MODERNISM 149

34 Petros Haris also writes on intellectual freedom in the *Anglo-Greek Review* (1/7 (September 1945), pp. 18–20).

35 Andreas Karantonis, *Μια Φωνή* (there is no date on the pamphlet but it must have been published before April 1949 when it was reviewed in the *Anglo-Greek Review* by Alkis Thrylos (4/3 (April 1949), pp. 119–20)). On the copy of the pamphlet that I consulted (housed in the University of Crete library), the following information has been added on the front cover by typewriter: Ἐπιστολή τοῦ συγγραφέως κ. Ἀνδρέα Καραντώνη πρός τούς ἀποπλανηθέντας ἤ βιαίως στρατολογηθέντας ὑπό τῶν κομμουνιστῶν κατά τῆς Πατρίδος' ['Letter from the author Mr Andreas Karantonis to those who have been duped or violently mobilized by the communists against the Homeland'].

36 Katsimbalis and Seferis, *'Αγαπητέ μου Γιώργο'*, vol. 2, p. 24. In his memoirs John Lehmann notes that the *Anglo-Greek Review* was 'not a propaganda sheet but a serious cultural review with first-class contributions, and a larger circulation than any other similar paper in the country' (*The Ample Proposition: Autobiography III* (London, 1966), p. 65).

37 G.P. Savidis, *Σπουδές, δράση και εργασίες. Υπόμνημα προς τη Φιλοσοφική Σχολή του Αριστοτελείου Πανεπιστημίου Θεσσαλονίκης για υποψηφιότητα στην έκτακτη αυτοτελή έδρα της Νεώτερης Ελληνικής Φιλολογίας* (Athens, 1966), p. 9.

38 Taylor, *The Projection of Britain*, pp. 125–26.

39 T.S. Eliot, 'The Responsibilities of the Man of Letters', *Anglo-Greek Review*, 1/3 (May 1945), p. 14.

40 There is only a short article by Costas Biris on 'The English Church in Athens', which was built in the nineteenth century, to the design of the Greek architect Stamatis Kleanthis, by the Danish architect Hans Christian Hansen (3/2 (June 1947), pp. 57–58).

41 Antiochos Evangelatos, Yeorgios Sklavos, Andreas Nezeritis, Theodoros Karyotakis, Menelaos Pallantios, Solon Michailides, Yannis Papaioannou, Yeorgios Kazasoglou, Nikos Skalkottas, Leonidas Zoras, Stavros Prokopiou, Alekos Kontis.

42 *Report of The British Council 1945–1946*, p. 37.

43 Katsimbalis and Seferis, *'Αγαπητέ μου Γιώργο'*, vol. 2, p. 220.

44 Ibid., pp. 290, 296, 308, 322.

45 Ibid., pp. 290, 296. In Ian Scott-Kilvert's report (31 December 1948/ 4 January 1949) it is acknowledged that 'Mr Katsimbalis needs some administrative help'.

46 'Κιτρινισμός, ένα συμπέρασμα' (3/5, September 1947), 'Η ελληνική Περιοχή' (3/6, October 1947), 'Ακριβολογία και ωραιολογία της κριτικής' (3/12). See also the article on the National Theatre by Petros Charis ('Ο απολογισμός μιας μάχης', 2/4 (June 1946)).

47 In the first issue an extract from 'Hymn to Liberty' by Solomos and two sonnets by Keats were published, followed by Kipling's 'If' and Sikelianos' 'The Sacred Way' in the second, 'Attic Morn' from *The King's Flute* by Palamas in the third and two poems by Byron in the tenth. In the second volume of the magazine

150   DIMITRIS TZIOVAS

short stories appeared by a number of British writers (John Galsworthy (no. 1), D.H. Lawrence (no. 2), Aldous Huxley (no. 3), Hugh Walpole (no. 4), Virginia Woolf (no. 6), Katherine Mansfield (no. 7) and Francis Brett Young (no. 8)). For some of the same authors as they appeared in the magazine *Prosperos* see Theodosis Pylarinos' chapter in this volume.

48 Alkis Thrylos reviewed very few post-war writers. Her reviews in the *Anglo-Greek Review* have now been reprinted in the volume Alkis Thrylos, *Κριτική: Πεζογραφία, Ποίηση, Δοκίμιο (1945–1965)* (Athens, 2010).

49 Odysseas Elytis, 'Πέντε κορυφαίοι νεοέλληνες λυρικοί: Σολωμός-Κάλβος-Παλαμάς-Καβάφης-Σικελιανός', *Anglo-Greek Review*, 1/7 (September 1945), pp. 23–24. See also the reservations of Linos Politis, 'Μορφές του νεοελληνικού λυρισμού', *Anglo-Greek Review*, 2/12 (February 1947), p. 420 and Andreas Karantonis, 'Παλαμάς-Καβάφης-Σικελιανός', *Anglo-Greek Review*, 4/7 (November-December 1949), pp. 261–62.

50 Katsimbalis wrote in (approximately spelt) French: 'Il faut seferiser les gens par petites doses, une trop violente innoculation pourrait les tuer. . . '. Katsimbalis and Seferis, *'Αγαπητέ μου Γιώργο'*, vol. 2, p. 113.

51 Alkis Thrylos, 'Τα βιβλία', *Anglo-Greek Review*, 3/7 (November-December 1947), p. 223.

52 Andreas Karantonis, 'Ένας νέος κριτικός', *Anglo-Greek Review*, 4/1 (January-February 1949), pp. 27–29.

53 Though she was a regular reviewer of books during the magazine's first period, her husband, the poet Costas Ouranis, contributed only four pieces and they were all published in the first two volumes.

54 Kenneth Young, 'The Contemporary Greek Influence on English Writers', *Life and Letters*, 64/149 (1950), pp. 53–64. For Seferis' poor opinion of this article see Katsimbalis and Seferis, *'Αγαπητέ μου Γιώργο'*, vol. 2, p. 215. Young was married to a Greek woman who died in the summer of 1950 (ibid., p. 211). In 1969 he published his book *The Greek Passion: A Study in People and Politics*, which tends to be supportive of the military junta in Greece (its third part 'contains the first full account of the events leading to the military coup d'état in Greece on 21st April 1967, and of the acts and aims of the Government since that time'). The reference to Katsimbalis 'practically dictating' an article to Young appears in Katsimbalis and Seferis, *'Αγαπητέ μου Γιώργο'*, vol. 2, p. 211. Richard Clogg calls Young's book 'an apology for the Colonels'. He adds that Young was an adviser to the Colonels on press legislation, and he even surmises that Young wrote his book at the behest of the military junta: Richard Clogg, *Greek to me: A Memoir of Academic Life* (London, 2018), pp. 60-61. Katsimbalis told Seferis that this article was to be published in the English magazine *World Review* in November or December 1950, but it failed to appear in either of these issues. It is not known whether it was ever published.

55 Ibid., p. 235. Warner actually published two books on Greece, one in 1950 (*Views of Attica and its Surroundings*) and another in 1953 (Rex Warner and Martin Hürlimann, *Eternal Greece* (London, 1953)).

56 The other magazine, *Prosperos*, published by the British Council in Corfu also included in its first issue (1949) translations of T.S. Eliot and Virginia Woolf.

57 Timos Malanos, *Η ποίηση του Σεφέρη: Κριτική μελέτη* (Alexandria 1951). See also Katsimbalis and Seferis, *'Αγαπητέ μου Γιώργο'*, vol. 2, pp. 198–201, 258–63.

58 Philip Sherrard, *'Η ποίηση του Τ.S. Eliot και του Σεφέρη: Μια αντίθεση'*, *Anglo-Greek Review*, 5/8 (November-December 1951), pp. 306–11. It is worth noting that when it was reprinted, almost fifty years later, the title was changed to: *'Τ.Σ. Έλιοτ και Σεφέρης: Ένας παραλληλισμός'* in his book *Η Μαρτυρία του Ποιητή* (Athens, 1998), pp. 79–102. See also the comment by K.Th. Dimaras, *'Αντίθεση και μίμηση'*, *Anglo-Greek Review*, 5/11 (May-June 1952), p. 451.

59 Rex Warner, *'Εισαγωγή στο έργο του Σεφέρη'*, *Anglo-Greek Review*, 3/7 (November-December 1947), p. 202. Louis MacNeice, reviewing Rex Warner's translation of Seferis' *Poems*, returns to the influence of Eliot on Seferis, saying 'Seferis as a young poet was inspired and influenced by Eliot's *Marina*, but in his own work the sea is both more personal and more Greek' (Louis MacNeice, 'A Modern Odyssey', *New Statesman*, 17 December 1960, p. 978).

60 Katsimbalis and Seferis, *'Αγαπητέ μου Γιώργο'*, vol. 2, pp. 72, 98, 112, 113, 143.

61 Ibid., pp. 125, 145.

62 Ibid., pp. 79, 180.

63 P.S. Spandonidis, *'Η "Κίχλη" του Γ. Σεφέρη'*, *Makedonika Grammata*, 4 (July-August 1951), pp. 22–31.

64 Timos Malanos, *'Η κριτική και η νέα μας ποίηση'*, *Νέα Εστία*, 51/590 (1 February 1952), pp. 194–95 (and the exchanges between Malanos and Petros Haris in subsequent issues). See also Yannis Hatzinis' review of Sherrard's study in *Νέα Εστία*, 52/600 (1 July 1952), pp. 899–900.

65 Katsimbalis and Seferis, *'Αγαπητέ μου Γιώργο'*, vol. 2, pp. 106, 212, 215, 219, 221, 258, 279, 441, 447.

66 In 1982 a former Greek Minister of Culture is quoted saying: 'The intellectual life of Athens after the war was formed by the British Council' (Donaldson, *The British Council*, p. 147). The year that the *Anglo-Greek Review* first appeared Aimilios Chourmouzios, following a trip to England, proposed the publication of an elegant magazine in English with translations of Greek literary texts (*'Η λογοτεχνία μας στην Αγγλία'*, *Νέα Εστία*, 38/436 (15 August 1945), pp. 721–22). Also in 1945 G. Georgiadis-Arnakis wrote in *Nea Estia* about medieval English literature.

67 In the 1940s some Greeks wrote on English culture, praised the role of England during and after the Second World War and suggested closer ties between the two countries. A characteristic example is the journalist and critic Lazaros Piniatoglou, *Αγγλικός πολιτισμός* (Athens, 1944) and *'Η Αγγλία και η Ελλάς στον πόλεμο και στην ειρήνη'* in his volume *Ελληνικά προβλήματα* (Athens, 1945), pp. 1–42). Both books were reviewed by Alkis Thrylos, *'Ομολογίες πίστης'*, *Anglo-Greek Review*, 1/4 (June 1945), pp. 28–29.

68 For more details about his movements during the 1940s see Minoo Dinshaw, *Outlandish Knight: The Byzantine Life of Steven Runciman* (London, 2016).

69 Harold Nicolson's talk on Byron's *Childe Harold* was published in the *Anglo-Greek Review* (1/10, December 1945).

152 DIMITRIS TZIOVAS

70 The Introduction was removed from subsequent editions of the translation. Ian Scott-Kilvert's Greek wife translated Elias Venezis, *Aeolia* (London, 1949), which was published with a preface by Lawrence Durrell.

71 Valaoritis, 'Modern Greek Poetry'.

72 Tasos Athanasiadis, 'Το μήνυμα της αγγλικής πεζογραφίας', *Anglo-Greek Review*, 1/10 (December 1945), pp. 9–10. See also the earlier article by Angelos Terzakis, 'Επιδράσεις στη νεοελληνική λογοτεχνία', *Anglo-Greek Review*, 1/4 (June 1945), pp. 14–15.

73 Kleon Paraschos, 'Προσανατολισμοί', *Anglo-Greek Review*, 2/1 (March 1946), pp. 27–28.

74 K. Th. Dimaras, 'Επαφές της νεώτερης ελληνικής λογοτεχνίας με την Αγγλική', *Anglo-Greek Review*, 3/1 (May 1947), pp. 18–22, 3/2 (June 1947), pp. 52–55. See also his article on *Ρωσσαγγλογάλλος*, 'Με πέντε Άγγλους στην Ελλάδα (1811–1814)', *Anglo-Greek Review*, 3/10 (May-June 1948), pp. 293–300.

75 George Seferis, 'Κ.Π. Καβάφης, Θ.Σ. Έλιοτ ·παράλληλοι', *Anglo-Greek Review*, 3/2 (June 1947), pp. 33–43, and John Mavrogordato, 'Σολωμός και Wordsworth', *Anglo-Greek Review*, 3/9 (March-April 1948), pp. 281–84.

76 Earlier Pantelis Prevelakis had given a lecture at the British Institute in Athens on modern trends in contemporary British sculpture (*Αγγλοελληνική Επιθεώρηση*, 2/12, February 1947).

77 George Seferis, *The King of Asine and Other Poems, Translated from the Greek by Bernard Spencer, Nanos Valaoritis, Lawrence Durrell; with an Introduction by Rex Warner* (London, 1948).

78 David Roessel notes that 'from one point of view Zorba was simply Katsimbalis dressed up as a peasant' and that Zorba 'did not replace Katsimbalis as the masculine personification of a new Greece until the middle of the 1960s' (David Roessel, *In Byron's Shadow: Modern Greece in the English and American Imagination* (Oxford and New York, 2002), p. 269).

79 T.S. Eliot, 'The Responsibility of the Man of Letters', *Anglo-Greek Review*, 1/3 (May 1945), pp. 2–5 and 14–15. The article was originally published with a slightly different title 'The Responsibility of the Man of Letters in the Cultural Restoration of Europe', *Norseman*, 4 (July-August 1944), pp. 243–48. It was reprinted as 'The Man of Letters and the Future of Europe', *Horizon*, 10/60 (December 1944), pp. 382–89, and in *The Sewanee Review*, 45/3 (Summer 1945), pp. 333–42.

80 Andreas Karantonis, 'Ένα δοκίμιο για το Σολωμό', *Anglo-Greek Review*, 3/9 (March-April 1948), pp. 291–92.

81 E.P. Papanoutsos, 'Ποίηση και σχόλια', *Anglo-Greek Review*, 5/1 (September-October 1950), pp. 26–27.

82 Rex Warner, 'Εισαγωγή στο έργο του Σεφέρη', *Anglo-Greek Review*, 3/7 (November-December 1947), p. 202.

83 Lehmann, *The Ample Proposition*, p. 60.

84 Sagos, *A Chronicle of the British Council Office in Athens 1938–1986*, pp. 29–33.

85 The British Council's offices in Athens, Thessaloniki and Corfu nevertheless continued to function (Donaldson, *The British Council*, p. 208).

BETWEEN PROPAGANDA AND MODERNISM 153

86 Katsimbalis and Seferis, *'Αγαπητέ μου Γιώργο'*, vol. 2, p. 304. For more details concerning the travel writings and attitudes of Greek writers to the US since the Second World War see Vassilis Lambropoulos, *'Το ταξίδι του Έλληνα διανοούμενου στην Αμερική'*, afterword in Giorgos Theotokas, *Δοκίμιο για την Αμερική* (Athens, 2009), pp. 237–56.

87 Julie Reeves, *Culture and International Relations: Narratives, Natives and Tourists* (London, 2004).

88 D. Capetanakis, 'The Greeks Are Human Beings', *Anglo-Greek Review*, 1/3 (May 1945), p. 14. On Capetanakis in England see the articles by Dimitris Papanikolaou, 'Demetrios Capetanakis: A Greek Poet (Coming out) in England', *Byzantine and Modern Greek Studies*, 30/2 (2006), pp. 201–23 and David Ricks, 'Demetrios Capetanakis: A Greek Poet in England', *Journal of the Hellenic Diaspora*, 22/1 (1996), pp. 61–75.

89 Rex Warner on the study of classics (2/3, May 1946), Ioannis Kakridis on the Homeric Question (2/5, July 1946), Arundell Esdaile on the Antiquities of the British Museum (2/8, October 1946), Angelos Sikelianos on the life and work of Pindar (3/7, November-December 1947 and Aeschylus (5/7, September-October 1951), Spyros Skiadaresis on the musical aesthetics and ethics of the ancient Greeks (4/7, November-December 1949) and V.N. Tatakis on Socratic rationalism (4/8, January-February 1950).

90 Steven Runciman, *'Άγγλοι ιστορικοί της μεσαιωνικής και της σύγχρονης Ελλάδας'*, *Anglo-Greek Review*, 2/4 (June 1946), pp. 106–10.

91 At the back of the first issue of volume 6 (Summer 1953) the articles published on Byzantium are listed.

92 Avi Sharon, 'New Friends for New Places: England Rediscovers Greece', *Arion*, 8/2 (Autumn 2000), pp. 42–62.

93 A representative example of this approach is seen in the study by J.C. Lawson, *Modern Greek Folklore and Ancient Greek Religion: A Study in Survivals* (Cambridge, 1910).

94 Edmund Keeley, *Inventing Paradise: The Greek Journey 1937–47* (New York, 1999), p. 122.

95 Perhaps the only exception to this appreciation of modern Greek literature is the review by C.M. Woodhouse of Rae Dalven's anthology of *Modern Greek Poetry* published in the *Times Literary Supplement* (22 September 1950). It begins by saying that 'the weaknesses of modern Greek poetry, considered as a manifestation of the nation's genius, are painfully apparent at first glance'.

96 Lawrence Durrell, 'Hellene and Philhellene', *Times Literary Supplement*, 13 May 1949, p. 305. The article was translated and published in the *Anglo-Greek Review* (*'Έλληνες και Φιλέλληνες'*, 4/5 (July-August 1949), pp. 188–91). See also the critical letter from Ian Scott-Kilvert (*Times Literary Supplement*, 3 June 1949, p. 365) in which he corrects some of Durrell's inaccuracies.

97 Cited in George Angeloglou, *This Is London, Good Evening – Edo Londino, Kalispera sas: The Story of the Greek Section of the B.B.C., 1939–1957* (Athens, 2003), p. 173.

98 Roessel, *In Byron's Shadow*, p. 275.

99 Rex Warner, *Views of Attica and Its Surroundings* (London, 1950), pp. 36–37. In the book's Introduction he compared the relative merits of the light in Greece and Italy thus: 'Compared with that Attic light, those noble and individual lines, that purity and beauty, the sky of Italy appeared to me garish, indeed intolerably vulgar, the line of coast and mountain was strangely uninteresting, Capri itself misshapen' (p. 18).

100 Ian Scott-Kilvert, 'Hellenic Revival', *United Nations United*, 1/9 (June 1949), p. 356.

101 Young, 'The Contemporary Greek Influence on English Writers'.

102 Quoted from Lawrence Durrell, *Prospero's Cell: A Guide to the Landscape and Manners of the Island of Corcyra* (London, 1945), p. 11.

103 In a brief article on Katsimbalis Philip Sherrard talks about a new type of Philhellene who was not so much bound to Greece's past as to its present. He points out that one day historians will speak of how for two decades from the late 1930s a number of English writers had begun to discover a Greek world entirely different from what had become the stereotype of the classical tradition. They started discovering a living Greece. (Philip Sherrard, 'Γιώργος Κατσίμπαλης', *Νέα Εστία*, 108 (1 October 1980), pp. 1426–27).

104 Warner and Hürlimann, *Eternal Greece*, pp. 14–15.

105 Robert Liddell, *Aegean Greece* (London, 1954), p. 26.

106 Osbert Lancaster, *Classical Landscape with Figures* (London, 1947), p. 11. The book has been reprinted several times.

107 Ibid., pp. 9–10.

108 Ibid., p. 9.

109 David Roessel points out that the word 'Dionysiac' occurs frequently in writing about Greece after 1940 (*In Byron's Shadow*, p. 332).

110 Stephen Spender, ' "Brilliant Athens and Us" ', *Encounter*, 2/1 (January 1954), p. 77. He lists as new Philhellenes Rex Warner, Louis MacNeice, Patrick Leigh Fermor, Osbert Lancaster, Laurence Durrell, Robert Liddell, Steven Runciman, Francis King, Bernard Spencer and John Craxton. It is worth noting that most of them featured in the pages of the *Anglo-Greek Review*.

111 Ibid., p. 78.

112 Roessel, *In Byron's Shadow*, p. 283.

113 I have in mind the 'philhellenism of the sun, the sea, and the bodies of boys' that David Roessel refers to in his contribution to the present volume.

114 Roessel, *In Byron's Shadow*, p. 252.

Chapter 6

The *Anglo-Greek Review*:
Some residual puzzles

Dimitris Daskalopoulos

It is a pity that the valuable public exchange of views about the British Council and the wider question of Anglo-Greek cultural relations at the colloquium which formed the basis of this volume never took place some years earlier, when more of the protagonists and other dramatis personae who took part in this fruitful intellectual exchange were still with us. We need only think of the valuable oral testimonies to this period which were provided at the colloquium by Messrs Geoffrey Graham-Bell and Nanos Valaoritis to be aware of this. So, with just a handful of reminiscences from those who actually lived through Greece's troubled decade 1945–55, the rest of us find ourselves commenting on a discrete, pre-packaged period, each of us seeking to reconstruct and, above all, interpret a cross-section of cultural history that binds the two countries together.

Some years ago Jonathan Bolton's study *Personal Landscapes* provided a discussion of the activity of the British writers and men of letters in Egypt during the Second World War who produced in Cairo the English-language magazines *The Citadel* and *Personal Landscape*.[1] When it comes to Greece at the same period it is unfortunate that we lack any comparable study; and it also happens to be the case that those who became actively involved in such publications or other activities in Greece never thought to bequeath us testimonies to their work in written form. In a variety of other texts that they did produce, however, one comes across a number of indirect or incidental mentions of the topics with which this volume is concerned. It is on such evidence, chiefly from Seferis' correspondence, that I shall rely in order to make some general comments and ask certain remaining questions, mostly about the *Anglo-Greek Review*, of which Dimitris Tziovas has produced such a full and cogent account in this volume.

I should point out, first, that before the *Anglo-Greek Review* commenced publication, the AGIS (Anglo-Greek Information Service) published for some months in Athens a four-page bulletin called *Photo-Nea* (*Photo-News*), distributed free of charge and featuring photographs of current Greek and international news, each photograph being accompanied by lengthy captions. A broadly similar publication, with more pages, had appeared in Cairo during the War under the Greek title *A.E.P.*, 'a fortnightly illustrated magazine'

156 DIMITRIS DASKALOPOULOS

for the Greek armed forces in the Middle East. Its title ingeniously brought together the initial letters of the Allies' names *Anglia, Ellada, Rosia* with an allusion to the war-cry *Aera!* used by the Greek soldiers during the Albanian campaign. Seferis himself had contributed pieces of an occasional character to this magazine while he was in Egypt.[2]

Following his usual tactic, G.K. Katsimbalis never allowed his name to appear in any number of the *Anglo-Greek Review* as the person officially responsible for the periodical, but it was an open secret that he was editor of its first series (1945–52). In October 1945 Maro Seferis wrote to Nanis Panagiotopoulos that Katsimbalis was 'going through a difficult time financially, and [was] working, for the first time in his life, for a periodical called *Anglo-Greek Review*'; she added the following improbable comment: 'It appears monthly, with a circulation of about 30 thousand copies in Greece.'[3] One wonders just how many copies of each number were in fact being printed. And one wonders, for that matter, just what Katsimbalis was being paid, given that he repeats every now and then in letters to Seferis that his involvement with the magazine is motivated by nothing more than a need for a livelihood. Indeed, he goes so far as to describe his salary as 'peanuts'.

From the same letters we glean various other important scraps of information. The translated and the unsigned items in the *Anglo-Greek Review* were on the whole the work of Katsimbalis himself or Nikos Gatsos.[4] Of which man in each case, we don't normally know; but beyond question four of the longer translations are Gatsos' work. Their quality probably gave Seferis his initial idea of translating *Murder in the Cathedral* in collaboration with Gatsos, before he set to writing the translation on his own. Careful study of Gatsos' archive, which is in the possession of his heir Agathi Dimitrouka, may throw up further information about the *Review*.

The Katsimbalis archive, too, needs thorough investigation. Let me give one example. In previous researches in the archive for other purposes, I located and transcribed a few letters and postcards exchanged between Katsimbalis and Nikos Kazantzakis. In 2005 these documents became the subject of my paper revealing the behind-the-scenes search for a translator of various reviews of Kazantzakis' work published in Sweden. These items from the Swedish press, translated by the well known student of place names Ioannis Thomopoulos, instead of I.Th. Kakridis, who was the original proposal, appeared as 'Swedish reviews of two books by N. Kazantzakis' in 1952 in the last number of the first series of the *Anglo-Greek Review*.[5]

This last number bears the dates July-September 1952. Between then and the summer of 1953, when the first number of the second series edited by G.P. Savidis appeared, months intervened. What went on during those months? How was the decision reached about the magazine's temporary cessation and, later, its continuation? Katsimbalis in his letters to Seferis seems as early as 1952 to have tired of it, and to have become fairly irritated with the indecisiveness of the British Council in relation to the *Review*, writing in May 1952,

THE *ANGLO-GREEK REVIEW* 157

'The high-ups in London have still not deigned to let us know their decision, despite the fact that the tax year ended on 31 March!' It is manifest that there had been some correspondence between the Council's Athens and London offices. A few months earlier, Seferis had informed Katsimbalis from London: 'Headquarters here is making more and more cuts. The other day when I saw [Kenneth] Johnstone I asked him about the *Anglo-Greek Review*, which of course has my support. He shook his head sadly.'[6]

Katsimbalis kept to himself the plan that Savidis would succeed him as editor. 'I hope you received the new *Anglo-Greek Review*,' he wrote to Seferis. 'I think my plan to have Savidis succeed me under my guidance was a good one. But it was a hell of a job to persuade that pig-headed Teitham [sic, for W.G. Tatham, Runciman's successor as the British Council's Representative in Athens]. As time goes on perhaps we'll be able to shift the *Anglo-Greek Review* into being simply the *Review* and get something really worthwhile on its feet.'[7] It is understandable that there should have been resistance to giving Savidis the editorship, given that he was a young man of just twenty-four who, for all his English education, had no editorial or journalistic experience to date. In the event, Savidis proved highly capable, and in his archives there are perhaps documents relating to his short but successful tenure.

As with the *Review*'s first series, so with its second, its cessation of publication was never announced to the readership. I am not at all sure that the decision to cease publication is simply to be ascribed to Savidis – a decision in which it has been said that Seferis alone encouraged him. I am inclined to think that the British Council in Athens must itself have felt uncomfortable with the anti-British climate which had started to prevail in the light of recent events in Cyprus.[8]

That magazine has now been the subject of an unpublished doctoral thesis by Marina Kokkinidou, which covers the period of its publication.[9] For my part, let me return to an idea I once put forward: the most interesting phase in the life of any magazine is the one that begins after it has ceased to appear.

Notes

1 Jonathan Bolton, *Personal Landscape: British Poets in Egypt During the Second World War* (London, 1997).

2 Giorgos Seferis, *Δοκιμές*, vol. 3 (Athens, 1992), pp. 70–77.

3 *Αλληλογραφία Γιώργου & Μαρώς Σεφέρη – Νάνη Παναγιωτόπουλου, 1938–1963*, ed. Dimitris Arvanitakis (Athens, 2006), pp. 169–70.

4 G.K. Katsimbalis and Giorgos Seferis, *Αγαπητέ μου Γιώργο: αλληλογραφία, 1924–1970* (Athens, 2009), vol. 2, p. 220.

5 Dimitris Daskalopoulos, 'Νίκος Καζαντζάκης – Γ.Κ. Κατσίμπαλης, Αλληλογραφικά τεκμήρια', *Μικροφιλολογικά*, 18 (2005), pp. 26–28.

6 Katsimbalis and Seferis, *Αγαπητέ μου Γιώργο*, vol. 2, pp. 290 and 308. [Editors' note: It would be worth investigating the British Council archives to find the internal correspondence between London and Athens regarding the *Review*.]

7 Ibid., vol. 2, p. 327.

8 On this point, one should mention the exceptional letter Seferis sent to Savidis giving his reasons for not allowing poems from his collection *Cyprus, Where it was Destined that I. . .* in the *Anglo-Greek Review*. For more details see the contribution by Dimitris Tziovas to the present volume.

9 Marina Kokkinidou, 'Το περιοδικό *Αγγλοελληνική Επιθεώρηση* (1945–1955)', unpublished Ph.D. thesis, Aristotle University of Thessaloniki, 2002.

Chapter 7

The magazine *Prosperos* and the British Council Corfu branch

Theodosis Pylarinos

This chapter examines four interlinked aspects of our subject. The first regards the creation of the journal *Prosperos*, its content and its contribution. The second and third involve a discussion of its prime movers, and particularly of its main contributor, Marie (Maria-Aspasia) Aspioti. Finally, I examine the journal's relationship with the British Council's wider operations in Corfu. While examining the fourth aspect, I will attempt, among other things, an appraisal of the magazine during that period of intellectual and ideological ferment and upheaval in post-war Greece. I shall also make a brief comparison with two related publications, *Anglo-Greek Review*, published in Athens as a 'monthly publication of intellectual culture', and *Symposio*, a journal of intellectual culture, published by the British Institute in Patras. The aim of all this output was to show Britain's lively interest in securing and extending its influence through the dissemination of its intellectual production. Besides the Greek capital, the centre of its efforts, it chose two cities which were culturally and geopolitically of key importance, Patras and Corfu. These two provincial cities were suitable for the development of cultural activities because of their educational traditions and their relatively moderate political climate in the years after the War and, in due course, the Civil War. This British intervention in Greek literary affairs was, as we shall see, reflected in a preference for and promotion of particular writers.

Prosperos, 'a publication on letters and the arts by the British Council', according to its subtitle, appeared in Greek in Corfu, irregularly and unpredictably, from 1949 (in fact, January 1950) until 1954.[1] It published nine issues, *fylladia* ('numbers') according to the old Corfiot term; the British Council branch in Corfu, which had been in operation on the island since 1945, is given as the publisher.[2] The main function of the Corfu branch was the provision of English language classes; but each evening after class a gathering in the Institute's reading room would follow: books and magazines, Greek and English, were to be found at its oblong table, opinions would be exchanged and conversation would ensue on everyday matters, but also on hot political issues, notably Cyprus. Apart from Marie Aspioti, other teachers included Spyridon Politis, Konstantinos Grollios and Mari Nikaki (the last an accomplished violinist whose occasional recitals were well known). Over and above this, the British Council organized talks from the outset: these were popularizing presentations on matters of cultural or broad intellectual interest. The talks took place regularly every week, with a wide variety of speakers. Among them was the soft-spoken Eirini Dentrinou. Her talk entitled 'The speaker and the listener' was legendary, though by design it lasted only a quarter of an hour; Patrick Leigh Fermor's talk, about the abduction of the German General Kreipe, was given at the Commercial School of Corfu in order to accommodate a larger crowd.

This was evidence of the wider role that the British Council would play and of the function of *Prosperos* from the end of 1949 within it. In essence, the 'Institute', as it was generally known in Corfu, constituted a more active continuation of the Anglo-Hellenic League in Corfu, where English had been taught since the 1930s.[3]

As I have pointed out elsewhere, and as he himself attested, the magazine's name derives from Lawrence Durrell's well-known book *Prospero's Cell*.[4] From internal evidence in the publication, as well as from oral testimony, it seems that the journal operated independently: the British Council only provided the paper for its printing, and was not involved, at least overtly, in the publication itself.[5] For all the suspicions that were occasionally expressed about the existence of British propaganda behind the publication, the magazine's editors, Marie Aspioti, the Director of the British Council branch (who had known Durrell from before the War and enjoyed his confidence), and Michail Desyllas (known in Corfu by his diminutive Lilis), the heart and soul of the magazine, never provided formal confirmation of such involvement.[6] The British Council's impeccable reputation, as well as the fact of Desyllas' socialist leanings – it is known that he was under surveillance by the Security Police for as long as he was active in the journal and in the cultural life of the Council – dispelled suspicions about the magazine's involvement in political matters, let alone any sense that it was British propaganda.[7] This must be seen as a British policy success. Furthermore, the collaboration of Greek patriots with their British allies during the course of the War renders any boundaries between agent, collaborator and ally somewhat blurred.[8]

When it comes to its range of contributors, *Prosperos* presents notable distinctiveness and originality, considering its modest scale. Its contributors were and remained, for the most part, unknown in the broader field of Greek letters. Nonetheless, a few gained a degree of recognition, and their success may in part be attributed to their presence in the magazine's pages. Such were not so much established writers as enquiring younger minds and the intellectually restless, most of whom had come into contact with English language and literature as amateurs, through attendance at the lectures and evening meetings in Theotokis Street. They were marked by a passion for learning, a love of the arts and a regenerative spirit after the bitter events of the war. Corfu had suffered from Italian bombardment and occupation in the early stages, but still more from the German firebombs, which obliterated significant parts of the town and destroyed monuments such as the well-stocked public library and the famous Municipal Theatre. In particular, contributors sought an acquaintance with the modern and the innovative, an inclination reinforced by contact with British work in literature, drama, and the visual arts. It was the Corfiot literati who staffed *Prosperos*, people mostly in their twenties, active participants in the lectures, dramatic performances, art exhibitions, and cinema screenings at the Institute, the intellectual hive from which the journal originated.[9] But the high point of the British Council's success in Corfu was the publication of *Prosperos* as its intellectual organ.

Marie Aspioti, who, in addition to her teaching role, directed the Institute and organized and participated in many of its events, was the driving force behind the Corfu branch.[10] Descended from a well-known Corfiot family, she was a cultured polyglot, and in her person the Corfiot tradition met with an innovative spirit nourished by British culture.[11] The choice of collaborators, as well as the warm and friendly atmosphere of the Institute, which soon became a meeting place for the island's enquiring minds, and especially the young, was due to Aspioti's force of character, ethos, sophistication and open-mindedness.[12]

Michail Desyllas, Aspioti's close collaborator and friend, was himself a man of culture and truly the heart and soul of the magazine. The planning and production of *Prosperos*, and indeed the magazine's broad orientation, derived from him. An erudite poet, his versions from English poetry appeared in the magazine. In Desyllas, its main inspirer and ideological guide, the indigenous tradition gave rise to a utopian commitment to a distinctive Corfiot cultural identity.[13] He sought to combine this local allegiance with a spirit of creative renewal and innovation, despite the unlikelihood that Corfu would ever constitute a central focus in the post-war revival of Greek intellectual life. It was a period when Corfiot writers expressed their grief for mankind and laid bare the painful experiences arising from the misfortunes of their birthplace.[14] In the pages of *Prosperos*, literary testimonies of this type were central. In a visionary frame of mind which owed much to the poet and mystic Angelos Sikelianos, Desyllas expressed such a faith and hope in mankind in difficult times in the last pages of each number of *Prosperos*, under his own name or in unsigned contributions.[15] A particularly important intellectual guide in this connection was T.S. Eliot; likewise the interior anxiety of the intellectual in the footsteps of Joyce, who had espoused the freedom of the artist as offering an escape from the stranglehold of derivative tradition.[16]

Dominant in the thought of the two prime movers and collaborators of *Prosperos* were notions of responsibility, moral integrit, and obligation, a legacy of the nineteenth-century Corfiot writer, translator and politician Iakovos Polylas and, to an even greater extent, of the Kantian poet and war hero Lorentzos Mavilis, who had himself been influenced by English thought. Nevertheless, the tenacity of what may be termed Corfiotism constituted a brake on the assimilation of new ideas and a hindrance to the influence of *Prosperos*. The magazine, with its innovative orientation, and in spite of clear efforts on the part of its contributors to present new aesthetic trends in the light of Corfu's longstanding Idealist tradition, did not receive an especially warm reception, except among a small section of the young. Following the first numbers, and in an attempt to counter this initially cool reception, the reinforcement by the editors of a certain regional flavour is clear, as a continuation of the Corfiot school through recourse to historical or biographical texts.[17] This was an indication of Corfu's general reluctance to embrace cultural innovation, and concessions were made in the face of this by the magazine's contributors. We know from oral testimony that the appearance of the magazine's first two issues was accompanied by sarcastic comments from the innately irreverent Corfiots about the incomprehensible and obscure texts here included.[18] Desyllas himself, in an honest acknowledgement of the nature of *Prosperos'* initial reception, referred to the lukewarm response there had been to the magazine's collective commitment to be an inspiration to others. Similar, if less barbed, opinions marked the reception of the British Council magazine in Patras, *Symposio*.[19]

Among frequent contributors to *Prosperos* was the poet Iason Depountis, who with his earlier collections *Uninhabited Night* and *From the Sea* had been among the Corfiot pioneers of experimental writing. The thematic content of his poems was Corfiot, inspired by the traumatic experiences of the recent war, but his writing innovative, with surrealist flourishes. The contributions of Spyros Nikokavouras and of Th.D. Frangopoulos (later a translator, with Rex Warner, of some of Seferis' essays) were in poetry; contributions in literary prose came from Tasos Korfis, I Korfiati (the pseudonym of E. Oikonomou), Gerasimos Chytiris, Babis S. Anninos and P.G. Kallinikos. The historical field was represented by Kostas Dafnis, the editor of *Kerkyraïka Chronika*. The publication of *Prosperos* was a lesson to him following after the failure of the *Filologika Nea*, a short-lived journal that he had brought out in 1945 to promote French poetry. The contributions by Nikos Leftheriotis, a well-known scholar and poet from the circle of Eirini Dentrinou, were of a historical character; other contributors included Konstantinos Grollios, who taught English language at the Institute and would later become Professor of Latin at the Aristotle University of Thessaloniki, and Tasos Papanastasatos, later of the University of Piraeus. Many of those mentioned here also published translations from English writers, and Liana Koulouri, who signed her name in the last issues as Liana M. Desylla (she was married to Michail Desyllas), appeared solely as a translator.

The visual arts were represented by two engravers, Virginia Ventouras and, from the magazine's sixth number, the avant-garde engraver Nikos Ventouras, who embellished its pages and covers with their work. However, there were few contributions on art: an essay by Pitsa Dendrinou on Indian painting, and an abridgement of the eighteenth-century work by Panagiotis Doxaras *On Painting*. This was a small harvest considering the early pledge that

Prosperos would feature contributions on the visual arts, a field also promoted by the British Council.

When it comes to British and Irish writers, it is not surprising that Eliot was an emblematic figure.[20] To Joyce, by contrast, a brief but pithy profile was devoted.[21] Yet attempts to acquaint the Corfiot public with other prominent British and Irish writers are also of interest. Among these were the poets W.H. Auden, Stephen Spender and Walter de la Mare, and the novelist Elizabeth Bowen.[22] Two British Council employees, the novelist Francis King and the poet and dramatist Louis MacNeice, also made their appearance.[23] Nor is it a surprise to find another writer with a continuing preoccupation with the Greeks, Robert Liddell.[24] From earlier generations we find the ubiquitous Wilde but also Shaw.[25] Among the Modernists appear Lawrence, along with Virginia Woolf, and Katherine Mansfield.[26] From among the English classics Shakespeare and Milton are represented.[27] Critical contributions came from the Byron Professor at the University of Athens, Arthur Sewell (with a study written especially for *Prosperos*), and from the younger Philhellenes Philip Sherrard and Patrick Leigh Fermor, alongside the senior figure of E.M. Forster.[28]

The examples cited vouch for the general literary level, yet they appeared in a truncated and sketchy fashion, giving some reference points but affording little opportunity even for the rudimentary understanding of the significance of such significant writers' work. For the intellectually conservative Corfiot public, what was seen as incomprehensible and innovative literature was to remain so.

Prosperos was, for a provincial publication, over-ambitious, and the marks of inexperience and amateurism are obvious, by contrast with the more systematic agenda of the *Anglo-Greek Review* and its more organized project, more varied content, and large number of well-known contributors. Adopting a literary canon by then well established, the *Anglo-Greek Review* trod firmly and persistently the royal road of Greek poetry: Solomos, Palamas, Cavafy, Sikelianos and Seferis.[29] By its very longevity it acquired *de facto* ideological stature, and it carried on the route opened up by the Generation of the Thirties. This was achieved through critical texts by Andreas Karantonis, Apostolos Sachinis, Kleon Paraschos and George Theotokas, and with reviews by Alkis Thrylos and Angelos Terzakis; and through Linos Politis and C.Th. Dimaras the magazine also gained considerable scholarly ballast. Yet the *Anglo-Greek Review* was rather lacking when it came to the Ionian Islands, which had been assigned to Fanis Michalopoulos, though, as appears from the number of relevant pieces, the Heptanesian contribution did not go unrecognized in its pages.[30] In *Prosperos*, meanwhile, the Ionian Islands tradition, though singled out as important, became anaemic and fruitlessly diluted by the inclusion of texts of a historical character. This lack of emphasis on the Corfiot literary tradition probably derives from a fear of exhibiting that brand of Corfiot provincialism which had been subject to a barrage of criticism from Athens over the previous two decades.[31]

It is, however, worth referring briefly to the case of Angelos Sikelianos, because *Prosperos* was the first magazine to dedicate a whole number to him immediately after his death in 1951.[32] Desyllas was obviously the prime mover of that number, to which no fewer than three British writers (Liddell, H.B. Forster and Sherrard) contributed – this in a climate when Sikelianos' national contribution had been called into question by the self-appointed champions of nationalism. Desyllas, who had a conciliatory temperament, comparable to and indeed indebted to Sikelianos' own, and who had similarly progressive political leanings, contributed to that number what was intended as a rehabilitation of the great poet, a rehabilitation in which the *Anglo-Greek Review* had played a role while he lived, installing him firmly in its literary canon.[33] Sikelianos, for that matter, had lectured at the British Council in Athens and contributed to the magazine.[34] This position taken towards Sikelianos by a magazine representing the educated Right seems to reflect not only its own affinities, but also the stance of the British Council.

Desyllas in particular had an intellectual affinity with Sikelianos, marked by a high-flown visionary vein and a commitment to the poet's sense of Hellenism, with its faith in mankind and its high-flown Apollonian vision. With intellectual origins that went back to Lorentzos Mavilis and came to him through Spyros Nikokavouras, Desyllas had grasped what he saw as the moral problem of his time and looked to a model, much indebted to Sikelianos, of ecumenical unity. His essay, 'The Sense of Purpose', is noteworthy because it reflects the influence of the *Anglo-Greek Review* in its constant reference to and promotion of emblematic poets as part of its modernist project. This effort to connect tradition with innovation was greatly stimulated by the influence of Anglo-American modernism and the avant-garde, and above all by T.S. Eliot.[35] Finally, we note the complete absence of the Left poets Yannis Ritsos, Nikiphoros Vrettakos and Manolis Anagnostakis as an indication of the magazine's political contours.

The discontinuation of *Prosperos* was prompted by the resignation of the Director of the British Council Corfu branch, who withdrew after a period of mental strain and a crisis of conscience. In the upheaval of the Cyprus crisis, Corfiot hotheads threw stones at the Institute and, during a demonstration, at the British Consul's car. In these circumstances, Aspioti resigned, torn between the Institute, on the one hand, where she had worked and in which she had invested intellectually, and her wounded patriotism regarding the Cyprus question, on the other. With the worsening of the Cyprus crisis Aspioti made clear her disagreement with Britain's position and actions through her resignation. In two letters, which are well-known today, written on 17 September and 5 October respectively, she explained the reasons for her resignation, emphasizing, apart from anything else, the rupture of the 'sacred bonds of long standing' that connected the two peoples, ties which *Prosperos* had been created to reinforce and for which she herself had laboured.[36] Taking this moral stand without fanfare, and seeing the betrayal of a goal for which she had worked body and soul, Aspioti left her position as Director and also refused to

PROSPEROS AND THE CORFU BRANCH

continue her teaching role, thus losing her main source of livelihood. And her admiration and love for Britain, which she had demonstrated also in her own historical and literary endeavours – the subjects of which relate to the period of British rule and more generally the British presence in Corfu – was shaken.[37]

Despite the intellectual breadth of its contributors and the support of the British Council, *Prosperos* was in essence very much a junior partner to the *Anglo-Greek Review* and broadly followed its cultural line. English letters constituted the common reference point between the two magazines. Despite a lack of documented communication or collaboration between the two magazines, Aspioti's acquaintance with the Lamprakis family must have lain behind *Prosperos*' creation. And the *Anglo-Greek Review* was evidently the main model for *Prosperos*, funded as it was by the British Council.

Yet its possibilities, financial as well literary, were of course limited. *Prosperos* did not have the security of regular publication: the meagre and uncertain income from the print run of 350 for each number was always the basis for the production of the next, with any shortfall being supplied from Aspioti's own funds. With the prestige of its contributors, its variety of topics, and the abundance of familiar names in its pages, whether Greek or British, the *Anglo-Greek Review* cannot be compared with the human resources available to *Prosperos*. As we have seen, *Prosperos* depended on local talent, a further disadvantage being that its contributors were for the most part unknown young persons, however promising, whose contribution was to bear fruit in Corfu only at a later date. Nor could the main contributors, Desyllas and Aspioti, be compared with names of the stature of an Andreas Karantonis or an Angelos Terzakis. The magazine's topics, furthermore, drew largely on a Corfiot regional tradition, despite the wide humanistic intentions of its founders, an additional disadvantage being the lack of breadth and intellectual resources to cover very many fields of interest. Despite a liberal openness to English-language poetry and prose, the shadow of Corfiot tradition was a negative factor: town and island remained stubbornly devoted to the former glories of the late phase of the Ionian School.

A further difference lay in the fact that the *Anglo-Greek Review* was a continuation of the *Ta Nea Grammata* and an organ of the enlightened right-wing intelligentsia.[38] In that sense not dissimilar in spirit to two excellent magazines of the Left at that time, *Eleftbera Grammata*, edited by Dimitris Fotiadis (1945–48), and *Epitheorisi Technis* (1954–67), the *Anglo-Greek Review* combated the right-wing excesses of Spyros Melas for example, whose *Elliniki Dimiourgia* appeared between 1948 and 1954.[39] *Prosperos*, by contrast, did not find itself caught between such stark ideological differences and for this reason could embrace enlightened bourgeois, such as Aspioti; progressive socialists, such as Desyllas (who had been inducted into the Left youth group EPON); and even men of the Left such as Iason Depountis.[40] They all managed to coexist in the magazine's pages and at the events of the British Council in Corfu, collaborating in an atmosphere of reconciliation made possible by the relatively mild nature of political confrontation in post-war Corfu. For its part, *Filologika*

Nea, published by Kostas Dafnis in 1945, with its low-key promotion especially of French poetry and its miscellaneous material, was not exactly a precursor of *Prosperos*, yet Desyllas' involvement as the main local translator of French poetry for the magazine gave him experience that bore fruit in *Prosperos*.[41]

In any case, we should not forget that the project of *Prosperos* and the events at the Institute was not without later impact. *To Proto Skali*, its title borrowed from Cavafy's poem, 'The First Rung', was a magazine brought out in mid-1954 by a group of young Corfiots. It followed in the footsteps and spirit of *Prosperos*, introducing foreign literary trends and disowning narrow Corfiotism, but was inferior in terms of quality. This is the first evidence of the Institute's contribution immediately after its closure and the discontinuation of its magazine. Very much later, in 1980, came the appearance of the Corfiot literary journal *Porphyras*, again with younger editors: the influence of Aspioti and Desyllas is clear from the magazine's opening pages, which honoured their historic contribution. *Porphyras* has sought to follow *Prosperos* in a gradual liberation from narrow regionalism, a creative respect for local tradition and an openness to foreign literature.

Prosperos and *Anglo-Greek Review* are not of commensurable significance. And this is not just a matter of the infrastructure or the contributors, nor even of the patchiness of the Corfu magazine compared to its fuller, more scholarly Athenian equivalent. It also lies in the subject matter. One cannot compare the wide overview of Greek and English poetry and prose in the *Anglo-Greek Review*, on the one hand, with the focus on Corfiot literary output in *Prosperos*. From *Prosperos* literary studies of this kind, along with theatre and music reviews were all absent; and the latter would in any case have been largely confined to Corfu. Yet there is in a sense a common spirit that permeates both publications. The impulse to innovate is clear in *Prosperos*, despite the unresponsiveness of the wider Corfu public. Yet it was obliged to follow an ambiguous strategy, appealing to a small and select readership with an appetite for innovation, and simultaneously to a more conservative wider public. In fact *Symposio*, the British Council magazine in Patras, was rather more rounded than *Prosperos*, with quite a few texts in English, and with a smaller proportion of contributors from Patras itself – and with contributions from some writers who are well-known even today. Such writers, in contrast to the Corfiots, produced notable work marked by greater formal variety and with more of an orientation to contemporary Greek reality; hence perhaps with a distinct preference for the short story as a genre.[42] We may also point to the collaboration in their translations of Greek poets into English by George Katsimbalis, the editor of *Anglo-Greek Review*, and Theodore D. Stephanides.[43] Yet *Symposio* too met with reservations from the public, as certain of its contributions make clear.[44]

To conclude, *Prosperos* reflects a deep commitment to artistic quality and free expression in the arts and letters on the part of a region of Greece by then marginal to literary production but with indisputable past achievements. It was a harbinger of innovations that reflected a keenly felt need to transcend the moral and cultural crisis that had come to a head in the Second World

PROSPEROS AND THE CORFU BRANCH

War. The magazine's whole enterprise is marked by an effort to alleviate the atmosphere of Greece in the years of civil war and after: men and women of differing ideological convictions co-existed harmoniously in its pages, just as they collaborated in the British Council's manifold related activities. It was fortunate that it fell to two politically aware intellectuals such as Desyllas and Aspioti to work together, despite their different ideological origins, thus exerting a balancing influence on the Corfiot *milieu* and moderating any political differences. We should recognize the discernment of the British Council in its recognition of that distinctive atmosphere and in maintaining a discreet presence, thanks to which the British influence, at least until the end of our period, grew stronger. Yet this influence was a delicate plant, as events were to show, with the reactions that broke out in Corfu immediately after the eruption of protests in Athens against Britain's Cyprus policy. This brought about a rupture in the political consensus that had earlier built on Greek-British cooperation during the War. The British Council, initially through the *Anglo-Greek Review*, showed its own literary preferences, naturally promoting English literature for the most part; and this was the common denominator between the three journals that were published in its name, and which operated, in conjunction with their Greek contributors, in the service of a certain ideological-political outlook.

The demise of *Prosperos* was brought about by events in Cyprus. But in any case the financial difficulties that the magazine faced were a problem that could never have been resolved simply by the generosity of Marie Aspioti. Furthermore, there was a shortage of contributors, which resulted in a certain monotony and a repetition of the same themes. This shortage presented a long-term impediment for Corfiot publications in general. The presence of certain lengthy texts in *Prosperos*, particularly those of a historical character, and also the scarcity of translators among its contributors, are evidence of its inability to gather material of sufficient significance and variety. To these, we must add the paucity of British contributors, which the *Anglo-Greek Review* had in good number. For all the well-intentioned efforts to palliate the fact, *Prosperos* remained trapped in a local Corfiot tradition, the roots of which lay deep. We may quote a few words by Desyllas from his statement announcing a future number of the magazine which would be devoted to modern Corfiot painters – a number that never appeared. He wrote, 'We thus repay a debt both to a place and to those who are building a new Corfiot culture.'[45]

Notes

1 I discuss the journal's name in the introduction to the volume *Πρόσπερος (1949–1954)*, ed. Theodosis Pylarinos (Corfu, 2007), pp. 9–10. See below for the clear connection to Lawrence Durrell's *Prospero's Cell* (1945).

2 The view that it was founded in 1946 probably does not stand up to examination. Tasos Papanastasatos, an expert on the period, gives 1945 as the year of its establishment.

168 THEODOSIS PYLARINOS

3 From an oral communication from Papanastasatos it seems that his father perfected his English there with an English teacher in 1938.

4 Periklis Pangratis, 'Ο Lawrence Durrell και μία μετάφραση από το «Κελί του Πρόσπερου»', *Πόρφυρας*, 93 (2000), p. 304: 'The magazine [*Prosperos*] is charming and nicely produced. Its title is flattering to me, and I think the poet of *The Tempest* would have felt the same way. I shall write an article for the magazine myself.' For Durrell's later connections with Corfu see pp. 303ff above on an introduction to his work by Michail Desyllas in the Corfu newspaper *Εφημερίς των Ειδήσεων*; in addition, for a previously unknown passage of a translation of *Prospero's Cell*, *Πόρφυρας*, 11 (1982), pp. 27–28, where he answers questions posed by the journal on literature. A text by Durrell, with the title 'Χαμένο ορόσημο', had earlier been published in a translation by Aspioti in *Πόρφυρας*, 5.

5 Personal communications from Professor Tasos Papanastasatos, the journalist Spiros Ziniatis and Periklis Pangratis, editor of *Porfyras*, to each of whom my thanks.

6 Aspioti, as Papanastasatos notes, 'was immediately after the Liberation working in the Anglo-Greek Information Service' (Pylarinos, *Πρόσπερος (1949–1954)*, p. 513). She, the scion of a rich family, had been tutored at home, both in Greek general education and in foreign languages. She acquired certification in English by sitting exams in Spetses and, in order to teach at the Institute, was later awarded the Proficiency as official proof of her good knowledge of the English language (Tasos Papanastasatos, personal communication). Proof of Durrell's personal trust in her is the assignment to her of the editing of his book *Prospero's Cell*, and he refers to her in a complimentary manner at the book's end.

7 In the little anthology of lyric poets of Corfu edited by Desyllas in 1946, his name as editor does not appear, in order to avoid political provocation.

8 To take just one example of the complexities of the period: Periklis Karidis, the lawyer and later chairman of the Reading Society, whose English wife Pat served as British consul in Corfu, had been one of a three-member secretariat of EAM in Corfu. Pat Karidis organized at the Institute an exhibition of contemporary photography from across Greece. See *Prosperos*, 6 (1951), p. 220.

9 Such as the musical evenings on Tuesdays or the literary events each Thursday, where works of modern Greek literature were presented and discussed, at a time when Seferis and Elytis were little known and Ritsos and Vrettakos lived in a climate of persecution. For the events of 1951 see *Prosperos*, 6 (1951), pp. 219–20, where there is also information about Desyllas' role. For events during the first five months of 1952 see *Prosperos*, 7 (1952), pp. 256–57.

10 See Tasos Papanastasatos, 'Μαρία Ασπιώτη (1909–2000): Μια ζωή, μια προσφορά', *Πόρφυρας*, 102 (2002), pp. 507–31. Events at the Institute were announced in the Corfu press; see also references in *Prosperos*, 3 (1950), p. 103 to two such.

11 In *Prosperos*, 3 (1950), pp. 102–3, Aspioti justifies the publication of Corfiot texts with reference to notions of Hellenism promoted by the Generation of the Thirties and especially Elytis.

PROSPEROS AND THE CORFU BRANCH

12 The creation of intellectual groups in Corfu goes as far back as the time of Polylas. For the Spianada as an intellectual meeting-place with emblematic significance see Lorentzos Mavilis, *Τα κριτικά κείμενα*, ed. Theodosis Pylarinos (Athens, 2007), pp. 51–53.

13 The most characteristic presentation of this utopian romanticism (if the term be permitted) was Desyllas' talk at the Institute, with the title, 'A town's destiny', referring to Corfu, published in *Prosperos*, 4 (1951), pp. 132–40. In an atmosphere charged by recent traumatic events, what is clear is the ardent patriotism of Desyllas and its affinities to Lorentzos Mavilis, a characteristic of all the representatives of the indigenous school: 'Corfu carries on, even in the chaos of her own destruction, her intense creative effort. . . . There is no selfishness to her intentions, no vested interest. She follows a faith which was ever her main characteristic.' Or again: 'This bent to existence – and when we say existence we do not mean mere continuation of life – is the best possible sign that the mark of decadence is fundamentally alien to this place.'

14 See the introductory note (probably written by Desyllas) to a short story by Iason Depountis, 'Χ.Α. Donnet, ο βομβαρδισμός μιας άμαχης πολιτείας', *Prosperos*, 3 (1950), pp. 76–82. The note and the short story alike convey the atmosphere of grief in Corfu after the War. See also Desyllas' poem, 'Το ναυάγιο της Ομίχλης', *Prosperos*, 4 (1951), pp. 110–17. Periklis Pangratis, 'Πολεμικές εμπειρίες και μεταπολεμική κερκυραϊκή λογοτεχνία', *Πορφύρας*, 1 (1980), pp. 19–24, surveys the literary texts of the period with their sense of pain. One may add the case of the poet Dimitris Sourvinos, whose poetry was later to become well known: see Theodosis Pylarinos, *Ι. Σουρβίνος «ο ασκούμενος της νυκτός»* (Corfu, 2006).

15 The same role was played by Desyllas' piece, 'Σχόλια στο περιθώριο του Πρόσπερου'. The title was also used later by Aspioti in a text of hers in 1951, published much later in the Corfiot newspaper *Ενημέρωση* 353–5 (1992), with historical information on the members of the Institute milieu.

16 C. Day Lewis had published 'The Poetry of T.S. Eliot', in *Anglo-Greek Review*, 1/5 (July 1945), pp. 17–18.

17 So Desyllas' piece, 'Από την άρνηση στη θέση', *Prosperos*, 7 (1952), pp. 255–56. Likewise, in *Prosperos*, 3 (1950), p. 102, with reference to the recent death of the poet Spiros Leftheriotis, Desyllas had dubbed hasty those who rushed to call Leftheriotis one 'of the last of the Corfiot school', preferring the term 'one of its veterans'.

18 Papanastasatos, 'Maria Aspioti', p. 519, compares the derisive reception of the first Greek surrealists: 'The word Prosperos, as an epithet, had become synonymous with misfit or simpleton.'

19 *Prosperos*, 2 (1950), p. 4: 'They make captious criticisms of our modern style, general spirit, language, everything.'

20 Translations from Eliot in *Prosperos* were 'A Song for Simeon', 1 (1949), pp. 1–2; 'Chorus' from *The Family Reunion* (4 (1951), pp. 120–21); and two choruses from *Murder in the Cathedral*, in a translation by Aspioti.

21 Joyce was presented to the readership in 'Απλό σημείωμα για τον Joyce', *Prosperos*, 2 (1950), pp. 44–55. He was a literary model for Desyllas, who had

170 THEODOSIS PYLARINOS

described disintegration as early as 1920, in a new language and form. The excerpt in *Prosperos* was from *A Portrait of the Artist as a Young Man*, and the interior anxiety that runs through it is clear. The use of a larger font is noteworthy.

22 *Anglo-Greek Review* had made reference to de la Mare and Auden, in an article by Stephen Spender, 'Η αγγλική ποίηση του μεσοπολέμου', 2/4 (1946), pp. 114–16. Spender himself is represented by a translation of his best-known poem, 'I Think Continually of Those Who Were Truly Great', *Prosperos*, 3 (1950), p. 87. Elizabeth Bowen's 'Η καστανιά' was an extract from *A World of Love*: *Prosperos*, 7 (1952), pp. 251–54.

23 MacNeice in *Prosperos*, (1950), pp. 91–94, with a piece about Birmingham with an autobiographical flavour: in *Anglo-Greek Review* there had been presentations of several British cities. See also p. 102, where it is noted that this was the first piece MacNeice had written especially for a Greek magazine; the author of the notes to contributions also draws attention to the link between the piece and the New Poetry. In *Prosperos*, 6 (1951), p. 213 appeared the translation of a poem by MacNeice as 'Ενοικιάζεται', by Aspioti.

24 Liddell contributed an article on Sikelianos, *Prosperos*, 5 (1951), pp. 189–91.

25 *Prosperos*, 4 (1951), pp. 105–9, with the start of the fifth scene of *Saint Joan*.

26 Aldous Huxley's article, 'D.H. Lawrence' had appeared in *Anglo-Greek Review*, 2/8 (1946), pp. 235–39. In *Prosperos*, 3 (1950), pp. 83–86, we find an extract from *The Rainbow* and in *Prosperos*, 4 (1951), p. 128 the poem 'Song of a Man Who has Come Through'. Katherine Mansfield is represented by 'Such a Sweet Old lady': *Prosperos*, 4 (1951), pp. 129–31; Virginia Woolf by an excerpt from *To the Lighthouse*: *Prosperos* 7 (1952), pp. 231–35. See also John Lehmann, 'Virginia Woolf', *Anglo-Greek Review*, 2/6 (1946), pp. 178–82.

27 Milton by an extract from *Paradise Regained*, in a translation by Grollios: *Prosperos*, 6 (1951), pp. 193–94.

28 *Prosperos*, 5 (1951), pp. 171–74 and 181–85.

29 This not to the exclusion of other important writers, such as Prevelakis; see Vas. Laourdas, 'Παντελής Πρεβελάκης', *Anglo-Greek Review*, 2/5 (1946), pp. 145–47.

30 E.g. 'Ιάκωβος Πολυλάς (1826–1896), ένας Έλληνας πουριτανός', *Anglo-Greek Review*, 2/1 (1946), pp. 19–22, 2/2 (1946), pp. 56–57, and 2/3 (1946), pp. 87–90, and 'Γεώργιος Τερτσέτης (1800–1874)', 2/7 (1946), pp. 207–8, and 2/8 (1946), pp. 254–56.

31 Theodosis Pylarinos, 'Κερκυραϊσμός η κορφίτιδα: αποδοχές και αντιρρήσεις προς την ταυτότητα των Κερκυραίων εκπροσώπων της Επτανησιακής σχολής', *Ιονικά Ανάλεκτα*, 1 (2011), pp. 215–29.

32 *Prosperos*, 5 (1951). In it six poems by Sikelianos (pp. 155–67) and the 'Delphic Summons' (pp. 147–54) were published, texts relating to 'his stance towards the moral and the intellectual problem' of the period. See also pp. 143–44 for the rationale for the publication of the special edition. The contributions, emotionally charged by the poet's recent death, constitute an appraisal of his work in relation to his life and personality.

33 Theodoros Xydis, 'Το ερωτικό στοιχείο στην ποίηση του Σικελιανού', *Anglo-Greek Review*, 1/11–12 (1946), pp. 12–16, critical opinions on *Αλαφροΐσκιωτος*

PROSPEROS AND THE CORFU BRANCH

(*The Light-Shadowed One*), 2/8 (1946), pp. 240–41; and 'Το πρώτο φανέρωμα του Σικελιανού', ibid., pp. 258–62, with appraisals by various contributors.

34 Angelos Sikelianos, 'Εικοστή Πέμπτη Μαρτίου 1821', *Anglo-Greek Review*, 2/1 (1946), pp. 1–2.

35 C.M. Bowra, 'Ο ποιητής Θ.Σ. Έλιοτ', *Anglo-Greek Review*, 2/5 (1946), pp. 136–42.

36 Papanastasatos, 'Μαρία Ασπιώτη', p. 520.

37 Of Aspioti's historical works on the period of British rule in Corfu two were published during her term of office at the Institute. Beyond this, there were pieces which she chose not to publish (Periklis Pangratis, personal communication). These were 'Το άσπρο σπίτι' (1950), referring to Durrell's house at Kalami, and 'Στο περιβόλι των ξένων' (1951), on the British Cemetery in Corfu.

38 Useful for an assessment of the inter-war magazines that had preceded *Anglo-Greek Review* and of their orientation is the article by Yannis Chatzinis, 'Περιοδικά του μεσοπολέμου', *Anglo-Greek Review*, 2/6 (1946), pp. 177–78). See also the article by A. Vousvounis about the journal *Tetradio*, in the same issue, p. 188.

39 See Theodosis Pylarinos, 'Ο Μάρκος Αυγέρης και τα Ελεύθερα Γράμματα του Δημήτρη Φωτιάδη', *Θέματα Λογοτεχνίας*, (May-August 2005), pp. 180–94.

40 Of Nikos Varotsis, who took part in events at the Institute – though his formation was very different, particularly with regard to the influence on him of Marxist writers – it is said that he had little affinity for the brand of modernism that prevailed in *Prosperos*. Nonetheless, he sensed that something new and significant was afoot and participated, following the example of his friends.

41 Of interest in this light is the short but dense piece 'Προσανατολισμοί' by Kleon Paraschos in *Anglo-Greek Review*, 2/1 (1946), pp. 27–28. In it are discussed foreign literary influences in nineteenth- and twentieth-century Greece: German, with a mention of Lorentzos Mavilis; French, to which *Filologika Nea* was orientated, thanks to Desyllas; and English, the promoters of which were (once again) Desyllas, alongside Aspioti and the British Council in Corfu. The same author ('Το Βρεταννικό Συμβούλιο', also on p. 27 of the same issue) notes the Council's contribution over ten years, with a mention of the reconstruction of the bombed buildings of Corfu.

42 The roll-call of names is impressive: Ilias Venezis, Apostolos Melachrinos, Nikos Gabriel Pentzikis, Zoi Karelli, Takis Sinopoulos, Takis Doxas, Nikos Kachtitsis, (who lived in Patras), Tasos Yannaras, I.M. Panagiotopoulos, Giorgos Athanas, Takis Papatsonis.

43 Stephanides was part of the Durrell circle in Corfu and a piece by him about Corfu, showing the influence of Durrell, appeared in *Prosperos*, 2 (1950), pp. 41–43.

44 *Prosperos*, 2 (1950), pp. 58–59, and *Symposio*, 2 (1951).

45 *Prosperos*, 2 (1950), pp. 66–67.

Chapter 8
The magazine *The Record* (1947–1955)

Dinos Christianopoulos

The British Council magazine *The Record*, which ran from 1947 to (it seems) 1955 was undoubtedly of a provincial cast, in appearance and content alike, in no way comparable to the remarkable *Anglo-Greek Review* in Athens or the congenial *Prosperos* of Corfu. That said, it gathered around it a number of Thessalonian writers who had an interest in literature in English, among them the fiction writer and essayist George Delios and the poet George Vafopoulos and, from a younger generation, Loula Anagnostaki, Kleitos Kyrou, Iphigeneia Chrysochoou and others. In 1947 I joined their number, interested as I greatly was in T.S. Eliot, but also in the British poets of the War. I was still a very young man and my contributions to the magazine were in the nature of juvenilia. Since I was penniless, I was permitted to enrol at the British Institute without paying. In those days (when the Institute was still at 2 Anaktoron Street) I was first and foremost spending time in its library, to which I was attracted less by the English language – of which I was a poor student – than by an interest in the works of the British painters Stanley Spencer and Feliks Topolski.[1]

The state of affairs after the German withdrawal in 1944 was pretty bad and remained so after the arrival of British troops. The notorious 'December events' exacerbated the hatred that a section of the population had for the British, though nothing of that sort took place up here in Thessaloniki, where the political leadership showed greater prudence. It was not long before the Cyprus rising broke out and gave the final blow to the so-called *Anglokratia* (British rule). Between these two dates a British literary influence squeezed itself in, culminating at the time of the award of the Nobel Prize to T.S. Eliot in 1948. This British influence, over the five years from 1946 to 1950 especially, played a certain role and took root gradually at the expense of the French language and its literature. I myself am an unbiased witness to this very development. My first poetry book, *A Time of the Lean Kine* (1950),[2] certainly shows a shaking off of French Surrealism and a cleaving to Eliot (the fact that the British were later to ignore my poetry, while Americans have translated me on two dozen occasions, is neither here nor there). As for *The Record*, despite the mediocre quality of my own contributions to it, I had the good fortune to translate the fine poem by Loula Anagnostaki (sister of Manolis Anagnostakis) 'A Stranger in the Bar', along with John Dos Passos' piece about Isadora Duncan – two translations which still give me satisfaction.[3]

Notes

1 Editors' note: It is interesting to recall that Stanley Spencer had spent time on the Salonica Front in the First World War, which inspired his most ambitious project as an artist: George Behrend, *Stanley Spencer at Burghclere* (London, 1991).

2 Dinos Christianopoulos, *Εποχή των ισχνών αγελάδων* (Thessaloniki, 1950).

3 Editors' note: Isadora Duncan had a connection to Greek letters through her relation by marriage to the great Greek poet (and contributor to *Anglo-Greek Review*) Angelos Sikelianos: Isadora's brother Raymond married Sikelianos' sister Penelope.

Chapter 9

Making friends for Britain?
Francis King and Roger Hinks at the
British Council in Athens

David Roessel

Neil Kinnock, in an introduction to a history of the organization, wrote that 'put simply the British Council exists to build trust between the UK and other countries and people and thereby make lifelong friends for Britain'.[1] Roger Hinks, as his tenure as Director of the British Council in Athens (from 1954 to 1957) came to a close, remarked, 'At the end of thirty months here [Athens] I have not made any Greek friends for England (which I was paid to do) because I have not made any Greek friends myself,'[2] adding, 'I do not flatter myself that my departure will be regretted by a single Greek.'[3] In his autobiography, *Yesterday Came Suddenly*, the novelist Francis King, who served under Hinks in Athens, stated that he spent 'more than seven years in Athens' working for the British Council, 'three more than the usual British Council period of duty'.[4] Unlike his superior, King reported that he had made some Greek friends, although it is far from clear whether he made any friends for Britain, which, one might think, he was also paid to do. It seems that this part of his job did not concern King as much as it did Hinks, if at all. If the years after the Second World were the Golden Age of the Council in Greece, a romanticized version of history that King follows in his autobiography,[5] King and Hinks represent the Council's Bronze Age in Athens, when the problems between Greece and Britain over Cyprus brought cultural relations to their nadir. Or as Hinks put it, 'the Byronic phase of Anglo-Greek relations is over, and we have entered the post-Byronic phase'.[6]

There is a problem with King's chronology of seven years in Athens with the Council. He was posted to Salonica from 1950 to 1952, and he was sent to Alexandria in 1956 just weeks before the Suez crisis. After three weeks in Egypt, he returned to Athens once more until another post was found in Finland. Further, King took a year's leave of absence after he received the Somerset Maugham Prize for his novel *The Dividing Stream* in 1952, and spent most of that year in Corfu and England. The logical dates for King's service in Athens are those provided by Jim Potts, 1953 to 1957.[7] This seems comparable to King's subsequent stay of four-and-a-half years as the Council's regional director at Kyoto in the early 1960s, despite King's stress that his time in Athens was more

176   DAVID ROESSEL

than the usual period of duty. King stretched his service in Athens in his memoir to make the following point:

> The Alliance Française takes the view that the longer one of its officers is resident in a country, the greater his usefulness. The British Council, on the other hand, is convinced that any officer who stays more than a few years in a country will inevitably go native – thus coming to represent not Great Britain but the country of his adoption. In this argument, I side with the Alliance Française. I remember the occasion when, during my third year in Athens, I was attempting to see the Greek Minister of Culture about some matter and was constantly being fobbed off with a junior official. 'But the Director of the French Institute tells me that he saw the Minister *twice* last week!' I eventually protested. The junior official smiled: 'The Minister was once the Director's student at the French Institute,' he explained.[8] That I was able to hang on for so long in Athens was merely because, unlike most of the other English members of the Council staff, I was fluent in Greek. 'We must have at least one person who can speak the language,' was the line taken.
>
> But this was a line that Roger Hinks was not prepared to take. He decided that – for my sake, not the Council's – it was essential that he should engineer a move. 'Francis has been here too long,' he told all and sundry. 'He's got stuck in a groove. It'll do his writing a world of good if he finds himself in a totally strange environment.' There he may have been right. To some people he went on to say, 'In any case, the relationship with Dino needs to be terminated. That boy is a pest and a drag on him.' There he was wrong. But for Dino, so uncomplicated, so generous-hearted and so affectionate, my life would have been far less happy.[9]

In his diary, Hinks offered a different reason for wanting to move King, one that was more for the Council's sake, not King's. As the situation in Cyprus worsened, the work of the Council diminished – certainly there was no further need for teachers at the British Institute when in 1956 it was, in Hinks's words, 'dead and just about to be buried'.[10] He made this comment before the Institute was officially closed down, after, as King related, 'a bomb had exploded . . . over the Christmas holidays, it killed no one but caused extensive damage'.[11] Hinks lamented that there was 'no intention of scaling down my establishment to what, in the present lamentable state of political circumstances, I should be the first to call reasonable proportions, and on the other hand, nobody has the slightest idea what tasks to give this enormous establishment'.[12] But at the time London was concerned that a reduction of the Council staff in Athens would be taken as a sign of failure of its handling of the Cyprus crisis. So the policy was 'the retention of so large a staff when there was nothing for them to do' and a refusal 'to face the issue whether there would ever again be anything for them to do'. Hinks lamented: 'That our programme is unrealizable, and that our establishment is superfluous, seems to concern them [London] not at all.'[13]

So it is hardly surprising that, according to King, when in 1956 he returned to Athens after only six weeks in Alexandria,

> Roger Hinks greeted me, with a notable lack of enthusiasm. Having worked so hard to get me posted, he was not unnaturally annoyed that political events had now annulled this achievement. 'I don't know what I'm going to do with you' . . . he went on. 'We're overstaffed already.' Because of this overstaffing, I spent the next few months in a limbo of doing virtually nothing at all.[14]

If Hinks's diary has any degree of accuracy, King was in a not too dissimilar situation of doing almost nothing at all before he was posted to Alexandria.

Hinks cannot avoid the Cyprus issue in his diary; how could he, when he was called to London to discuss it?[15] Anyone would have had a difficult time as Director of the Council in Greece during the Cyprus crisis, but it was a particularly hard challenge for someone with the personality of Hinks even if he had not been involved in the bungled cleaning of the Parthenon marbles in 1937–38.[16] Hinks's successor Ronald Bottrall (1906–89), 'blustery, ebullient, matey and given to making noisy scenes – was far more to the taste of Greeks', in King's opinion.[17] Hinks commented that Bottrall 'will get on much better with Katsimbalis'.[18] As this is the only time that the latter name appears in Hinks's diary it seems clear there was room for improvement in the relations between George Katsimbalis and the Council after the Hinks years. But King would later observe, when Bottrall became the Director of the Council in Japan, that 'Ronald Bottrall was so unsuited to Japan, both physically and temperamentally, that it is unlikely that any organization other than the British Council would have ever thought of dispatching him there'.[19]

King has less to say about Cyprus. He notes that his close association with Marie Aspioti, whom he met in Corfu in 1952 (where he contributed poems, stories and essays to the journal *Prosperos*), ended when she visited Athens and he became angry with her for defending acts of terrorism in Cyprus. King remarked, 'Apart from Marie and a Greek diplomatist who, no doubt for career reasons, abruptly dropped me, I can truthfully say that I never lost a single Greek friend because of the political troubles.' But beyond his comment that he would defuse tension in bars by offering Greeks a cigarette and saying, 'If I had Cyprus, I'd give it to you. Like this', he does not discuss Greek concerns about the island nor what he thought about them personally or professionally.[20] Nor does he acknowledge that, if he did not lose any Greek friends because of political troubles, Britain in fact lost many. Where Hinks saw a link between the personal and professional in making friends, King did not.

King did not provide an inside look at the working of the Council in Athens or Salonica in his fiction as he had for Florence in *The Ant Colony*. In that novel, the non-local teachers hired for the Institute 'knew little about English-Language teaching',[21] and there was little attention to the question of whether they were suited to their posts or not. For example, there is the following conversation between two teachers who have just arrived. 'How did you get on?' 'I've no idea . . . it's called a conversation course but how do you teach people to converse? . . . And you?' 'Mine was a class in business English. I never knew there was a special kind of English for business.'[22] In his autobiography King has very little to say about his duties while in Greece. Of his time in Salonica, which he disliked, he remarked only that

> My students in Salonika were very different from my students in Florence. After the occupation and the years of civil war, only the wealthiest of the women showed any elegance. Men and women alike often irritated me with that characteristically Greek assumption that everything is simpler and easier than it is. When, to an advanced literature class, I tried to explain, say, the whole spectrum of critical interpretations of a Hamlet soliloquy, a look of fretful boredom would appear on all but a few of their faces. 'Yes, yes, that's obvious, that's clear, get on with it,' they seemed to be chiding me.'[23]

Daniel Nash, also stationed in Salonica a bit later, had a more charitable view of the students and their struggles. In his novel *My Son is in the Mountains*, he wrote that the students 'moved through all the workings of the Institute as through a cloud, guided along their courses and towards their examinations by their British lecturers. It was pitiful, Gordon thought, how many of them late in life were making the hopeless effort to master English, cherishing the belief that a qualification in the language might help them escape from the grinding difficulties of life in their own country'.[24]

Hinks, although not as sympathetic to the students, came to a similar conclusion that their goals were practical and not cultural; he thought the students wanted to learn not English but 'business English, and that the Americans can teach them',[25] noting elsewhere, 'It is futile to suppose that you can have a British "Institute of Higher Studies" in a country where lower studies were on so low a level as they are in Greece.'[26] In his memoir, King never discusses the aspirations of his students in Greece. He has one short story, 'So Hurt and Humiliated', set in Salonica, in which a Greek boy, whose 'one idea is to get himself to England', seduces the daughter of the chairman of the examining board in an unsuccessful attempt to 'fix' the results of a Council scholarship.[27] In his fiction, King suggests that 'it is only guilt in the search of pleasure' that creates a sense of vice and squalor, and for his Greek characters 'guilt, though so terrible a reality to the ancient Greeks, is fortunately almost unknown to their descendants'.[28] But guiltless vice and squalor were not the sole province of the Greeks in King's work, but also of the Italians. He would later include a similar scenario in *The Ant Colony*, in which an Italian seduces an English teacher who is later fired after stealing examination questions.

MAKING FRIENDS FOR BRITAIN?

Of his duties teaching for the Institute in Athens, a city which he loved, King had even less to say:

> At first my duties were to teach English language and literature at the British Institute. I think that I was efficient; and I think that I was also popular with my students. But it was a far from exacting job, and my free time was ample. Having previously read a book every two or three days, I am ashamed to say during this period of my life I read virtually nothing. Nor did I write all that much. There was a dangerously seductive air of *dolce fa* [sic] *niente*, which, during the hours of the day when I was not teaching, would lure me out of my flat to one of the cafés on Kolonaki square, to Zonar's just by the Grande Bretagne Hotel, or to a bar called Apotsos. There I would be certain of meeting people, both foreign and Greek, as idle as myself, with whom I would drink and talk for hours, literally, on end.[29]

Hinks, in his diary, remarked that the philhellenism of the 1950s was reduced to the fact that Greece offered 'the sun, the sea, and the bodies of the boys. All the bathing and buggering was done in Greece. Philhellenism was never offset by a comparable amount of anglophilism.'[30] And, while he never quite managed to find a way to do it, Hinks did worry that the Council was not addressing its goal to create anglophilism in Greece. As the head of the Council in Greece, he expressed concern that the Greeks might come to 'feel exploited, degraded, corrupted, trifled with and abandoned. Greece is like Ariadne on Naxos'.[31] Further, Hinks suggested that the Greeks 'often felt impatient and contemptuous of philhellenic sentimentality'.[32] This is certainly the picture one gets from King's novels *The Man on the Rock*[33] and *The Dark Glasses*,[34] in which the Greek characters exhibit disdain for the foreigners, such as King himself, whom they attempt to exploit. The difference was that King, unlike Hinks, was sentimental about a world of Greek rogues taking advantage of starry-eyed foreigners.

In his introduction to a new edition of his 1948 novel, *An Air that Kills*, King said that when he was near graduation from Oxford he informed his godfather that he wanted to join the Foreign Service. He was told that he might be too 'unconventional' to be a diplomat, but that he should try the British Council because 'they don't demand the same standard of conventionality from their people'. King then praised the Council as 'an organization for which I can only be grateful for its tolerance and humanity in an age when most institutions were so intolerant and inhumane about the "illness" (as many people then saw it) from which I was suffering'.[35] Although King does not say so directly, it is clear that he did not think that Roger Hinks was the most tolerant and humane superior, and with some reason. In Athens, Hinks recorded his 'profound dislike of the homosexual circle in which I find myself, and also a certain compassion for it', again signalling his impatience with 'sentimental pederasty masquerading as philhellenism'.[36] This remark might not have been directed only at Francis King, but there is no question that he was a target. Indeed, King, in the quote above, indicated that Hinks thought that King needed to be transferred to end a long-term gay relationship. If King's story 'Getting Ready' is, as I think, a fictional account of a conversation between Hinks and King, then, rightly or wrongly, Hinks thought that King's actions might also be a drag and a pest on the Council. The superior in the story says, 'From time to time I heard things; one does in this kind of job. I ignored them. But now . . . frankly, I'm worried. We can't afford scandals. And especially not in a country like this where they detest us anyway and can be relied upon to exploit them.'[37] When the junior says that 'we've been together now for more than eighteen months' and he cannot just end the relationship, the response is, 'Then I have no alternative but to ask Personnel to transfer you . . . I have no wish to harm your career, you've always seemed to me to be an excellent officer. I shall think of something – health or the need of a fresh environment, something like that.'[38]

By his own account, King threw himself with abandon into gay life in Athens with little caution or circumspection. 'I would often go to some working-class taverna, where both the food and the wine were vile, but where I would see some spectacular dancing and where, with luck I would pick up some sailor, soldier, airman, or manual worker eager both to enjoy himself and to make some money. On the page it sounds squalid; but there was friendship, joy, and, yes, a kind of innocence in those encounters on some deserted beach below the noisy taverna or in some woodland behind it.'[39] Indeed, his long relationship with Dino began as a cash transaction and, despite King's protests, could be said to have continued as one. King described it as follows: 'Dino was in no way mercenary; but, inevitably, since his family were so poor, I used to give him and them gifts.'[40]

King went on to say, 'Unlike many of my friends in Athens in similar situations, I made no to attempt to educate Dino. . . . Inevitably, the relationship could not stand such cultural bombardment.'[41] In his novel *The Firewalkers*, King put it this way: 'Greeks must have the courage to be Greeks and not inferior imitations of Americans or Englishmen.'[42] The protagonist of King's novel *The Man on the Rock* skips the English classes at the British Institute for which his boss, who had a 'mania for improving those nearest to him', had paid because young Greek men don't 'want to give up an hour and a half of one's evening to sit in a stuffy class room'.[43] It might, perhaps, be worth noting that someone who was paid for six years to teach English to Greeks seemed to question whether Greeks should be taking those classes.

And, of course, King gave no consideration to taking Dino with him when he left Greece. In King's story 'The Bitter End', an American about to leave Greece mused about a Greek whose life had been changed by their relationship. 'America would ruin you; and you are something I don't want ruined. Or is it, more subtly and infinitely more dangerous – at that moment the thought first came to him – that I just don't want you there?'[44] It all seems so perfectly

Cavafian that one feels the Alexandrian poet was King's guiding spirit, as he was for King's closest friend in Athens, Robert Liddell.

It is certainly true that in his attitude towards his duties King differed from some of his fellow grecophiles only in his sexual preference. For example, according to King, during his time in Athens Louis MacNeice 'had even less to do than I had' and 'could not be bothered to do it'.[45] But it seems fairly clear that King's gay life style is a reason, and perhaps the main reason, he is rarely, if ever, mentioned among the British literary post-war philhellenes. Indeed, as far as I know, King appears on such a list only once. In a piece in 1954, Stephen Spender provides the following list of new philhellenes, and, as one reads the names, it is bit surprising to see King's name among the group: 'Rex Warner, Louis MacNeice, Patrick Leigh Fermor, Osbert Lancaster, Lawrence Durrell, Robert Liddell, Steven Runciman, Francis King, Bernard Spencer, and John Craxton.' Spender goes on to say that the new philhellenes approached Greece through 'poets like Seferis, Sikelianos, and Elytis, and painters like Ghika and Tsarouchis'.[46] It seems hardly possible that King could have worked at the British Council and spent so many hours in Apotsos and not have met Katsimbalis, or Seferis, or Gatsos, or Ghika, or Savidis, or have not known of the work of Sikelianos or Elytis. But, despite seven years in Greece, he never mentions in his memoir the work of any modern Greek author, nor does he record meeting them. The only Greek that King singles out for special notice in his autobiography is Thanos Veloudios, who King also fictionalized as the main character in *The Firewalkers*. 'Everyone in Athens knew Colonel Grecos,' the narrator of *The Firewalkers* declares, 'with the possible exception of the Colossus of Maroussi he is the best-known figure in Athens.' British literary figures coming to Greece certainly had heard of Katsimbalis.[47] But if everyone in Athens knew Veloudios, no one except King ever mentions him; the only exception I know of is by Patrick Leigh Fermor in a footnote to *Mani*.[48] And Leigh Fermor is the only one of the famous British literary philhellenes who, in the company of Veloudios, would visit King at his Athens apartment.[49] In *The Firewalkers*, Grecos tells a visiting dignitary that he will have a soirée at which he will play some of his own music, and the guests would include perhaps 'Madame Venizelou, Nicholas Ghika, Seferis – if he has returned from England, – Spiro Harocopos, and, of course, my very good friend, the Colossus of Maroussi'. Impressed by the list, the dignitary agrees to attend. Later, when asked how he would get the guests he had mentioned, Grecos responds, 'Oh, It needn't be *exactly* those.'[50] And, of course, none of those people appear at the event. Clearly both Veloudios and King had met and knew the people mentioned, but, as the novel suggests, there was not a great deal of social contact between the groups.

As King described him, Veloudios was the grand old man, or colossus, of gay Athens. 'People who disliked Thanos – often those whose parties he had gate-crashed – tended to say he was "shameless" or "wicked". That he was the first of these things, no one could deny; but his shamelessness was, for me, part of his lurid charm. At a cocktail party at the British Embassy, he would

182   DAVID ROESSEL

proposition or even grope a waiter with little or no attempt at concealment.'[51] King's novel *The Firewalkers* is, as the quote above suggests, an answer to Miller's heterosexual Katsimbalis. But it is equally evokes Robert Liddell's *Unreal City*, with Veloudios as the disreputable Christo/Cavafy figure.[52]

The one Greek artist on Spender's list who receives even a passing reference from King is Yannis Tsarouchis. In *The Firewalkers*, on the outside of the door of Colonel Grecos' dwelling was an 'enormous figure of a military policeman . . . wearing shorts, and his naked thighs and knees gleamed through the darkness'. The figure also had a 'square-jawed face, with horizontal line of a mustache, its eyes set close together and the high peasant cheek-bones; the same kind of stylisation as is achieved on the male Greek face is achieved on the cover of Esquire with the American female one. . . . In a corner was the single Greek work: Ela!' Grecos tells the narrator that 'Tsarouchis made it for me. I particularly like the position of the knocker.' This would seem to place Tsarouchis, along with King, in Veloudios' circle, but as it is King's only mention of the artist in print it is difficult to ascertain how close they might have been. There are no letters in the King Papers at the Ransom Center at the University of Texas at Austin from Tsarouchis, nor is there a folder for correspondence with Veloudios. Hinks said that his relations with those he saw most often in Greece – 'Ghika, Dragoumis, and Dimaras' – were 'cordial acquaintances' that 'will not long survive our separation'.[53] While King may proclaim that he made deeper friendships in Greece, from the epistolary evidence the one that clearly survived the separation was with Robert Liddell, not any of his Greek friends.

The Firewalkers caused some commotion in the Council at Athens. In the introduction written for a new edition in the Gay Modern Classics series, King says,

> When in obedience to a regulation of the time, I submitted the manuscript . . . to my then employers, the British Council, I was faced with an ultimatum. I could resign and publish the book under my own name; I could stay in the British Council and publish it under another name; or I could stay in the British Council and not publish it at all. It was clear that it was the last of these three alternatives that the Council favoured.

> There were two reasons for this severity. The first – and how ludicrous it seems in these libertarian days, nearly thirty years later – was that the book dealt (as one of the British Council officers responsible for acting as its censors put it to me), with 'murky, and, to many people, distasteful aspects of sexuality'. The second was that it was all too plainly a *roman à clef*.[54]

King published the novel under the pseudonym Frank Cauldwell – a reference to a character in his first novel, *To the Dark Tower*,[55] which contained one of the first accounts of an act of fellatio in English literature – a novel, we

MAKING FRIENDS FOR BRITAIN? 183

should note, that was published under the name of Francis King before he was hired to work for the British Council.

Roger Hinks passed the following judgment on the novel in his diary: 'One is bored with books written without imagination, even when they refer to subjects in which one is slightly interested like *The Firewalkers*.'[56] In another entry, Hinks remarked that Robert Liddell 'said that King was "clever without being intelligent" and I added that he was "inquisitorial without being curious"; what we both meant was that he was lacking in imagination. And his books prove it'.[57] From Hinks's perspective, *The Firewalkers* was embarrassing, but not necessarily for the reasons that King thought. But Hinks's verdict was undoubtedly affected by the fact that the book celebrated a philhellenism of the sun, the sea, and the bodies of the boys that he found so lamentable.

Indeed, Hinks surprisingly has more to say about modern Greek poetry in his diary than King does in any of his work. He records a long discussion about the merits of Cavafy's erotic poetry over his historical pieces with Robert Liddell and a George [perhaps Savidis]; a discussion about the oral nature of modern Greek verse with Constantine Dimaras, and a critique of an article by Patrick Leigh Fermor on the work of Ghika. But these three are like little flares in the diary which are all the more unexpected for the lack of any sustained discussion of Greek art. Hinks's diary elicits no real interest in the modern Greek cultural world; the best one can say is that one could not be a member of the Council in Greece and not experience it to some degree. All the more surprising then that King, who portrays himself as 'going native', has even less to say about Greek intellectuals in his published work. It highlights the fact that King intentionally and studiously avoided comment on Greek literary acquaintances to showcase his connection to Greek authenticity. But this could also indicate that, while King felt free to express his sexuality in certain places in of Athens, the higher literary circles of Athens were not among those them.

*

King went native in Japan as well. ('I came to feel so much at home in Japan that I often used to say that I was sure that, in some previous existence, I must have been Japanese.'[58]) For King, the key fact of his employment with British Council, as he himself makes clear, was that it allowed him to escape from Britain and a British culture he found awful and confining to the liberating air of Greece or Japan, where he was much more 'at home' (and in this he was not unlike many of his heterosexual Council colleagues).[59] King was aware of the problems in his thinking. In his novel *The Man on the Rock*, the Greek protagonist talks of the many expatriates who say, 'I am at home here' and that these were 'all people who felt there was no place for them in the countries of their origin. They settled in Greece firstly because Greeks are individualists, and respect, instead of despising, oddity; and secondly because they would delude themselves that their oddity was not something innate . . . but simply the natural result of being a foreigner'.[60] Here one can see the spectre of Hinks once again asking how do people who feel there is no place for themselves in Britain further the work of the Council in making friends for Britain? Yet Hinks himself was not much better. 'It would be easy to be a philhellene if one sees nothing but country folk,' Hinks asserted, 'The difficulty is to endure the business man, the party man and the university professors. It is they who have turned Athens into what Constantine Dimaras calls 'the cancer of Hellas'. But it is also with them that we have to deal professionally.'[61] He noted, 'If Greece were ruled by people like Mimi, and Nitsa, and Irini, and not by crooks and politicasters and clerics, it would be a happier country.'[62]

Hinks and King shared, along with other British in Greece, preconceptions and prejudices about Greeks and education – including a belief that the education offered by the Council somehow made Greeks more Western and thus less genuine and real. Here there was a fundamental collision between philhellenic feeling and sentimentality, and the goal of the British Council in Greece. How could one put one's heart and soul into establishing a British Institute of Higher Studies when one thought that the success of that enterprise would mean the end of everything good about Greece? This celebration of the rural Greeks as the real Greeks was part of a philhellenic myth developed during the Golden Age of the British Council after the War. As the Council entered its Age of Bronze, Hinks saw one advantage over the Golden Age that had gone before. 'It is a great advantage, of course, to have no philhellenic past – one is spared the disillusionment of love gone sour.'[63] Yet, despite this advantage, Hinks and King, however different they might have been, made few friends for Britain during their service in Greece.

Notes

1 Ali Fisher, *A Story of Engagement: The British Council 1934–2009* (London, 2009), p. 2.

2 Firestone Library Rare Book and Manuscript Collection, Princeton University, Roger Hinks diary, G 30 p. 102.

3 Firestone Library, Hinks diary, G 30 p. 84.

4 Francis King, *Yesterday Came Suddenly* (London, 1993), p. 148.

5 Ibid., pp. 127–28.

6 Firestone Library, Hinks diary, D 27 p. 61.

7 Jim Potts, 'Truth will Triumph: The British Council and Cultural Relations in Greece', in David Wills (ed.), *Greece and Britain Since 1945* (Newcastle, 2010), p. 115.

8 The French kept Octave Merlier in his position as Director for 30 years. See Firestone Library, Hinks diary, G 30 p. 21.

9 King, *Yesterday*, p. 148.

10 Firestone Library Rare Book and Manuscript Collection, Princeton University, Roger Hinks diary, E 28 p. 68.

MAKING FRIENDS FOR BRITAIN? 185

11 King, *Yesterday*, p. 141.

12 Firestone Library, Hinks diary, D 27 pp. 59–60.

13 Firestone Library, Hinks diary, D 27 p. 60.

14 King, *Yesterday*, p. 153.

15 Firestone Library, Hinks diary, D 27 p. 57.

16 King rather cattily related the incident as follows. One day, Hinks, as Deputy Keeper of Greek and Roman Antiquities at the British Museum, noticed that the Elgin marbles looked a bit 'off colour' and told the staff: 'Those could do with a clean.' Hinks always claimed that he was not responsible, but he resigned over the incident. King, *Yesterday*, p. 128.

17 Ibid., p. 153.

18 Firestone Library, Hinks diary, G 30 p. 89.

19 King, *Yesterday*, p. 173.

20 Ibid., pp. 141–42.

21 Francis King, *The Ant Colony* (London, 1991), p. 23.

22 Ibid., p. 25.

23 King, *Yesterday*, p. 112.

24 Daniel Nash, *My Son Is in the Mountains* (London, 1955), p. 11. For more on this novel by Daniel Nash (pen name of W.R. Loader) see Jim Potts's chapter in this volume.

25 Firestone Library, Hinks diary, E 28 p. 70.

26 Firestone Library, Hinks diary, G 30 p. 32.

27 Francis King, *So Hurt and Humiliated, and Other Stories* (London, 1959), p. 14.

28 Ibid., p. 158.

29 King, *Yesterday*, pp. 126–27.

30 Firestone Library, Hinks diary, E 28 p. 70.

31 Firestone Library, Hinks diary, E 28 p. 71.

32 Firestone Library, Hinks diary, E 28 p. 38.

33 Francis King, *The Man on the Rock* (London, 1957).

34 Francis King, *The Dark Glasses* (London, 1954).

35 Francis King, *An Air That Kills* (Kansas City, 2008), p. VIII.

36 Firestone Library, Hinks diary, G 30 p. 35.

37 King, *So Hurt*, p. 182.

38 Ibid., p. 183.

39 King, *Yesterday*, p. 127.

40 Ibid., p. 144.

41 Ibid.

42 Francis King, *The Firewalkers* (London, 1985), p. 54.

43 King, *Man*, p. 101.

44 King, *So Hurt*, p. 175.

45 King, *Yesterday*, p. 127.

46 Stephen Spender, ' "Brilliant Athens and Us" ', *Encounter*, 2/1 (January 1954), p. 78.

47 David Roessel, *In Byron's Shadow: Modern Greece in the English and American Imagination* (Oxford and New York, 2002), pp. 252–55.

48 Patrick Leigh Fermor, *Mani, Travels in the Southern Peloponnese* (London, 1958), p. 190.

49 King, *Yesterday*, p. 142.

50 King, *Firewalkers*, pp. 114–15.

51 King, *Yesterday*, p. 143.

52 Robert Liddell, *Unreal City* (London, 1952).

53 Firestone Library, Hinks diary, G 30 p. 58.

54 King, *Firewalkers*, p. (I).

55 Francis King, *To the Dark Tower* (London, 1946).

56 Firestone Library, Hinks diary, G 30 p. 96.

57 Firestone Library, Hinks diary, E 28 p. 40.

58 King, *Yesterday*, p. 185.

59 At the age of nine, like other Anglo-Indian children, King was sent 'home' to England for school 'since otherwise you might go native'. If 'England was always home to English expatriates, however humble they were and however many generations the families had been resident in India', the young Francis King was not 'at home' there. He was one of those 'who felt there was no place for them in the countries of their origin', if as an Anglo-Indian he did in fact come to accept that Britain was the country of his origin. King, *Air*, p. VI.

60 King, *Man*, p. 25.

61 Firestone Library, Hinks diary, C 26 p. 55.

62 Firestone Library, Hinks diary, C 26 p. 54.

63 Firestone Library, Hinks diary, C 26 p. 54.

Chapter 10
Cultural relations and the 'non-political' problem: Some personal reflections, with a glance at two novels from the period 1945–1955[1]

Jim Potts

In the field of cultural relations, it is instructive to note the changing uses of language: concepts and terms which have been fashionable, pejorative or ideologically loaded at various times. Such terms include 'cultural propaganda', 'cultural diplomacy', 'public diplomacy' – the last used in its modern sense from around 1965 – and, since 1990 (the term coined by Joseph Nye), 'soft power'.[2]

When it comes to the more old-fashioned term 'propaganda', J.M. Mitchell writes as follows:

> In spite of the threat to Britain's existence, the Council's rapid expansion during the war was accomplished without surrender of its independence. . . . This remarkable fact reflects the general understanding that the Council was not to be involved directly in propaganda. In the Introduction to the Annual Report 1940/4, for example, it was stated that 'the Council was prepared to let facts speak for themselves, to abstain from all political propaganda. . .'[3]

In similar vein, C.A.F. Dundas, the Representative for the Middle East, visited Athens in 1939 and wrote to HQ on 20 October 1939:

> The whole of my wanderings since the beginning of the war have confirmed that the usefulness of the British Council's work at the present time depends almost entirely on its institutions refraining from any kind of active political propaganda or connection with political activities.

Again, on 23 December 1940, A.R. Burn, the Representative in Athens, wrote to HQ: 'Perhaps my chief difficulty is that the British Council gets no credit whatever for its scrupulous refusal to take part in politics.' Indeed, at this critical time in world affairs, the Council was criticized and reproached by Anglophile Greeks for *not* making more propaganda.

188   JIM POTTS

On the Council's own website, in the *History* section, one could find until quite recently a short article by Nicholas J. Cull entitled 'Propaganda?':

> The British Council was founded as an organ of international propaganda. During the late 1920s an influential group of civil servants became convinced that 'British' values of parliamentary democracy could be subsumed [sic] by the rising tide of fascism. . . . Particular Council initiatives included the teaching of English, but political messages always came along with the language tuition.[4]

Such messages were often about parliamentary democracy and other British values. After the end of the War, Cull argues, the Council had a 'new incarnation as truth teller and fount of fair play'.

It is true that the Council was founded in 1934 against a background of the rise of Fascism and National Socialism and largely thanks to the conviction of a few individuals that Britain should do more to promote liberal and democratic values to help preserve the free world, to speak up for 'the British way of life' in a time of increasing propaganda of the type associated with Mussolini and Goebbels. As Lord Kinnock, then Chairman of the British Council, put it in 2009: 'At that time, some European states were manifesting their approach to international relations with the aid of rearmament, marching songs and aggressive declarations about *mare nostrum* and *Lebensraum*.'

In December 2010 the British Council released online an archive of 1930s and 1940s 'Propaganda films' about the British way of life. This is how the BBC framed it: 'The films were a form of propaganda to showcase the best of British life at a time when fascism was gaining strength in Europe. The documentaries deal, among other things, with the subtleties of cricket and the delights of Kew Gardens.'[5] It is clear that, if Council staff were ever obliged occasionally to become involved in forms of what some might choose to term propaganda, it was as reluctant propagandists.

Nicholas Cull argues, 'The Council helped to ensure a cultural place for Britain in the modern world beyond that justified by its economic or political power: it has been a central organ of. . . "soft power".' Indeed Joseph Nye, in his lecture at Portcullis House, London, 20 January 2010 on 'Soft Power and Public Diplomacy' said of soft power, 'The British Council discovered [soft power] and has been practising it effectively since 1934.' To quote Cull once again, 'During the Cold War the British Council . . . provided a point of contact with western ideas in the non-aligned world and, when thaws permitted, the Eastern Bloc.'

That is true, even before the thaws. But how were the Council's activities perceived in Central and Eastern Europe, as late as the 1980s, before the fall of Communism in that region? Jaroslav Kučera, for example, writing in 1986, in the still-frozen Cold War atmosphere of that period (the same year I was

CULTURAL RELATIONS AND A PROBLEM

posted to Prague as Cultural Attaché and British Council Director, Czechoslovakia), stated,

> State propaganda institutions in capitalist states have, in a way, a similar or identical position to the secret services. Just as the activities of the special services, the activity of external propaganda institutions is relatively independent of the composition of bourgeois governments, of which political party or coalition is in power. In Great Britain, for example, governments come and go but the British Council, directing British propaganda abroad, remains.[6]

The non-political, 'arms-length' status and integrity of the British Council are held sacred, both in terms of the staff's own activities and in the professional practice of cultural relations. Staff members have never been authorized to express overt political opinions, to engage in political activity or to publish their own work without clearance – these were once fundamental conditions of service. In the case of those who served with the Council in Greece, both Francis King[7] and W.R. Loader (writing as Daniel Nash) used pen names for certain of their novels.

The British Council was founded in 1934 and granted a Royal Charter by Parliament in 1940. The Council has charitable, non-governmental status. A recent version of the British Council website has stated,

> We operate independently from the UK government. Our approach is rooted in our commitment to building mutually beneficial relationships – with our partners internationally and across the UK. We believe that the best way to win greater appreciation and understanding of the UK as a trusted and creative partner is to demonstrate a desire to listen to and learn from the people we engage with. Throughout our history – in Suez, in South Africa under apartheid, in central Europe during the Cold War and today in the aftermath of September 11th – this reputation for internationalism and integrity has enabled us to nurture long-term relationships which might otherwise have been impossible.

This statement from today's setting should be borne in mind by the reader of this chapter. My theme is the 'non-political problem' in the context of cultural relations, mutual respect, trust-building and exchange, with regard to Greece in the period 1945–55.

I refer to trust-building in the spirit of the foreword by Lord Kinnock referred to earlier: 'The trust-building efforts, the public diplomacy efforts, of the British Council are obviously not conducted in a political vacuum – nothing is. But they are people-to-people rather than government-to-government.' Maybe the term was at its most fashionable peak in my last decade with the Council. (I retired at the end of 2004.) Publications such as the Foreign Policy

Centre's *Public Diplomacy*[8] and Counterpoint's *Mutuality, Trust and Cultural Relations*[9] capture the mood of that time.

But perhaps that strikes too reassuring a note: Greece and Britain did not enjoy an easy relationship in this period. The cultural allure of Britain in post-war Greece was strong, encompassing as it did the refined tastes of the English gentleman, tweed jackets and brogues, clubs, Burberry, Shakespeare, Oxford and Cambridge, respect for tradition and democratic institutions, as often featured in Eckersley's English teaching text-books. Yet, as George Seferis wrote in 'Salamis in Cyprus' (written 1953), here in the version by Edmund Keeley and Philip Sherrard:

> It doesn't take much time
> for the yeast of bitterness to rise
> . . . talking does no good;
> who can change the attitude of those with power?
> Who can make himself heard?
> Each dreams separately without hearing anyone else's nightmare.[10]

Not even the most alluring manifestations of soft power and the closest of old friendships would be able to sustain trust and good relations in times of international conflict, mistrust, suspicion and hostility.

After the German withdrawal from Athens the Council's office opened there at the very time that British troops were on active service in the Greek capital and became involved in the Battle of Athens (December 1944). The office was reopened by Colonel K.R. Johnstone, himself on active service at the time. (It is interesting that in *Men of Stones*, Rex Warner's Director of the Cultural Mission is also given the rank of Colonel.) In Athens the Council's Institute of English Studies and the British Institute of Higher Studies opened officially in October 1945. In Thessaloniki the Council reopened in 1945, and John Elliott arrived as Director of the British Institute there around July 1945.

The British ambassador who was anxious to see a resumption of British Council work in Greece was Sydney-born Sir Reginald (Rex) Leeper, who had played a formative role in the creation of the British Council in 1934. He had been involved in the new field of 'cultural propaganda' from 1931 and was much involved with the development of the Council until about 1939. He later served as British ambassador to Greece from 1943 to 1946, and in the epilogue to *When Greek Meets Greek* he wrote, 'I was liable at any moment to stir up waves of philotimo against me.'[11] There would be times when his 1930s brainchild, the British Council, would also make a few waves.

Kenneth Johnstone published an obituary of Leeper in *Home and Abroad*, the British Council Staff Journal. It concludes,

> It might be said that, while Leeper's view of the Council was always from the political angle, his conception of it was always more than political. The

CULTURAL RELATIONS AND A PROBLEM

Council owes it to him that what might have been just another vague essay in international goodwill or just another national advertising campaign was accepted as making political sense but at the same time seen to be something distinct from foreign policy or propaganda.

It could be argued, with hindsight, that things were not quite so clear-cut. Let me give a few examples from our period to bring this out.

In *An Affair of the Heart* (1957), Dilys Powell gives an account of her visit to Salonica in 1945 to give lectures for the British Council:

> It was easy to cause political mischief in the Salonika of 1945. Every phrase uttered was quoted on behalf of one or other of the parties, and after a lecture in which, remembering the loyalty I owed when abroad, I had spoken with respect of the policy of the Labour Government then in power in Britain, I was startled to find myself hailed as a supporter by the Communist newspapers. Once again I was out of my depth in a savage political current. . . . In the streets, on the quayside, the eyes were hostile. . . . Nobody in Salonika smiled back. . . . For the first time in Greece I felt I was taken for an enemy. The drum-beat in the air grew louder.[12]

By the same token, Nikos Kazantzakis' British Council-sponsored visit to Britain in 1946 (discussed by David Holton in his contribution to this volume), created some political controversy about the plebiscite issue. His widow Helen Kazantzakis records that at the end of August 1946 the British Council gentlemen were annoyed that their guest had cabled his vote (in the plebiscite) in support of the Republic. 'You promised us not to get involved in politics during your stay in England,' they told him. Kazantzakis was forced to explain that 'he had not given up his civil rights when he accepted their amiable invitation'. 'To take part in a plebiscite on which the future of one's country depends is, it seems to me, the foremost duty of any responsible person!'

Earlier that year there had been an article, in Greek, about the work of the Council, in the first number of the *Anglo-Greek Review* (my translation):

> The aims of the British Council are neither political, nor economic, nor propagandistic – unless we are using the word propaganda in a different sense . . . humanistic aims . . . mutual understanding, respect and love between the peoples of the world. And that, above all, is the Propaganda of Peace.

Yet actual manifestations of cultural interaction could at times cause frictions. For instance, the exhibition of the naïve painter Theophilos at the British Council in Athens in May 1947 caused political reactions from the Left and the Right alike, as Rex Warner recalled in *Views of Attica and its Surroundings*. A glance at two English-language novels of the period, both published by major trade publishers, can help illuminate some of the atmosphere of the time and the

192 JIM POTTS

issues with which British Council staff were forced to engage. The first is Rex Warner's *Men of Stones: a Melodrama,* published in London by The Bodley Head in 1949.

*

Rex Warner served as Director of the British Institute in Athens in 1945–47. George Seferis, who first met Warner at this time, wrote of him in his journal, on 25 January 1947: 'There is something solid about this man; I feel a steadily growing friendship for him.'[13] Years later, in 1968, Seferis would recall in a poem, 'Letter to Rex Warner':

> . . . I sensed who you were and we became friends.
> We were in a country devastated by the war –
> they'd crippled even the dolls of children.[14]

In his introduction (dated Athens, 1946) to George Seferis' *The King of Asine and Other Poems* Warner wrote of Greece and its history:

> There is something disturbing and oppressive as well as inspiring in the thought of such a weight and variety of history. . . . As important to the Greek and European spirit as the Parthenon are the vast rock structures of Mycenae, the palace dripping with the blood of kindred slain by kindred, the wealth and savagery of the house of Atreus.

Such a view colours *Men of Stones*. The novel is an allegory of human nature which could be described as, in essence, a parable about soft power against hard power – the plays and love poetry of Shakespeare versus oppression and military force; the pen versus the sword. It sets out to ask whether love, gentleness, decency and goodness are forces that are in any way a match for cruelty, savagery, fear, atrocities and absolute power. It is about fundamental differences of world-view between people with very different or opposing senses of mission and morality. The novel also seems to embody and dramatize many of the points made by Plato in the section of *The Republic* that deals with tyranny and despotism and with the tyrannical man capable even of parricide when faced with resistance to his tyrannical 'master-passion' and programme.

The moral justification for the exercise of hard power and brute force is a theme that had long preoccupied Warner. Yet the experience of the savagery of the Second World War and of the fratricidal Greek Civil War had made everything much more complicated. He explores the issues in depth in his essay *The Cult of Power* (1946), which is something of a blueprint for *Men of Stones*. The essay begins as follows:

> The worship of violence, of absolute power, of lawlessness, the setting-up of the individual against the universe – all these are old things. Socrates argued

CULTURAL RELATIONS AND A PROBLEM

against them: Marlowe was fascinated by them. Today they seem to have returned, with their old strength newly armed, and more dangerous than before.[15]

Warner argues that what is most remarkable is

the rapidity with which generally accepted ideals of the early twentieth century such as toleration, kindliness, objective truth, freedom, have been replaced in many people's minds by their exact opposites. More remarkable still is the enthusiasm with which people have accepted the substitution. It is true that we see this process most clearly in fascism and, amongst fascist states, most clearly of all in Germany; but it would be most unwise to regard it as a process that is wholly alien from ourselves. . . . Fascist ideals appear in the most unlikely place.

Men of Stones is set in an island prison, formerly a medieval castle. The novel was inspired no doubt by events in Greece, by the attempts to rehabilitate political prisoners held on islands like Makronisos, Trikeri and Aï-Stratis, by involving them in the staging of classical Greek dramas and some 'well-regarded foreign classics' in order to bring about 'moral salvation' – as recently discussed in Gonda Van Steen's *Theatre of the Condemned*[16] – as well as by post-war disgust and disillusionment concerning man's behaviour to man, the atrocities and the burning of villages, the horrors of concentration camps, starvation and suffering in other parts of Europe.

The novel dramatizes issues of totalitarianism, morality, religious faith and freedom. Mr Goat, 'a young lecturer in literature attached to one of the foreign cultural missions', goes to the island, with his liberal ideals, to assist the Governor with his disguised prison reform project, directing the prisoners in a production of *King Lear*; once there, he has an affair with the Governor's wife, Maria, who comes across at first as an amoral but seductive young woman. Finally, he himself is obliged to perform the role of Lear, and Maria the part of Cordelia. At the end of the performance, her dead body is placed in Lear's arms.

She has been killed by the Governor, a mad dictator intent upon seizing power through a *coup d'état* and upon achieving a new world order based on a ruthless programme of moral regeneration or re-armament and a selectively appropriated Christianity, and on his own absolute, God-like power and unchallenged divinity. His absurd plans, born from his coldly calculating but clear-headed form of insanity, include the birth of a redeemer-child, and the use of his liberated but thoroughly brainwashed prisoners as the missionaries of his new religion and as the vanguard of a general uprising and revolution.

Perhaps, the novel suggests, we are all men of stones, with collective responsibility, or varying degrees of individual responsibility, for the deaths of innocent Cordelia figures, for not preventing world wars and civil wars, for not resisting dictators, but rather for helping to create the conditions for

194 JIM POTTS

conflicts and *coups d'état*. Mr Goat, the British lecturer, is quite unable to face the facts – the very real threats and danger posed by those wielding hard power, in a world where words like 'civilized' and 'uncivilized', 'good' and 'evil', have lost their meaning:

> As for the people, disorganised and perplexed by years of civil war and of devastation, it was by no means certain that this extraordinary propaganda, directed with energy and skill, might not enjoy among them a certain success.

At an earlier stage, the Governor has insisted that

> We have had three thousand years of poetry and philosophy and love. Which of your poets and philosophers and lovers would have imagined the final age, the age of the concentration camp and of the atomic bomb? Is it not clear that, apart from some few exceptions, men are not interested in poetry or philosophy or love?

His brother Marcus, who has himself endured great suffering, claims that, alongside the despair and misery he has experienced and witnessed, he has seen at the same time 'what is really meant by love and pity, and that they, in a way that is impossible to explain, are in the end stronger than your fire and your prisons – both stronger and more real'.

Attending the performance of *King Lear* is the director of the foreign cultural mission, Colonel Felson, who has responsibility for Mr Goat. Felson thinks only of the Mission's role, and his desire to bring people together, 'more important than all else was his simple directive – to be non-political'. 'With some part of his mind he wished that this was not so. He was not convinced that, at all times and all places, the pen was mightier than the sword.' In spite of constant protestations that his interests are only cultural and entirely non-political, we are told that he attaches great importance, 'from the point of view of propaganda, to the performance which he and a number of foreign journalists were to watch that evening'. Mr Goat is killed in the ensuing bombardment of the island by the Governor's political rival, which marks the beginning of a new round of civil war. Colonel Felson reflects that 'this temporary discouragement should not be allowed to affect in any way the existing arrangements for the future of the Mission'.

Perhaps the most human and attractive character *in Men of Stones* is Captain Nicholas, the bibulous literary critic and lecturer on poetry, whose portrayal at times suggests that Warner had in mind some attributes of a fictionalized Katsimbalis character. (Katsimbalis, as Avi Sharon's contribution to the present volume reminds us, was readily mythologized.) Towards the end of the novel, when the group is swimming in the sea, Mr Goat and Maria comment 'on the huge frame of Captain Nicholas, who for long floated on his back, like some aquatic beast, singing to himself or spouting water into the air'. Warner

CULTURAL RELATIONS AND A PROBLEM

manages to combine philosophical allegory with considerable suspense in this *tour de force*. It is no easy matter to make an amateur or prison inmates' production of *King Lear* the convincing central point of so much political intrigue and drama.

Although it is nowhere specified that *Men of Stones* is set in Greece or indeed in any specific country, there are sufficient markers about the landscape, cuisine, civil wars and a national Church to imply a Greece-like country as one of the most likely Mediterranean settings. One drawback to that interpretation – for the literal-minded reader – is the necessity to suspend one's disbelief when reading the allegory, given the implausibility of the play being acted in English. Would any government minister or prison governor from such a real, or imaginary, foreign country, assume that prisoners would command sufficient English at that period to act in a difficult Shakespeare tragedy in the original? French might have been a possibility.

Before the *dénouement* of the novel, the Minister for Public Instruction, who had originally conceived the idea of the scheme for prisoners to act in regular productions of Shakespeare's plays as a normal part of prison discipline, praises the work done by the staff of Colonel Felson's cultural mission and expresses the hope for his own country – in a jocular way – that 'in the future, the criminal instincts of his countrymen might be permanently diverted by the harmless imitations of crime and folly that were the themes of dramatic literature'. The Colonel himself had much earlier asked the rhetorical question 'Who can estimate the possible effect on the most unlikely minds, of great poetry?'

Dwelling on such questions, Warner was to recall only a few years later that

> In Athens at the time of which I am writing one could laugh at what often seems the ridiculous intrusions of politics into the spheres of literature or of art; . . . the obscure processes of creation can certainly not be regulated by political or moral standards. . . . And so, it seems to me, we should urge our politicians and administrators to expect, if they expect anything, rather criticism and opposition from the arts than any obvious support or acclamation.[17]

Warner faces squarely an issue which was – if one may add a short parenthesis on how this themes comes into the poetry of the period – to preoccupy John Press. Press had been Lecturer at the Council's Athens Institute of English Studies from 1946 to 1947 before transferring to Salonica from 1947 to 1950. In his editorial for the British Council magazine, *The Record*, in December 1949 Press wrote,

> Here, in Salonika, we cannot cloister ourselves in an academic paradise. This does not mean that we should dabble in political speculation. The Record, by its very nature, is precluded from expressing any formal views on political affairs. Yet even those who fancy that their interests are purely literary or

aesthetic find, sooner or later, that political implications lie folded in their subject. . . . We can hope to exert little or no influence upon the jungle-world of barbed-wire frontiers, manipulated currencies, passports, visas and preparations for destruction in which we find ourselves. We can at least remind ourselves that there are other worlds, less hideous and more permanent, worlds in which science is not the agent of militarism, literature the slave of authority and learning the weapon of cynical power.

In his collection *Uncertainties, and Other Poems*, published just one year after the end of our period, Press does permit himself to write on political themes, and with some animus. 'Aftermath of Civil War' is about an old man crouching with two candles beneath two icons:

> Day after day he kneels there to recite
> The names of martyrs and to dedicate
> A pair of candles, like an acolyte,
> To some malignant god of rancorous hate.
> This loving scrutiny of festering wrongs
> That shapes the rite of self-inflicted pain
> Is timeless in its cruelty; it belongs
> To prehistoric epochs, and we gain
> A dreadful revelation of the same
> Intense, primaeval brooding on revenge
> That, smouldering with a dark, inhuman flame,
> Inspired the liturgies upon Stonehenge.[18]

This precisely is the theme of the second novel by a less well known British Council employee to which I now briefly turn: Daniel Nash's *My Son is in the Mountains*, published in London by Jonathan Cape in 1955. The author, whose real name was W.R. (Bill) Loader (1916–73), served in Greece, in Crete (as Regional Director, 1946–1947) and then in Thessaloniki (1947–49), where he was a British Council lecturer in English Literature at the Aristotle University.

My Son is in the Mountains involves Derek Gordon, a lecturer at the British Institute in Thessaloniki, in the last years of the Greek Civil War. It describes the Communist underground and the activities of the communist-led Democratic Army, of guerrillas and rebels striking against the 'Monarcho-Fascists' and 'plutocrats'; killings, acts of sabotage and bombings, including the attempted bombing of the British Consulate-General, and attempted strikes by the Democratic Army against Edessa and Salonica. The British Council Institute features in a central way. The novel would make a gripping film. Chapter 8 is of particular interest in terms of the pretensions of cultural relations work, as perceived by the author, perhaps from the satirical standpoint of a university lecturer. (Kingsley Amis' *Lucky Jim* had appeared in 1954.)

CULTURAL RELATIONS AND A PROBLEM

There the Director, 'a shortish, plump man, with a shining pink face and a head that was developing a tonsure of baldness', stands at the lectern in the library, with his back to the grand piano, and finishes his lecture, to a small audience, on 'Aspects of British Culture', in the following vein:

> Our Institute, and the little meetings we have here, shines like a beacon in the distressing darkness which has fallen over Northern Greece . . . it would be improper for me to reflect on the political cleavage which now divides this country, but may I say what a great joy it is to me that here in the Institute we have one piece of, as it were, neutral territory where political opponents may come together and forget their differences in a common act of worship before the shrine of culture. Here we do not know politics. We know only the purpose of truth and the love of beauty.

The Commander of the Gendarmerie, attending the lecture because he thinks that he has been invited by the British Consul-General rather than by the British Council – the two were commonly confused – comments to another Greek,

> Are not the English superb? If Greece were about to slide under the waves there would still be a British lecturer on top of Mount Olympus, talking of Keats or parliamentary democracy. There is some sort of missionary spirit which afflicts them.

Derek Gordon, the lecturer, lives in a top-floor apartment overlooking the Thessaloniki waterfront, near the White Tower. To him, it seems like a besieged city, offering few intellectual or cultural diversions or compensations. Gordon is not unlike Goat, the young lecturer in *Men of Stones*, although Goat is more susceptible to feminine charms. In Nash's novel, Maroula, a young woman on the run from the security police, can also be compared to some extent with Maria in *Men of Stones*: both have been active participants in civil wars, the promiscuous Maria herself having fought in the mountains from the age of fifteen, with an anti-government band, and herself capable of revenge atrocities.

The murder takes place of Gordon's school contemporary John Fawcett, a visiting British journalist who was staying at his flat while trying to make contact with the Communist underground in order to write a story. Fawcett is shot in the back of the head and found in the Thermaic Gulf; this was inspired in part by the murder of the American CBS radio correspondent George Polk in May 1948. In some ways Derek Gordon is a typical Beaverbrook Press British Council caricature of the time, rather precious and effeminate; an inexperienced, long-nosed, supercilious Englishman, largely uninterested in women, an Oxford graduate more interested in his books, gramophone records and cultured conversation with his male university friends: 'He did not want this savage world of fighting and killing to impinge on his own cultured existence.'

It begins to dawn on Gordon, however, that political violence is 'more the rule than the exception in Greek history', and the idea of corruption gradually becomes less foreign to him: 'Already students had offered him presents if he would expedite their passage through examinations.' Gordon only narrowly escapes being liquidated himself, not so much for political reasons (although the British are perceived as anything but neutral), but because he has aroused the intense jealousy of Nikos, a cowardly but hot-headed Communist extremist, a wireless operator who desires Maroula, whom Gordon finds himself harbouring out of compassion. Eventually Maroula loses her sense of gratitude and respectful devotion to Gordon, who has sheltered her, seeing him in an unattractive new light and 'not liking what she saw'. She turns her back on the comforts of the bourgeois city lifestyle option, and goes in search of Nikos, even though he has betrayed his friends, partly out of a desperate, unrequited longing for her; for, at the end of the day, he is a surviving comrade in need, one of those who has not yet been executed or imprisoned.

Although there are elements of caricature and stereotyping in all the characters, Greek and British, they are all sufficiently convincing to be capable of engaging our sympathy and antipathy in turn. There are some comments or dialogue suggesting gender, class and ethnic chauvinism, characteristic perhaps of the period, even when meant ironically or satirically, but they do not seriously detract from the excitement and documentary realism of much of the narrative, which is set a year (or two) before the end of the Greek Civil War. Needless to say, the tragedy of the situation in the country is felt throughout, and the love and anxiety of a Salonica father for his son who has joined the guerrillas in the mountains of Epirus is poignantly drawn. The author, too, has a sound knowledge of twentieth-century Greek history.

I have, then, sought to bring out some of the moral and political issues which British Council employees faced and to illustrate these with reference to two neglected novels produced by two of their number in our period. Though very much of their time, they repay rereading today.

Notes

1 Parts of this chapter draw on and expand my earlier discussion, 'Truth Will Triumph: The British Council and Cultural Relations in Greece', in David Wills (ed.), *Greece and Britain Since 1945* (Newcastle, 2010), pp. 99–129.

2 Joseph Nye, *Soft Power: The Means to Success in World Politics* (New York, 2004).

3 J.M. Mitchell, *International Cultural Relations* (London, 1986), pp. 50–51.

4 Nicholas J. Cull, 'Propaganda?', http://archive.li/Xk00J.

5 'Rare Propaganda Films of 1940s Britain Released Online', www.bbc.co.uk/news/entertainment-arts-11997847.

6 Jaroslav Kučera, *'Unlimited Exchange' or Information Imperialism?* (Prague, 1986), p. 43.

CULTURAL RELATIONS AND A PROBLEM

7 See David Roessel's contribution to the present volume.

8 Mark Leonard, with Catherine Stead and Conrad Smewing, *Public Diplomacy* (London, 2002).

9 Martin Rose and Nick Wadham-Smith, *Mutuality, Trust and Cultural Relations* (London, 2004).

10 George Seferis, *Complete Poems*, trans. Edmund Keeley and Philip Sherrard (Princeton, 1995).

11 Reginald Leeper, *When Greek Meets Greek* (London, 1950), p. 239.

12 Dilys Powell, *An Affair of the Heart* (London, 1957).

13 Giorgos Seferis, *Μέρες Ε΄. 1 Γενάρη 1945–19 Απρίλη 1951* (Athens, 1977), p. 88.

14 George Seferis, *Complete Poems*.

15 Rex Warner, *The Cult of Power* (London, 1946), p. 7.

16 Gonda Van Steen, *Theatre of the Condemned* (Oxford, 2011).

17 Rex Warner, *Views of Attica and Its Surroundings* (London, 1950), pp. 78–79.

18 John Press, *Uncertainties and Other Poems* (London, 1956), pp. 28–29.

Chapter 11
MacNeice in Greece

David Ricks

'This place is really the other end of the world': 'Am disappointed by the Greek intelligentsia whom I'd heard much of but perhaps we haven't met the right cliques yet.'[1] These comments in letters a few months into Louis MacNeice's Athens secondment from the BBC to direct the British Institute in 1950 hardly breathe the Philhellenism which was such a feature of many – notably Rex Warner, or Kenneth Johnstone before that – who were part of that Athens setting; and they might suggest that a generally dyspeptic attitude to Greece prevailed on MacNeice's part.[2] That, however, would be a simplification. In this chapter I aim to tease out some of the implications of MacNeice's frustrations with the Institute and the Council, and by extension their Greek setting, in the immediate aftermath of the Civil War. It may be that, without the pre-war or war-time experience of Greece possessed by some of his British colleagues, and without their conversance with the modern language, MacNeice found it harder to marry his classical background with the contemporary experience. (By contrast, Lawrence Durrell's very lack of a classical background seems to have disinhibited his rapport with Greece.) That would account for some of the dialogue-of-the-deaf feeling to his reports of the cultural milieu and what he felt could be but a minor British contribution to it. It may be, too – as critics have argued – that the poet's Athens stay coincided with, even was intended to compensate for, a dry period 'in the middle way' of his poetic career.[3] But it seems worth taking seriously the fact that he built his most architectonic book, *Ten Burnt Offerings* (1952), around a Greece formed, not just by a store of classical allusions, but by the Greece around him – about which he had some sharply, though covertly, political things to say.[4] Here I aim briefly to set the poems that emerged from this period in the context of, and in contact with, contemporary Greece and, above all, the poetry of George Seferis.

MacNeice's comment on the Greek intelligentsia stands in contrast with a brisk bit of stereotyping made by Reginald Leeper back in 1931, shortly before the British Council's formation, when the Poet Laureate John Masefield was to be sent over: 'We have just secured Masefield to lecture on English poetry both at Angora and at Athens. We told him that at the former place the standard of intelligence would not be high, while at the latter it would be. He will vary his lecture accordingly.'[5] Yet Leeper's role in the creation of the British Council, and its objectives in countering Fascist propaganda, were by no means at odds with the fact that Athens came to secure the services of the series of eminent

202   DAVID RICKS

men of letters (and one woman, Alethea Hayter) who are at the heart of this volume.[6] Where does MacNeice fit in?[7]

In a personal retrospect on the work of the Council, written some time before 1956, W.R.L. Wickham opined that 'a Representative should be something of a personality in his own right'.[8] At the time when MacNeice was seconded from the BBC, from January 1950 to June 1951, (initially as Director of the British Institute, until September 1950, and subsequently as Assistant Representative) he certainly qualified as such a personality, rather more so than Warner and Leigh Fermor at that stage, or indeed (in literary circles) than Runciman. In fact, as most surveys of his work acknowledge, MacNeice was both an established figure and, at the same time, one whose reputation was now rather on the wane – this, not so much in spite of as in the light of, his *Collected Poems 1925–1948*.[9]

MacNeice found himself at the helm of an outfit that he described as functioning smoothly.[10] Just as well, since Frances Donaldson's official history of the British Council expresses the view that 'The record suggests that Messrs Runciman, Warner and Leigh Fermor may not have been by nature suited to the administration of the Council finances.'[11]

In Athens, the great machine of English language teaching, heavily oversubscribed, ground on in a Cold War setting; and the importance of the library for spreading English literary work and tastes is clear.[12] MacNeice for his part was there to bring something of contemporary British literary life to Greece. (Really to Athens: in practice, his interest in the provincial branches seems to have been minimal: and this was perhaps a difference of perspective from that of Runciman and other old hands in Greece.)[13]

The biggest fish MacNeice might have landed for an Athens visit – though he did bring an important Henry Moore exhibition – was that of his publisher, and 1948 Nobel Laureate, Mr Eliot. Writing to Eliot, the younger man buttered him up: 'You have a very strong following in Athens who would flock to hear you on anything.'[14] This was undoubtedly true, in a climate influenced by the *Anglo-Greek Review*; and a visit by Eliot might have had a greater impact even than the influential visit of William Faulkner later in the decade (1957).[15] But MacNeice had his doubts about whether Eliot's influence in Greece was entirely positive, and this fits in with a broader negative assessment he made five months in (15 May 1950), to his fellow Ulsterman and Hellenist E.R. Dodds:

> The poets, of whom there are too many, all seem to think that T.S. Eliot liberated poetry from tradition (!) and that Free Verse is empress for ever. And the painters are of many styles but seem with some notable exceptions, not only derivative but dreary. Music, Hedli [MacNeice's second wife] thinks, is poor except for a humble little group that performs in the Byzantine tradition. Architects there seem to be none although there is an immense amount of building (walking along the streets one's nostrils get full of cement). And the University, so everyone tells me, is still quite Teutonic & opposed to all ideas.[16]

We're not on oath when we write letters, but this paragraph contains much to offend a whole gamut of constituencies. MacNeice was clearly right to protest against one-sided readings of Eliot, and his own work of the time is particularly preoccupied with variety of verse form. (This in part reflects his interest in broadcast verse and the BBC years which were no more than punctuated by his Athens posting.) Yet Zissimos Lorenzatos, admittedly living outside Greece at that time, was starting to engage with Eliot's criticism, and in particular his notion of tradition, in ways of which MacNeice clearly had no inkling.[17] When it came to painting, MacNeice did evidently make a welcome exception for Nikos Hadjikyriakos-Ghika, with whom he became friends; and one may note here that contacts in the world of the visual arts played significant role in the development of literary affinities: think only of the Ghika portrait of Seferis and the John Craxton's illustrations to the *King of Asine* volume which had introduced Seferis to an English-speaking audience in 1948.[18] When it comes to art music, MacNeice was surely correct, but his hint in this passage at an unnamed Simon Karas will be taken up by me later. His picture of architecture ignores Dimitris Pikionis and others, though in fairness Pikionis' celebrated Acropolis approach project had not been begun; and it is hard to imagine, unless I do that institution an injustice, that MacNeice would have found fellow-feeling in the National and Capodistrian University of Athens of those days. If MacNeice had tired of English classical scholars, he would have found Athenian ones less congenial still.

MacNeice, we must not forget, came to Greece with, of course, a sound classical pedigree, having taught ancient Greek at the University of Birmingham (where he remembered the strange Hellenist Nicholas Bachtin) and at Bedford College in London.[19] That certainly distinguished him from the likes of Durrell. But he came also with a preconception, shaped by his troubled sense of English classical education as a class construct under which 'a gentleman never misplaces his accents', that there had been a decline in Greece over the centuries.[20] It is given famous expression in section IX of *Autumn Journal* (1939):

> And for a thousand years they went on talking
> Making such apt remarks,
> A race no longer of heroes but of professors
> And crooked business men and secretaries and clerks.[21]

It was not long before MacNeice had been forced to eat these words by the events of 1940–1941: in fact, his first radio play on moving to the BBC, *The Glory that is Greece*, aired on 28 October 1941, the first anniversary of the Greek entry into the war with Metaxas' famous *ochi* ('no') to the Italians presents the present-day ordinary Greeks as indeed a race of heroes.[22] The whole historical episode may have swung the poet's decision to go to Athens a decade later; yet marrying this sense of recent heroism to the realities of post-war

204 · DAVID RICKS

Greece – something of the same 'morning after' quality had affected many foreign observers after the War of Independence – proved not always easy.

As so often, Seferis gives a couple of interesting hints here. He noted that MacNeice was hardly the sort of man to appeal to the rumbustious and influential Katsimbalis.[23] Part of this was a matter of personal reserve, which in MacNeice's case was normally unlocked only when, in Irish idiom, there was drink taken. Gregariousness, especially of the Kolonaki socialite variety, was horrible to him – and that is surely a problem for a cultural representative.[24] (Runciman, by contrast, derived sardonic enjoyment from the social side.) On 13 May 1950 MacNeice writes, a touch ungallantly, 'Now thank God, the Culture Season (which largely means smiling at a lot of old ladies) is ending.'[25] Seferis also describes a reading by MacNeice which only really caught fire once he moved on from other poets such as Yeats to his own work.[26]

Part of the problem with Katsimbalis, though, may have been his implacably right-wing views following the civil war: once in Athens, MacNeice was getting a rather different angle on 'the grim realities of Modern Greek history' from the young American Kevin Andrews, who was telling the MacNeices about Makronisos not long after their arrival.[27] This prompted a piece about the infamous prison island by MacNeice in the *New Statesman* in November 1950; and a sense that the places of recent tribulation should be visited undoubtedly helped determine the choice of the celebrated Cretan village of Anoyia which had been burned by the Germans as the subject of a BBC programme, 'In search of Anoyia' (Third Programme, 11 December 1951) after the poet's return to England.[28] MacNeice's biographer Jon Stallworthy records a later difficult evening with the classically educated veteran of the British military intervention C.M. Woodhouse, when the *froideur* may have had a political aspect.[29]

Yet if MacNeice felt a degree of unease in Anglophile Greek circles, it is hard to imagine that he could as a Briton of pale-pink views ever have found himself comfortably at home in the circles of the Greek literary Left either. The British Council in Greece has sometimes found itself the target of direct animosity (outside our period, I can remember seeing its Thessaloniki premises fire-bombed by sympathizers of the Provisional IRA); and I find it hard to imagine that any official representative of Britain at that time, even one whose poems had sympathized with the Spanish Republic (see *Autumn Journal* VI) and who had objected to the Metaxas régime, could have had close relations with Greek Left writers, especially anyone linked to the Greek-Soviet League. In any case, many of these Left writers were imprisoned or interned at the time.[30] And, as other contributors to this volume remind us, there was a requirement (sometimes, of course, breached) for British Council staff to avoid political involvement.

MacNeice's links to the fate of the Greek Left seem to have been indirect, through sympathizers like Kevin Andrews, or by chance contact, as when the family travelled with their maid Ariadne to her island Ikaria and heard

MACNEICE IN GREECE

tubercular political prisoners, some of them women and children, coughing in the night.[31] I shall come back to this in relation to MacNeice's related poem 'The Island'; but the lesson all this has for a dominant nation's cultural links with another divided society will not be lost on us. In any case, MacNeice did not find himself among those Britons who regretted the outcome of the civil war in itself; writing to Dodds on 15 May 1950, he comments acerbically on his old friend Reginald Smith's assessment of things:

> Of course there is injustice done (with some pretty nasty frills) but there is *not* complete suffocation as in Reggie's pet places due north of us. Nor can everything that happens here be fitted into the stock ideological equations.[32]

A further more banal reason for reserve was simply MacNeice's tongue-tied state in Greece. He writes to Dodds, 'Not that we as yet can cope with Greek (modern), at any rate as regards talking; I just haven't had time to take lessons & in Athens one can get on without it.' I think this last point was precisely the problem, and MacNeice puts his finger on this as one reason why (apart from the fact that he saw the British Council colleagues as 'tiresome people in many ways', and apart from the painful amalgamation of the Institute under the British Council) he came to feel that the Council was 'in general an excellent idea which is being at least 50% wasted'.[33]

Perhaps then it is not surprising that, despite his eminence, MacNeice does not show up in retrospective surveys of the British Council's global activities; perhaps, however, he was being too hard on himself: R.L.O. Macfarlane is reported as saying that 'he worked wholeheartedly at the job, taking an influential part in the intellectual life of Athens'.[34] If the jury is still out on the question, that need not inhibit us from looking briefly at the other side of the coin: what was the artistic payback for MacNeice from his intermittently frustrating stay in a now post-heroic Greece? And how far was this in the nature of a genuine cultural exchange? My answer will be a tentative but not a negative one.

Perhaps not over-encumbered with duties, despite his recurrent complaints, MacNeice was able to work rapidly and systematically on what was to become his elaborately ordered collection of longish poems, *Ten Burnt Offerings*, which appeared in 1952, the year after his return from Greece. A letter of 20 September 1950 to Eliot outlines the initial plan for this volume, originally to have been called *Panegyrics*.[35] Though MacNeice hedges the word 'about' in quotation marks in his outline for Eliot, there is no doubt that each poem is indeed 'about' a particular theme; and both early reviews and much recent criticism have tended to assess this as over-systematic, even contrived.[36] Stallworthy in particular deems the poems better fitted for radio broadcasting – some were broadcast, over a two-month period – than for the page.[37] It is hard to disagree with this assessment, and the more modest poems that Greece inspired in MacNeice's schoolfellow Bernard Spencer, recently re-edited to critical acclaim, have worn better as more deeply grounded responses to Greece and the Greeks.[38]

MacNeice seems uneasily aware, in the lines, 'This middle stretch / Of life is bad for poets' – with its echo of Eliot – that he must compensate for lack of inspiration.[39] Yet Seferis perhaps helped to provide some solidarity in a Greek voice: *Mythistorema*, published when the Greek poet was thirty-five, is, among other things, a poem of middle life.[40] MacNeice's book can be seen as planting the seed of an engagement with Seferis' work which issued in a quiet allusion in MacNeice's last period: 'Ravenna', as I have noted elsewhere.[41] MacNeice's highly favourable review of Rex Warner's still estimable versions of Seferis in 1960, moreover, together with his setting up of the Greek poet's first meeting with Eliot in 1951, may well have played a behind-the-scenes role in Seferis' Nobel Prize nomination – now, that *would* be a real mark left on Greek literary life by an acquaintanceship made through the British Council.[42] MacNeice comments in some detail on the existing Seferis versions, showing a close engagement with the poems to match his admiration; and it is hard to believe that he had pitched up in Athens without the *King of Asine* volume to hand.[43]

For reasons of space but also of relevance my brief observations about *Ten Burnt Offerings* will be largely confined to three of the poems: 'Areopagus', 'The Island' and 'Day of Returning', for it is in those, rather than the flabby poem about Byron or the flat one about the poet's dead cat that we will find significant, as opposed to what one might call touristic, Greek detail.[44]

To begin with, though, I would stress that we can read a submerged civil war theme as running through the book as a whole; and it might allow us read a sense a sense of scorched earth into the book's title. The opening poem, 'Suite for Recorders', bears the epigraph from *As You Like It*: ' . . . it strikes a man more dead than a great reckoning in a little room'.[45] Always haunted by the close and divided ground of the North of Ireland, MacNeice also hints here at the Greek civil war aftermath, something the echoes of Whitman's *Drum-Taps* and *Calamus* confirm: 'What faint echoes drift to us / Of muffled drums or calamus.' And the linkage between violence and pastoral here takes on a Greek colour in the sense of showing a pastoral setting riven by modern war: 'Come, my flocks, but shun the rusty wire, the tank-traps.'[46] It could be said to prefigure the early work of Michalis Ganas (1944-), though that will be coincidence.

'Areopagus', the second poem, is a sustained and more successful meditation on how Christian and pagan heritages might be reconciled in a modern doubting mind that now sees things anew in a Greek setting.[47] But the Athenian scene is not mere opportunism, for here Paul is placed, not over against a vaguely defined paganism (as in Hardy's 'In the British Museum') but against the Aeschylean chthonic deities and especially the Furies.[48] MacNeice, as scholar and verse translator, knew his Aeschylus, of course, but his approach also seems to bear an affinity with Seferis 'Mycenae', a poem bringing Aeschylus into the present; and I suspect he may have taken a cue from that poem. Take these lines: 'Once avenging, later beneficent, / With tousled vipers, gravestone eyes, / The Kind Ones turned in their sleep' and compare (from the version in the volume *The King of Asine*): 'When the Furies started whistling / In the scarce grass / I have seen snakes coupled with vipers.'[49]

In 'Areopagus', which is in part a reparation to his cleric father, who had died in 1942, MacNeice finds both Oriental fatalism and modern political propaganda wanting, compared with the *Oresteia*'s final appeasing of the furies of civil war; and Orestes becomes here in effect a redeemed Cain: 'This starlit court / None the less cut one just, one divine, impeachment short.'[50] The hint at the Greek civil war is as unmistakable as the one quietly present at the end of Seferis' *'Thrush'* five years earlier.[51] 'Cock o' the North', the poem on Byron, in turn emphasizes Greek divisions: 'Mavrocordato, Colocotroni, faction, fiction and all', and the link between Byron's death at Missolonghi and Meleager's burnt brand at Calydon is coloured by the fact that Meleager dies as a result of internecine conflict.[52] But it is 'The Island' – again possibly in spirit more a radio script than a poem – which contains within it the sharpest sense of the Civil War.[53]

Set on Ikaria, as the early reference to Icarus signals, the end of section 1 already contains a hint at political repression under the ostensible description of a primordial peasant fatalism: 'Where labouring wisdom / Then as now, ready to leave / Things till tomorrow, asked of tomorrow / No freedom, only reprieve'.[54] Here the fate of the interned *dilosies* who were coerced to forswear their Party allegiance is captured, just as the scars of past conflicts endure with the figure of 'the time-worn baker, / Burnt out of Smyrna'. Not least from that hint, one may detect a Seferian background, imparted especially by *Mythistorema* and 'The King of Asine', in section 2 of MacNeice's poem, where 'a tall woman / Strides out of Homer over the pine-needles'.[55] In the section that follows, the visitor's reverie is troubled by the sawmill noise of the cicadas (like Seferis' 'Trizonia', this section is in tercets: by coincidence?), and it ends with a clear though smuggled-in political statement: 'And there are prisoners really, here in the hills, who would not agree / To sign for their freedom, whether in doubt of / Such freedom or having forgotten or never having known what it meant to be free.' The claim needs more space than I have here, but I would argue that 'The Island' is an authentically, if not tightly, post-Seferian poem.[56]

'Day of Returning' is the eighth (and, in the original and better plan, the last) of the *Ten Burnt Offerings* sequence: clearly this is the Homeric *nostimon hēmar*. But the whole business of *nostos* will be read differently by someone whose Homeric recollections have been adjusted and made more present, and perhaps more poignant, by *Mythistorema*. The first section of 'Day of Renewal' takes the Odysseus of Calypso's island, her entrancing voice now a nightmare: as Seferis has it, 'of the day which could not die'.[57] In the second section we jump – rather successfully – back to the Ulster setting, seen as authentic home compared with the false paradise – in fact a prison – of southern exile. MacNeice's Odysseus seems even to dream of conflict as Tennyson's Ulysses does of adventure: he muses on turning his fabled craft 'to the earth that bred it, a new threshing floor/Or setting up boundary stones, for even the best/ Neighbours encroach – and I like to have someone to argue with.' His final vocation, to produce 'by-products perhaps such as shall we say honey' might even be seen as echoing the humble objects, 'these carvings of a humble art' that the voyagers bring back in the opening poem of *Mythistorema*.[58] Here Mac-Neice finds from Seferis an attractively hard-bitten modesty by contrast with the over-schematic pretensions of much of *Ten Burnt Offerings*.

Rennell Rodd's enjoyable anthology of 1910, *The Englishman in Greece* (it contains just two Irishmen, Aubrey de Vere and Oscar Wilde), contains, not – as one might expect – poems of travel or personal experience but simply poems on ancient Greek themes: the idea that autopsy might be relevant, the idea that as Demetrios Capetanakis plaintively announced, 'the Greeks are human beings', is quite alien to such a book.[59] I think one can make a case for saying that *Ten Burnt Offerings* does manifest a new kind of engagement with Greece on MacNeice's part different from the allusive detail and facility of his earlier encounters with ancient Greece. The Seferian vein of agnosticism, in particular, seems to affirm MacNeice's sense of where his own vocation lies. His editor Peter McDonald writes,

> The dialectic of *Ten Burnt Offerings* . . . is such as to ensure that religious goals are glimpsed rather than achieved. Other aspects of myth, the historical and personal, compromise the movement of religious motifs by making clearer the implications of sacrifice and appeasement in secular contexts.[60]

The words fit Seferis like a glove, and it would be rewarding to see good Greek translations of these poems of MacNeice which find themselves 'in conversation with Seferis' from beyond the barrier of language.[61]

It is not perhaps surprising, however, that this lapsed Anglican son of a bishop devoted his simplest and most heartfelt pages about Greece to something he felt was really new to him there: it's a *Radio Times* article describing the wedding of the musicologist Simon Karas (5 September 1952). Emphasizing the (supposedly) classless nature of Karas' musical enterprise, Mac-Neice ends this affectionate little piece, which might seem on the face of it touristic in flavour, with a description that seems to find the Yeatsian ideal of the dance out there in the real life of a living Greece and in an aspiration, never to be renounced, to something that lies beyond this life: 'The two white bridal crowns hung on the wall as the guests danced in at one door and out at another, with excitement and yet with dignity, round and round with Karas himself leading them.'[62]

To conclude, one of Frances Donaldson's anonymous sources for her official history of the British Council (it may have been C.A. Trypanis) wrote that 'the intellectual life of Athens after the war was transformed by the British Council'.[63] If there was such a transformation, then MacNeice himself cannot be thought to have had more than a walk-on part when it came to personal

MACNEICE IN GREECE

209

contacts and the ability to inspire cultural engagement, let alone intimacy. The dominant poetic influence from Anglo-American poetry on Greek poets in the post-war period was to remain that of Eliot and Pound, right up to the early 1960s when the Beat poets made their presence felt. MacNeice remains a little-known figure in Greece. Yet I hope to have shown that through a handful of poems and broadcasts, and as part of a climate that fostered the *Anglo-Greek Review*, he formed an important footnote to the story told in this volume. *Ten Burnt Offerings* – the title evocative to the attentive reader of the suffering that Greece had endured in the 1940s – were offered to their first readers with a specific acknowledgement that they were made in, and for, Greece as a living thing, and for the Greeks as real people: 'These ten poems were written in Greece between March 1950 and April 1951 and are printed here in the order they were written.'[64] The volume represented an exchange of gifts, *xenia*, in a way that was most appropriate for the British Council to promote.

Notes

1 *Letters of Louis MacNeice*, ed. Jonathan Allison (London, 2010), pp. 524 (2 March 1950), 528 (15 May 1950). I am grateful to Sir Michael Llewellyn-Smith, whose reading of a draft of this chapter has helped me put MacNeice in the Athens context.

2 For Johnstone's perspective see briefly Gioula Koutsopanagou's contribution to the present volume. Rex Warner of course had a particular affinity for Greece and a gift for friendship with Greek artists. He is to some extent the forgotten man in the British Council story (and his entry in the *Oxford Dictionary of National Biography* is scarcely enlightening on the topic).

3 I quote Eliot's *East Coker* V to identify a poem, as well as a feeling, that was something of a shadow over MacNeice. The view that the latter was now running out of steam is widely held: see Peter McDonald, *Louis MacNeice: The Poet and His Contexts* (Oxford, 1991), p. 130; a more hostile account is that of D.B. Moore, *The Poetry of Louis MacNeice* (Leicester, 1972), pp. 139–63.

4 *Ten Burnt Offerings* are now to be found in Louis MacNeice, *Collected Poems*, ed. Peter McDonald (London, 2007), pp. 314–70.

5 In Frances Donaldson, *The British Council: The First Fifty Years* (London, 1984), p. 19.

6 Over time, of course, the United States, with far greater resources (including, notably, the provision of university scholarships such as the Fulbright), and a larger 'hyphenated' 'Greek-American' diaspora, was to exert a stronger pole of attraction and a greater cultural and literary influence on Greece.

7 The fullest account of the personalities is Anastasios Sagos, *A Chronicle of the British Council Office in Athens 1938–1986* (Athens, privately reproduced typescript 1995). Sagos draws attention (p. 16) to the homosexual atmosphere of the milieu, which MacNeice will have found uncongenial, though his letters do not attest to this.

8 In A.J.S. White, *The British Council. The First 25 Years 1934–1959: A Personal Account Written for the Unformation of Council Staff* (London, 1959), p. 134.

9 When MacNeice arrived in Athens on 1 January 1950 this volume had just appeared: Jon Stallworthy, *Louis MacNeice* (London, 1995), p. 376.

10 Stallworthy, *Louis MacNeice*, p. 377.

11 Donaldson, *The British Council*, pp. 146–47.This assertion is challenged, as regards Runciman, by Michael Llewellyn-Smith in the present volume; Sagos, *A Chronicle*, p. 14 is a little negative.

12 It would have been extremely illuminating to have access to the borrowing details in the form of stamps in English-language books, but the library is now dispersed.

13 This could be said to be a real failing, given the intermittent vigour and importance of the branches in Patras, Thessaloniki and perhaps especially Corfu.

14 The Moore visit is recalled in *Selected Prose of Louis MacNeice*, ed. Alan Heuser (Oxford, 1990), p. 22. The letter to Eliot appears in MacNeice, *Letters*, p. 531.

15 For Faulkner's visit see Joseph Blotner, *William Faulkner: A Biography* (2 vols, London, 1974), vol. 2, pp. 1644–55. Interestingly, Greek views of Eliot at this period do not seem to have been much concerned with his political views. Nor indeed is it the recollection of contemporaries that strong Leftists shunned the British Council premises.

16 MacNeice, *Selected Letters*, p. 528. MacNeice's view about Eliot's influence is tendentious but understandable given the emphasis of the *Anglo-Greek Review*.

17 See David Ricks, 'Lorenzatos and Eliot', *Sobornost*, 32/2 (2011), pp. 6–18.

18 George Seferis, *The King of Asine and Other Poems*, translated from the Greek by Bernard Spencer, Nanos Valaoritis and Lawrence Durrell, with an introduction by Rex Warner (London, 1948).

19 On Bachtin, see *Selected Letters*, p. 528: the latter's eccentric *Introduction to the Study of Modern Greek* (Cambridge, 1935) would not have made a useful primer had MacNeice laid hands on it.

20 MacNeice, *Collected Poems*, p. 130. Christopher Stray, *Classics Transformed* (Oxford, 1998) is an illuminating account of the 'classics and class' question.

21 MacNeice, *Collected Poems*, p. 121.

22 This and other Greek-related plays contributing to the Allied cause have now been collected as Louis MacNeice, *The Classical Radio Plays*, eds. Amanda Wrigley and S.J. Harrison (Oxford, 2013). *The Glory That Is Greece* was (probably not by coincidence) the title of a later propaganda volume edited by Hilda Hughes (London, 1944).

23 Roderick Beaton, *George Seferis: Waiting for the Angel* (New Haven, 2003), p. 294; Stallworthy, *Louis MacNeice*, p. 381.

24 Geoffrey Graham-Bell, employed by the British Institute at this period, speaks of 'essentially a snobbish institution' and of MacNeice as 'quite out of place' in it (oral communication, 27 January 2012). This would fit with MacNeice's gibe (*Letters*, pp. 524 and 525) that Athens was stuck in 1913 – implicitly, in a world of 'Georgian' hebetude.

MACNEICE IN GREECE   211

25 MacNeice, *Letters*, p. 525.

26 Giorgos Seferis, *Μέρες Ε'. 1 Γενάρη 1945–19 Απρίλη 1951* (Athens, 1977), p. 231.

27 Stallworthy, *Louis MacNeice*, p. 379. Andrews' recollections of the civil war and its effects are vividly presented in *The Flight of Ikaros* (1959; repr. Philadelphia, 2004); a recent biography is Roger Jinkinson, *American Ikaros: The Search for Kevin Andrews* (London, 2010).

28 Stallworthy, *Louis MacNeice*, pp. 378–79; 'Makronisos', *New Statesman* 4 (November 1950), p. 409.

29 Stallworthy, *Louis MacNeice*, p. 385.

30 MacNeice, *Collected Poems*, pp. 112–14. It may also be relevant to note that, aside from his lifelong Stalinism, Yannis Ritsos made no serious contact with the ancient Greek world that came instinctively to MacNeice, until the 1960s, but did so then with great astuteness and trenchancy.

31 Stallworthy, *Louis MacNeice*, p. 383; he perhaps unfairly feels that the visit made too little of an impression on MacNeice's poetry.

32 MacNeice, *Letters*, p. 538. MacNeice's assessment of his University of Birmingham protégé (at whose wedding to the novelist Olivia Manning he had been best man) does not seem out of place: it is surprising that a Communist Party member should ever have been employed by the British Council, as Smith was in Bucharest before the War (*ODNB* Reginald Donald Smith). A biography of Smith by Gerry Harrison is in course of preparation.

33 Both quotations from MacNeice, *Letters*, p. 538.

34 In William T. McKinnon, *Apollo's Blended Dream: A Study of the Poetry of Louis MacNeice* (London, 1971), p. 35 n.1.

35 MacNeice, *Letters*, p. 537. MacNeice no doubt has the related modern Greek word for a fiesta, *panegyri*, in mind, and his sense of coming upon a country in which ritual still matters is both characteristic of a classical scholar and indicative of a yearning in himself.

36 Reviews were disappointing: see Robyn Marsack, *The Cave of Making: The Poetry of Louis MacNeice* (Oxford, 1982), p. 96; but in making his 1959 selection, *Eighty-Five Poems, Selected by the Author* (London) MacNeice still thought *Ten Burnt Offerings* his best book (ibid., p. 97), and 'Didymus' and 'Day of Returning' appear there: pp. 111–16, 124–28.

37 Stallworthy, *Louis MacNeice*, p. 387. For him, this is a criticism; but it is worth considering whether the poems in question in fact work better that way and are best read in conjunction with the earlier radio plays on Greek themes: see n. 22 above.

38 Bernard Spencer, *Complete Poetry, Translations and Selected Prose*, ed. Peter Robinson (Tarset, 2011).

39 MacNeice, *Collected Poems*, p. 349.

40 MacNeice's acquaintance with the collection will have been through the version in *The King of Asine* volume, but it is inconceivable that he hadn't scanned through some of the Greek text too. It is worth noting that MacNeice had

reviewed Tambimuttu's *T.S. Eliot: A Symposium* (1948), which contained a contribution from Seferis: see now *Selected Literary Criticism of Louis MacNeice*, ed. Alan Heuser (Oxford, 1987), pp. 148–53.

41 MacNeice, *Collected Poems*, p. 589, with David Ricks, 'Simpering Byzantines, Grecian Goldsmiths, et al.: Some Appearances of Byzantium in English Poetry', in Robin Cormack and Elizabeth Jeffreys (eds.), *Through the Looking-Glass: British Responses to Byzantium* (Aldershot, 2000), pp. 223–35.

42 Beaton, *George Seferis: Waiting for the Angel*, p. 294.

43 MacNeice, *Selected Criticism*, pp. 220–23. One of the *King of Asine* translators, Nanos Valaoritis, had been working for the BBC Greek Service in the 1940s and had made MacNeice's acquaintance by that point (oral communication, 27 January 2012).

44 For a sample of responses covering that spectrum see Don Schofield (ed.), *Kindled Terraces: American Poets in Greece* (Kirksville, MO, 2004).

45 MacNeice, *Collected Poems*, p. 315.

46 Ibid., p. 319. A Seferian echo of much this kind – perhaps triggered by MacNeice's interest – is to be found in the poem by his compatriot Derek Mahon, 'A Disused Shed in Co. Wexford', *Collected Poems* (Dublin, 1999), pp. 89–90, with comment in Hugh Haughton, *The Poetry of Derek Mahon* (Oxford, 2004), pp. 118–19. For more detail see Joanna Kruczkowska, *Irish Poets and Modern Greece: Heaney, Mahon, Cavafy, Seferis* (n.p., 2017).

47 MacNeice, *Collected Poems*, pp. 321–25.

48 Thomas Hardy, *Collected Poems*, ed. James Gibson (London, 1976), pp. 381–82.

49 Seferis, *The King of Asine*, p. 50.

50 MacNeice, *Collected Poems*, p. 325.

51 Roderick Beaton, *George Seferis* (Bristol, 1991), p. 116.

52 MacNeice, *Collected Poems*, p. 326; *Iliad*, 9.524ff.

53 MacNeice, *Collected Poems*, pp. 343–48.

54 Compare more recently the Greek-American poet George Contogenis' powerful riposte to Auden's 'Musée des Beaux Arts': 'There Are No Ploughshares on Ikaria', in Christopher Ricks (ed.), *Joining Music with Reason* (Chipping Norton, 2010), p. 73.

55 Compare Seferis, 'The King of Asine', in the volume of that name, pp. 71–73 and poem 7 of *Mythistorema*, pp. 24–25.

56 Jim Potts in the present volume quotes a less circumspect response to the same historical milieu on the part of another poet who served in the British Council in Athens: John Press's 'Aftermath of Civil War' (1955), though ostensibly anti-Royalist, in effect expresses dismay at Orthodoxy as an opiate of the Greek people.

57 Seferis, *The King of Asine*, p. 17.

58 Ibid.

MACNEICE IN GREECE

59 Rennell Rodd (ed.), *The Englishman in Greece, Being a Collection of the Verse of Many English Poets* (Oxford, 1910); Demetrios Capetanakis, *A Greek Poet in England* (London, 1947), pp. 43–48.

60 McDonald, *Louis MacNeice*, p. 145.

61 I take the term from the anthology *Synomilontas me ton Kavafe*, ed. Nasos Vayenas (Thessaloniki, 2001). It may be time for a (smaller) volume of the same type covering Seferis' poetic influence around the world: in it, the poems of MacNeice, Spencer, Durrell and others of this period would have a pioneering place.

62 MacNeice, *Selected Prose*, pp. 184–86.

63 Donaldson, *The British Council*, pp. 126–27 and 395 n. 16. For Trypanis' advice to the British authorities on cultural matters back in 1945 see Gioula Koutsopanagou's contribution to the present volume. He joined MacNeice in Faber's poetry stable with *The Stones of Troy* (London, 1957).

64 MacNeice, *Collected Poems*, p. 806.

Chapter 12
Kazantzakis in Cambridge

David Holton

In the summer of 1946 Nikos Kazantzakis travelled to England as the guest of the British Council. He set out by ship from Piraeus on 2 June and arrived in London on 8 June. His stay was longer than originally intended and lasted until 28 September, when he left for Paris. During the first half of his visit he was based in London, but made short trips to Cambridge, Oxford and Stratford-upon-Avon. From 30 July until 19 September he was living in Cambridge and mainly devoting himself to his writing.[1] For information about his activities in England we are almost entirely dependent on the letters he wrote, particularly to his wife Eleni (whom he had married on 11 November of the previous year), but also to a number of friends, including Pantelis Prevelakis, Angelos Sikelianos, Nikos Veis (Beis) and Yannis (J.Th.) Kakridis.[2]

It was not his first visit to England. That had taken place in 1939, after the British Ambassador in Athens, Sir Sydney Waterlow, had secured him an invitation from the British Council. It resulted in a travel work,[3] published first in newspaper articles,[4] and then in 1941 as a book dedicated to Waterlow.[5]

The 1946 visit was arranged as a kind of compensation for the fact that his 1939 trip was curtailed by the outbreak of war. The official invitation arrived in late April 1946, soon after Kazantzakis had returned to Aegina from Athens, following what Peter Bien has aptly called his 'abortive foray into politics'.[6] One person who was closely involved reports that the trip to England would have taken place earlier but was delayed by two complicating factors: first, Kazantzakis' brief period as a minister in the Sofoulis government; and second, by the fact that, at that time, Italy was not issuing transit visas to Greek citizens for diplomatic reasons.[7] A route therefore had to found which avoided Italy. Our source for this information is Vasilis Kazantzis,[8] who was then working for the British Council in Athens.[9] The solution was for Kazantzakis to travel by sea to France, in one of the so-called 'bride ships' which carried women from various Mediterranean countries, who had married, or were going to marry, British citizens. Kazantzakis was virtually the only male passenger. Kazantzis escorted him to Piraeus to see him off. Kazantzakis had been hoping that Prevelakis, another British Council guest, would travel with him to London, and in a letter of 28 April he asked Kazantzis to try to arrange it.[10] It did not happen, though Kazantzakis continued to hope that Prevelakis would catch up with him in England.[11]

Kazantzakis would arrive in England at a time when there was considerable interest in contemporary Greece amongst intellectuals and the wider public, as is attested elsewhere in this volume. For example, *The Listener*, an organ of the BBC, carried a number of items of Greek interest, in most cases based on radio programmes, during the summer and autumn of 1946. There were two travel pieces by Bernard Spencer (published on 25 July, with related correspondence in the next two issues, and on 5 September), and another on Cyprus by Laurie Lee (20 June). There was a talk entitled 'Aegean Afternoon' by Gordon Winter, a member of the British Military Mission in the Aegean (13 June), and another of more political relevance by Kenneth Matthews, entitled 'Brigands in Greece' (16 May). John Mavrogordato's translations of two Cavafy poems, 'In the Month of Athyr' and 'On Board Ship', were published in successive months (16 May and 13 June), and there was even a recipe for moussaka (1 August) – with potato and no aubergine!

Arrival in London: meetings and visits

Kazantzakis arrived in London on 8 June and made contact with his British Council hosts. His avowed aim during his stay was to write a book which he described as 'Post-war conversations with English intellectual personalities'.[12] To this end the British Council arranged a series of meetings – in London, Cambridge and Oxford – with prominent academics, writers and artists. Prevelakis provides a long list of names (which includes David Garnett, Graham Greene, Walter de la Mare, Henry Moore, Stephen Spender and many others), though it is impossible to know whether all the meetings took place. However, several are referred to explicitly in Kazantzakis' letters and notebooks kept at the time. In London there were meetings with David Garnett, Laurie Lee, Stephen Spender, John Masefield, John and Rosamond Lehmann and others.[13] In Cambridge, where he stayed from 21 to 24 June, he met the classical scholar and Provost of King's College J.T. Sheppard, the Master of Trinity G.M. Trevelyan, and the classically trained English don and Fellow of King's F.L. Lucas.[14] Further information about this first trip to Cambridge has been given by the ancient historian N.G.L. Hammond, who acted as local host. Hammond, a fellow of Clare College who had served as a member of the military mission to Greece during the Occupation, received a telephone call from the British Council asking him to look after Kazantzakis during his stay. Kazantzakis requested – and Hammond arranged – the meeting with the Provost of King's, which took place over tea on 21 June. His question 'Who are the intelligentsia in Cambridge?' did not go down well:

> Sheppard was angered by this question and somewhat disgusted, replying that the 'intelligentsia' was not an ideal having any value. Cambridge, he continued, was concerned with basic truth and not with posing as intellectuals.

He sarcastically suggested that Kazantzakis may find the 'intelligentsia' at Oxford.[15]

A little over a week later Kazantzakis was indeed in Oxford pursuing his quest. In a letter to Vasilis Kazantzis he mentions that he spent ten days there.[16] The visit began on 1 July, as he writes in a letter of 25 June to Tea Anemoyanni: 'Yesterday I returned from Cambridge, where I met three fine, erudite men. . . . On 1 July I leave for Oxford, where I'll see Krinio and will try to get her term of stay renewed, since it's in danger of being cut in half.'[17] On 1 July John Mavrogordato recorded in his diary that Krinio Papastavrou (who was studying music at Oxford with a bursary from the British Council) brought Kazantzakis to meet him at Exeter College and that he gave him a tour of the College before introducing him to R.M. Dawkins (his predecessor as Bywater and Sotheby Professor of Byzantine and Modern Greek Language and Literature).[18] On 4 July Kazantzakis wrote to Tea Anemoyanni from Oxford about his meeting with Sir John Myres, 'an old man 80 years old, who can no longer talk clearly and who is striving day and night to read the Minoan script'.[19] He also had a lengthy discussion with Maurice Bowra. Although he writes enthusiastically about these meetings, in both Oxford and Cambridge, it is clear that his interlocutors did not react favourably to his proposal for an international pressure group of intellectuals and the naive questionnaire to which he asked them to respond.[20]

In addition to these face-to-face meetings arranged by the British Council, there were also radio broadcasts. On 13 June, in a letter to Eleni, Kazantzakis announces that he will speak on the BBC 'in a few days'.[21] In fact there are references to a number of broadcasts, which he made at this time, though the facts are somewhat sketchy. Eleni mentions that Michalis Cacoyannis had invited Nikos to give a series of talks on the BBC, 'in the Greek broadcast for Cyprus'.[22] Cacoyannis, unable to return to Cyprus during the war, had found a position working for the Greek Service of the BBC, while continuing to take acting and directing classes at the Old Vic. Eleni reports that there were about ten broadcasts ('une dizaine'), of which the first was the appeal to intellectuals to join an '*Internationale* of the spirit'. That broadcast appears to have gone out on 18 July; in her biography Eleni reproduces the text of the talk and the seven questions.[23] It was published in September of the same year in the literary magazine *Life and Letters*.[24] The second talk focused on Angelos Sikelianos, but I have not been able to discover when it was broadcast. Kazantzakis repeatedly states that Sikelianos is the only Greek writer he mentioned on the BBC, the reason being, of course, their joint candidacy for the Nobel Prize.[25] The third talk was on George Bernard Shaw, on the occasion of his ninetieth birthday, and this is of particular interest. It was published in two forms, the first in Greek in *Nea Estia* on 1 September of the same year.[26] An editorial note states that the talk was given on 'the Radio Station of London' ('από το Ραδιοφωνικό Σταθμό του Λονδίνου') on 26 July, which was indeed Shaw's birthday and both the

218 DAVID HOLTON

Home Service and the Light Programme carried celebratory broadcasts that day. But Kazantzakis' talk went out on the Overseas Service, as clearly stated when the English text was published, with Eleni's permission, in *The Shaw Review* some twenty-nine years later.[27] Kazantzakis' relationship with Shaw has not, as far as I know, been fully researched.[28] In this radio talk there are hints of a close affinity:

> At first, we feel somewhat uncomfortable in his presence, a little repulsed even, a little cold. As though we were drawing near the other face of God – Satan. We feel that Shaw is having a game with us, distorting and over-magnifying truth, to make us laugh and feel ashamed. But little by little we understand – we understand that all this is but the hard shell, and that deep down, the heart that beats is so sensitive, that it could not have gone on living, unless it had been protected all round by the impenetrable shield of laughter. The wit worn on Bernard Shaw's heart is a mask – a gas-mask to keep him immune from the world's poisonous fumes.

> And when one has discovered this secret of Shaw's, one begins to feel a great love for him. For then, Shaw reveals himself in his three successive personalities; first as the Revolutionary; second, as the Prophet; and finally, in his present personality, as the old grandfather – a benign dragon, holding the ever childish humanity by the hand, and leading it through the wood...

The third role, that of kindly grandfather, was one that Kazantzakis would perhaps have had some difficulty casting himself in, but otherwise – as Revolutionary and Prophet – he may well have regarded himself as a Shaw-like figure (albeit without the beard).[29]

Of the other seven talks – if indeed they ever took place – there is no trace. It seems likely that the three whose subjects we know about were broadcast either on the Overseas Service, presumably in English, or on the Greek Service in Greek. An invitation to 'talk on the BBC' may mean many things; it does not necessarily give direct access to a British audience or constitute a sign of recognition by the British establishment.

In Cambridge

Kazantzakis' stay in England was meant to last about six weeks (one and a half months he says in a letter to Kakridis on 25 May).[30] It's not entirely clear what caused the change of plan: the political situation in Greece, or a feeling that he had not discharged his obligations to the British Council, or perhaps an invitation that was too good to turn down? On 5 September, in a letter to Nikos Veis, he says he extended his stay unwillingly ('χωρὶς νὰ το θέλω') and had withdrawn to the 'green serenity of Cambridge', where he had written 'a book, which is being translated into English to be published here'.[31] Writing to Kazantzis on 1 September, and apologizing for not returning earlier, he was more explicit: 'I remained here, withdrawing myself to green Cambridge in order to write a book – the book which I owed to the Br. (sic) Council. . . '[32]

Kazantzakis preferred not to stay in a hotel so lodgings were found for him in Chesterton Lane. The house, which belonged to Clare College, was called Castlebrae (Kazantzakis always writes 'Castle Bray' in his letters) and had – and still has – a certain resemblance to a Scottish baronial hall. In his letter of 30 July to Eleni, Kazantzakis describes some of its curious internal features, for example the Greek inscriptions 'ΧΑΙΡΕ ΧΥΤΡΑ' and 'ΧΑΙΡΕ ΦΙΛΙΑ' over the entrances to the kitchen and another room, the function of which remained unclear to him.[33] Built in 1889, Castlebrae had been the home of Mrs Agnes Lewis and Mrs Margaret Gibson, twin sisters born in Scotland (which explains the architecture and name of the house), who acquired a considerable reputation as biblical scholars and experts in Semitic languages. They also knew Greek (hence the inscriptions). Their greatest achievement was the discovery, in St Catherine's Monastery, Sinai, of the oldest extant Syriac text of the gospels.[34] Their interest in things Greek also manifested itself in their endowment of a lectureship in Modern Greek at the University of Cambridge: the Lewis-Gibson Lectureship. But Kazantzakis appears to have known none of this.

Most of his time in Cambridge was spent writing. He very quickly decided that the projected book on British intellectuals was not feasible. In the letter of 30 July he tells Eleni,

> I've got the plan of the book. It will be a novel, because the intellectuals here haven't given me any material. Three parts: Crete, England, Solitude. And I myself will answer the questions I asked. I don't know whether here in this house I will find the climate I want. Fortunately, the little window of my study looks out on a beautiful garden – and there's an enormous apple tree in front of me.[35]

The new project was clearly to have an autobiographical slant, with 'Solitude' representing the hoped-for return to Aegina.[36] More information is found in a letter of 19 August, also to Eleni: after describing his writing regime, which begins at 5:30 am, he goes on: 'By now I'm two thirds of the way through. By the end of August, I'll have finished. In the third part, I'll include the whole of the Spiritual Exercises. . . '[37]

By 1 September, in a letter to Kazantzis, he can refer to the book as already finished: 'It is already being translated into English and I hope to find a publisher here. Something which is extremely difficult.'[38] And a few days later to Veis, 'I have written a book, which is being translated into English to be published here. If I returned to the "Kingdom" of Greece, I would certainly have had no pleasure or desire for writing; now I've finished the book, I've found calm (ησύχασα).'[39]

The book had the title *O Ανήφορος* but was never published. One chapter appeared in *Νέα Εστία* the following year, under the title 'Ο Θάνατος του παπού',[40] and was subsequently incorporated in *Καπετάν Μιχάλης* (*Freedom and Death*).[41] An article about the fortitude of the Cretans under German Occupation was perhaps also part of the unpublished 'novel'. It was certainly written in 1946 and almost certainly in England.[42]

While he was in Cambridge, his first major novel, *Βίος και Πολιτεία του Αλέξη Ζορμπά* (*Zorba the Greek*), was finally published. On 20 June, in a letter to Eleni from London, he was asking impatiently, 'What's happening with Zorba? Has it been printed? That book especially offers hopes for publication in English.' Five days later he wrote to Tea Anemoyanni, 'Has Zorba been printed? If not, will you do me the favor of going to Dimitrakos's and telling him how much that infuriates me? There would be a chance for it to be translated here. If it has been printed, will you send me a copy immediately?'[43] But it was not until 14 August that he actually received a copy. On the following date he wrote to Chrysanthi Cleridou, who was then working in the Greek Service of the BBC:

> Yesterday I received my novel, which was printed this month and about which I was talking to you regarding the possibility of its being translated and our finding a publisher in England. I believe it will be very popular. Thus if you have time and appetite to undertake this task, I beg you to write to me and I'll send the book to you. . . .
>
> I will be very pleased if you are the one to translate it because I know that you have what is needed to understand and to render a text: strength, poetic comprehension, freshness, and a daring mind.[44]

By 12 September he is also planning to write to Börje Knös about the Swedish translation,[45] which would appear in 1949, three years before the English one (1952 – done from the French by Carl Wildman).

Another issue that was occupying him throughout his time in England was his joint candidacy with Sikelianos for the Nobel Prize for literature. Because the whole affair has been well covered by Peter Bien,[46] I will not go into it here, save to say that Kazantzakis repeatedly brings up the issue in letters from London and Cambridge, to Eleni, Prevelakis, Nikos Veis, Kakridis and of course to Sikelianos himself.

One other event should be mentioned from this period. On 30 July he writes to Eleni that on the following Saturday he is to go to London to have dinner with Philip Noel-Baker, Minister of State at the Foreign Office, who wants to seek his views on the situation in Greece.[47] Despite the fact that Noel-Baker was a self-confessed Philhellene, Kazantzakis was pessimistic: 'I know my opinion won't influence them at all. Nevertheless, I shall express it and, as is my habit at critical moments, abruptly and without mincing words.' It has

KAZANTZAKIS IN CAMBRIDGE

been claimed that, as a result of the replies he gave to Noel-Baker and his colleague Hector McNeil (shortly to be his successor), as well as the public statement he sent to Greece at the time of the plebiscite, he was declared *persona non grata*.[48] It may well be the case that issuing a statement to the Greek public was seen as violating his undertaking not to engage in politics while he was in Britain; Eleni specifically mentions that,[49] but she does not say that he was ordered to leave in consequence. The affair has probably been exaggerated for political ends.

As his stay in Cambridge drew to an end he was increasingly concerned about the fate of Greece, but also the threat of nuclear war. In his last letter to Eleni from Cambridge, he writes, 'The situation in Greece and the whole world disturbs me terribly. I'm beginning to be afraid that a new war could possibly break out. . . . Perhaps the new war will be brief, but it will be terrible. Certainly few will survive and many will be driven insane.'[50] In a very different mood, just three days later, he wrote to Tea Anemoyanni, 'What plunder am I taking with me as I leave Cambridge? A book, the vision of the colleges and, above all, the heavenly greenness – the grass in the college courtyards – a miracle so simple and so profound that no word can ever contain it.'[51] We must now consider what in fact he had achieved.

Conclusions

On the face of it Kazantzakis' stay in England chalked up a series of resounding failures. He was rebuffed by the British intelligentsia and his *Internationale* of the Spirit was a very damp squib. As a result, he failed to gather any material for the book on 'Post-war conversations with English intellectual personalities' that was supposed to be the purpose of his stay, and it was never written.[52] He wrote what he called a 'novel', *Ο Ανήφορος*, but that too was never published, either in Greek or in the projected English translation. His hopes of finding a translator for *Zorba* while in England failed to materialize. His candidacy for the Nobel Prize, to which he devoted a good deal of time and ink, came to nothing. Although he did publish an article in English relating to his grand project, the magazine in which it appeared, *Life and Letters*, did not have a particularly dazzling list of contributors – and they got his name wrong![53]

Much of this could have been predicted. The label 'intellectual' has always been treated with suspicion in Britain. And Kazantzakis' English was probably inadequate to put his message across: it appears that many of his discussions were actually conducted in French. His work was virtually unknown in Britain at this time, as nothing had been translated into English. Even in 1952 Rex Warner – no less – who had met Kazantzakis 'several times' in Athens in 1945–6, was unfamiliar with the range of his work: in thanking John Lehmann for sending him a copy of *Zorba*, which he 'enjoyed immensely', he comments, 'But I'd always thought of him as a poet rather than a novelist.'[54] Kazantzakis

222   DAVID HOLTON

the thinker and Kazantzakis the novelist meant nothing to the British literary and academic establishment in 1946. There is no trace of his visit in the
archives I have been able to consult.[55]

So are we to conclude that Kazantzakis achieved nothing? There may
be an alternative way of looking at this liminal period between Greece and
France. Kazantzakis never returned to Greece from the moment he embarked
for England. Eleni joined him in Paris in late 1946 and in 1948 they settled in
Antibes. When he went to England he had, more or less, retired from active
involvement in Greek politics. Vasilis Kazantzis puts it like this: 'This timely
departure [from Greece in 1946] was decisive (σημαδιακή) for the whole of
Kazantzakis' post-war development as, by now, a European writer.'[56] There
were a few more distractions while he was in Paris (the UNESCO post), but it
is indeed true that Kazantzakis was now firmly committed to novel-writing.
Those seven weeks of hard slog in Cambridge were decisive for the germi-
nation of *Kapetan Michalis*. During the same period *Zorba* was published and
Kazantzakis immediately set his sights on having it translated. It is perhaps no
exaggeration to say that he had finally come to believe in himself as a novelist.
But there was still the need to earn a living and for both Eleni and Nikos an
academic post was a persistent attraction. On 12 September 1946 he wrote
to Eleni, 'I, too, wrote to [Jean] Herbert, asking if he can find me a place in
some university. We'll see. Maybe something will turn up.'[57] In the *Biography*,
Eleni wrote, 'After the grayness and hubbub of London, Nikos reveled in the
green serenity of Cambridge. On Aegina, I was still hoping for some miracle –
for example, a chair of Modern Greek literature at Oxford or Cambridge –
to take us far away from Aegina.'[58] This was not as far-fetched as one might
think, though his age was perhaps against it. Two posts were in fact filled
in 1947: Constantine Trypanis was elected to the Bywater and Sotheby Chair
of Byzantine and Modern Greek Language and Literature at Oxford and
Stavros Papastavrou was appointed Lewis-Gibson lecturer in Modern Greek
at Cambridge. Now if Kazantzakis had been appointed instead of one of them,
the history of Modern Greek studies in Britain might have been rather different.

Notes

1 For the dates see, most conveniently, Pantelis Prevelakis, *Τετρακόσια γράμματα
   του Καζαντζάκη στον Πρεβελάκη*, 2nd edn (Athens, 1984), p. 531.

2 Wherever possible, I cite the letters in the recent English edition: *The Selected
   Letters of Nikos Kazantzakis*, ed. and trans. Peter Bien (Princeton, 2012) (hereafter
   Bien, *Letters*). I am most grateful to Peter Bien for giving me access to unpublished letters before publication of this volume and for his helpful comments on
   an earlier draft of this paper.

3 Nikos Kazantzakis, *Ταξιδεύοντας Γ´: Αγγλία* (Athens, 1941).

4 The first extract appeared in *Νέα Εστία*, 26 (Christmas 1939), and then a further
   32 instalments in *Η Καθημερινή* from July to December 1940.

KAZANTZAKIS IN CAMBRIDGE 223

5 On Kazantzakis' travel writing, see Konstantinos A. Dimadis, 'Τέχνη και εξουσία: παρατηρήσεις σε τέσσερα ταξιδιωτικά έργα του Νίκου Καζαντζάκη', in Roderick Beaton (ed.), *Εισαγωγή στο έργο του Καζαντζάκη: Επιλογή κριτικών κειμένων* (Heraklion, 2011), pp. 271–310. The article is now available in English in the author's collected volume: Konstantinos A. Dimadis, *Power and Prose Fiction in Modern Greece* (Athens, 2016), pp. 193–236. Dimadis calls the volume on England 'a hymn to the liberal traditions of British society' ('Τέχνη και εξουσία', p. 289). See also Peter Bien, *Kazantzakis: Politics of the Spirit*, vol. 2 (Princeton, 2007), pp. 16–21. For valuable insights concerning Kazantzakis' two visits to England see Afroditi Athanasopoulou, 'Kazantzakis's Perception of England (1939, 1946)', in Liana Giannakopoulou and E. Kostas Skordyles (eds.), *Culture and Society in Crete: From Kornaros to Kazantzakis* (Newcastle upon Tyne, 2017), pp. 77–102.

6 Peter Bien, 'Kazantzakis's Abortive Foray into Politics in Liberated Athens, 1944–46', *Κάμπος: Cambridge Papers in Modern Greek*, 13 (2005), pp. 1–19.

7 Diplomatic relations between Greece and Italy were actually resumed on 5 June 1946, when the Italian government declared that it had no objections to the cession of the Dodecanese to Greece. See Stephen G. Xydis, *Greece and the Great Powers 1944–1947: Prelude to the 'Truman Doctrine'* (Thessaloniki, 1963), pp. 214–15.

8 For this and further details of Kazantzakis' departure see Vasilis Kazantzis, 'Τρία ανέκδοτα γράμματα του Ν. Καζαντζάκη', *Νέα Εστία*, 74/865 (15 July 1963), pp. 906–7. Kazantzis later became a well-known journalist, writing χρονογραφήματα (short articles on matters of topical, often cultural, interest) under the nom de plume of 'Index'. He was also a versatile translator: his translations include works by Emily Brontë, Aldous Huxley, Arthur Koestler, Norman Mailer and Henry Miller. Kazantzakis also mentions, in a letter of 25 May to Yannis Kakridis, that he was ready to leave for England but still waiting for a visa to enter Italy; Bien, *Letters*, p. 614. For the original see '84 γράμματα του Καζαντζάκη στον Κακριδή', *Νέα Εστία*, 102 (Christmas 1977), pp. 257–300 (hereafter Kazantzakis – Kakridis, '84 γράμματα'), at p. 277. Earlier in the month, however, he apparently refused a British Council request to leave at twenty-four hours' notice; Helen Kazantzakis, *Nikos Kazantzakis: A Biography Based on his Letters* (Oxford and New York, 1968), p. 439 (hereafter H. Kazantzakis, *Biography*). For an evaluation of this biography see Georgia Farinou-Malamatari, 'Τέσσερεις γυναίκες βιογραφούν τον Καζαντζάκη', in Stamatis Philippidis (ed.), *Ο Καζαντζάκης στον 21ο αιώνα: Πρακτικά του Διεθνούς Επιστημονικού Συνεδρίου «Νίκος Καζαντάκης 2007: Πενήντα χρόνια μετά»* (Heraklion, 2010), pp. 291–338.

9 See Prevelakis, *Τετρακόσια γράμματα*, pp. 527–28; Bien, *Letters*, p. 601.

10 He also mentions his request in a letter of the same date to Prevelakis: Bien, *Letters*, p. 611; Prevelakis, *Τετρακόσια γράμματα*, p. 527.

11 Prevelakis did not arrive in London until 3 October, several days after Kazantzakis' departure. (See E. Kasdaglis, 'Συμβολή στη χρονολογία του βίου του Παντελή Πρεβελάκη', *Νέα Εστία*, 119/1427 (Christmas 1986), p. 12.) Yet another British Council guest from Greece that year was the novelist, playwright and critic George Theotokas. He gives an account of his stay in Britain,

224 DAVID HOLTON

from 23 August to 29 September 1946, in his journal: Giorgos Theotokas, *Τετράδια ημερολογίου 1939–1953*, introduced and edited by Dimitris Tziovas (Athens, n.d.), pp. 585–99. During a brief visit to Cambridge he, like Kazantzakis, met N.G.L. Hammond.

12 Prevelakis, *Τετρακόσια γράμματα*, p. 531; in his letter of 9 June to Eleni (Bien, *Letters*, p. 616) he qualifies it: 'if I obtain sufficient documentation'. Elsewhere, in an editorial note, it is referred to as 'a book on intellectual England after the war'; see Kazantzaki[s], 'The Immortal Free Spirit of Man', *Life and Letters*, 50/109 (1946), pp. 123–26.

13 H. Kazantzakis, *Biography*, pp. 447–48.

14 Together with his wife, Lucas had written a book, to which Kazantzakis refers, about his travels in Greece: F.L. and Prudence Lucas, *From Olympus to the Styx* (London, 1934).

15 Lewis Owens, ' "Who Are the Intelligentsia in Cambridge?" The Hostile Reception to Kazantzakis' Desire for an "International of the Spirit" ', *The Cambridge Review*, 119/2331 (November 1998), pp. 91–92, where further details of the encounter, as recollected by Nicholas Hammond, may be found.

16 Kazantzis, 'Τρία ανέκδοτα γράμματα', p. 907.

17 Bien, *Letters*, p. 619.

18 I am grateful to Peter Mackridge for this information, which is based on his research in the John Mavrogordato archive in the Bodleian Library, Oxford (Bodleian Library, Papers of John Mavrogordato, MS Dep. Mavrogordato 51).

19 H. Kazantzakis, *Biography*, p. 450.

20 G.M. Trevelyan, for example, angrily refused to answer and screwed up the questionnaire. See H. Kazantzakis, *Biography*, p. 447; Bien, *Politics*, vol. 2, pp. 274–75.

21 H. Kazantzakis, *Biography*, p. 441.

22 Eleni N. Kazantzaki, *Νίκος Καζαντζάκης, ο ασυμβίβαστος: βιογραφία βασισμένη σε ανέκδοτα γράμματα και κείμενά του* (Athens, 1977), p. 518, n. 1. Cf. Eleni N. Kazantzaki, *Le Dissident: biographie de Nikos Kazantzaki* (Paris, 1968), p. 468; H. Kazantzakis, *Biography*, p. 455. (The three versions of the biography have some differences between them.)

23 H. Kazantzakis, *Biography*, pp. 442–45. The Greek version in E. Kazantzaki, *O ασυμβίβαστος*, pp. 522–24, has some cuts.

24 Kazantzaki[s], 'The Immortal Free Spirit of Man'. The text differs from that in the *Biography*, which is presumably a translation by Amy Mims from the Greek original.

25 In a letter to Yannis Kakridis dated 31 July: 'The other day I spoke about our intellectual life on the BBC and he was the only one of all of us to whom I referred, speaking of "Sikelianos's elevated poetic form".' See Bien, *Letters*, p. 625. Similarly in a letter to Nikos Veis dated 5 September: Mairi N. Vei, 'Δύο επιστολαί του Νίκου Καζαντζάκη προς τον Νίκο Βέη', *Νέα Εστία*, 74 (15 November 1963), p. 1690.

KAZANTZAKIS IN CAMBRIDGE

26 Nikos Kazantzakis, 'Μια ελληνική φωνή για τον Μπέρναρντ Σω', *Νέα Εστία*, 40/460 (1 September 1946), p. 953.

27 See E. Kazantzaki, *Ο ασυμβίβαστος*, p. 518, n. 1; in its published English version the talk is entitled 'The Homeric G.B.S.', *The Shaw Review*, 18/3 (September 1975), pp. 91–92. This was a special issue for the twenty-fifth anniversary of Shaw's death.

28 Farinou-Malamatari, 'Τέσσερεις γυναίκες βιογραφούν τον Καζαντζάκη', p. 296, n. 7, briefly refers to interesting parallels between the lives of Shaw and Kazantzakis. In a private communication Peter Bien points out that Kazantzakis' very early play *Ξημερώνει*, like Shaw's early play *The Philanderer*, is based on Ibsen and treats the liberation of women.

29 Did he actually meet Shaw? In a letter to Prevelakis dated 18 July, he writes: 'Μεθαύριο – θεωρήθηκε μέγας θρίαμβος – θα δω τον B[ernard] Shaw' (Prevelakis, *Τετρακόσια γράμματα*, p. 543; Bien, *Letters*, p. 662). But I can find no evidence that the meeting took place.

30 Kazantzakis – Kakridis, '84 γράμματα', p. 277; Bien, *Letters*, p. 614.

31 Vei, 'Δύο επιστολαί', p. 1690.

32 Kazantzis. 'Τρία ανέκδοτα γράμματα', p. 907.

33 E. Kazantzaki, *Ο ασυμβίβαστος*, pp. 531–32; H. Kazantzakis, *Biography*, pp. 451–53; *Le Dissident*, pp. 464–65.

34 See the biography by Janet Soskice, *Sisters of Sinai: How Two Lady Adventurers Found the Hidden Gospels* (London, 2009); see also A. Whigham Price, *The Ladies of Castlebrae: A Story of Nineteenth-century Travel and Research* (Gloucester, 1985).

35 H. Kazantzakis, *Biography*, p. 452.

36 In a letter of 31 July to Kakridis (Bien, *Letters*, p. 626) he writes, 'I've withdrawn to Cambridge, where I'm going to write a book; afterwards I'll come to the beloved soil that is bleeding once more.' And further down, 'Here in Cambridge it's quiet, green lawns everywhere, but rainstorms and cold. I don't feel any pleasure. I'm impatient to see Aegina again. When? This drudgery might last another two months.'

37 H. Kazantzakis, *Biography*, p. 453.

38 Kazantzis, 'Τρία ανέκδοτα γράμματα', p. 907.

39 Letter dated 5 September 1946; Vei, 'Δύο επιστολαί', p. 1690.

40 Nikos Kazantzakis, 'Ο θάνατος του παπού', *Νέα Εστία*, 41 (15 March 1947), pp. 327–34. A footnote on the first page reads: 'Ένα κεφάλαιο από το τελευταίο βιβλίο που γράφτηκε στο Cambridje (sic): «Ο Ανήφορος».' Concerning *Ο Ανήφορος*, see also Prevelakis, *Τετρακόσια γράμματα*, p. 531, G. K. Katsimbalis, *Βιβλιογραφία Ν. Καζαντζάκη*, vol. 1 [and only]: 1906–1948 (Athens, 1958), no. 99; Bien, *Politics of the Spirit*, vol. 2, pp. xiii, 90, 290, 378, 520, 537; and Bien, *Letters*, pp. 638, 638n, 643, 644, 645, 647, 653, 658.

41 It became part of chapter XIII.

42 Nikos Kazantzakis, 'Η Κρήτη', *Νέα Εστία*, 66 (Christmas 1959), pp. 39–42.

226 DAVID HOLTON

43 Bien, *Letters*, pp. 619 and 620.

44 Bien, *Letters*, p. 626.

45 He mentions it in a letter to Eleni; see Bien, *Letters*, p. 627. He actually wrote to Knös on 4 October, in Paris (ibid., pp. 628–29), but the translation of *Zorba* was not mentioned until later letters.

46 Bien, *Politics of the Spirit*, vol. 2, pp. 248, 261–63, and in his article 'Kazantzakis's Abortive Foray', pp. 8–10.

47 H. Kazantzakis, *Biography*, pp. 452–53.

48 See Dimadis, 'Τέχνη και εξουσία', 290–5, and *Power and Prose Fiction*, 215–20. See also Jim Potts, 'Truth will Triumph: The British Council and Cultural Relations in Greece', in David Wills (ed.), *Greece and Britain since 1945* (Newcastle, 2010), p. 114.

49 H. Kazantzakis, *Biography*, pp. 453–54.

50 Letter dated 12 September 1946; see Bien, *Letters*, pp. 627.

51 H. Kazantzakis, *Biography*, p. 455.

52 There are about a dozen books in his library that we can assume were acquired while he was in England. They include: C.M. Bowra, *A Classical Education*; John Donne, *Complete Poetry and Selected Prose* (given to him – then or later? – by Stavros and Flora Papastavrou); Graham Greene, *The Power and the Glory*; Laurie Lee, *The Sun My Monument* (with personal dedication); John Lehmann (ed.), *Penguin New Writing*; Arthur Ransome, *Swallows and Amazons*; Henry Reed, *The Novel Since 1939* and Stephen Spender, *Poetry Since 1939* (both British Council publications); and four novels by H.G. Wells. See: Georgia Katsalaki, *Η βιβλιοθήκη του Νίκου Καζαντζάκη στο Ιστορικό Μουσείο Κρήτης*. Εισαγωγικό σημείωμα Θεοχάρης Δετοράκης (Heraklion, 1997).

53 To be fair, 'Nikos Kazantzaki' was the form of his name that he normally used in French, but in English he was 'Kazantzakis'.

54 Stephen E. Tabachnik, *Fiercer than Tigers: the Life and Works of Rex Warner* (East Lansing, 2002), p. 286. In a BBC Third Programme talk, given on 27 August 1948 and entitled 'Aspects of contemporary Greek poetry', Warner devoted a paragraph to Kazantzakis; the only specific work he mentioned was *The Odyssey*, although he added, 'This vast volume is only a fragment of the poet's works. Poems, dramas and translations stream continually from his fecund pen; and he finds time for politics as well.' See Rex Warner, *Personal Impressions: Talks on Writers and Writing*, ed. Marion B. McLeod (Sydney, 1986), p. 18.

55 For example, the diaries, correspondence and visitors' book of the Provost of King's College, Cambridge.

56 Kazantzis, 'Τρία ανέκδοτα γράμματα', p. 907.

57 Bien, *Letters*, p. 627. Cf. H. Kazantzakis, *Biography*, p. 454.

58 Ibid., p. 446. Sir Sydney Waterlow had lobbied for Kazantzakis to be elected to the Bywater and Sotheby Professorship in 1939 and also, apparently, for a Readership to be established for him at the University of London. See Bien, *Letters*, p. 520.

Chapter 13
The Institut français d'Athènes 1945–1955: Cultural exchanges and Franco-Greek relations

Lucile Arnoux-Farnoux

The Institut français d'Athènes[1] was created in 1907 and quickly expanded its mission to encompass more than the teaching of French language and culture to young Greeks. It was to become a centre of philhellenism and, in that spirit, of the promotion of Greek culture as much as French culture. For example, between 1918 and 1924, Louis Roussel,[2] a former member of the Ecole française d'Athènes and teacher at the Institut supérieur d'Etudes françaises, the future IFA, gave lectures on Karagiozis, the subject of his second thesis, and created a review, *Libre*, dedicated entirely to Greek language and literature. It was the arrival of Octave Merlier in 1925, however, that allowed this policy of dual cultural openness to blossom. Because the history of the Institute was inextricably bound up with that of this great philhellene from then until his return to France in 1961, a brief overview is appropriate here.

Octave Merlier (1897–1976) arrived in Greece in January 1925 to succeed Louis Roussel as principal professor at the Institut supérieur d'Etudes françaises. In 1935 he became responsible for the entire pedagogical and cultural direction of the establishment and, in 1938, was named administrator of the Institute. During those years he increased the number of classes offered by the Institute from 16 to 182 hours per week. Since 1930, moreover, the Institute had been training French teachers for Greek secondary education in a 'Special Course'. In parallel, the Institute's cultural arm was being developed through the provision of numerous lectures.

In 1939 Merlier was drafted into the French forces while remaining in post. He managed to ensure that the Institute was not requisitioned and continued to fulfil his teaching mission in Athens. When General de Gaulle called the French to arms in 1940 he responded immediately, becoming his secret correspondent a few months later. Nevertheless, in July 1941, he was summoned back to France by the Vichy government because of his rallying to Free France and his support of the Greek Resistance. He was obliged to reside in Aurillac and forbidden to return to Greece; he did not go back there until 1945. Meanwhile Robert Demangel, the director of the Ecole d'Athènes, took over the interim management, aided by the director of studies and secretary general of the Institute, Roger Milliex (1913–2006), the de facto director between 1941 and 1945.

On his return to Greece in July 1945, Merlier immediately resumed the directorship of the Institute. Its pedagogical activities – which had continued uninterrupted throughout the war, despite extremely difficult conditions – intensified in response to an even greater demand on the part of the Greek public. The number of registered students jumped from twelve hundred in 1939 to three thousand four hundred in 1945, while more than a thousand applications remained unprocessed due to lack of available places. To meet this demand the Institute opened fifteen new annexes in the Athens suburbs, experiencing an unprecedented expansion.[3] Yet Merlier nursed an even more ambitious project: he wished to offer particularly brilliant Greek students the possibility of extending their higher education in France itself, thus sparing them the troubles of the civil war and its disastrous effects on society. This would be doubly beneficial, since a generation in danger of being sacrificed to the prevalent political and social conditions in Greece would be saved and well educated and, on returning to Greece, would constitute an élite immersed in French culture and, thereby, a natural ally of France.

The voyage of the *Mataroa* and the Greek grant-holders of the French State[4]

Because of his forced exile in France until the summer of 1945, Merlier knew that the political context was favourable for the implementation of his idea: the French government wanted to take advantage of the fact that Germany was no longer a focus for foreign students – up until the war German universities had attracted large numbers of these – in order to spread French influence, while simultaneously countering the growing influence of Britain and the United States. For this reason, it had already put in place a policy of very generous scholarships, for that year in particular. Merlier was quick to grab the opportunity and even succeeded in increasing their number: from the 45 originally allocated for Greek students, he finally obtained 154, a number that would never be repeated; in 1947 only 40 scholarships were granted, and a mere 30 in 1948.[5] The applications, however, by far exceeded the available grants: 950 applied in the summer of 1945, whereas only 350 candidates applied for British grants that same year.

Besides the 154 grant-holders, 59 other students were authorized to go and study in France at their own expense, while benefiting, once there, from the same facilities as their comrades: university residences, access to university refectories and coverage of social services. Moreover, they were allowed to travel with the other group – no small advantage at a time when international transport had quite some way to go before returning to normal. Organizing the travel arrangements turned out to be a real headache for Merlier, and it took him several months to bring them to fruition.

THE INSTITUT FRANÇAIS D'ATHÈNES 1945–1955   229

In the event, the New Zealand ship *Mataroa* took them across from Piraeus to Taranto, whence the young Greeks travelled by rail through Italy and Switzerland, finally reaching Paris on 28 December, having left Piraeus six days earlier. Though this is not the place to discuss it, the voyage of the *Mataroa* came to take on almost mythical proportions.[6] Nevertheless, the very positive consequences of this initiative for Franco-Greek cultural relations cannot be overemphasized. The Greek students arriving in Paris at the end of December 1945 represented most scientific and artistic domains: apart from future teachers of French, for whom a certain number of grants had been earmarked, there were architects, sculptors, actors or directors, musicians, specialists in the humanities – literature, history, philosophy, sociology – as well as numerous scientists, medical students, students of chemistry, physics, mathematics and engineering. Because the civil war lasted until 1949, the majority of the students stayed on in France much longer than planned. Some of the brightest among them, finding particularly favourable conditions in France, settled there permanently with careers either as liberal professionals or working in the various teaching and research establishments (such as the Centre national de la recherche scientifique, the Ecole des hautes études en sciences sociales, the Ecole pratique des hautes études and the universities).[7] Thenceforth they became part of the French intellectual and artistic élite. Cases in point are the well-known philosophers Kostas Axelos, Cornelius Castoriadis and Kostas Papaïoannou, the historian Nicolas Svoronos and the writer Mimika Kranaki, to whom should be added the engineer and musician Ianis Xenakis, who joined them in 1947. Their oeuvres built a bridge between the two countries and the two cultures, and constituted the most visible part of the phenomenal cultural transfer that made up the success of Merlier's project. But a far greater number did return to Greece after some years, having completed their education in France, and contributed to the cultivation of ties between the two countries, just as the director of the Institute had foreseen.

Activities in Athens

In Athens, alongside the educational activities of the Institute, Merlier pursued a cultural policy of openness and even-handedness. As he had said in 1936 to the young Roger Milliex, newly arrived from France: 'If we wish France to be loved by the Greeks, then we must ourselves love Greece.'[8] And to love her one must know her.

As early as 1945, he created the 'Collection de l'Institut français d'Athènes' where he published Greek as well as French works: Greek literature in French translation or in bilingual editions, French classics (Villon, Descartes, Molière, Rabelais and others) in bilingual editions, studies in Greek or French concerning domains as diverse as law, history, history of art and, of course, literature.[9]

Characteristically, the first two volumes, published in 1945, were translations of the Greek poets Dionysios Solomos[10] and George Seferis[11] by Robert Levesque,[12] who was teaching at the IFA at the time. As far as Merlier was concerned, it was just as important to make modern Greek literature known to the French as it was to make classic French literature familiar to Greek youth. The third volume, published in 1946, was the work of a contemporary Greek poet, Angelos Sikelianos, this time translated by Octave Merlier himself.[13] There is a story behind this translation. One hundred hand-written copies of Sikelianos' collection *Akritika* (1941–42) had been circulated secretly in Athens in 1942, illustrated with woodcuts by Spyros Vassiliou. A limited number of copies of this work, which Merlier translated during his assigned residence at Aurillac, were printed in 1944, although their sale was prohibited by the Vichy government. In 1946, Merlier had his translation reprinted, including Vassiliou's woodcuts and a short introduction. During the war, a public reading of the French translation of the poet's poem Μήτηρ Θεού as *Mater Dei* had taken place at the Institute, organized by Robert Levesque.[14] In 1951, Merlier translated Nikos Kazantzakis' *Askitiki*[15] and, in 1953, published a prose text by Seferis in a bilingual Greek and French edition: *Trois jours dans les églises rupestres de Cappadoce*,[16] which Seferis had originally written for the volume published in homage to Octave and Melpo Merlier.[17]

That same year, the cultural exchanges promoted by the Institute were exemplified by the first volume of *Ellinogallika* [Greco-French Studies], published in Greek by Roger Milliex. This volume consisted of two texts which symbolized this exchange: 'Adamantios Korais on French civilization' and 'Victor Hugo, a faithful friend of Greece'. After the title page came the following double dedication, laid out *en face*:

> To the memory of Sotiris Skipis/(1881–1952) poet of Attica and Provence/faithful friend of France/in sorrow as in days of joy
>
> and in honour of/Octave and Melpo Merlier/whose labours I have watched for sixteen years/for the two merged motherlands/I dedicate this first notebook which unites them.[18]

Publications followed one another at a rapid pace: after just ten years, in 1955, the Collection de l'Institut Français d'Athènes had reached one hundred publications, the catalogue of titles testifying to the constant linguistic and cultural exchange going on between the two nations. It is an impressive achievement, even more so if we bear in mind that at the time, from 1946 onwards, the Institute published the *Bulletin Analytique de Bibliographie Hellénique*, thus presenting Greece with a bibliographical tool which had previously been lacking. Nothing in the British Council's record is comparable.

Aside from the Franco-Greek publications, there were exhibitions that rendered homage to the great figures of modern Greek literature. The first,

THE INSTITUT FRANÇAIS D'ATHÈNES 1945–1955   231

dedicated to Sikelianos, took place immediately after the poet's death in 1951. The exhibition contained personal objects, editions of his works, photographs and other memorabilia of the recently departed poet. Another exhibition followed in 1956, in honour of Aristotelis Valaoritis (1824–79), while the exhibition for the centenary of the death of Solomos, in 1957, was particularly significant and attracted many visitors to the French Institute.

As far as Merlier was concerned, Greek culture was not limited to Greece's political borders. Through his wife, the musician and musicologist Melpo Logotheti-Merlier, a native of Constantinople, Merlier's horizons opened onto the Hellenism of Asia Minor. The French Institute actively supported the Centre for Asia Minor Studies created by Melpo Merlier in 1930 for the preservation and study of the Greek civilization of Asia Minor. With the permission of the Direction Générale des Relations Culturelles de France, the Institute allocated funds annually for the subvention of the Centre. For a very long time these funds remained its sole financial support.[19] Melpo Merlier ran a series, within the Collection of the French Institute, called 'Archives of popular music and folklore of Asia Minor', in which she published a paper explaining the history of these archives.[20]

Homage to Greece

The most spectacular event of those years, however, apart from the voyage of the *Mataroa*, was the 'Exhibition of works offered by French artists in Homage to Greece', which opened its doors at the French Institute on 17 April 1949. It was the perfect sequel to the *Mataroa* adventure: in 1945 two hundred young Greeks had made the voyage from Athens to Paris to study and, four years later, the voyage from Paris to Athens was undertaken by forty works by French artists. This time the initiative was due to the other great personality of the Institute, Roger Milliex. Having arrived in Greece in 1936, he became the director of studies in 1940. Like Merlier, he was an exceptional modern Greek scholar and a great philhellene and, again like Merlier, he had married a Greek, the writer Tatiana Gritsi. The Milliexes were in France[21] during the winter of 1945–46. There they gathered testimonials from French intellectuals in honour of the Greek resistance:

> At the time we were only thinking of a written monument, a kind of *Livre d'Or* in which French people from all walks of life and all cultural levels could express the admiration, devotion, and fraternal solidarity that they had felt, in silence, between 1940 and 1944, when faced with Greece's exemplary stance during the war.[22]

However, while testimonials began to reach the Milliexes, the painter André Fougeron, whose contribution they had requested, suggested that they choose between a short manuscript and a painting signed by him. Then Henri Matisse offered them an illustration for Henry de Montherlant's play *Pasiphaé*, which he had done during the war, followed by 'Chant de Minos', on which, he told them, he 'had worked with passion, trying hard to imagine an old Cretan'. In a postscript, he asked humbly if 'one of [his] drawings would be accepted for the Modern Museum of Athens', and added, 'Could you perhaps accept this advice: ask some skilled artists[23] for drawings for the Athens museum in honour of Greek intellectuals.'[24] Thus the idea of having the written homage accompanied by a pictorial homage was thanks to the encouragement of Henri Matisse and André Fougeron – the latter opening doors to younger painters as well – but also of Christian Zervos, who was 'doubly interested in this Franco-Greek project'.[25] Roger and Tatiana set out to make the rounds of the Parisian studios, 'delighted to have been offered this unlooked for mission: a quest on behalf of the Athens museum in the interests of Greece, its people and its intellectuals'.[26] Thirty years later, Milliex still recalled that time with exaltation, specifying the names of the artists who had been asked to contribute:

> And there we were, as brother seekers, making the rounds of the studios of Picasso, Marquet, Lhote, Marchand, Gromaire, Desnoyer, and others, not forgetting Bourdelle, and writing to Bonnard, Braque, Gimond, Survage, et al. to solicit material, and soon their gifts to Greece, with matching heartfelt dedications to the Greek people, accumulated in a narrow room, in the attic of student lodgings, at 3 rue de l'Odéon. . .[27]

Finally, Milliex and his wife managed to collect 'twenty-nine canvases, engravings, drawings, sculptures and art books offered to Greece by twenty-six French artists (or French by "adoption" like Galanis and Mario Prassinos), joined by Madame Sébasto-Bourdelle, who donated a beautiful bronze "Pallas" on behalf of her husband as a posthumous homage to the land of his spiritual and physical attachment'.[28] Apart from these twenty-nine works, an additional donation was made by the General Direction of Cultural Relations of the French Ministry of Foreign Affairs, which took over from Milliex's personal initiative, bringing the total to 46 pieces (28 canvases, 12 engravings or drawings, four sculptures and two books),[29] which were exhibited from 17 to 29 April 1949 at the French Institute, before being solemnly handed over to the Greek Minister of Education at the time, Constantine Tsatsos, and deposited in the National Gallery.

The exhibition proved to be a two-fold event. First of all, as homage from French artists to the Greek Resistance, it had a moral significance. Milliex underlined this at the very start of his foreword to the 1949 catalogue:

> The works of contemporary French art which our Institute is presenting to the Greek public for a few days is an exhibition unlike any other. It should be shielded from the usual criteria and appreciated in a most particular fashion,

THE INSTITUT FRANÇAIS D'ATHÈNES 1945–1955   233

one which will give those for whom it is destined, namely, all our Greek friends, a brief review of the conditions under which it has been brought together.[30]

It must not be forgotten that in April 1949 the civil war was not over and that this exhibition was taking place in a highly charged social and political context. The right-wing press criticized it not only for the aesthetic tendencies that were represented but also because communist artists had participated. This was precisely why Octave Merlier decided to withhold publication of the famous 'Livre d'Or' containing the testimonials gathered by the Milliexes, judging 'in his prudent wisdom that the publication of certain texts whose signatories (French writers) had taken a position in the internal struggles of Greece (1946–49) would damage the unanimity of Greek public opinion – the unanimity that the publication of the Homage was intended to encourage'.[31] It was only in 1979, five years after the return of democracy to Greece and thirty years after the exhibition, that the texts which made up this Homage were finally published.[32] What is most striking about these texts is the diversity of their authors. All political tendencies are represented in them, from the most conservative right, with Jacques de Lacretelle or Gabriel Boissy, to the left, which encompassed the majority, and the communist party, with Eluard and Guillevic, and even certain intellectuals of Catholic allegiance, among them Jacques Maritain and Emmanuel Mounier, the founder of the review *Esprit*. Numerous writers responded, whether they had joined the resistance or not, such as Georges Bernanos, René Char, Georges Duhamel, Roger Martin du Gard, Louis Guilloux, François Mauriac, André Maurois, Francis Ponge, Jules Romains and Vercors, among others. Some of them did so simply with a letter; others with a poem (Paul Eluard, Guillevic, Tristan Tzara), a prose poem (René Char, André Suarès), even a play (Paul Claudel). Among them were also several journalists, publishers or men of letters, like Jean Ballard, the editor of the *Cahiers du Sud*; Jean Cassou; Jean Cayrol; Max-Pol Fouchet, editor of the review *Fontaine* in Algiers; Jean Paulhan; and Pierre Seghers. There were also Hellenists (Mario Meunier), philhellenes (Philéas Lebesgue) and scholars of the Greek language (André Mirambel, Hubert Pernot), as well as scientists such as Robert Debré, Louis de Broglie and Louis Pasteur Vallery-Radot, the grandson of Louis Pasteur. In his contribution the architect Le Corbusier recalled his arrival in Athens in 1933 on the occasion of the fourth International Congress for Modern Architecture. Finally, the rector of the University of Paris sent an official letter, as well as the students of the Ecole Normale Supérieure.

The tone of the different types of homage was less varied, however. Most of them consisted of rather vague praise of Greek heroism during the war, often resorting (unsurprisingly) to ancient references. Nevertheless, some of the better informed and more committed alluded directly to the civil war. The poems by Eluard and Guillevic both refer to the bloody events of December 1944, while several correspondents expressed their wishes for the triumph of liberty

234   LUCILE ARNOUX-FARNOUX

and democracy in Greece. One can understand why, in 1949, Merlier considered it wise to withhold the publication of these texts.

Even though the value of the 1949 exhibition was primarily a moral one, it nevertheless introduced contemporary French art into Athenian cultural life and as such had an obvious aesthetic impact. There had been a precedent, two years earlier, when the French Institute had backed an exhibition organized by the very active Union Franco-Hellénique des Jeunes in July 1947: 'French engravers 1808–1947', which had shown 135 works by Daumier, Manet, Rodin, Lautrec, Matisse, Rouault, Galanis, Villon and many others.[33] But in 1949, the point was not to exhibit but to donate works which might form the nucleus of a permanent collection. At the time, this aspect was almost entirely overlooked in Athens. Only the review *Nea Estia* devoted a positive review to the event, in its issue of 15 May 1949, which contained reproductions of some of the works shown. The journalist who covered the exhibition called it an 'important artistic event'. He also referred to Roger Milliex's even more ambitious project to create a room in the National Gallery entirely dedicated to French contemporary art, of which, he emphasized, hardly any examples existed in Greece at that time. He acknowledged that even though these new artistic forms were not yet highly appreciated in Greece, they nevertheless represented a world movement, and one could not ignore the fact that they would probably have a decisive influence on the next generation. Such a collection would constitute, he concluded, 'a school of the highest importance for our art and our culture'.[34] Other events presenting contemporary French art at the IFA would follow, such as the exhibition at the end of 1955 of drawings and lithographs by Fernand Léger to honour this artist, who had died a few months earlier. But that of 1949 remains unique in its history and significance.[35] Twenty years later, the painter Panayotis Tetsis stated, 'The aim was not to promote French art in Greece for the benefit of France. On the contrary, the aim was to enable Greek artists to benefit from this contact [with French art].'[36]

Conclusion

As we have seen, the decade 1945–55 was a period of intense activity for the Institut français d'Athènes. This was thanks to the two exceptional personalities of Octave Merlier and Roger Milliex, both of whom exercised a seemingly inexhaustible energy and an uncommon inventiveness and sensitivity in the service of the Institute. With these men the Institute no longer confined itself to being an instrument for promoting the French language and culture, but became a veritable intercultural focus or, put more simply, a place of culture: 'For a certain period the square formed by Sina, Arachovis and Prassa Streets was flooded by Greece and for twenty years dominated the intellectual life of Athens and of the country as a whole – particularly in the difficult post-war years, which were filled with hopes and disillusionments,' Tetsis

THE INSTITUT FRANÇAIS D'ATHÈNES 1945–1955 235

still remembers.[37] It was precisely during those years that the cultural policy pursued by Merlier and Milliex, at the head of the French Institute, caused a continual to and fro of Greek and French people between Paris and Athens. This 'double journey'[38] continued the journey that began between the two world wars but was enhanced by a feeling of urgency that had not been originally present. To publish contemporary Greek literature in French translation, to collect from French intellectuals testimonials of admiration for the Greek Resistance, and to do all this in the middle of the Greek civil war, meant also to help French people who knew little about Greece to become familiar with Greek reality. These actions, as well as many others, attempted, within their more general objectives, to enlighten French public opinion with a view to finding a political solution to the civil war.[39]

This cultural policy did not fail to arouse a reaction from the most conservative Greek circles, where Merlier and Milliex were seen as allies of the Greek communist party. From 1945 on, the Greek authorities were insistently demanding that the two men be replaced while, in France, at the French Ministry of Foreign Affairs, there was disquiet at seeing the Institute more concerned with promoting Greek culture in France than French culture in Greece. The fact that Merlier, in spite of everything, managed to maintain his directorship of the IFA not only during the decade 1945–55 but right up to 1960 was due, no doubt, to his supporters in both France and Greece. Certain high-profile politicians in the conservative Greek government supported him, such as Constantine Tsatsos, who emphasized the extremely positive role he played in Franco-Greek relations.[40] Merlier was finally recalled to France in 1961, while Roger Milliex had been obliged to quit his post as assistant director of the Institute even earlier, in 1959, in order to take up the post of cultural attaché in Cyprus. Each man felt his departure from Greece to be nothing less than an exile and each returned to Greece after the fall of the dictatorship in 1974.

Notes

1 It was only after the Second World War that it was thus named. In 1907 permission was granted to establish an Ecole primaire française. This was built thanks to the legacy left by the engineer Giffard to the French state and was administered by the director of the Ecole française d'Athènes. In 1915 the Ecole primaire was transformed into the Institut supérieur d'Etudes françaises, commonly called the 'Institut Giffard', yet remained under the tutelage of the EFA. From 1935 onwards the Institute became autonomous in matters of pedagogy and cultural policy while still remaining financially dependent on the EFA. Finally, in 1945, it became officially the Institut français d'Athènes under an independent administration. For a more complete history of the IFA see Roger Milliex, 'L'Institut français d'Athènes, fils spirituel de l'Ecole française', *Bulletin de Correspondance Hellénique*, 120 (1996), pp. 69–82; Lambros Flitouris, 'Ο Octave Merlier και ο ρόλος του στην προώθηση των ελληνογαλλικών σχέσεων (1925–1961)', *ΚΑ΄ Πανελλήνιο Ιστορικό Συνέδριο (26, 27, 28 Μαΐου*

236 LUCILE ARNOUX-FARNOUX

2000) (Thessaloniki, 2001), pp. 383–94; Lambros Flitouris, 'L'institut français d'Athènes pendant la Seconde Guerre mondiale', *Guerres mondiales et conflits contemporains*, 218 (April 2005), pp. 37–52.

2 Louis Roussel (1881–1971), a Hellenist and a member of the Ecole française d'Athènes (1906–08), specialized in the study of modern Greek. He taught French at the Institut supérieur d'Etudes françaises from 1918 to 1924 before obtaining the Greek chair at the University of Montpellier. From 1923 to 1936 he edited, first in Athens and then in Montpellier, the monthly review *Libre* (later bimonthly), which published Greek linguistic and literary news.

3 Nicolas Manitakis, 'Ξένες κρατικές υποτροφίες: πολιτιστική προπαγάνδα στην Ελλάδα του Εμφυλίου', in Christos Hatziiosif (ed.), *Ιστορία της Ελλάδας του 20ου αιώνα, 4.2: Ανασυγκρότηση – Εμφύλιος – Παλινόρθωση 1945–1952* (Athens, 2009), p. 139.

4 Detailed accounts of the sending of Greek grant-holders of the French State to France in 1945 and the voyage of the *Mataroa* are given in several well-documented articles. See in particular Manitakis, 'Ξένες κρατικές υποτροφίες'; and Nicolas Manitakis, 'L'exil des jeunes Grecs et le rôle de l'Institut français: un exil doré?', in Servanne Jollivet, Christophe Premat, and Mats Rosengren (eds.), *Destins d'exilés: Trois philosophes grecs à Paris – Kostas Axelos, Cornelius Castoriadis et Kostas Papaïoannou* (Paris, 2011), pp. 45–61. See also Flitouris, 'Ο Octave Merlier και ο ρόλος του', and *Le Voyage du Mataroa: Portrait d'une génération en exil*, study day organized by the Ecole française d'Athènes, 11 October 2013 (forthcoming).

5 By way of comparison, the British Council offered 15 grants to Greek students for studies in the United Kingdom for the year 1947–48, and 11 for the year 1948–49. As for American universities, they offered eight grants in 1945 and 23 in 1946 (Manitakis, 'Ξένες κρατικές υποτροφίες', p. 144).

6 Apart from the articles already mentioned, see the accounts of two female passengers of the *Mataroa*: Nelli Andrikopoulou, *Το ταξίδι του Mataroa, 1945: Στον καθρέφτη της μνήμης* (Athens, 2007); and Mimika Kranaki, *Mataora à deux voix: Journal d'exil* (Athens, 2007). Besides these there is the latter author's fictionalized evocation of the voyage in *Φιλέλληνες: είκοσι τέσσερα γράμματα μιας Οδύσσειας* (Athens, 1998) [1st edn 1992].

7 Manitakis, 'L'exil des jeunes Grecs', pp. 56–60.

8 Milliex, 'L'Institut français d'Athènes', p. 75.

9 See Lucile Arnoux-Farnoux, 'Το εκδοτικό έργο του Ο. Μερλιέ (1945–1961)', *Athens Review of Books*, 42 (July-August 2013), pp. 44–47.

10 Solomos, *Introduction, proses et poèmes [par] R. Levesque* (Athens, 1945) (Collection de l'Institut Français d'Athènes no. 1).

11 Georges Seferis, *Choix de poèmes, traduits et accompagnés du texte grec avec une préface de Robert Levesque* (Athens, 1945) (Collection de l'Institut Français d'Athènes no. 2).

12 Robert Levesque (1909–75) first taught French at the Anargyrios School on Spetses (1938–41), then at the IFA from 1941 to 1947. He published translations of Seferis (1945), Elytis (1945), Solomos (1945) and Sikelianos (1946), as well as

an anthology of contemporary Greek poetry, *Domaine grec: 1930–1946* (1947). In 1948 he presented and translated a selection of texts in the special issue of *Cahiers du Sud*, entitled 'Permanence de la Grèce.'

13 *Le Serment sur le Styx: Cinq poèmes de Sikelianos (1941–1942): Bois de Spyro Vassiliou, traduction d'Octave Merlier* (Athens, 1946) (Collection de l'Institut Français d'Athènes no. 3).

14 Milliex, 'L'Institut français d'Athènes,' p. 81.

15 Nikos Kazantzakis, *Ascèse: salvatores dei: Traduit du grec et présenté par Octave Merlier* (Athens: Institut Français d'Athènes, 1951) (Collection de l'Institut Français d'Athènes no. 27).

16 Georges Seferis, *Trois jours dans les églises rupestres de Cappadoce* (Athens, 1953) (Collection de l'Institut Français d'Athènes no. 78A).

17 *Mélanges offerts à Octave et Melpo Merlier à l'occasion du 25e anniversaire de leur arrivée en Grèce* (3 vols, Athens, 1956–57) (Collection de l'Institut Français d'Athènes, nos 92, 93 and 94). Seferis' contribution is in vol. 3, pp. 185–215.

18 Roger Milliex, *Ελληνογαλλικά, I: Αδαμάντιος Κοραής – Victor Hugo* (Athens, 1953) (Collection de l'Institut Français d'Athènes no. 77).

19 Melpo Merlier, *Présentation du Centre d'Etudes d'Asie Mineure: Recherches d'ethnographie*, 2nd edn, ed. P. Kitromilidis (Athens, 2011), p. 20 (1st edn 1951).

20 Melpo Merlier, *Το αρχείο της Μικρασιατικής λαογραφίας: πώς ιδρύθηκε, πώς εργάστηκε* (Athens, 1948) (Collection de l'Institut Français d'Athènes no. 7).

21 In fact, Roger Milliex was recalled to France on leave of absence from August 1945 to June 1946 as a result of pressure from certain Greek government quarters. He returned in the summer of 1946 as vice-director, a post he filled until 1959. Towards the end of 1959, he was made cultural attaché for the French Embassy in Nicosia; then in 1971 he became the director of the French Cultural Centre in Genoa. He came back to Greece as soon as the dictatorship fell, in the summer of 1974 (Christophe Chiclet, 'Hommage à Roger Milliex (1913–2006)', *Confluences Méditerranée*, 59 (Autumn 2006), pp. 189–90); on Milliex see also Lucile Arnoux-Farnoux, 'Relations intellectuelles et artistiques entre la France et la Grèce au XXe siècle: l'action de deux philhellènes, Octave Merlier (1897–1976) et Roger Milliex (1913–2006)', in Ourania Polycandrioti (ed.), *Figures d'intellectuels en Méditerranée (XIXe-XXe siècles)* (Rives Méditerranéennes, 50 (2015), pp. 53–64.)

22 Roger Milliex, Introduction to the catalogue: *Exposition des œuvres offertes par des artistes français en hommage à la Grèce, du 17 au 29 avril à l'Institut français d'Athènes* (Athens, 1949), p. 7.

23 The original manuscript specifies: 'such as Bonnard, Picasso, Braque, Laurens, [. . .] Rouault, Dufy, Gromaire' (letter from Henri Matisse, 3 December 1945, Roger Milliex archive, ELIA, Athens).

24 Letter from Henri Matisse to Roger Milliex, 3 December 1945, published in Roger Milliex (ed.), *Hommage à la Grèce 1940–1944. Textes et témoignages français* (Athens, 1979), p. 220.

25 Milliex, Introduction to *Exposition des œuvres offertes*, p. 8.

238   LUCILE ARNOUX-FARNOUX

26 Ibid.

27 Milliex, 'Avant-Propos', in *Hommage à la Grèce 1940–1944*, pp. 9–10.

28 Milliex, Introduction to *Exposition des œuvres offertes*, p. 9.

29 The names of André Masson and Francis Picabia should be added to those already mentioned.

30 Milliex, Introduction to *Exposition des œuvres offertes*, p. 7.

31 Milliex, 'Avant-Propos', in *Hommage à la Grèce 1940–1944*, p. 10.

32 Ibid.

33 Evgenios Matthiopoulos, 'Οι εικαστικές τέχνες στην Ελλάδα τα χρόνια 1945–1953', in Hatziiosif (ed.), *Ιστορία της Ελλάδας του 20ου αιώνα*, 4.2, p. 217.

34 D.E. Evangelidis, 'Εκθέσεις', *Νέα Εστία*, 525 (15 May 1949), pp. 675–77.

35 It would take thirty years for this to be fully recognized. From then on the exhibition has been repeated several times: at the National Gallery from 4 to 28 February 1980; at the Municipal Gallery of Patras from 12 April to 30 July 2003; at the Macedonian Museum of Contemporary Art in Thessaloniki from 9 December 2003 to 1 February 2004; at the Corfu annex of the National Gallery from 3 May to 30 June 2004; and, most recently, from 5 June to 5 July 2007, once more at the National Gallery, in connection with the centenary of the IFA. It was also shown in Paris from 2 October to 30 November 2008, at the Mémorial Leclerc-Musée Jean Moulin, under the title 'Hommage à la Grèce résistante'.

36 Panayotis Tetsis, *Αφιέρωμα στους Μιλλιέξ*, special issue of *Τομές*, 2nd series, 12–13 (May-June 1977), p. 53.

37 Ibid. [Editors' note: Sina, Arachovis, Prassa and Didotou Streets form the boundaries of the EFA and the IFA. The relevant section of Arachovis has since been renamed in honour of Octave Merlier, while Didotou is named after the French printer and Philhellene Ambroise Firmin Didot.]

38 Cf. the title of the colloquium 'Paris-Athènes 1919–1939: le double voyage', organized in Athens from 19 to 21 January 2012 by the EFA, the Benaki Museum and the Institut d'Etudes Méditerranéennes (publication forthcoming).

39 Flitouris, 'Ο Octave Merlier και ο ρόλος του', p. 391.

40 Ibid., p. 392.

Bibliography

Electronic sources

Cameron, Averil, 'Runciman, Sir James Cochran Stevenson [Steven]', *Oxford Dictionary of National Biography* online (2004), http://ezproxy-prd.bodleian. ox.ac.uk:2167/view/10.1093/ref:odnb/9780198614128.001.0001/odnb-9780198614128-e-74911?rskey=FCkKC8&result=6.

Cull, Nicholas J., 'Propaganda?', http://archive.li/Xk00J

'Rare Propaganda Films of 1940s Britain Released Online', www.bbc.co.uk/news/entertainment-arts-11997847

Thomas, Jeanette, 'Smith, Reginald Donald', *Oxford Dictionary of National Biography* online (2004), http://ezproxy-prd.bodleian.ox.ac.uk:2167/view/10.1093/ref:odnb/9780198614128.001.0001/odnb-9780198614128-e-65435?rskey=DCfhuE&result=1.

Warnock, G.J. (revised), 'Warner, Reginald Ernest [Rex]', *Oxford Dictionary of National Biography* online (2009), http://ezproxy-prd.bodleian.ox.ac.uk:2167/view/10.1093/ref:odnb/9780198614128.001.0001/odnb-9780198614128-e-39846?rskey=0Hhsyi&result=1.

Printed sources

'84 γράμματα του Καζαντζάκη στον Κακριδή', *Νέα Εστία*, 102 (Christmas 1977): 257–300.

Aldrich, Richard J., 'Putting Culture into the Cold War: The Cultural Relations Department (CRD) and British Covert Information Warfare', in Giles Scott-Smith and Hans Krabbendam (eds.), *The Cultural Cold War in Western Europe, 1945–1960* (London: Routledge, 2003): 109–33.

Aldrich, Richard J., *The Hidden Hand. Britain, America, and Cold War Secret Intelligence* (Woodstock: Overlook Press, 2002).

Alexander, G.M., *The Prelude to the Truman Doctrine: British Policy in Greece, 1944–47* (Oxford: The Clarendon Press, 1982).

Alexander, Peter F., *William Plomer: A Biography* (Oxford: Oxford University Press, 1989).

Allison, Jonathan (ed.), *Letters of Louis MacNeice* (London: Faber, 2010).

Andrews, Kevin, *The Flight of Ikaros* (Philadelphia: Paul Dry Books, 2004 [1st edn 1959]).

Andrikopoulou, Nelli, *Το ταξίδι του Ματαρόα, 1945: Στον καθρέπτη της μνήμης* (Athens: Estia, 2007).

BIBLIOGRAPHY

Angeloglou, George, *This Is London, Good Evening – Edo Londino, Kalispera sas: The Story of the Greek Section of the B.B.C., 1939–1957* (Athens: Eftstathiadis, 2003).

Argyriou, Alexandros, 'Introduction', in *Η μεταπολεμική πεζογραφία: Από τον πόλεμο του '40 ώς τη δικτατορία του '67*, vol. 1 (Athens: Sokolis, 1996).

Arnakis, George Georgiadis, 'An Autobiographical Sketch by George G. Arnakis', *Neo-Hellenika*, 4 (1981): 9–28.

Arnoux-Farnoux, Lucile, 'Relations intellectuelles et artistiques entre la France et la Grèce au XXe siècle: l'action de deux philhellènes, Octave Merlier (1897–1976) et Roger Milliex (1913–2006)', in Ourania Polycandrioti (ed.), *Figures d'intellectuels en Méditerranée (XIXe-XXe siècles)* (*Rives Méditerranéennes*, 50 [2015]): 53–64.

Arnoux-Farnoux, Lucile, 'Το εκδοτικό έργο του Ο. Μερλιέ (1945–1961)', *Athens Review of Books*, 42 (July-August 2013): 44–7.

Athanasopoulou, Afroditi, 'Kazantzakis's Perception of England (1939, 1946)', in Liana Giannakopoulou and E. Kostas Skordyles (eds.), *Culture and Society in Crete: From Kornaros to Kazantzakis* (Newcastle upon Tyne: Cambridge Scholars, 2017): 77–102.

Atherton, Louise, 'Lord Lloyd at the British Council and the Balkan Front, 1937–1940', *The International History Review*, 16/1 (February 1994): 25–48.

Attlee, C.M., *Philosophy in Educational Theory* (Birmingham: Cornish Brothers, 1932).

Bachtin, Nicholas, *Introduction to the Study of Modern Greek* (Cambridge: Cambridge University Press, 1935).

Barros, James, *Britain, Greece and the Politics of Sanctions: Ethiopia, 1936–36* (London: Royal Historical Society, 1982).

Beaton, Roderick, *George Seferis* (Bristol: Bristol Classical Press, 1991).

Beaton, Roderick, *George Seferis: Waiting for the Angel: A Biography* (New Haven, CT and London: Yale University Press, 2003).

Behrend, George, *Stanley Spencer at Burghclere* (London: National Trust, 1991).

Bien, Peter, 'Kazantzakis's Abortive Foray into Politics in Liberated Athens, 1944–46', *Κάμπος: Cambridge Papers in Modern Greek*, 13 (2005): 1–19.

Bien, Peter, *Kazantzakis: Politics of the Spirit*, vol. 2 (Princeton: Princeton University Press, 2007).

Bien, Peter (ed. and trans.), *The Selected Letters of Nikos Kazantzakis* (Princeton: Princeton University Press, 2012).

Bikelas, Demetrios, *Loukes Laras: Reminiscences of a Chiote Merchant During the War of Independence*, translated from the Greek by J. Gennadius (London: Macmillan, 1881).

Blotner, Joseph, *William Faulkner: A Biography* (2 vols, London: Chatto and Windus, 1974).

Bolton, Jonathan, *Personal Landscape: British Poets in Egypt During the Second World War* (London: Palgrave, 1997).

BIBLIOGRAPHY

Bowra, Maurice, *New Bats in Old Belfries* (Oxford: Robert Dugdale in association with Wadham College, 2005).

Bryer, Anthony, 'James Cochran Stevenson Runciman', *Proceedings of the British Academy*, 120 (2003): 365–81.

Bryer, Anthony, 'Steven Runciman – Proem: The Problem of Oratory; Being a Brief Thesis on the World, Oral, Written and Remembered; in a Word History', in *Αφιέρωμα στον Sir Steven Runciman*, special issue of *The New Griffon* (Athens: American School of Classical Studies), new series, 5 (2002).

Burn, A.R., *A Traveller's History of Greece* (London: Hodder and Stoughton, 1965).

Burn, A.R., *The Modern Greeks* (London: Nelson, 1944).

Capell, Richard, *Simiomata: A Greek Note Book, 1944–45* (London: Macdonald, n.d.).

Cardiff, Maurice, *Friends Abroad: Memories of Lawrence Durrell, Freya Stark, Patrick Leigh-Fermor, Peggy Guggenheim and Others* (London: Radcliffe Press, 1997).

Cavafy, C.P., *Poems*, trans. John Mavrogordato (London: Hogarth Press, 1951).

Chandler, Geoffrey, *The Divided Land: An Anglo-Greek Tragedy* (Norwich: Michael Russell, 1994).

Chiclet, Christophe, 'Hommage à Roger Milliex (1913–2006)', *Confluences Méditerranée*, 59 (Autumn 2006): 189–90.

Chorchoulis, Dionysios, 'High Hopes, Bold Aims, Limited Results: Britain and the Establishment of the NATO Mediterranean Command, 1950–1953', *Diplomacy and Statecraft*, 20/3 (2009): 434–52.

Christianopoulos, Dinos, *Εποχή των ισχνών αγελάδων* (Thessaloniki: Kochlias, 1950).

Clogg, Richard, *Anglo-Greek Attitudes: Studies in History* (Basingstoke: Macmillan, 2000).

Clogg, Richard, *Bearing Gifts to Greeks: Humanitarian Aid to Greece in the 1940s* (Basingstoke: Palgrave Macmillan, 2008).

Clogg, Richard, *Greek to Me: A Memoir of Academic Life* (London: I.B. Tauris, 2018).

Close, David H., 'War, Medical Advance and the Improvement of Health in Greece, 1944–53', *South European Society and Politics*, 9/3 (Winter 2004): 1–27.

Collins, Ian, *John Craxton*, introduction by David Attenborough (Farnham: Lund Humphries, 2011).

Cooper, Artemis, *Patrick Leigh Fermor: An Adventure* (London: John Murray, 2012).

Craxton, John, 'Obituary: Nikos Ghika', *The Independent*, 7 September 1994.

Cruickshank, Charles, *Greece, 1940–41* (London: Davis-Poynter, 1976).

Cull, Nicholas J., 'Public Diplomacy Before Gullion. The Evolution of a Phrase', in Nancy Snow and P.M. Taylor (eds.), *Routledge Handbook of Public Diplomacy* (London: Routledge, 2009): 19–23.

242 BIBLIOGRAPHY

Daskalopoulos, Dimitris, 'Βιβλιογραφία Γ.Κ. Κατσίμπαλη', *Νέα Εστία*, 108 (1980): 1484–1548.
Daskalopoulos, Dimitris, 'Νίκος Καζαντζάκης – Γ.Κ. Κατσίμπαλης, Αλληλογραφικά τεκμήρια', *Μικροφιλολογικά*, 18 (2005): 26–8.
Defty, Andrew, *Britain, America and Anti-Communist Propaganda 1945–53: The Information Research Department* (London: Routledge, 2004).
Demetrios Capetanakis, A Greek Poet in England (London: John Lehmann, 1947).
Dimadis, Konstantinos A., *Power and Prose Fiction in Modern Greece* (Athens: Armos, 2016).
Dimadis, Konstantinos A., 'Τέχνη και εξουσία: παρατηρήσεις σε τέσσερα ταξιδιωτικά έργα του Νίκου Καζαντζάκη', in Roderick Beaton (ed.), *Εισαγωγή στο έργο του Καζαντζάκη: Επιλογή κριτικών κειμένων* (Heraklion: Panepistimiakes Ekdoseis Kritis, 2011): 271–310.
Dimaras, Alexis, *Η μεταρρύθμιση που δεν έγινε, 2: 1895–1967* (Athens: Ermis, 1974).
Dimitrakopoulos, Fotis and Vasiliki D. Lambropoulou (eds.), *Γιώργος Σεφέρης, P.L. Fermor & J. Rayner: Αλληλογραφία (1948–1971)* (Nicosia: Kentro Epistimonikon Erevnon, 2007).
Dinshaw, Minoo, *Outlandish Knight: The Byzantine Life of Steven Runciman* (London: Allen Lane, 2016).
Donaldson, Frances, *The British Council: The First Fifty Years* (London: Jonathan Cape, 1984).
Dorril, Stephen, *MI6: Inside the Covert World of Her Majesty's Secret Intelligence Service* (New York: Simon and Schuster, 2000).
Dorril, Stephen, *MI6: Fifty Years of Special Operations* (London: Fourth Estate, 2000).
Durrell, Lawrence, *Bitter Lemons* (London: Faber and Faber, 1957).
Durrell, Lawrence, *Blue Thirst* (Santa Barbara: Capra Press, 1975).
Durrell, Lawrence, 'Hellene and Philhellene', *The Times Literary Supplement*, 13 May 1949: 305–6.
Durrell, Lawrence, *Prospero's Cell: A Guide to the Landscape and Manners of the Island of Corcyra* (London: Faber and Faber, 1945).
Durrell, Lawrence, *Reflections of a Marine Venus: A Companion to the Landscape of Rhodes* (London: Faber and Faber, 1953).
Durrell, Lawrence, *Six Poems from the Greek of Sekilianos [sic] and Seferis* (Rhodes, privately printed, 1946).
Durrell, Lawrence, *Tunc* (London: Faber, 1968).
Economidis, Phivos, *Πόλεμος, διείσδυση και προπαγάνδα* (Athens: Orfeas, 1992).
Eliot, T.S., 'The Man of Letters and the Future of Europe', *Horizon*, 10/60 (December 1944): 382–89, and *The Sewanee Review*, 45/3 (Summer 1945): 333–42.
Eliot, T.S., 'The Responsibility of the Man of Letters in the Cultural Restoration of Europe', *Norseman*, 4 (July-August 1944): 243–48.

BIBLIOGRAPHY

Ellwood, D.W., ' "Showing the World What It Owed to Britain": Foreign Policy and "Cultural Propaganda", 1935–1945', in N. Pronay and D.W. Spring (eds.), *Propaganda, Politics and Film* (London: Macmillan, 1982).

Evangelidis, D.E., 'Εκθέσεις', *Νέα Εστία*, 45 (1949): 675–77.

Exposition des œuvres offertes par des artistes français en hommage à la Grèce, du 17 au 29 avril à l'Institut français d'Athènes (Athens: Institut Français d'Athènes, 1949).

Farinou-Malamatari, Georgia, 'Τέσσερεις γυναίκες βιογραφούν τον Καζαντζάκη', in Stamatis Philippidis (ed.), *Ο Καζαντζάκης στον 21ο αιώνα: Πρακτικά του Διεθνούς Επιστημονικού Συνεδρίου "Νίκος Καζαντάκης 2007: Πενήντα χρόνια μετά"* (Heraklion: Panepistimiakes Ekdoseis Kritis, 2010): 291–338.

Fisher, Ali, *A Story of Engagement: The British Council 1934–2009* (London: Counterpoint, 2009).

Flitouris, Lambros, 'L'Institut français d'Athènes pendant la Seconde Guerre mondiale', *Guerres mondiales et conflits contemporains*, 218 (April 2005): 37–52.

Flitouris, Lambros, 'Ο Octave Merlier και ο ρόλος του στην προώθηση των ελληνογαλλικών σχέσεων (1925–1961)', in *ΚΑ΄ Πανελλήνιο Ιστορικό Συνέδριο (26, 27, 28 Μαΐου 2000)* (Thessaloniki: Elliniki Istoriki Etaireia, 2001): 383–94.

Ford, Mark, 'Review of Spencer, "Complete Poetry" ', *London Review of Books*, 17 November 2011.

Forster, E.M., 'In the Rue Lepsius', *The Listener*, 5 July 1951: 28–29, reprinted as 'The Complete Poems of C.P. Cavafy', in *Two Cheers for Democracy* (London: Edward Arnold, 1951): 247–50.

Gallant, Thomas W., *Experiencing Dominion: Culture, Identity, and Power in the British Mediterranean* (Notre Dame, IN: University of Notre Dame Press, 2002).

Gardikas, Katerina, 'Relief Work and Malaria in Greece, 1943–1947', *Journal of Contemporary History*, 43/3 (2008): 493–508.

Giannuli, Dimitra, ' "Repeated Disappointment": The Rockefeller Foundation and the Reform of the Greek Public Health System, 1929–1940', *Bulletin of the History of Medicine* 72/1 (1998): 47–72.

Golani, Matti (ed.), *The End of the British Mandate, 1948: The Diary of Sir Henry Gurney* (Basingstoke: Palgrave Macmillan, 2009).

Gomme, A.W., *Greece* (London: Oxford University Press, 1945).

Hamilton, Keith and Patrick Salmon (eds.), *The Southern Flank in Crisis, 1973–6* [Documents on British Policy Overseas, series III, vol. V] (London: Foreign and Commonwealth Office, 2006).

Hammond, Nicholas, *Venture into Greece with the Guerrillas, 1943–44* (London: W. Kimber, 1983).

Hardy, Thomas, *Collected Poems*, ed. James Gibson (London: Macmillan, 1976).

Hatziiosif, Christos (ed.), *Ιστορία της Ελλάδας του 20ου αιώνα, 4.2. Ανασυγκρότηση – Εμφύλιος – Παλινόρθωση 1945–1952* (Athens: Vivliorama, 2009).

244 BIBLIOGRAPHY

Haughton, Hugh, *The Poetry of Derek Mahon* (Oxford: Oxford University Press, 2004).

Hayter, Alethea, *A Sultry Month: Scenes of London Literary Life in 1846* (London: Faber and Faber, 1965).

Henderson, Mary, *Xenia: A Memoir* (London: Weidenfeld and Nicolson, 1988).

Hermione, Countess of Ranfurly, *To War with Whitaker: The Wartime Diaries of the Countess of Ranfurly, 1939–45* (London: Heinemann, 1994).

Heuser, Alan (ed.), *Selected Literary Criticism of Louis MacNeice* (Oxford: Oxford University Press, 1987).

Hionidou, Violetta, *Famine and Death in Occupied Greece, 1941–1944* (Cambridge: Cambridge University Press, 2006).

Holland, Robert, *Blue-Water Empire: The British in the Mediterranean Since 1800* (London: Allen Lane, 2012).

Holland, Robert, *Britain and the Revolt in Cyprus, 1954–58* (Oxford: Clarendon Press, 1998).

Holland, Robert, *The Pursuit of Greatness: Britain and the World Role, 1900–1970* (London: Fontana Press, 1991).

Holland, Robert and Diana Markides, *The British and the Hellenes: Struggles for Mastery in the Eastern Mediterranean, 1850–1960* (Oxford: Oxford University Press, 2006).

Hourmouzios, Aimilios, 'Η λογοτεχνία μας στην Αγγλία', *Νέα Εστία*, 38 (1945): 721–22.

Hughes, Hilda (ed.), *The Glory That Is Greece* (London: Hutchinson, 1944).

Iatrides, J.O., *Ambassador MacVeagh Reports: Greece, 1933–1947* (Princeton: Princeton University Press, 1980).

Jeffreys, Peter (ed.), *The Forster-Cavafy Letters: Friends at a Slight Angle* (Cairo and New York: American University in Cairo Press, 2009).

Jinkinson, Roger, *American Ikaros: The Search for Kevin Andrews* (London: Racing Horse Press, 2010).

Johnstone, Kenneth, 'Obituary, Sir Reginald Leeper, CBE, KCMG', *Home and Abroad* [British Council Staff Journal], 14 (May 1968): 52–54.

Johnstone, Pauline, *Greek Island Embroidery* (London: A. Tiranti, 1961).

Jordan, R.R., *Writers and Their Other Work* (Cambridge: Lutterworth Press, 2006).

Kallinis, Yiorgos, ' "Αγαπητή Μέλπω": Οκτώ επιστολές του Κοσμά Πολίτη προς τη Μέλπω Αξιώτη', *Νέα Εστία*, 155 (2004): 741–53.

Kallinis, Yiorgos, *Σχεδίασμα βιβλιογραφίας Κοσμά Πολίτη (1930–2000)* (Thessaloniki: University Studio Press, 2008).

Kasdaglis, E., 'Συμβολή στη χρονολογία του βίου του Παντελή Πρεβελάκη', *Νέα Εστία*, 119 (Christmas 1986): 2–33.

Katsalaki, Georgia, *Η βιβλιοθήκη του Νίκου Καζαντζάκη στο Ιστορικό Μουσείο Κρήτης: Εισαγωγικό σημείωμα Θεοχάρης Δετοράκης* (Heraklion: Etairia Kritikon Istorikon Meleton, 1997).

BIBLIOGRAPHY

Katsimbalis, G.K., *Βιβλιογραφία Ν. Καζαντζάκη*, vol. 1 [and only]: 1906–1948 (Athens: no publisher, 1958).

Katsimbalis, G.K. and Giorgos Seferis, *'Αγαπητέ μου Γιώργο': Αλληλογραφία (1924–1970)*, ed. Dimitris Daskalopoulos (2 vols, Athens: Ikaros, 2009).

Kazantzaki, Eleni N., *Le Dissident: biographie de Nikos Kazantzaki* (Paris: Plon, 1968).

Kazantzaki, Eleni N., *Νίκος Καζαντζάκης, ο ασυμβίβαστος: βιογραφία βασισμένη σε ανέκδοτα γράμματα και κείμενά του* (Athens: Ekdoseis Elenis N. Kazantzaki, 1977).

Kazantzakis, Helen, *Nikos Kazantzakis: A Biography Based on His Letters*, trans. Amy Mims (Oxford: Cassirer; and New York: Simon and Schuster, 1968).

Kazantzakis, Nikos, *Ascèse: salvatores dei: Traduit du grec et présenté par Octave Merlier* (Athens: Institut Français d'Athènes, 1951) (Collection de l'Institut Français d'Athènes no. 27).

Kazantzakis, Nikos, 'Η Κρήτη', *Νέα Εστία*, 66 (Christmas 1959): 39–42.

Kazantzakis, Nikos, 'Μια ελληνική φωνή για τον Μπέρναρντ Σω', *Νέα Εστία*, 40 (1946): 953.

Kazantzakis, Nikos, 'Ο θάνατος του παπού', *Νέα Εστία*, 41 (1947): 327–34.

Kazantzakis, Nikos, *Ταξιδεύοντας Γ': Αγγλία* (Athens: Pyrsos, 1941).

Kazantzaki[s], Nikos, 'The Immortal Free Spirit of Man', *Life and Letters*, 50/109 (1946): 123–26.

Kazantzakis, Nikos, 'The Homeric G.B.S.', *The Shaw Review*, 18/3 (September 1975): 91–92.

Kazantzakis, Nikos, *Zorba the Greek*, trans. Carl Wildman, with an introduction by Ian Scott-Kilvert (London: John Lehmann, 1952).

Kazantzis, Vasilis, 'Τρία ανέκδοτα γράμματα του Ν. Καζαντζάκη', *Νέα Εστία*, 74 (1963): 906–7.

Keeley, Edmund, *Inventing Paradise: The Greek Journey 1937–47* (New York: Farrar, Straus and Giroux, 1999).

Kenner, Hugh, *The Pound Era* (London: Faber, 1971).

King, Francis, *An Air That Kills* (Kansas City: Valancourt Books, 2008).

King, Francis, *Introducing Greece* (London: Methuen, 1956).

King, Francis, *So Hurt and Humiliated, and Other Stories* (London: Longmans, 1959).

King, Francis, *The Ant Colony* (London: Constable, 1991).

King, Francis, *The Dark Glasses* (London: Longmans, 1954).

King, Francis, *The Firewalkers* (London: GMP, 1985).

King, Francis, *The Man on the Rock* (London: Longmans, 1957).

King, Francis, *To the Dark Tower* (London: Home and Van Thal, 1946).

King, Francis, *Yesterday Came Suddenly* (London: Constable, 1993).

Kitroeff, Alexander, 'Documents: Cyprus, 1950–1954: The Prelude to the Crisis, Part I: 1950', *Journal of the Hellenic Diaspora*, 15/1–2 (Spring-Summer 1988): 71–102.

246 BIBLIOGRAPHY

Kokkinidou, Marina, 'Το περιοδικό *Αγγλοελληνική Επιθεώρηση* (1945–1955): περίοδοι, στόχοι και συμβολή του στη μεταπολεμικη πολιτισμική ζωή', unpublished doctoral dissertation, Aristotle University of Thessaloniki, 2002.

Kolocotroni, Vassiliki and Efterpi Mitsi (eds.), *Women Writing Greece: Essays on Hellenism, Orientalism and Travel* (Amsterdam and New York: Rodopi, 2008).

Kornaros, Vitzentzos, *Erotocritos: circa 1640 A.D.*, trans. Theodore Ph. Stephanides (Athens: Papazissis Publishers, 1984).

Kostiou, Katerina (ed.), *'Κυπριακές' επιστολές του Σεφέρη (1954–1962): από την αλληλογραφία του με τον Γ.Π. Σαββίδη* (Nicosia: Politistiko Idryma Trapezis Kyprou, 1991).

Koutsopanagou, Gioula, 'Πολιτογράφηση και νομική θωράκιση του ελληνικού προσκοπισμού, 1917–1920', in Vangelis Karamanolakis et al. (eds.), *Η ελληνική νεολαία στον 20° αιώνα: Πολιτικες διαδρομές, κοινωνικές πρακτικές και πολιτιστικές εκφράσεις* (Athens: Themelio, 2010): 379–99.

Koutsopanagou, Gioula, 'Προπαγάνδα και απελευθέρωση: Το Βρετανικό Συμβούλιο και ο Ελληνοσοβιετικός Σύνδεσμος στις παραμονές του εμφυλίου πολέμου (1945)', *Μνήμων*, 22 (2000): 171–90.

Koutsopanagou, P., 'The British Press and the Greek Crisis, 1943–1949', unpublished Ph.D. thesis, LSE, University of London, 1996.

Kranaki, Mimika, *Mataroa à deux voix: Journal d'exil* (Athens: Museio Benaki, 2007) (in Greek and French).

Kranaki, Mimika, *Φιλέλληνες: είκοσι τέσσερα γράμματα μιας Οδύσσειας* (Athens: M.I.E.T., 1998) [1st edn 1992].

Krontiris, Tina, ' "Henry V" and the Anglo-Greek Alliance in World War II', in Graham Bradshaw and Tom Bishop (eds.), *The Shakespearean International Yearbook*, 8 (2008): 32–50.

Kruczkowska, Joanna, *Irish Poets and Modern Greece: Heaney, Mahon, Cavafy, Seferis* (n.p.: Palgrave Macmillan, 2017).

Kučera, Jaroslav, *'Unlimited Exchange' or Information Imperialism?* (Prague: Orbis Press Agency, 1986).

Lambropoulos, Vassilis, 'Το ταξίδι του Έλληνα διανοούμενου στην Αμερική', in Giorgos Theotokas (ed.), *Δοκίμιο για την Αμερική* (Athens: Estia, 2009): 237–56.

Lancaster, Osbert, *Classical Landscape with Figures* (London: John Murray, 1947).

Lawson, J.C., *Modern Greek Folklore and Ancient Greek Religion: A Study in Survivals* (Cambridge: University Press, 1910).

Le Serment sur le Styx: Cinq poèmes de Sikélianos (1941–1942): Bois de Spyro Vassiliou, traduction d'Octave Merlier (Athens: Icaros, 1946) (Collection de l'Institut Français d'Athènes no. 3).

Lee, J.M., 'British Cultural Diplomacy and the Cold War: 1946–61', *Diplomacy and Statecraft*, 9/1 (1998): 112–34.

BIBLIOGRAPHY

Leeper, Reginald, 'British Culture Abroad', *Contemporary Review*, 148 (July-December 1935): 201–7.

Leeper, Reginald, *When Greek Meets Greek* (London: Chatto and Windus, 1950).

Lehmann, John, *The Ample Proposition: Autobiography III* (London: Eyre and Spottiswoode, 1966).

Leigh Fermor, Patrick, *Mani, Travels in the Southern Peloponnese* (London: Murray, 1958).

Leonard, Mark and Andrew Small, with Martin Rose, *British Public Diplomacy in the 'Age of Schisms'* (London: Counterpoint, 2005).

Leonard, Mark with Catherine Stead and Conrad Smewing, *Public Diplomacy* (London: Foreign Policy Centre, 2002).

Lewin, Ronald, *The Chief: Field-Marshal Lord Wavell, Commander-in-Chief and Viceroy, 1939–1947* (London: Hutchinson, 1980).

Liddell, Robert, *A Treatise on the Novel* (London: Jonathan Cape, 1947).

Liddell, Robert, *Aegean Greece* (London: Jonathan Cape, 1954).

Liddell, Robert, *Cavafy: A Critical Biography* (London: Duckworth, 1974, revised edn 2000).

Liddell, Robert, *Mainland Greece* (London: Longmans, 1965).

Liddell, Robert, *The Morea* (London: Jonathan Cape, 1958).

Liddell, Robert, *Unreal City* (London: Jonathan Cape, 1952).

Liebeschuetz, Wolfgang, 'William Hugh Clifford Frend 1916–2005', *Proceedings of the British Academy*, 150 (2007): 37–54.

Lincoln, John [Maurice Cardiff], *Achilles and the Tortoise: An Eastern Aegean Exploit* (London: Heinemann, 1958).

Llewellyn-Smith, Michael, Paschalis M. Kitromilides and Eleni Calligas (eds.), *Scholars, Travels, Archives: Greek History and Culture Through the British School at Athens* (London: British School at Athens, 2009).

Lucas, F.L. and Prudence Lucas, *From Olympus to the Styx* (London: Cassell, 1934).

Mackridge, Peter, 'Χρονολόγιο Κοσμά Πολίτη (Πάρι Ταβελούδη)', *Διαβάζω*, 116 (10 April 1985): 8–12.

MacNeice, Louis, 'A Modern Odyssey', *New Statesman*, 17 December 1960: 978–79.

MacNeice, Louis, *Collected Poems*, ed. Peter McDonald (London: Faber, 2007).

MacNeice, Louis, *Eighty-Five Poems, Selected by the Author* (London: Faber, 1959).

MacNeice, Louis, 'Makronisos', *New Statesman*, 4 November 1950: 409.

MacNeice, Louis, *Selected Prose of Louis MacNeice*, ed. Alan Heuser (Oxford: Oxford University Press, 1990).

MacNeice, Louis, *The Classical Radio Plays*, eds. Amanda Wrigley and S.J. Harrison (Oxford: Oxford University Press, 2013).

MacNeice, Louis, *The Strings Are False* (London: Faber and Faber, 1965).

MacNiven, Ian, *Lawrence Durrell: A Biography* (London: Faber and Faber, 1998).

Mahon, Derek, *Collected Poems* (Dublin: Gallery Books, 1999).

248 BIBLIOGRAPHY

Malanos, Timos, 'Η κριτική και η νέα μας ποίηση', Νέα Εστία, 51 (1952): 194–95.

Malanos, Timos, Η ποίηση του Σεφέρη: Κριτική μελέτη (Alexandria: Mitsanis, 1951).

Malone, G.D., *Political Advocacy and Cultural Communication: Organizing the Nation's Public Diplomacy* (Boston: University Press of America, 1988).

Manitakis, Nicolas, 'L'exil des jeunes Grecs et le rôle de l'Institut français: un exil doré?', in Servanne Jollivet, Christophe Premat, Mats Rosengren (eds.), *Destins d'exilés: Trois philosophes grecs à Paris – Kostas Axelos, Cornelius Castoriadis et Kostas Papaïoannou* (Paris: Editions Le Manuscrit, 2011): 45–61.

Manitakis, Nicolas, 'Ξένες κρατικές υποτροφίες: πολιτιστική προπαγάνδα στην Ελλάδα του Εμφυλίου', in Hatziiosif (ed.), Ιστορία της Ελλάδας του 20ου αιώνα, 4/2 (Athens: Vivliorama, 2009): 133–57.

Manning, Olivia, *The Balkan Trilogy; The Great Fortune* (London: Heinemann, 1960); *The Spoilt City* (London: Heinemann, 1962); *Friends and Heroes* (London: Heinemann, 1965).

Marsack, Robyn, *The Cave of Making: The Poetry of Louis MacNeice* (Oxford: Oxford University Press, 1982).

Matthiopoulos, Evgenios, 'Οι εικαστικές τέχνες στην Ελλάδα τα χρόνια 1945–1953', in Hatziiosif (ed.), Ιστορία της Ελλάδας του 20ου αιώνα, 4/2 (Athens: Vivliorama, 2009): 182–237.

Mavilis, Lorentzos, Τα κριτικά κείμενα, ed. Theodosis Pylarinos (Athens: Syllogos pros Diadosin Ophelimon Vivlion, 2007).

McDonald, Peter, *Louis MacNeice: The Poet and His Contexts* (Oxford: Oxford University Press, 1991).

McKinnon, William T., *Apollo's Blended Dream: A Study of the Poetry of Louis MacNeice* (London: Oxford University Press, 1971).

Mélanges offerts à Octaves et Melpo Merlier à l'occasion du 25e anniversaire de leur arrivée en Grèce (3 vols, Athens: Institut Français d'Athènes, 1956–57) (Collection de l'Institut Français d'Athènes nos 92, 93 and 94).

Merlier, Melpo, *Présentation du Centre d'Etudes d'Asie Mineure: Recherches d'ethnographie*, 2nd edn, ed. P. Kitromilidis (Athens: Centre d'Etudes d'Asie Mineur, 2011, 1st edn 1951).

Merlier, Melpo, Το αρχείο της Μικρασιατικής λαογραφίας: πώς ιδρύθηκε, πώς εργάστηκε (Athens: Ikaros, 1948) (Collection de l'Institut Français d'Athènes no. 7).

Miller, Henry, *The Colossus of Maroussi* (San Francisco: Colt Press, 1941).

Milliex, Roger, Ελληνογαλλικά, Ι: Αδαμάντιος Κοραής – Victor Hugo (Athens: Institut Français d'Athènes, 1953) (Collection de l'Institut Français d'Athènes no. 77).

Milliex, Roger (ed.), *Hommage à la Grèce 1940–1944: Textes et témoignages français* (Athens: Institut Français d'Athènes, 1979).

Milliex, Roger, 'L'Institut français d'Athènes, fils spirituel de l'Ecole française', *Bulletin de Correspondance Hellénique*, 120 (1996): 69–82.

BIBLIOGRAPHY 249

Mitchell, J.M., *International Cultural Relations* (London: Allen and Unwin, in association with The British Council, 1986).

Mitchell, Leslie, *Maurice Bowra: A Life* (Oxford: Oxford University Press, 2009).

Modern Greek Poems, Selected and Rendered into English by Theodore Ph. Stephanides and George C. Katsimbalis (London: Hazell, Watson and Viney, 1926).

Moore, D.B., *The Poetry of Louis MacNeice* (Leicester: Leicester University Press, 1972).

Nash, Daniel, *My Son Is in the Mountains* (London: Jonathan Cape, 1955).

Noutsos, Charalambos, *Ο δρόμος της καμήλας και το σχολείο: Η εκπαιδευτική πολιτική στην Ελλάδα: 1944–1946* (Athens: Vivliorama, 2003).

Nye, Joseph, *Soft Power: The Means to Success in World Politics* (New York: Public Affairs, 2004).

Owens, Lewis, ' "Who Are the Intelligentsia in Cambridge?" The Hostile Reception to Kazantzakis' Desire for an "International of the Spirit" ', *The Cambridge Review*, 119/2331 (November 1998): 91–92.

Pangratis, Periklis, 'Πολεμικές εμπειρίες και μεταπολεμική κερκυραϊκή λογοτεχνία', *Πόρφυρας*, 1 (1980): 19–24.

Pangratis, Periklis, 'Ο Lawrence Durrell και μια μετάφραση από το "Κελί του Πρόσπερου" ', *Πόρφυρας*, 93 (2000).

Papanastasatos, Tasos, 'Μαρία Ασπιώτη (1909–2000): Μια ζωή, μια προσφορά', *Πόρφυρας*, 102 (2002): 507–31.

Papanikolaou, Dimitris, 'Demetrios Capetanakis: A Greek Poet (Coming out) in England', *Byzantine and Modern Greek Studies*, 30/2 (2006): 201–23.

Peri, Massimo, *Τα Νέα Γράμματα: Lettere Nuove (1935–1945)* (Rome: Edizioni dell'Ateneo, 1974).

Petraki, Marina, *Βρετανική πολιτική και προπαγάνδα στον ελληνοϊταλικό πόλεμο* (Athens: Patakis, 2011).

Piniatoglou, Lazaros, *Αγγλικός πολιτισμός* (Athens: Ellinikon Aima, 1944).

Piniatoglou, Lazaros, *Ελληνικά προβλήματα* (Athens: Xenos, 1945).

Plomer, William, *Collected Poems* (London: Jonathan Cape, 1960).

Potts, Jim, *Corfu Blues* (Stockholm: Ars Interpres, 2006).

Potts, Jim, 'Truth Will Triumph: The British Council and Cultural Relations in Greece', in David Wills (ed.), *Greece and Britain Since 1945* (Newcastle: Cambridge Scholars Publishing, 2010): 99–129.

Powell, Dilys, *An Affair of the Heart* (London: Hodder and Stoughton, 1957).

Press, John, *Uncertainties and Other Poems* (London: Oxford University Press, 1956).

Prevelakis, Pandelis, *The Tale of a Town*, trans. Kenneth Johnstone (London and Athens: Doric Publications, 1976).

Prevelakis, Pantelis, *Τετρακόσια γράμματα του Καζαντζάκη στον Πρεβελάκη*, 2nd edn (Athens: Ekdoseis Elenis N. Kazantzaki, 1984).

Price, A. Whigham, *The Ladies of Castlebrae: A Story of Nineteenth-century Travel and Research* (Gloucester: A. Sutton, 1985).

Pylarinos, Theodosis, *Ι. Σουρβίνος "ο ασκούμενος της νυκτός"* (Corfu: Etaireia Kerkyraikon Spoudon, 2006).

250   BIBLIOGRAPHY

Pylarinos, Theodosis (ed.), Πρόσπερος (1949–1954) (Corfu: Ionio Panepistimio, 2007).

Pylarinos, Theodosis, 'Κερκυραϊσμός η κορφίτιδα: αποδοχές και αντιρρήσεις προς την ταυτότητα των Κερκυραίων εκπροσώπων της Επτανησιακής σχολής', Ιονικά Ανάλεκτα, 1 (2011): 215–29.

Pylarinos, Theodosis, 'Ο Μάρκος Αυγέρης και τα Ελεύθερα Γράμματα του Δημήτρη Φωτιάδη', Θέματα Λογοτεχνίας, 29 (2005): 180–94.

Reeves, Julie, *Culture and International Relations: Narratives, Natives and Tourists* (London: Routledge, 2004).

Report of The British Council 1945–1946 (Name of Representative: The Hon. Steven Runciman) (London: September 1946).

Report of The British Council 1946–1947 (Name of Representative: W.G. Tatham M.C.) (London: September 1947).

Report of The British Council 1947–1948 (Name of Representative: W.G. Tatham M.C.) (London: June 1948).

Rhoides, Emmanuel, *Pope Joan: A Historical Study*, translated with a preface by C.H. Collette (London, 1886).

Ricks, Christopher (ed.), *Joining Music with Reason* (Chipping Norton: Waywiser Press, 2010).

Ricks, David, 'Demetrios Capetanakis: A Greek Poet in England', *Journal of the Hellenic Diaspora*, 22/1 (1996): 61–75.

Ricks, David, 'Lorenzatos and Eliot', *Sobornost*, 32/2 (2011): 6–18.

Ricks, David, 'Simpering Byzantines, Grecian Goldsmiths, et al.: Some Appearances of Byzantium in English Poetry', in Robin Cormack and Elizabeth Jeffreys (eds.), *Through the Looking-Glass: British Responses to Byzantium* (Aldershot: Ashgate, 2000): 223–35.

Rodd, Rennell (ed.), *The Englishman in Greece, Being a Collection of the Verse of Many English Poets* (Oxford: Clarendon Press, 1910).

Roessel, David, *In Byron's Shadow: Modern Greece in the English and American Imagination* (Oxford and New York: Oxford University Press, 2002).

Roessel, David, ' "This Is Not a Political Book" ': "Bitter Lemons" as British Propaganda', *Byzantine and Modern Greek Studies*, 24 (2000): 235–45.

Rose, Martin and Nick Wadham-Smith, *Mutuality, Trust and Cultural Relations* (London: Counterpoint, 2004).

Roussou-Sinclair, Mary, *Victorian Travellers in Cyprus: A Garden of Their Own* (Nicosia: Cyprus Research Centre, 2002).

Royidis, Emmanuel, *Pope Joan: A Romantic Biography*, translated from the Greek by Lawrence Durrell (London: D. Verschoyle, 1954).

Runciman, Steven, *A History of the Crusades* (3 vols, Cambridge: Cambridge University Press, 1951, 1954, 1955).

Runciman, Steven, *A Traveller's Alphabet: Partial Memoirs* (London: Thames and Hudson, 1991).

Runciman, Steven, *Byzantine Civilisation* (London: Edward Arnold, 1933).

Runciman, Steven, 'Some Personal Memories', *Labrys*, 8 (1983): 47–49.

BIBLIOGRAPHY

Runciman, Steven, 'Zante and Its Capital Zakynthos Destroyed in the Recent Earthquake', *Architectural Review* (October 1953): 214–20.

Sagos, Anastasios, *A Chronicle of the British Council Office in Athens 1938–1986* (Athens: privately reproduced typescript, 1995).

Schofield, Don (ed.), *Kindled Terraces: American Poets in Greece* (Kirksville, MO: Truman University Press, 2004).

Scott-Kilvert, Ian, 'Hellenic Revival', *United Nations United*, 1/9 (June 1949): 356–59.

Seferis, George, *Choix de poèmes, traduits et accompagnés du texte grec avec une préface de Robert Levesque* (Athens: Icaros, 1945) (Collection de l'Institut Français d'Athènes no. 2).

Seferis, George, *Complete Poems*, trans. Edmund Keeley and Philip Sherrard (Princeton: Princeton University Press, 1995).

Seferis, George, *On the Greek Style: Selected Essays in Poetry and Hellenism*, trans. Rex Warner and Th. D. Frangopoulos, with an introduction by Rex Warner (London: Bodley Head, 1967).

Seferis, George, *Poems*, translated from the Greek by Rex Warner (London: Bodley Head, 1960).

Seferis, George, *The King of Asine and Other Poems*, translated from the Greek by Bernard Spencer, Nanos Valaoritis, Lawrence Durrell, with an introduction by Rex Warner (London: John Lehmann, 1948).

Seferis, Georges, *Trois jours dans les églises rupestres de Cappadoce* (Athens: Institut Français d'Athènes, 1953) (Collection de l'Institut Français d'Athènes no. 78A).

Seferis, Giorgos, *Δοκιμές*, vol. 3 (Athens: Ikaros 1992).

Seferis, Giorgos, *Μέρες Ε΄: 1 Γενάρη 1945–19 Απρίλη 1951* (Athens: Ikaros, 1977).

Sharon, Avi, 'New Friends for New Places: England Rediscovers Greece', *Arion*, 8/2 (Autumn 2000): 42–62.

Sherrard, Philip, 'Γιώργος Κατσίμπαλης', *Νέα Εστία*, 108 (1980): 1426–27.

Sherrard, Philip, *Η Μαρτυρία του Ποιητή* (Athens: Indiktos, 1998).

Solomos, Dionysios, *Introduction, proses et poèmes [par] R. Levesque* (Athens: Icaros, 1945) (Collection de l'Institut Français d'Athènes no. 1).

Soskice, Janet, *Sisters of Sinai: How Two Lady Adventurers Found the Hidden Gospels* (London: Chatto and Windus, 2009).

Spandonidis, P.S., 'Η "Κίχλη" του Γ. Σεφέρη', *Makedonika Grammata*, 4 (July-August 1951): 22–31.

Spencer, Bernard, *Aegean Islands and Other Poems* (London: Editions Poetry London, 1946).

Spencer, Bernard, *Complete Poetry, Translations and Selected Prose*, ed. Peter Robinson (Tarset: Bloodaxe, 2011).

Spencer, Terence, *Fair Greece, Sad Relic: Literary Philhellenism from Shakespeare to Byron* (London: Weidenfeld and Nicolson, 1954).

Spender, Stephen, ' "Brilliant Athens and Us" ', *Encounter*, 2/1 (January 1954): 77–80.

252   BIBLIOGRAPHY

Stallworthy, Jon, *Louis MacNeice* (London: Faber, 1995).

Stray, Christopher, *Classics Transformed* (Oxford: Oxford University Press, 1998).

Tabachnick, Stephen, *Fiercer than Tigers: The Life and Works of Rex Warner* (East Lansing, MI: Michigan State University Press, 2002).

Taylor, Philip M., 'Cultural Diplomacy and the British Council, 1934–1939', *The British Journal of International Studies*, 4/3 (October 1978): 244–65.

Taylor, Philip M., *The Projection of Britain: British Overseas Publicity and Propaganda 1919–1939* (Cambridge: Cambridge University Press, 1981).

Tetsis, Panayotis, Αφιέρωμα στους Μιλλιέξ, special issue of *Τομές*, 2nd series, 12/13 (May-June 1977).

Thaniel, George, *Seferis and Friends*, ed. Ed Phinney (Stratford, Ontario: Mercury Press, 1994).

Theotokas, George, *Argo*, translated from the Greek by E. Margaret Brooke and Ares Tsatsopoulos (London: Methuen, 1951).

Theotokas, Giorgos, 'Η φοβερή κλίκα', *Νέα Εστία*, 42 (1947): 969–71.

Theotokas, Giorgos, Τετράδια ημερολογίου 1939–1953, ed. with introduction by Dimitris Tziovas (Athens: Estia, n.d.).

Thorpe, Andrew, ' "In a Rather Emotional State": The Labour Party and British Intervention in Greece, 1944–45', *English Historical Review*, 121 (2006): 1075–1105.

Thrylos, Alkis, Κριτική: Πεζογραφία, Ποίηση, Δοκίμιο (1945–1965) (Athens: Idryma Ourani, 2010).

Trypanis, C.A., *The Stones of Troy* (London: Faber, 1957).

Tuch, H.N., *Communicating with the World: U.S. Public Diplomacy Overseas* (New York: St. Martin's Press, 1990).

Valaoritis, Nanos, 'A Memoir', *Agenda*, 43/2–3 (2008).

Valaoritis, Nanos, 'Modern Greek Poetry', *Horizon*, 13/75 (March 1946): 205–16.

Valaoritis, Nanos, 'Remembering the Poets: Translating Seferis with Durrell and Bernard Spencer', in Anna Lillios (ed.), *Lawrence Durrell and the Greek World* (Selinsgrove, PA: Susquehanna University Press, 2004): 46–53.

Valaoritis, Nanos and Giorgos Seferis, Αλληλογραφία (Athens: Ypsilon, 2004).

Van Steen, Gonda, *Theatre of the Condemned* (Oxford: Oxford University Press, 2011).

Vassiliou, Maria, 'Politics, Public Health and Development: Malaria in 20th Century Greece', D.Phil. thesis, University of Oxford, 2005.

Vei, Mairi N., 'Δύο επιστολαί του Νίκου Καζαντζάκη προς τον Νίκο Βέη', *Νέα Εστία*, 74 (1963): 1688–91.

Venezis, Elias, *Aeolia*, trans. E.D. Scott-Kilvert (London: Campion, 1949).

Vikelas: see Bikelas.

Warner, Rex, 'Introduction', in Seferis, *The King of Asine and Other Poems*.

Warner, Rex, *Men of Stones: A Melodrama* (London: Bodley Head, 1949).

Warner, Rex, *Personal Impressions: Talks on Writers and Writing*, ed. Marion B. McLeod (Sydney: Wentworth Press, 1986).

BIBLIOGRAPHY 253

Warner, Rex, *Poems and Contradictions* (London: Bodley Head, revised edn 1945).

Warner, Rex, *The Cult of Power* (London: Bodley Head, 1946).

Warner, Rex, *Views of Attica and Its Surroundings* (London: John Lehmann, 1950).

Warner, Rex and Martin Hürlimann, *Eternal Greece* (London: Thames and Hudson, 1953).

White, A.J.S., *The British Council: The First 25 Years 1934–1959: A Personal Account Written for the Information of Council Staff* (London: British Council, 1959).

Wills, David, *The Mirror of Antiquity: 20th Century British Travellers in Greece* (Newcastle: Cambridge Scholars Publishing, 2007).

Wilson, Henry Maitland, *Eight Years Overseas, 1937–47* (London and New York: Hutchinson, 1950).

Woodhouse, C.M., *Apple of Discord* (London: Hutchinson, 1948).

Woodhouse, C.M., *The Struggle for Greece, 1941–1949* (London: Hart-Davis, MacGibbon, 1976).

Xydis, Stephen G., *Greece and the Great Powers 1944–1947: Prelude to the "Truman Doctrine"* (Thessaloniki: Institute for Balkan Studies, 1963).

Young, Kenneth, 'The Contemporary Greek Influence on English Writers', *Life and Letters*, 64/149 (1950): 53–64.

Young, Kenneth, *The Greek Passion: A Study in People and Politics* (London: Dent, 1969).

Ziegler, Philip, *Mountbatten: The Official Biography* (London: Collins, 1985).

Αλληλογραφία Γιώργου & Μαρώς Σεφέρη – Νάνη Παναγιωτόπουλου, 1938– 1963, ed. Dimitris Arvanitakis (Athens: Mouseio Benaki, 2006).

Εθνικό και Καποδιστριακό Πανεπιστήμιο Αθηνών, Τμήμα Αγγλικής Γλώσσας και Φιλολογίας: 56 χρόνια παρουσίας (Athens: University of Athens, 2008).

Index

Abbott, G.F. 142
Adam, Robert 78, 85, 108
Aegina 215, 219, 222, 225
Aeschylus 206
AGIS *see* Anglo-Greek Information
  Service
Alexandria 112, 115, 175, 177, 181
Alice, Princess 89–91
America *see* USA
Amis, Kingsley 196
Anagnostaki, Loula 173
Anagnostakis, Manolis 164
Andrews, Kevin 204, 211
Andrić, Ivo 19
Andriotis, N.P. 15
Anemoyanni, Tea 217, 220–1
Angelou, Alkis 135
Anglo-Greek Cultural Convention 40,
  51, 66, 80
Anglo-Greek Information Service 11,
  19, 27, 40–1, 43, 45, 51, 72, 95, 120,
  126, 155, 168
Anglo-Greek Review 4–5, 11–12, 14–15,
  78, 81, 111, 117, 120, 123–59, 163–7,
  191, 202, 208
Anglo-Hellenic League 8, 28, 46–7, 103,
  147, 160
Anninos, Babis S. 162
Antoniou, D.I. 95, 112
Apotsos 75–6, 179, 181
Argyriou, Alexandros 135
Arnakis, George Georgiadis 46, 60, 151
Asia Minor 9, 231
Aspioti, Marie 109, 159–61, 164–9,
  171, 177
Athanasiadis, Tasos 137–8
Athena 126
Athens, University of 5, 28, 41, 57, 61,
  63, 89, 137; Byron Chair 2, 7, 40,
  42–4, 48–50, 70, 77, 81, 89, 124, 145,
  163, 175, 203; Chair of British Life
  and Thought 49–50, 62; Chair of
  French Literature 64
Attlee, Clement 30–1

Attlee, C.M. 43–4, 49, 62–3, 73
Auden, W.H. 12, 112, 137, 163, 212

Bachtin, Nicholas 203, 210
Badenoch, Cameron 83
Balzac, Honoré de 114
Barker, George 12
BBC 6–7, 13, 20, 27, 39, 116, 133, 142,
  201–3, 216–17, 220, 226
Beaton, Roderick 82
Beveridge, William 128
Bevin, Ernest 27, 85
Bien, Peter 215, 220, 225
Blackstone, Bernard 19, 64
Blunden, Edmund 128
Boase, T.S.R. 40
Boissy, Gabriel 233
Bolton, Jonathan 155
Bottrall, Ronald 177
Bowen, Elizabeth 128, 163, 170
Bowra, Maurice 17, 75, 79, 89, 108–9,
  137–8, 217
Brandram, Richard 90, 93
British School at Athens 21, 40, 50,
  123, 136
Britten-Jones, Joyce 74, 76, 92, 93–4, 106
Brooke, Rupert 112
Burke, Thomas 128
Burn, A.R. 70–1, 103, 124, 187
Bury, J.B. 69
Byron, Lord 1, 29, 77, 111, 141, 145, 149,
  175, 206–7
Byron, Robert 120
Byron Chair *see* Athens, University of

Caccia, Harold 28, 51, 65
Cacoyannis, Michael 137, 217
Cairo 1, 3, 5, 8, 12, 23–4, 40, 58, 69, 72,
  115, 125, 155
Cambridge 12, 69–70, 101, 190, 215–26
Campbell, Roy 12
Capell, Richard 14, 28
Capetanakis, Demetrios 12, 76, 140–1,
  143, 208

256 INDEX

Cardiff, Maurice 5, 43, 47–8, 51, 58, 72, 75, 78, 83, 95, 97, 104, 128
Castoriadis, Cornelius 229
Catherine, Princess 89–94
Cavafy, C.P. 1, 6–7, 10, 17–18, 112, 134, 137–8, 143, 166, 181–3, 216
Centre for Asia Minor Studies 231
Cephalonia 3, 13
Chalcis 97
Chandler, Geoffrey 30
Chatzidakis, Manolis 141
Chatzimichail, Theophilos 10, 18, 80, 132, 191
Chourmouzios, Aimilios 59, 134, 138, 151
Chourmouzios, Stylianos-Loukianos 59
Christianopoulos, Dinos 11
Chrysochoou, Iphigeneia 173
Churchill, Winston 22–4, 27, 124
Chytiris, Gerasimos 162
Cicellis, Kay 13, 135
civil war, Greek 1, 11, 15, 26–7, 29–30, 32, 35, 73, 79, 98–9, 130, 133, 143, 159, 167, 192, 196, 198, 201, 204, 206–7, 228–9, 233, 235
Cleridou, Chrysanthi 220
Clogg, Richard 123, 150
Close, Reginald 70
Cold War 15, 31, 140, 188–9, 202
Compton, Fay 13
Connolly, Cyril 12–13, 19, 112, 117
Constantine, Prince 91–2
Constantinidis, N.P. 58
Contogenis, George 212
Corfu 8, 10–11, 21, 45, 113–14, 150, 152, 159–71, 173, 175, 177, 210
Craxton, John 8–9, 13, 18, 75–6, 94, 105, 107, 132, 181, 203
Crete 12, 24, 29, 71, 196, 220
Crichton, Ronald 18, 75, 80, 89, 98
Cull, Nicholas J. 188
cultural diplomacy 4, 39, 56, 70, 124–5, 133, 187
Cyprus 1, 7–8, 12, 15, 21, 26, 28–9, 33–4, 58, 71, 130, 139, 147, 157, 159, 164, 167, 173, 175–7, 216–17, 235

Dafnis, Kostas 162, 166
Dakin, Douglas 70
Dalton, Hugh 31
Dalven, Rae 136
Davies, Homer 47, 60–1
Davies, S.J. 43, 49

Dawkins, R.M. 217
Day-Lewis, Cecil 137
Dekemvriana (December 1944 events) 1, 9, 24–6, 30, 173
Delios, George 173
Demangel, Robert 227
Dendrinou, Pitsa 162
Denmark 124
Dentrinou, Eirini 160, 162
Depountis, Iason 162, 165
Desyllas, Michail 160–1, 164–71
Diamantopoulos, Alexis 13
Dimaras, C.Th. 5, 75, 134, 136, 182–4
Dimitrouka, Agathi 156
Dodds, E.R. 202, 205
Dodecanese 8, 24, 29, 72, 86, 223
Donaldson, Frances 82, 202, 208
Dos Passos, John 173
Doxaras, Panagiotis 162
Dragoumis, Ion 138
Duncan, Isadora 173
Dundas, C.A.F. 71, 187
Durrell, Lawrence 5–8, 11–13, 16, 18, 70–1, 76, 95, 105, 111–15, 117–18, 135, 138, 141–3, 145, 160, 168, 171, 181, 201, 203, 213

EAM (National Liberation Front) 4, 11, 19, 41, 48, 57, 66, 73, 86, 103, 105
Eden, Anthony 22, 33
EDES (National Republican Greek League) 25
education 40, 42–3, 45–50, 52, 54–5, 79, 81, 84, 89, 97–8, 133, 159, 184, 227–9
Egypt 5, 7, 22, 24, 71, 115, 130, 155–6
ELAS (Greek Popular Liberation Army) 11, 19, 25, 30, 103
Elefthera Grammata 165
Eliot, T.S. 1, 10, 12–13, 17–18, 112–13, 115, 132, 135–9, 150–1, 156, 161, 163–4, 169, 173, 202–3, 205–6, 209–10
Elliniki Dimiourgia 165
Elliott, John 190
Eluard, Paul 233
Elytis, Odysseus 7, 9, 13, 17, 76, 112, 116, 134, 143, 168, 181
Embiricos, Andreas 2, 13
English language teaching 2, 27, 45–6, 54–5, 63–4, 70–1, 81–2, 159, 162, 178–9, 202
Engonopoulos, Nikos 7, 13, 143

INDEX

EOKA (National Organization of Cypriot Struggle) 1, 16
Epirus 22, 29, 104, 198
Epitheorisi Technis 165
EPON (youth resistance organization) 52, 165
Erotokritos 11, 132

Faulkner, William 202, 210
Fedden, Robin 70
Fielding, Xan 76, 117
Filolologika Nea 162, 166
FitzGerald, Edward 113
Foreign Office 5, 28, 30, 39–46, 48, 50–1, 53–5, 70, 72, 76, 78, 125, 220
Forster, E.M. 17, 112, 143, 163
Fotiadis, Dimitris 165
Fougeron, André 231–2
France 12, 14, 48, 52–3, 55–6, 61, 81, 123–5, 141, 184, 227–38
Frangopoulos, Th.D. 6, 162
Frederika, Queen 33, 74, 89–90, 92–3
French Institute *see* Institut français
Frend, W.H.C. 50
Freud, Lucien 105
Friar, Kimon 136

Galanis, Dimitrios 232
Ganas, Michalis 206
Garnett, David 216
Gatsos, Nikos 128, 156, 181
de Gaulle, Charles 227
Generation of 1930, 4, 9–10, 136, 163, 168
Gennadius, Ioannes 137
Georgakis, Ioannis 53, 66–7
George II 4, 25, 70, 73, 74–5, 87–94, 106
Germany 1, 22, 123–5, 130–1, 141, 143, 160–1, 228
Ghika *see* Hadjikyriakos-Ghika, Nikos
Gibson, Margaret 219
Goebbels, Joseph 188
Goethe 138
Grady, Henry F. 31
Graham-Bell, Geoffrey 6, 8, 155, 210
Grant, Michael 44, 73, 102, 104–5
Greek-Soviet League 51–3, 124, 204
Greene, Graham 216
Grivas, George 26, 29
Grollios, Konstantinos 159, 162
Guillevic 233
Gurney, K.T. 42

Hadjikyriakos-Ghika, Nikos 9–10, 13, 75, 76, 80, 107, 113, 181–3, 203
Hammond, Nicholas 73, 104–5, 216, 224
Hardy, Thomas 206
Hayter, Alethea 75, 77, 106, 202
Hedley, H.M. 42, 44, 46, 51
Henderson, A.J. 44
Henderson, Mary 28
Herbert, Jean 222
Hinks, Roger 175–80, 182–6
Hitler, Adolf 23
Homer 207
homosexuality 58, 73, 179–83, 209
Horizon 13, 117, 137
Hugo, Victor 230
Hürlimann, Martin 143, 145
Hydra 114

Ikaria 204, 207
Imvrioti, Rosa 52
Institut français 12, 14–15, 41, 52, 60, 176, 227–38
Ionian Islands 1, 11, 136–7, 163, 165
Ireland 206–7
Istanbul 6, 44, 70, 96
Italy 22–4, 26, 40, 57–8, 123–5, 154, 203, 215, 223
Ithaca 3

Japan 183
Jenkins, Romilly 73, 104–5, 134, 137–8
Johnson, Samuel 112, 118
Johnstone, Kenneth 11, 19, 41–4, 46, 48–9, 51, 54, 56, 58, 65, 68, 72–3, 78, 82, 104, 109, 120, 157, 190, 201
de Jongh, Brian 75
Jonson, Ben 138
Joyce, James 1, 113, 135, 138, 161, 163, 169–70

Kakridis, I.Th. 156, 215, 218, 220, 224–5
Kalamata 5, 23, 71
Kallinikos, P.G. 162
Kalvos, Andreas 137
Kanellopoulos, Panayiotis 75
Karagatsis, M. 5, 12, 140
Karagiozis 10, 80, 227
Karamanlis, Constantine 77
Karantonis, Andreas 9, 19, 131, 133–4, 139
Karas, Simon 203, 208
Karidis, Pat 168

258 INDEX

Karidis, Perklis 168
Katakouzinos, Angelos 75
Katsaitis, Petros 15
Katsimbali, Aspasia 117, 120
Katsimbalis, G.K. 5–6, 8–9, 11–12,
  17–18, 75–6, 78, 82, 95, 111–21, 128,
  131–6, 140, 147, 149–50, 152, 154,
  156–7, 166, 177, 181–2, 194, 204
Kavalla 97, 108
Kazantzakis, Helen 191, 215, 217–22,
  224, 226
Kazantzakis, Nikos 12, 17, 52, 75, 95,
  109, 137, 139, 143, 152, 156, 191,
  215–26, 230
Kazantzis, Vasilis 215, 217–19, 223
Keats, John 147, 149, 197
Keeley, Edmund 82, 190
Kenner, Hugh 119
King, Ernest 24
King, Francis 3, 7, 163, 175–86, 189
Kinnock, Neil 175, 188–9
Kitsikis, Nikos 51–2
KKE (Greek Communist Party) 5, 11,
  19, 23, 25, 28, 48, 51, 81, 207, 235
Knös, Börje 220, 226
Kokkinidou, Maria 157
Kolonaki 6, 10, 71, 179, 204
Kontoglou, Fotis 75
Korais, Adamantios 230
Korfis, Tasos 162
Kornaros, Vintzentzos 11
Kostas Axelos 229
Koukoules, Phaidon 15
Koulouri (Desylla), Liana 162
Kranaki, Mimika 135, 229
Kreipe, Heinrich 160
Kriaras, Emmanouil 141
Krontiris, Tina 2
Kučera, Jaroslav 188–9
Kyrou, Kleitos 173

Lacretelle, Jacques de 233
de la Mare, Walter 163, 216
Lambridi, Elli 12, 52
Lancaster, Osbert 27, 29, 54–5, 65, 68,
  108, 144–5, 181
Laourdas, Vasilis 135
Larbaud, Valery 113
Laskey, D.S. 51
Lawrence, D.H. 163, 170
Lear, Edward 6
Le Corbusier 233
Lee, Laurie 117, 216

Leeper, Reginald (Rex) 3, 11, 19, 39,
  40–6, 49, 53, 55–6, 59, 65, 70, 72–4,
  103–4, 125–6, 147, 190, 201
Leftheriotis, Nikos 162, 169
Léger, Fernand 234
Lehmann, John 12–13, 17, 19–20, 75–6,
  77, 89, 107, 112–13, 117–18, 137, 139,
  149, 216, 221
Lehmann, Rosamund 117, 216
Leigh Fermor, Patrick (Paddy) 7–8,
  18, 28, 34, 75–6, 78–9, 82, 89, 105,
  108–9, 112, 117–18, 137, 160, 163,
  181, 183, 202
Levesque, Robert 15, 134, 139, 230,
  236–7
Levidis, Dimitrios 74, 92
Lewis, Agnes 219
Lewis, Wyndham 119
Liddell, Robert 5, 7, 70–1, 103, 118, 144,
  163–4, 170, 181–3
Listener, The 216
Lloyd, Lord 70–2, 124
Loader, W.R. 178, 189, 196–8
Lorenzatos, Zissimos 13, 134, 137, 203
Loukatos, Dimitris 128
Lucas, F.L. 216, 224
Lutyens, Elizabeth 13
Lymberaki, Margarita 135

Macedonia 25, 30, 129
MacElroy, Katherine 47
Macfarlane, R.L.O. 205
MacNeice, Louis 7, 12, 13, 71, 112, 135,
  137, 151, 163, 170, 181, 201–13
MacVeagh, Lincoln 22
Mahon, Derek 210
Makarios, Archbishop 7, 140
Makriyannis 132
Makronisos 193, 204
Malanos, Timos 135–6
Malta 26
Manning, Olivia 28, 71, 211
Mansfield, Katherine 163, 170
Marinatos, Spyridon 63–64
Maritain, Jacques 233
Markezinis, Spyros 86, 88
Masefield, John 201, 216
Mataroa 14, 124, 228–9, 231
Matisse, Henri 232
Matthews, Kenneth 216
Mavilis, Lorentzos 161, 164, 169, 171
Mavrogordato, John 6, 17, 66, 77,
  107, 216

INDEX

McDonald, Peter 208
McNeil, Hector 30, 51, 221
Megara 98
Melas Spyros 165
Meleager 207
Merlier, Melpo 14, 230–1
Merlier, Octave 14–15, 52, 61, 66, 184,
  227–31, 233–5
Metaxas, Ioannis 4, 48, 70, 130, 203–4
Michalopoulos, Fanis 135, 163
Michelis, P.A. 141
Miller, Henry 8, 17, 112–15,
  117–18, 141
Milliex, Roger 14–15, 227, 229,
  231–5, 237
Milliex, Tatiana Gritsi 14, 231–3
Milton, John 170
Mitchell, J.M. 187
Molotov, V.M. 86
Montagu-Pollock, William H. 39, 43–6,
  48, 50, 53, 57
Montherlant, Henry de 232
Moore, Henry 131, 202, 210, 216
Morand, Paul 113
Morgan, Dr 79, 84, 109
Mortimer, Raymond 75, 77, 95
Mounier, Emmanuel 233
Mussolini, Benito 22, 188
Mykonos 114
Myres 217

Nash, Daniel *see* Loader, W.R.
National Technical University 51, 81
Navarino, battle of 1
Nea Estia 118, 151, 217, 234
Nea Grammata, Ta 9, 11, 113–14, 119,
  134, 165
Nelly's (Elli Sougioultzoglou) 113
Nicolson, Harold 77, 89, 137
Nikaki, Mari 159
Nikokavouras, Spyros 162, 164
Nikolareizis, Dimitris 134
Nobel Prize 6, 9, 113, 134, 173, 202, 206,
  217, 220–1
Noel-Baker, Philip 53, 220–1
Norton, Clifford 9, 32–3, 35, 68, 74–6,
  78, 81, 93–5, 105, 108
Norton, 'Peter' 9, 33, 74–6, 81, 93–5,
  105, 107
Nye, Joseph 16, 187–8

Occupation (of Greece by the Axis) 2, 4,
  8–9, 14, 25, 97, 130, 138, 160, 216, 220

Oikonomou, E. 162
Ourani, Eleni 5, 134, 150
Ouranis, Costas 125, 128, 146–7, 150
Owen, Wilfred 120
Oxford 49, 77, 101, 179, 190, 209,
  216–17, 222, 226

Palamas, Kostis 113, 116, 134–5, 149
Panagiotopoulos, I.M. 5, 118–19
Panagiotopoulos, Nanis 156
Panteios School 65–7
Papagos, Alexandros 31, 33
Papaïoannou, Kostas 229
Papanastasatos, Tasos 162, 167–8
Papandreou, George 25, 40
Papanikolaou, Mitsos 134
Papanoutsos, Evangelos 45, 61, 139
Papastavrou, Krinio 217
Papastavrou, Stavros 222
Paraschos, Kleon 134, 138
Pares, Bernard 130
Paris 215, 222, 229
Parthenon 111, 177, 192
Patras 10–11, 16, 45, 95–6, 110, 159,
  162, 166, 210
Patton, George 32
Paul, King 33, 74, 87, 89–90, 92–3,
  100–1
Payne, Humfry 21, 35
Peloponnese, Runciman's tour of
  98–100
Peranthis, Michalis 134–5
philhellenism 141–5, 154, 179, 181,
  183–4, 201, 227
Philip, Prince 89–90
Picasso, Pablo 113
Pikionis, Dimitris 203
Pipinelis, Panagiotis 90, 92
Plastiras, Nikolaos 11
Plato 192
Plomer, William 43, 58, 118
Politis, Kosmas *see* Taveloudis, Paris
Politis, Linos 134, 137, 139
Politis, Spyridon 159
Polylas, Iakovos 161, 169
Polytechnic *see* National Technical
  University
Porphyras 166
Potts, Jim 123
Pound, Ezra 138, 209
Powell, Dilys 21, 35, 77, 89, 191
Prassinos, Mario 232
Press, John 195–6, 212

260 INDEX

Prevelakis, Pantelis 12, 19, 80, 109, 152, 215, 220, 223, 225
Pring, Julian 70–1
Prosperos 11, 159–71, 173
Proto Skali, To 162
Pryce-Jones, Alan 117, 120
Pylarinos, Savvas 51

Raine, Kathleen 12
Rangavis, Alexandros Rizos 137
Rayner, Joan 109, 117
Record, The 11, 173–4, 195
Rhodes 8, 72
Ridley, M.R. 73
Riggs, Ernest 47, 60
Ritsos, Yannis 164, 168, 211
Rizospastis 10, 81
Robertson, Malcolm 42, 78
Rodas, Michail 5, 130
Rodd, Rennell 142, 208
Roessel, David 142, 145, 152
Roidis, Emmanuel 8, 114, 139
Ross, Alan 117, 121
Rotas, Vasilis 2
Rothschild, Barbara 107, 117
Rousseau, Henri 10, 80
Roussel, Louis 227, 236
Runciman, Leslie 79, 83–4, 101–2
Runciman, Steven 5, 13, 17, 44–5, 49–50, 53, 66, 69–110, 115, 137, 141, 157, 181, 202
Runciman, Viscount 69
Runciman, Viscountess 69, 83, 85, 91, 101–2
Russell, Bertrand 128
Russia *see* USSR

Sachinis, Apostolos 128, 134, 137–8
Sagos, Anastasios 70, 139, 209
Salonica 5, 7, 10–11, 25, 33, 45–9, 52–3, 71–2, 81, 89, 96, 130, 140, 152, 173–5, 177–8, 190–1, 195, 204, 210; University of Thessaloniki 50, 139, 141, 162, 196
Sargent, Orme 30
Savidis, G.P. 12, 128, 131, 135, 141, 147, 156–8, 181
Scobie, Ronald 11, 25, 73–4, 105
Scott -Kilvert, E.D. 152
Scott-Kilvert, Ian 129, 137, 143, 148–9, 152
Sébasto-Bourdelle, Mme 232

Second World War 2, 3, 5, 9, 11, 24, 32, 111, 151, 155–6, 160, 162, 166–7, 173, 187, 192, 201, 203, 231, 233
Seferis, George 2, 6, 7–10, 12–13, 15, 17–20, 34, 64, 75–6, 78, 82, 106, 108, 112–16, 128, 131, 133–6, 138–40, 143, 145, 147–8, 150–1, 155–8, 162, 168, 181, 190, 192, 201, 203–4, 206–8, 212–13, 230
Seferis, Maro 156
Selby, William 33
Sewell, W.A. 50, 63–4, 77, 163
Seymour, Richard 43–5, 48, 105
Shakespeare, William 2, 74, 91, 131, 178, 193–5, 206
Shaw, G.B. 131, 138, 163, 217–18, 225
Shelley, P.B. 140, 142
Sheppard, J.T. 216–17
Sherrard, Philip 111, 118, 135, 154, 163–4, 190
Shillan, David 41–2, 45–6
Shukman, Ann 73, 102
Siapkaras-Pitsillidès, Thémis 15
Sikelianos, Angelos 5, 15, 17, 20, 75, 95, 116, 128, 134, 138, 143, 149, 161, 164, 170–1, 174, 181, 215, 217, 220, 224, 230–1
Sinopoulos, Takis 135
Sitwell, Edith 12
Smith, Reginald 71, 202, 211
Smuts, J.C. 120
Socrates 112
SOE (Special Operations Executive) 24, 57, 73, 79, 104–5
Sofoulis, Themistocles 87–8, 215
soft power 16, 188
Solomos, Dionysios 7, 15, 132, 134, 139, 147, 149, 230–1
Sourvinos, Dimitris 169
Soviet Union *see* USSR
Spain 27, 204
Spandonidis, Petros 136
Speaight, Robert 75
Spencer, Bernard 5–7, 12–13, 112, 114, 118, 135, 143, 181, 205, 216
Spencer, Stanley 173–4
Spencer, Terence 70
Spender, Natasha 117
Spender, Stephen 12, 19, 64, 112–13, 137, 145, 163, 170, 181–2, 216
Stallworthy, Jon 204–5
Stephanides, Theodore 112, 114, 120, 132, 147, 166, 171

INDEX

Stieglitz, Alfred 113
Stratou, Dora 95
Svoronos, Nikos 141, 229
Sweden 124, 156
Symposio 11, 159, 162, 166

Tambimuttu 12, 212
Tatakis, V.N. 141
Tatham, W.G. 78, 82, 157
Taveloudis, Paris 4–5, 113, 128, 147
Taylor, Philip 131
Tennyson, Alfred 207
Terzakis, Angelos 12, 79, 138
Tetsis, Panayotis 234
Thaniel, George 6
Theodorides, Ch. 52
Theodoropoulou, Avra 132
Theophilos *see* Chatzimichail,
  Theophilos
Theotokas, George 2, 5, 9, 12, 75, 118,
  138–40, 147, 223–4
Thessaloniki *see* Salonica
Thomas, Dylan 12, 138
Thomopoulos, Ioannis 156
Thompson, F.Y. 49
Thrylos, Alkis *see* Ourani, Eleni
Tomadakis, N.B. 64, 134
Topolski, Feliks 173
Trelawney, Edward 142
Trevelyan, G.M. 216, 224
Truman declaration 4, 31, 77, 86,
  88, 107
Trypanis, C.A. 51, 65–6, 77, 101, 107–8,
  118, 208, 213, 222
Tsaldaris, Constantine 74, 86–7,
  105–6
Tsaldaris, Nadine 87
Tsaldaris, Panagis 105–6
Tsarouchis, Yannis 137, 181–2
Tsatsos, Konstantinos 75, 232, 235
Turkey 23, 29, 32, 44, 88, 96, 130

University of Athens *see* Athens,
  University of
UNRRA (United Nations Relief and
  Rehabilitation Agency) 25, 61
USA 3–4, 6, 24, 27, 31–3, 35, 47–8, 53,
  55, 60, 81, 88–9, 209, 228
USSR 4, 24, 39, 51, 55, 81, 88–9, 124, 130

Vafopoulos, George 173
Valaoritis, Aristotelis 231

Valaoritis, Nanos 6, 7, 9, 12–13, 19–20,
  112, 114, 137–8, 145, 155, 212
Van Fleet, James 31
Van Steen, Gonda 193
Varkiza agreement 11, 19, 25–6, 28
Varotsis, Nikos 171
Vassiliou, Spyros 230
Veis, Nikos 141, 215, 218–20, 224
Velitchansky, Leonid 51–2
Veloudios, Thanos 181–2
Venezis, Elias 5, 138–40
Venizelos, Eleftherios 21
Ventouras, Nikos 162
Ventouras, Virginia 162
de Vere, Aubrey 208
Vikelas, Dimitrios 137, 139
Vrettakos, Nikiphoros 164, 168

Wallace, David 71, 104
Wallace, Prudence 71, 104
Waller, John 112
Warner, Rex 3, 6, 10, 13, 15, 17, 18, 20,
  71, 73, 75–6, 78–80, 82, 89, 95, 97,
  103, 109, 112, 115–18, 135–9, 143–5,
  150–1, 154, 162, 181, 190–5, 201–2,
  206, 209, 221, 226; marriages 107
Waterlow, Sydney 21–2, 29, 215
Wavell, Archibald 22
Welland, Malcolm 71
Whitman, Walt 206
Wickham, Charles 26
Wickham, W.R.L. 42–4, 54, 202
Wilde, Oscar 131, 163, 208
Wildman, Carl 220
Wilson, Henry Maitland 23
Winter, Gordon 216
Woodhouse, C.M. 3, 24, 70, 103,
  153, 204
Woolf, Leonard 17
Woolf, Virginia 1, 135, 140, 142,
  150, 170

Xenakis, Ianis 229

Yeats, W.B. 112, 135, 141, 204, 208
Young, Kenneth 135, 143
Yugoslavia 22

Zakynthos 1, 3, 6
Zakythinos, Dionysios 51, 141
Zervas, Napoleon 25
Zervos, Christian 232